"*Unveiling the Sixth Station of the Cross* will enlighten readers to the history and richness of this treasured, but nearly forgotten, devotion to the Holy Face of Our Lord. The Venerable Archbishop Fulton J. Sheen spoke of the mission of Veronica, who dared to brave a violent mob to refresh the Savior and, in reward, received on her towel the imprint of the Face that saved the world. Like Veronica, Mary Jane Zuzolo's zeal shines through, engaging the reader's mind and heart. May this holy book be the catalyst in raising up a generation of 'Veronicas' who will take up the desperately needed work of reparation to Our Lord in this time in history."

***Allan Smith**, Publisher*, BishopSheenToday.com; *Radio Host*

"I am extremely edified by Mary Zuzolo's presentation of the devotion to the Holy Face of Christ, and I strongly recommend it to all the faithful. Mary beautifully chronicles the history and power of this devotion, linking the lives of its most illustrious propagators, the holy people who have gone before us and who now behold the Face of God in Heaven. This little work will lend impetus to the resurrection of this marvelous devotion to the Lord, who still reaches out to us in the fullness of His humanity and seeks to show us mercy through His Holy Face."

***Mother Abbess Cecilia Snell**, O.S.B., Benedictines of Mary, Queen of Heaven, Gower, Missouri*

"Every human face is an incomparable icon, one that reveals the human person behind it. The eyes are windows of the soul. The human Face of Jesus is even more: it is the icon that reveals a Divine Person, the Second of the Holy Trinity. Are you lost? Well, take up this book by the great-great-great-niece of a famous French Carmelite, the nun who inspired the Church and the world with the revelations she received concerning the Holy Face. In this book great things will be presented to you — unveiled before the eyes of your soul — and a great new adventure will commence."

***Abbot Philip Anderson**, O.S.B., Our Lady of Clear Creek Abbey, Oklahoma*

"During this time of 'unfettered testing by Satan,' this magnificent book provides the guidepost and inspiration to navigate modernity. Mary Jane Zuzolo delineates in convincingly beautiful and moving prose the message of the Holy Face Devotion, which serves as a battle plan to defeat the forces of evil. I urge you to embrace *Unveiling the Sixth Station of the Cross*; it will deepen your faith, enliven your spiritual life, and embolden your soul as you walk along with Jesus on His Via Crucis."

Elizabeth Yore, Attorney and Child Rights Advocate

"*Unveiling the Sixth Station of the Cross* takes the reader on a fascinating historical, biographical, and theological journey that places the devotion to the Holy Face in the context of each of these areas. Readers will come to understand that these messages to a humble Carmelite nun in a monastery in Tours, France, in the 1840s is part of a larger picture of the way God is working to prepare the way to address what is happening in the Church and in the world today. This book is critical to bringing to light a devotion that has been mostly hidden and unknown at the very time for which it was intended and when it is needed most urgently. The devotion to the Holy Face was promised as the remedy to the primary ills of our time and helps us to recognize the great gift our Lord has granted us to be part of His work of reparation, redemption, and salvation."

— *Fr. Robert Altier*, Author, God's Plan for Your Marriage: An Exploration of Holy Matrimony from Genesis to the Wedding Feast of the Lamb

"What a spiritual feast! In this book come together different devotions — to the Holy Face, to the Infancy of Christ, to the Immaculate Heart of Mary — all of which increase in us the sense of their interwovenness in God's salvific fabric. God's humility shines beautifully through, by way of His Holy Face, which was so besmirched; by way of His infancy; and by way of His most intimate bond with His Mother, from whom He is inseparable. This book is a gift for anyone who yearns to grow in spiritual childhood, for, unless we become like little ones, we will not enter into His Kingdom. All of this has a special meaning to my family. It was this Holy Face devotion that we practiced the last eight months of my husband's earthly life, praying for a holy end of life and a holy death. God and His Mother gave abundantly. Childlike, my husband left, provided for with all the riches of the sacraments, to be embraced by Mary on a First Saturday. Thus, I can testify that this devotion is special, and we owe it to Mary Jane Zuzolo, a relative of Sr. Marie of St. Peter, that she is presenting it to us in this unique and interwoven way. Let us not forget here also St. Thérèse of Lisieux, whose special devotion was to the Holy Face and to the Child Jesus!"

— *Dr. Maike Hickson*, Widow of Dr. Robert Hickson; Writer, LifeSiteNews.com

"This book gives an excellent treatment of the relationship between the Holy Face Devotion, major Marian apparitions, and the Divine Mercy Devotion and its scriptural roots. Many today often fail to think about God's justice and its need to be appeased. This book captures the absolute necessity of making reparation for our sins and the sins of mankind, utilizing the infinite merits of Our Lord and Our Lady to draw down His unfathomable mercy upon us. As St. Paul tells us, "Where sin abounded, grace abounded all the more," and so Our Lord always offers a remedy. The Holy Face Devotion, explained so well in this book, will greatly help to repair and atone for the countless sins committed against Our Lord; thus, it will help us to console the Sacred Heart of Jesus, imprint His image within us, convert many sinners, and help us 'to shine with a particular splendor in Heaven.'"

Fr. Gregory Zannetti, Parish Priest of the Diocese of Metuchen

"This book is fruit of a generous love. In the first place, it is the fruit of love of the Holy Face of Jesus, the merciful gaze of God on man that is salvation itself. In the second place, it is the fruit of a great love of the Church, which is judged now more than ever to be in need of rediscovering the human gaze of Christ. Finally, this book is the fruit of a devoted love of Sr. Mary of St. Peter, a blood relative of the author, through whom the devotion to the Holy Face is inextricably bound."

Dr. Aaron Riches, Theologian, Benedictine College;
Author, Ecce Homo: On the Divine Unity of Christ

"Through its various delicacies and intricacies, the human face reveals and identifies the human person. It is by gazing upon and studying the face of another that we come to know that person and sense his or her heart. Thus have countless love letters and poems expressed the lover's insatiable desire to behold the face of his beloved. This lover's desire is surpassed only by the cry of every human to see God. It is a cry that is answered by God in the mystery of the Incarnation, which gives us the face of God in the human face of Jesus Christ. While devotion to the Sacred Heart is rightly well-known, devotion to the Holy Face of Jesus is less popular. Now, thanks to the passionate work of author Mary Zuzolo, every Catholic can discover the rich history of this devotion and the great graces that await those who practice it."

Abbot James R. Albers, O.S.B., St. Benedict's Abbey, Atchison, Kansas

UNVEILING the SIXTH STATION of the CROSS

Mary Jane Zuzolo

UNVEILING the SIXTH STATION of the CROSS

Reparation to the Holy Face, Mother of All Devotions

SOPHIA INSTITUTE PRESS
Manchester, New Hampshire

Copyright © 2024 by Mary Jane Zuzolo

Printed in the United States of America. All rights reserved.

Cover by LUCAS Art & Design, Jenison, MI.

Cover image: *Face of Christ*, 1649 engraving by Claude Mellan (1598–1688) / wikimedia commons

Scripture quotations are taken from the Douay-Rheims Bible and from the Catholic Edition of the Revised Standard Version of the Bible, copyright 1965, 1966 by the Division of Christian Education of the National Council of the Churches of Christ in the United States of America. Used by permission. All rights reserved.

No part of this book may be reproduced, stored in a retrieval system, or transmitted in any form, or by any means, electronic, mechanical, photocopying, or otherwise, without the prior written permission of the publisher, except by a reviewer, who may quote brief passages in a review.

Nihil obstat: Curtis Keddy
Censor Librorum

Imprimatur: ✠ Joseph F. Naumann
Archbishop of Kansas City in Kansas
November 17, 2023

The *nihil obstat* and *imprimatur* are declarations that the work is considered to be free from doctrinal or moral error. It is not implied that those who have granted the same agree with the contents, opinions, or statements expressed therein.

Sophia Institute Press
Box 5284, Manchester, NH 03108
1-800-888-9344
www.SophiaInstitute.com

Sophia Institute Press is a registered trademark of Sophia Institute.

paperback ISBN 979-8-88911-112-2

ebook ISBN 979-8-88911-113-9

Library of Congress Control Number: 2023952500

First printing

*In thanksgiving for my most loving husband and family,
without whose support this book would never have been written.*

*In memory of my parents, and especially my mother,
who passed away one year ago today. She was the ancestral link to
Sister Marie de St. Pierre as well as my mentor in searching the depths
of the devotion during a time in which it was all but forgotten.*

*In tribute to Sister Marie de St. Pierre, whose great-great-great-niece
I am humbled—and honored—to be.*

*In dedication to the veiled treasures of the Holy Face of Christ,
aids to spiritual union with God: that all may deign
to embrace them, as unveiled. And to the unfathomable
love of God manifested in His justice and mercy,
so magnificently and mysteriously intertwined in the
devotion of reparation to Him, which serves as a remedy
for the ills of the modern era. Also, to Our Lady of the Holy
Name of God, through whom the Almighty chose to bestow the
graces flowing from the devotion, toward the salvation of
all—the reclaiming of all—in her celestial battle with Satan.*

*Mary Jane Zuzolo
October 28, 2023*

Acknowledgment

My husband Michael. Our children: Frances and Zachary Myslinski; Thomas Zuzolo; Joseph Zuzolo; Peter Zuzolo; Anthony Zuzolo. Byron Bullock. Don Shotland and RealZeal.org. Paulyn Ripp. Father Lawrence Carney. Charles McKinney and Sophia Institute Press staff. Archbishop Naumann. Curtis Keddy. Amy Huerter. Scott and Kary Newbolds. Mark and Theresa Jirak. Spencer and Denise Taylor. Eric and Sarah Klingele. Sue Sachse. Becky Hund. Aaron and Melissa Riches. Paul and Elizabeth Slobodnik. John and Maggie Haigh. Mark and Julia Zia. James and Danielle Blosser. Matt and Megan Fassero. Stacey White. President Steve Minnis and Benedictine College. Abbot James and St. Benedict's Abbey of Atchison, Kansas. Abbess Cecilia Snell and Benedictines of Mary, Queen of Apostles of Gower, Missouri. Abbot Philip Anderson and Benedictine Abbey of Our Lady of Clear Creek of Hulbert, Oklahoma. Father Robert Altier. Father Gregory Zannetti. Liz Yore. Maike Hickson. Allan Smith. David Annunziato. Gene Zanetti. Steve Cunningham. Ted and Joanne Sabourin. Christian Colby and Peter Kelly. Michael and Jeannie Cowan. Virginia Greecher, O.C.D.S., and prayer group. Jule Lane and prayer group. Mary Anne Bredemann. Judy Shutzman. Brenda Taheri and prayer group. Joel and Donna Sue Berry and prayer group. Kathleen Heckenkamp. Melanie Schafer. Father Scott DuVall. Dawn Marie Roeder and prayer group. John and Karen Wood. Paul and Deanna McNamara. Tom and April Hoopes. Darrin and Dina Muggli. Deacon Charles and Lynn Welte.

Andrew and Sabitha Salzmann. Dwight and Ellen Stephenson. Litte Brothers and Sisters of the Lamb. Brother Joachim. Cardinal Philippe Barbarin, archbishop emeritus, Diocese of Lyon. Myron and Valerie Fanton. Peter and Anne Neulieb. Father Tom Shoemaker. Joe Moniz and prayer group. Joan Bicknel and prayer group. Pam Jackson and prayer group. Mary Kay Farran. Len and Paula Hornung. Pam Lambert. Robert and Jeanna Faulhaber. Paula Zurawski, O.C.D.S., and prayer group. Carmelite Monastery of St. Thérèse, Michigan. Paul Gilbert. Clare McGrath-Merkle, O.C.D.S. Lisa Parents and prayer group. Michelle Galushka. Cathy Maloney-Hills. Cathy Delk. Valerie Lukasik-Bozzo. Joanie Ruppel. Theresa and Chuck Shelby. Mark and Stephanie Ruppel. Francis and Eileen Ruppel. Dan Ruppel. Chris and Seemein Ruppel. Jo Ellen and Keith Obermeyer.

Contents

Acknowledgment xi

About the Cover of the Book xv

Preface xix

The Holy Face Devotion Outlined by Parallels to the Book of Job. xxxi

1. St. Joan of Arc: Forerunner of Sister Marie de St. Pierre, Forebearer of the Holy Face Devotion 3

2. A Fitting Birthplace of the Devotion and Sister St. Pierre's New Home: The Carmel of Tours. 19

3. The "Donkey" Ambassadress of Christ 37

4. The Mission 55

5. The Holy Face and the Salvation of France 73

6. Sister St. Pierre, St. Thérèse, and the Holy Face 93

7. Mother of Mercy and the Pinnacle Devotion 135

8. The Holy Face "Face-Off" with Communism. 207

9. The Death and Legacy of Sister St. Pierre 225

Appendix I: The Cross of Lorraine. 237

Appendix II: Circular of Sister Marie de St. Pierre 239

Appendix III: How to Say the Holy Face Chaplet. 255

About the Author 261

About the Cover of the Book

Unveiling the Sixth Station of the Cross

The Way of the Cross, also known as the Via Crucis, uses a series of images, or stations, depicting events immediately surrounding Our Lord's Passion. In imitation of the Via Dolorosa in Jerusalem, a traditional processional route symbolic of Christ's way to Mount Calvary, the stations are to help the faithful to meditate upon Our Lord's suffering during His Passion. The Way of the Cross is prayed publicly during Lent and especially on Good Friday, since the prayers and meditations used reflect a spirit of reparation for the sufferings that Christ endured for man's salvation. A valiant and compassionate woman is commemorated in the sixth station as using her veil to wipe the spittle, dust, sweat, and blood from the suffering Holy Face of Christ on His way to crucifixion. In return for her act of kindness, Christ left the imprint of His exact likeness upon her veil. Because of this, she has come to be referred to as *Veronica*, meaning "true icon." St. Veronica, as she is now known, is designated by Christ in Church-approved private revelations as a protectress and patron of the Holy Face devotion in that she was the first to make reparation to His wounded Countenance. "Unveiling the Sixth Station of the Cross" is indicative of the veil symbolizing the merciful love Veronica both gave and received from the Savior, which summates the very essence of the devotion. Additionally, it is reminiscent of the "veiled treasures" of the Holy Face, which are aids toward mystical objectives of the Carmelite tradition, especially those of St. Thérèse of Lisieux.

Neither the loving act of Veronica nor her history is written about in the Gospels, though tradition holds that she was the woman with the flow of blood who was healed by touching the hem of the garment of Christ (Matt. 9:20). Her veil, however, is preserved in the Vatican Basilica of St. Peter and has received every honor and veneration from the beginning of the Christian era as one of the most precious relics of Christ's sacred Passion. The Veronica's veil image on the cover is a photo of one of many distributed copies of an artistic rendering depicting the "Miracle of the Vatican" in 1849, during which the veil became miraculously "enlivened" and distinct from its usual centuries-old fading for a period of three hours during a Christmas octave exhibition. The event was notarized by canons at the basilica and entered in its daybook.[1] One of these images was used in the countless miracles performed at the hands of Ven. Dupont, as acknowledged by Pope Bl. Pius IX.[2]

According to the private revelations from Christ to initiate the Holy Face devotion, all the blasphemies now hurled against the Divinity, whom they cannot reach, fall back, so to speak, like the spittle of the impious, upon the Face of Our Lord, who offered Himself as a victim for sinners. Christ, "seeking Veronicas,"[3] implores the devout to imitate the zeal of the pious Veronica, who had so courageously braved the crowd of His enemies to console Him. Christ revealed that by making reparation for current acts of blasphemy (as prohibited in the first three commandments), which renew the injuries to His Face, devotees render Him the same service as this heroic woman, and He regards those who do so "with the same complacent eyes as He gazed upon her when on His road to Calvary."[4] He promises that by His Holy Face, devotees will work wonders.[5] He moreover reveals that when one offers His Face to the Eternal Father in reparation, nothing will be refused, and the conversion of many sinners will be obtained.[6] As He imprinted His likeness upon the veil of Veronica in return for her kindness, He promises to imprint His likeness on the souls of those who console Him in this way, giving His Holy Face as a recompense in proportion for

---

[1] Pierre Désiré Janvier, *The Holy Man of Tours* (Baltimore: John Murphy, 1882), 218–219.
[2] Pope Pius IX referred to Dupont as "perhaps one of the greatest miracle workers in Church history."
[3] Sister St. Pierre, *Life of Sister St. Pierre*, ed. Rev. P. Janvier (Baltimore: John Murphy, 1884), 210.
[4] Ibid., 218.
[5] Ibid., 225.
[6] Ibid., 268.

these acts of reparation, while also revealing this exchange as the "greatest source of grace second to the sacraments."[7]

REPARATION TO THE HOLY FACE

The Holy Face is the figure, the mirror, and the expression of the Divine Godhead.[8] For the Face of Christ represents not only His redemptive suffering endured in the Passion, but also the Face of the Mystical Body of Christ (the Church), as well as the Divine Trinity itself, for as St. Paul says, the head of Christ is God (1 Cor. 11:3). The faithful are thus called to make reparation to the Holy Face — reparation to the Godhead — by presenting the suffering Face of Christ to the Father in reparation for current sins of blasphemy to appease the Father's justice and to draw mercy for sinners. This is appropriate in that, as specified in the Holy Face revelations, one should not present himself before the Eternal Father without being accompanied by a portion of the precious merits of His Son.[9] Offering the merits and love, veiled in the wounded Countenance of Christ, is thus an offering *of God to God* by man, mirroring the Consecration at Mass, in which Christ (as represented by the priest) presents Himself as a perfect offering to be made to His heavenly Father. In the devotion (as distinct from a sacrament),[10] as an extension of the work of the Redemption, "a new Work for atonement of new crimes,"[11] man utilizes the merits and love of Christ, as offered to the Father, the head for the members, thereby combining the power of God with the cooperation of man in drawing mercy for sinners.

MOTHER OF ALL DEVOTIONS

Finally, Mary's role of Mother of Mercy establishes her as the underlying link in all devotions to Christ and Mary, as was most clearly designated and honored in the private revelations surrounding the Holy Face devotion. This, together with the devotion's singularity in making reparation to the Godhead (verses aspects of Christ's sacred humanity) for modern offenses against the first three

---

[7] Ibid., 226.
[8] Ibid., 222.
[9] Ibid., 273.
[10] Devotions are forms of popular piety outside the liturgy, which is, however, their origin and aim.
[11] Sister St. Pierre, *Life of Sister St. Pierre*, 287.

commandments (exclusively concerning the rights of God), makes it foundational to all others. Offered in union with the Sacred Heart in the Most Holy Sacrament of the Altar, the Holy Face devotion is its complement, while also giving it its greatest honor and consolation.[12] Given by God to appease justice for unparalleled times of iniquity, according to Christ, and as an extension of the Redemption, it sets forth the pattern of reparation or atonement first, followed by mercy, which is to flow through Mary (as is even true of the Divine Mercy devotion).[13] Though the devotee is called to selflessly assist in his brother's salvation by participating in this work, his own soul is transformed in the process, receiving the imprint of Christ's likeness in proportion for his acts of reparation.[14] These indicators, in addition to the devotion's unparalleled promises and miracles, and per the words of Christ Himself, reveal reparation to the Holy Face as no less than the pinnacle devotion — the devotions' devotion.[15] As the highest devotion, and given to mankind by Our Lady, through whom the merciful graces for conversion of sinners flow, the title "Mother of All Devotions" takes on dual significance.

---

[12] Sister Mary St. Peter, *Life of Sister Mary St. Peter*, ed. Rev. P. Janvier (France, 1884), 127–130. (It "wounds [his] Heart most lovingly" in consolation for that which injures him more than all else: blasphemy; it also "accomplishes his desire, that of honoring his Sacred Heart and the holy Heart of his Mother.")

[13] For full discussion, see chapter 7.

[14] Sister St. Pierre, *Life of Sister St. Pierre*, 88, 232, 233, 278.

[15] Sister Mary St. Peter, *Life of Sister Mary St. Peter*, 198.

Preface

IN FULLY CHURCH-APPROVED PRIVATE revelations, Christ describes the Holy Face devotion[16] as "the most beautiful work that has yet appeared on the face of the earth."[17] He also likens it analogously to "the miraculous wine served at the end of the wedding feast at Cana" — in contrast to the "common wine" of other devotions.[18] Certainly, all devotions are invaluable and interrelated, however. In fact, the Holy Face devotion emanates from and complements the Sacred and Immaculate Hearts,[19] while also affording them their greatest honor[20] and consolation.[21] Christ additionally states that this reparation to the Holy Face is "the sole means of appeasing His Father"[22] (in the face of chastisement) and is the "most noble and necessary work of our times."[23] Christ warns that, consequently, Satan will do everything in his power to stamp it out.[24] Intimately allied to the Redemption[25] and offered in union

---

[16] Devotions are forms of popular piety outside the Catholic liturgy, which, however, is its origin and aim.

[17] Sister Mary St. Peter, *Life of Sister Mary St. Peter*, ed. Rev. P. Janvier (France, 1884), 311–312.

[18] Ibid., 329–330.

[19] Ibid., 121, 124, 130, 149.

[20] Ibid., 127–130. To praise and bless the name of God *is* to honor the Sacred and Immaculate Hearts.

[21] Ibid., 124, 130, 153.

[22] Ibid., 290.

[23] Ibid., 312.

[24] Ibid., 154, 181.

[25] Ibid., 312.

with Christ in the Most Holy Sacrament of the Altar,[26] the Holy Face devotion is celestial armament for the era to assist man in doing his part to reclaim all for Christ. It is a spirituality of co-redemption — of reparation — composed by God Himself for modern times, which He refers to as unparalleled in moral depravity. The devotion, moreover, is prefigured in the book of Job, complements Fatima, encompasses the spirituality of St. Thérèse, crowns insights of the great Carmelite mystics, affirms the Mariology of St. Louis de Montfort (at a time when his writings were just resurfacing), and has produced more miracles than Lourdes.[27] Extraordinarily, Christ bestows His wounded Countenance as the object of adoration in the devotion as "the greatest source of grace second to the sacraments."[28] Christ also promises that in proportion to acts of reparation offered, He will imprint His likeness upon the devotee's soul.[29] This is reminiscent of His imprinting His likeness upon Veronica's veil in return for her act of consolation. *Unveiling the Sixth Station of the Cross* is indicative of the merciful love given and received by Christ in reparation, as well as the "veiled treasures" of the Holy Face, which become mystical aids toward union with God. And in that the devotion is "fraught with so much necessity and honor for God,"[30] Christ desires that His Mother have the privilege of giving it to mankind, as a new pledge of mercy.[31] Finally, Christ revealed that all graces flowing from this devotion come through Mary[32] and honors her with the title Our Lady of the Holy Name of God.[33] Unlike any other, it is a devotion centered on reparation to the Godhead itself (versus various aspects of Christ's sacred humanity).[34] In its preference by God to all other devotions,[35] and in its revealing Mary as the link of mercy in these devotions, it becomes, in a dual sense, the *mother of all devotions*.

---

[26] Ibid., 158.
[27] More than six thousand miracles were documented, and as many as ten thousand were performed in the presence of Dupont. Countless more were performed by way of the vials of Holy Face oil that Dupont sent worldwide, upon request. The estimated number of miraculous healings at Lourdes is around seven thousand, with seventy being officially recognized by the Church.
[28] Sister Mary St. Peter, *Life of Sister Mary St. Peter*, 246–247.
[29] Ibid., 254.
[30] Ibid., 327.
[31] Ibid., 333.
[32] Ibid., 356–359.
[33] Ibid., 333.
[34] Ibid., 198, 329.
[35] Ibid., 198, 311, 329.

Yet today, a time in which, according to Christ, "iniquity has never reached such a degree,"[36] very few know about the Holy Face devotion. This is especially regrettable given that its purpose is to repair "the most offensive affronts against God,"[37] those "wounding Christ's heart more than all others,"[38] "those renewing the injuries to His Face."[39] These most heinous sins in the eyes of God are *current* affronts against the first three commandments[40] — those forbidding idolatry, blasphemy, and irreverence. For some decades after its approval, the devotion was enormously popular. Satan has perhaps at long last, however, done all he can to stifle it (at the very time in which it is most needed). Though at the center of some of the greatest miracle-working in Church history — as attested by Pope Bl. Pius IX[41] — and immediately[42] approved for the whole world by Pope Leo XIII in 1885, the devotion has in recent decades most assuredly fallen into obscurity.

Sister Marie de St. Pierre of the Holy Family was the young French Carmelite nun who received revelations from Christ to initiate the now neglected and virtually unknown Holy Face devotion. I first learned of it because Sister Marie de St. Pierre (Sister St. Pierre, as commonly referred to in Carmel) is also my great-great-great-aunt.[43] There is no merit in merely being a relation of a very holy person, but I have always felt a familial obligation to at least understand and

[36] Ibid., 159.
[37] Ibid., 124.
[38] Ibid., 127, 311.
[39] Ibid., 238, 244, 245. The Face of Christ represents the Divinity as well as the "Face of the Church" or her doctrine, the essence of the Christian Faith. Renewed injuries wound the Mystical Body of Christ, the Church.
[40] Ibid.
[41] Pius IX referred to Dupont as "perhaps the greatest miracle worker in Church history."
[42] Pope Leo XIII broke with tradition by not approving the devotion more incrementally — initiating with the diocese of origin, then the country, etc. Instead, he approved the devotion immediately for the whole world: "*Non tam pro Galia, quam ubique*" (not only for France, but for everywhere).
[43] The first ancestor on my mother's side to live in America was Sister St. Pierre's brother, another of the twelve children born to Pierre and Francoise Portier, Prosper Michel Louis Marie Eluere, who emigrated from France to "Vincennes of America" in 1840. Prosper accompanied the second bishop to Vincennes, Rev. Célestine de la Hailandière, who had returned to Rennes, France, to find artisans to help him complete the St. Francis Xavier Cathedral in Vincennes, the first capital of the Indiana Territory. Prosper was a skilled blacksmith and later established a business in Vincennes, where he and his wife Mary Louise (Bayard) raised eight children, my great-great-grandfather, Edward L. M. Eluere, being the eldest. Prosper was also well acquainted with and did artisan work for the first Indiana saint, Mother Théodore Guérin of the Sisters of Providence in Terre Haute, Indiana, who was founding the convent and school at Saint Mary-of-the-Woods at the time.

practice the devotion to the best of my ability, as well as to pass along what I know to my children. I was content with this level of commitment until I read a biography of Ven. Leo Dupont to my sons.

Ven. Dupont is the "other half" of the story regarding the Holy Face devotion. He used his fortune and status to propogate it, and it was at his hands that thirty years of the Church's greatest miracle-working were manifested.[44] The miracles were effected through prayers consistent with[45] the devotion and oil from a lamp burning in front of a Holy Face image, which had been touched to Veronica's veil in the Vatican. This original veil had become miraculously "enlivened" for three hours during a Christmas octave exposition.[46] (The Holy Face image linked to the devotion is from a hand-drawn copy of this "Miracle of the Vatican.") Ven. Dupont played no small part in helping to show the credibility of the revelations, not just by virtue of these countless miracles[47] but also by way of his heroically virtuous life, marked by his extraordinary practice of and zeal for the Holy Face devotion. Unlike Sister St. Pierre, Dupont lived to see the newly appointed archbishop of Tours initiate approval of the devotion in 1876; Dupont died the same year. The Archconfraternity of the Holy Face was established in 1885.

[44] Pope Pius IX declared Dupont "perhaps the greatest miracle worker in Church history." Pope St. John Paul II declared Dupont Venerable. The miracles began in 1851.
[45] The prayers listed in the *Manual of the Archconfraternity of the Holy Face* had not yet been approved.
[46] Pierre Désiré Janvier, *The Holy Man of Tours* (Baltimore: John Murphy, 1882), 218–219. "In the month of January 1849, during the exile of Pius IX at Gaeta, public prayers, by order of the Holy Father, were offered in all the churches of Rome, to implore the mercy of the Omnipotent on the Pontifical States [due to the revolutions of 1848]. On this occasion, they exposed in St. Peter's the wood of the true cross and the veil of St. Veronica. On the third day of the exposition, the canons appointed to the charge of the precious relics, noticed in the Holy Face, the impression of which on the veil is so faint as to be scarcely visible, a remarkable change. Through another veil of silk which covers it, and absolutely prevents the features from being distinguished, the divine Face appeared distinctly, as if living, and illumined by a soft light; the features assumed a death-like hue, and the eyes, deep-sunken, wore an expression of great pain. The canons immediately notified the clergy of the Basilica; the people were called in. Many wept; all were impressed with a reverential awe. An apostolic notary was summoned; a certificate was drawn up attesting the fact; a copy of it was sent to the Holy Father at Gaeta. For many days this prodigy, which lasted three hours, was the sole topic of conversation at Rome. On the evening of the same day, some veils of white silk, on which is represented the Holy Face, were applied to the miraculous veil. These veils [were] sent to France."
[47] As mentioned in footnote 27, more than six thousand miracles were documented. As many as ten thousand were performed in the presence of Dupont. Countless more were performed by way of the vials of Holy Face oil that Dupont sent worldwide, upon request.

I thought that my sons would relate better to an overall introduction to the devotion by way of Ven. Dupont's life, rather than to that of Sister St. Pierre's, so I read to them Dorothy Scallan's *Holy Man of Tours*, a readily available, short biography of him. As teens, they quickly questioned how the author could have known certain details of Dupont's life and thoughts. I also began to wonder. I researched Scallan's bibliography and was delighted to be able to locate some (very long) biographies of Dupont, written close to the time of his death by those who knew him, which used as sources hundreds of letters, interviews, and even writings of Dupont himself.

Then more acquainted with Ven. Dupont's life, I was saddened to realize that the writer not only added much in the way of literary license to "novelize" his life, but she also left out amazing known facts, which would have dramatically enhanced the illustration of his remarkably holy and endearing soul. Furthermore, Scallan's writing style of the 1950s (including giving dialect to the slaves) would never stand up to the scrutiny of these times. I am forever indebted to the author, however, for recounting anew the amazing role Ven. Dupont played in spreading the devotion and for re-familiarizing the world with the truly "Holy Man of Tours." The book does read like a novel and is surely meant as only an introduction to the devotion and Dupont's life, yet the overall impression from a current reading seems to be a dated book that barely scratches the surface of Dupont's great depth of soul. I felt resolved to update Dupont's life story for the modern reader, but as I researched further to do so, a much, much more urgent need came to light: *to help reacquaint the world with the devotion itself.*

The Holy Face devotion was revealed to Sister St. Pierre by Our Lord in response to the "enlightened," freethinking notions concurrent with the French Revolution, which left an aftermath of atheistic and blasphemous ideology, now the norm. The freethinking ideology in which the "autonomy" of reason was substituted for the authority of Church dogma has clearly led to a decline of morals,[48] which at best is a confused notion of objective sin and at worst a total disregard of it. This rationalism, in which "truth" is understood through argumentation, paved the way for modernism, in which "truth" is understood as dynamic and even as

---

[48] The Reformation substituted "faith alone" and the "Bible alone" for the authority of the Church and its tradition. The freethinking ideology of the French Revolution took anti-Church concepts a step further, substituting, in effect, a new faith, the "autonomy" of reason for the authority of Church dogma and Christian society. Having separated morals from faith, the autonomy of reason led to a steady decline in morals.

perceived by personal feeling, which has further devolved into today's moral relativism and wokeism in which there is no objective truth at all.[49] Communism shares tactics of infiltration with modernism, and the various postmodernisms, and its anti-God, anti-family, and anti-man system has in fact become the deadliest in the history of man.[50] These systems have the explicit purpose of the de-spiritualization of Christian civilization and are warned about in Isaiah 5:20: "Woe to you that call evil good, and good evil." Reparation to the Holy Face was given to defeat these ideologies, making it extremely pertinent today.

Indeed, considering that the blasphemous thinking of nineteenth-century France (for which God initially requested reparation be made) was the catalyst to current, often even more pervasive and egregious affronts to God, the devotion is also — if not ultimately — intended for the third millennium. Though it was initiated in France, for France, Christ revealed that the Holy Face devotion is to be an ongoing practice by all the devout to save souls and nations throughout the world.[51] The divine communications given to Sister St. Pierre made clear that the practice of reparation for fresh offenses to the Godhead, by offering the merits residing in Christ's wounded Countenance to the Father,[52] should be an *essential element of Christian life*,[53] a newly revealed, timely aspect of Christian spirituality meant for the entire body of the Church. As testament to this, Pope Leo XIII broke from tradition by approving the Archconfraternity of the Holy Face by papal brief *immediately for the whole world* — for all times and peoples.

---

[49] Denial of genders is an example of a make-believe "reality."

[50] Paul Kengor, *The Politically Incorrect Guide to Communism: The Killingest Idea Ever* (Washington, D.C: Regnery, 2017), 9–13.

[51] Sister Mary St. Peter, *Life of Sister Mary St. Peter*, 172. Sister St. Pierre mentions prayers (of the devotion) that Our Lord wished to have propagated "over the whole world." Sister Mary Emmanuel, *Life of Sister Marie de St. Pierre of the Holy Family, Carmelite of Tours, 1816–1848: A Forerunner of St. Thérèse of Lisieux* (London: Burns, Oates & Washbourne, 1938), 147. Sister St. Pierre refers to the work (the Holy Face devotion) that is to "disarm the Justice of God and save France and the world." And Ibid., 184. Writing only in 1938, the author references "a new era [after that of Sister Saint Pierre's time] of blasphemy and hatred of God, seemingly unequaled in any preceding age, call[s] for a new era of Reparation and love."

[52] Sister Mary St. Peter, *Life of Sister Mary St. Peter*, 290. Our Lord to Sister St. Pierre: "If you knew how efficacious, how full of virtue is my divine Face! I have taken upon my head the sins of mankind, that my members may be spared.... Offer my Face to My Father, for it is the *sole means of appeasing him*.... I desire [the] Work of Reparation [to My Holy Face]." My emphasis.

[53] Sister Mary Emmanuel, *Life of Sister Marie*, 1–2.

The devotion, then, is to make reparation for ever-increasing, current blasphemous offenses against the Trinity, as prohibited in the first three commandments. Obeying the first three, which concern the rights of God, is foundational to the practice of the last seven, which concern the rights of men, though, assuredly, many — if not most people — today *at best* feel that the last seven can stand on their own. Again, this denial of the significance that God and the Church play in truth and morality is essentially the problem of relativism in which each person decides for himself what is "true" and "just," making of himself a god. Relativism gives way to socialism, Communism, atheism, and satanism, for they all deny to varying degrees the absolute truth of God, manifested in natural law, which allows for the deduction of the universal, God-given values and rights of men. These systems of thought are grave offenses to the Triune Divinity, and Communism, as particularly mentioned in the revelations, is an especial evil to defeat in that it is, according to Christ, "the sworn enem[y] of the Church and of ... Christ."[54] Communism is an unprecedented affront to the majesty of God in its *explicitly* atheistic and blasphemous foundation. (That is, it is designed to be *overtly anti-God, anti-Christian*: it has not "just" fallen into godlessness or become un-Christian because of sin and weakness.) Mankind is to "repair" its (and all) offenses against the Almighty in this reparation to the Godhead, defeating via spiritual, not material, combat — resulting in the conversion, not death, of the enemy.

Offenses against the Godhead (as represented by the Holy Face) are also offenses against the "Face of the Church," or her doctrine, such that all blasphemy endured by the Church are as renewed wounds to the Countenance of Christ (the Face of His Mystical Body).[55] The infectious blasphemy of Communism and

---

[54] Sister Mary St. Peter, *Life of Sister Mary St. Peter*, 319. These are Our Lord's words to Sister Marie St. Pierre. He recommended a specific (additional) means of combating Communists: offering the Cross and all instruments of His Passion in reparation to the Godhead. It may be confusing to the reader why a book published in 1884 should be referenced in referring to Communism; the *Communist Manifesto* was not published until the year Sister St. Pierre died (1848), the Russian and Chinese revolutions had not taken place, and there were no countries at that time referred to as Communist. And Ibid., 318–319. France, however, was the center of the "revolutionary and anti-social" spirit that had spread over Europe, "assuming different names at different epochs to suit the caprice of the moment; at one time styling themselves Socialists, then Liberals, and again Nihilists.... Toward the end of the reign of Louis Philip, at the period of ... the life and communications of Sr. Mary St. Peter, ... they bore the appellation of Communists."

[55] Ibid., 244–245.

modernism was alluded to in the apparitions of Fatima,[56] among others, foretelling of the "errors of Russia" spreading if Our Lady's requests were not met. This "infiltration" has also been warned against by various modern popes.[57] Reparation to the Holy Face is the "*most noble* and the most necessary work for our times,"[58] for God is demanding a new effort, a new cooperation on the part of man, whose object is to repair these most loathsome crimes of modern society, which He describes as "deep-rooted impiety and absolute incredulity."[59]

The Holy Face devotion, the work of reparation designed to reorient man to God, offered by man *in union with Christ* to the Father, by virtue of the merits of Christ's dolorous Face, is intrinsically linked to the Redemption of Christ. "The most beautiful work that has yet appeared on the face of the earth"[60] does not, therefore, somehow trump the beauty of Christ's Redemption, for it is an extension of it.[61] It is evidently both pleasing and fitting in God's eyes that mankind should take a more specific role in co-redemption, given how grave his offenses to God have become in modern times.[62] It is the most beautiful work in that it is Christ who is giving us, in mercy, His Face to be offered by mankind to appease the justice of God and to bring salvation to men, a completion of the circle: man is to assist in the redemption of his neighbor by offering in reparation the wounded Countenance of Christ to the Father. It is a most powerful

---

[56] In her apparition of July 13, 1917, Our Lady of Fatima told Sister Lucy that "Russia will spread its errors throughout the world, raising up wars and persecutions against the Church. The good will be martyred, the Holy Father will have much to suffer, and various nations will be annihilated."

[57] In the nineteenth and twentieth centuries, popes have expressed concern for this purported infiltration: Pope Leo XIII after his vision of 1884 in which Satan was given permission by God to attempt to destroy the Church (and which consequently led him to compose the St. Michael Prayer); Pope St. Pius X in his 1907 encyclical *Pascendi Dominici Gregis* in which he warns of modernists who "put their designs for her ruin into operation not from without but from within"; and Pope St. Paul VI who stated in 1972 that the smoke of Satan had entered the Church, perhaps referring to "anti-communism documents of Vatican II not being published." Paul Kengor, *The Devil and Karl Marx* (Gastonia, NC: TAN Books, 2020), 142–143. There is also the well-known testimony of Bella Dodd, former Communist, who spoke extensively of the infiltration of the Church by Soviet agents and *The Memoirs of the Communist Infiltration into the Church* by Marie Carré, etc.

[58] Sister Mary St. Peter, *Life of Sister Mary St. Peter*, 312.

[59] Ibid., 311–312.

[60] Ibid.

[61] Sister St. Pierre, *Life of Sister St. Pierre*, ed. Rev. P. Janvier (Baltimore: John Murphy, 1884), 287.

[62] Ibid.

offering, for it allows man to utilize the merits and love of Christ, veiled in His wounded Countenance, to satisfy the Father's justice, drawing mercy for sinners, thereby uniting the power of God with the cooperation of man. Appeased by the most adorable and beloved Face of His Son, disfigured by current blasphemies, and consoled by this offering,[63] the Father has pity on man's face, disfigured by sin. The devotee is formed to the likeness of Christ, becoming more and more a vessel of reparation and love in which he, in Christ, becomes a mediator between God's justice and mercy, empowered to further aid in the salvation of his brethren, while he himself is transformed in the process.

The Holy Face devotion as such is not merely a collection of prayers. It is a *spirituality of atonement* — of reparation — forming the devotee as a "victim" of justice and love, annihilating him into the Sacred and Immaculate Hearts, thereby destroying all but that which is of Christ. It (further) complements the spirituality of St. Thérèse by offering to Christ "the wine of compassion and the oil of charity"[64] — in fact becoming of greatest consolation to Him![65] (Consolation and compassion and charity toward Christ are the very hallmarks of St. Thérèse's victimhood to merciful love.) Moreover, Christ related that if one dedicates himself to this exercise of reparation, He would bestow upon him "a kiss of love," which would be a "pledge of the eternal union."[66] Encompassing for man the goal of the great Carmelite mystics, Our Lord appears to indicate that reparation to the Holy Face — appeasement of God's justice — is above all an act of profound *love*, for which He is prepared to return to the generous heart a most tender and lavish devotion, a cascading of — even a union with[67] — divine merciful love.

The merits hidden in the wounded Countenance of Christ — to be offered to the Father in reparation for current offenses against the first three commandments — is consolation for God and mercy for man. It is an act of selfless love of God and neighbor, yet God in His goodness allows for the devotee himself to become more Christlike in the process. Whoever makes this reparation will be performing the office of the pious Veronica, and Christ, in turn, pledges to care for these souls, disfigured by sin, by reproducing His image in them, in

---

[63] Sister Mary St. Peter, *Life of Sister Mary St. Peter*, 198, 329.
[64] Ibid., 260.
[65] Ibid., 260–261.
[66] Ibid., 260.
[67] Ibid., 279.

proportion to the care they take in offering reparation.[68] By making reparation for the offenses against the first three commandments, one is honoring the majesty of God in a way most pleasing to the Father — exhibiting fear of the Lord, quintessentially.

Likewise pleading for mankind to exhibit proper fear of the Lord, the Marian apparitions of La Salette pick up where the revelations of Christ to Sister St. Pierre leave off. They are linked not only in content but also in manner, for they came as a direct appeal from Sister St. Pierre to Our Lady, asking her to inform someone else of the messages for concern that her bishop would not approve the devotion.[69] Our Lady of La Salette conveys the extreme offense that sins of blasphemy and the profanation of Sunday give to Our Lord and how His hand of justice will not be held back forever. The La Salette messages echo the revelations of Sister St. Pierre in which reparation for sins of blasphemy — the opposite of fear of God — is consequently demanded of the faithful for themselves, and especially for others.

The interweaving of these and other Church-approved private revelations of Christ and Marian apparitions — especially Fatima — helps put into celestial context the current declining state of human morality, as well as an inevitable period of correction. They do, however, also give humanity hope for better times to come, a time of great peace and purity that Our Lady has promised will follow, as outlined in Fatima: the crown apparition and complement devotion to that of the Holy Face. To usher in that time, man has an essential part to play in drawing down mercy for himself and others; there is a responsibility for each to help save as many souls as possible by way of reparation, which also affords mitigation of God's merciful chastisement.[70] For, according to Christ, Communism is both the enemy of God and an allowed chastisement by Heaven as punishment for unprecedented modern sins of blasphemy, which includes all sin and ideology that denies the transcendence of the Almighty in lieu of man making himself a "god." It is perhaps only in this era, from a hindsight perspective, and with the benefit of successive devotions to Christ and Mary, each augmenting and complementing the foundational Holy Face revelations, that the full treasury of this reparation to the Godhead may now be appreciated. It is only now, in this apparent (ongoing)

---

[68] Ibid., 254.
[69] Ibid., 277–278.
[70] Sister Mary St. Peter, *Life of Sister Mary St. Peter*, 285.

"worst of times," that the effect of neglecting the devotion is being realized, as well as the ever-increasing necessity of it as remedy.

It is through the practice of the devotion by the humble devout that mercy for the conversion of others will be drawn. Our Lord told Sister St. Pierre, "Sinners, as clouds of dust borne on the wind, are whirled from this world, and precipitated into hell. Have pity on your brethren and pray for them!"[71] Our Lady of Fatima also implored, "Pray very much and make sacrifices for sinners; for many souls go to hell because there is no one to pray and make sacrifices for them."[72] It is a chilling reality check. God is all-just, all-good, and all-merciful, so this is not a description of an "unfair" scenario, but rather a call for solidarity, a call for all to pray and make sacrifices for our fellow brethren as co-redeemers in Christ. Lost souls are a real consequence of neglecting man's duty as members of the communion of saints in which each member contributes to the good and welfare of all. In that God is both all-merciful and all-just, reparation must come before mercy.

This book is a reintroduction for the faithful of the third millennium to a most efficacious tool by which man may do his part in bringing about the conversion of the masses, while also bringing blessings upon himself[73] — during these, the latter times. Indeed, it is urgently requested by Our Lord, for He cautioned Sister St. Pierre, "Woe to those [cities that] do not make reparation!"[74] The Holy Face devotion is to be an essential element of Catholic spirituality designed by God Himself for the modern era. It is for those engaged in the seriousness of the age, providing hope and a means for man to assist in reclaiming all for Christ. Complementing Fatima, it is a battle plan to assist Our Lady in the current spiritual war against evil, yet capping key understanding of the great

---

[71] Ibid., 309.
[72] Spoken to the children visionaries during the August 1917 apparition of Fatima.
[73] Sister Mary St. Peter, *Life of Sister Mary St. Peter*, 291, 254. Our Lord promises: "According to the diligence you will manifest in repairing my image disfigured by blasphemers, so will I have the same care in repairing your soul which has been disfigured by sin. I will imprint thereon my image, and I will render it as beautiful as when it came forth from the baptismal font." This is but one of many unparalleled promises given by Our Lord to those who practice the devotion.
[74] Ibid., 161. Our Lord said that since the sin of blasphemy (to include each of the first three commandments) is publicly committed, the reparation must likewise be made in "every village and in every hamlet." And, Ibid., 152, 172. Though He is specifically speaking of France in this instance, the revelations make clear that this is a devotion for the whole world and for the whole of mankind. (*Woe* as used biblically indicated terrible afflictions as in chastisements.)

Carmelite mystics, true devotion to Mary, and the promises and revelations surrounding the devotion itself, it is a most valuable aid in man's own individual salvation as well.

Mary Jane Zuzolo
Kansas, U.S.A.
May 13, 2023
Feast of Our Lady of Fatima

The Holy Face Devotion Outlined by Parallels to the Book of Job

Lo, we have seen him, and there is no beauty in him, nor comeliness. He is despised and rejected, a man of sorrows, his face full of grief. He is worn out by suffering, like one in whose presence the people hide their faces. He is scorned and disdained. His appearance is that of one tortured beyond human endurance. And yet he is fairer than all the sons of men, and by his wounds we are healed.

— *The Way of the Cross*[75]

Sin as Old as Time[76]

Paradoxically, the errors of modernism are not confined to the period of modernity. They originate in Lucifer's desire to be like God. Though "merely" borrowing from Satan's hallmark sin, they do comprise, however, an unprecedented ideology of blasphemy on the part of man. As such, Pope St. Pius X referred to modernism as "the synthesis of all heresies." Spawning from rationalism and embracing naturalism, modernism attacks revelation, faith, Scripture, and the authority of the Church in

---

[75] *The Way of the Cross: Adapted from an Old Latin Compilation of Liturgical and Biblical Texts*, rev., 2nd ed. (Collegeville, MN: Liturgical Press, 1978), 15.

[76] Much of the first three sections of this introduction were first published as a *Latin Mass* article: Mary Jane Zuzolo, "The Holy Face Devotion Prefigured in the Book of Job," *The Latin Mass: The Journal of Catholic Culture and Tradition* 31 (Winter–Spring 2022): 50–53.

its belief that doctrine not only evolves but should have subjective feelings, rather than the immutable truth of God, as its basis. Its inherent atheism attempts the destruction of the Faith from within, promoting an easy, feel-good religion in place of the absolute dogma of the Church. Modernism desires to characterize the Catholic Church as a purely social, rather than a supernatural, establishment.

Modernism's tactics of infiltration are exemplified by the socioeconomic systems of socialism and Communism, which tout an authoritarian ideology openly hostile to traditional values but also seek the subversion of tradition from within both Church and State. These systems are an anti-human, anti-family, and anti-God endeavor. They are responsible for the killing of nearly one hundred million victims to date and in the twentieth century account for double the martyrs of the previous nineteen centuries combined.[77] Marx's ideology is the enemy of humanity and Christianity, an adversary of the Almighty.

Modernism furthermore gives rise to today's moral relativism, which posits that there is no absolute truth but only individual "truths." (Yet in the fashion of Marxism's dictatorial dogmatism, this "tolerance" of different "truths" ends by imposing its own — the "dictatorship of relativism."[78]) In his desire to create his own truth and morality, man succeeds in "modernizing" Satan's primordial sin. Man embraces the same sin of blasphemy under the guise of ever new modernist ideologies to effectively join with the enemy again and again in declaring himself "like unto God."

It is specifically these "updated" sins of modernism for which man is called to atone in the Holy Face devotion. The devotion is a work of reparation given to man to repair *current* offenses against the first three commandments, those concerning the rights of God. The (approved) private revelations to initiate the devotion were given to Sister Marie de St. Pierre by Christ in response to the blasphemous ideology concurrent with the French Revolution, which became quite normalized in the years following (and remains so today). God chooses[79]

---

[77] Paul Kengor, *The Politically Incorrect Guide to Communism: The Killingest Idea Ever* (Washington, D.C.: Regnery, 2017), 9–13.

[78] A phrase coined by Pope Benedict XVI.

[79] Man's role in co-redemption is in no way equal to Christ's; it is categorically different in that nothing man can do can add to the Redemption. God *desires*, however, that man be a cooperative worker of salvation, a free participant in the redemption of his fellow man through prayer, sacrifice, and suffering. The mystery of co-redemption is highlighted in the New Testament, particularly by St. Paul, though arguably prefigured in the book of Job as well (among other books in the Old Testament), and will be discussed more in the main body of the book.

to give man a special role to play in the salvation of his brethren as an extension of the Redemption, given that, according to Christ, "iniquity has never reached such a degree."[80] Man is to offer to the Father the suffering Countenance of the Son — His merits and love — in reparation for offenses against the majesty of God. This offering of atonement, with the wounded Countenance as the sensible object of devotion in so doing, is described by Christ as "the greatest source of grace second to the sacraments"[81] and as "the most beautiful work that has yet appeared on the face of the earth."[82]

Given the importance Christ places upon the devotion, it is not surprising that it may have been prefigured in the Bible. While the irreverence of man being punished by God is a common theme in the Old Testament, the apparent, specific foreshadowing of the devotion presents itself in a surprising place: the book of Job.

Lessons of Job

Surely there are few more endearing characters in all biblical and literary history than Job. Mankind universally identifies with the conundrum of innocent suffering and the questions it brings. Though the person of Job in the Old Testament is a historical one,[83] the book of Job itself, irrespective of a literal interpretation,[84] is regarded as one of the great wisdom literary masterpieces of all time, written mostly in the form of didactic poetry to address the age-old problem of why bad things happen to good people.

From the land of Hus, possibly a king, and living around the time of the patriarchs, Job is not an Israelite, but he worships the true God and is described as "simple and upright, and fearing God, and avoiding evil" (1:1). His wealth and general blessings are singular, as is his piety. Satan challenges God by suggesting that were Job to be stripped of these copious blessings, he would curse God to His Face. God permits Job's great deprivation. Job loses his wealth, his children, and his own health to leprosy, is subjected to the wrongful accusation

---

[80] Sister Mary St. Peter, *Life of Sister Mary St. Peter*, ed. Rev. P. Janvier (France, 1884), 159.
[81] Ibid., 246–247.
[82] Ibid., 311–312.
[83] "Job ... is mentioned as such in Ezechiel, Tobias, Ecclesiasticus and the epistle of St. James." John Laux, *Introduction to the Bible* (Charlotte, NC: Saint Benedict Press, 1990), 62.
[84] Arguments for a literal interpretation of the book of Job are beyond the scope or purpose of this writing.

of his friends (who believe his turn of fortune must be a consequence of his sin), and undergoes the temptation of his wife to "curse God, and die" (2:9, RSVCE).

Not only does Job refrain from blaspheming God amid his unspeakable suffering, but he also does not doubt nor deny His existence. Rather, he affirms his faith in making his famous declaration, "The Lord gave, and the Lord hath taken away.... Blessed be the name of the Lord" (1:21). There is joy at the heart of Job's sorrow, "the joy of his belief in the presence of God."[85] Job knows that his "Redeemer" lives and even indicates belief in the resurrection of the dead.[86]

In the Old Testament, suffering and evil are at times synonymous in that the cause of evil is sometimes seen as the transgression, which is the position of Job's friends.[87] Given Job's incomparable calamity, his friends therefore cannot reconcile their understanding of a just God without insisting upon Job's guilt. The friends join punishment with guilt, not unlike Satan joining prosperity to piety.[88]

Job defends his innocence while attesting to God's justice during considerable debate with his friends. A youth eventually interjects that "suffering may be sent by God as a means of probation and purification for higher glory."[89] God Himself is then revealed in the storm wind and explains that since man cannot comprehend the greatness and wisdom of the Creator and Ruler of the universe, he should in affliction and suffering bend humbly and trustingly under the hand of the Almighty.[90] God warns that Job must therefore be careful, in attempting to justify himself, not to "condemn" his Creator (40:3).

Job does penance for at first not confessing properly his lack of humility in speaking too much of his own afflictions and not enough of God's goodness toward him when seeking an explanation from God for his loss[91] (tantamount to complaints that God had unjustly smitten him). Job is not free to judge God, for

---

[85] Joseph Fichtner, *Forerunners of Christ* (Milwaukee, WI: Bruce Publishing, 1965), 114.
[86] Job 19:25–27: "For I know that my Redeemer liveth, and in the last day I shall rise out of the earth. And I shall be clothed again with my skin, and in my flesh I shall see my God. Whom I myself shall see, and my eyes shall behold, and not another: this my hope is laid up in my bosom."
[87] Javier Lozano Barragán, "A Christian Understanding of Pain and Suffering," Eternal Word Television Network, September 7, 2005, accessed February 12, 2019, https://www.ewtn.com/catholicism/library/christian-understanding-of-pain-and-suffering-9911.
[88] Fichtner, *Forerunners*, 112.
[89] Laux, *Introduction to the Bible*, 67.
[90] John Laux, *Chief Truths of the Faith* (Charlotte, NC: Saint Benedict Press, 1990), 30.
[91] Job 39:34.

God is the highest standard of justice.[92] Wisdom, instead of scrutinizing the behavior of God, is rather, practicing "fear of the Lord" and "depart[ing] from evil" (28:28). Fear of the Lord consists in adhering to His laws of morality in humility. Man, therefore, is not free to determine right and wrong. God alone has that right and is not subject to the moral "constraints" of man.

God is pleased with Job's penance and humility and praises him, while Job's friends are reprimanded for not speaking "the thing that is right before [God], as [His] servant Job hath" (42:7). The friends offend God, even while endeavoring to "defend" Him; they are rebels against the truth, "which they imagine they are serving by their false assertions."[93] By ignoring the truth of Job's innocence, in attempting to prove that God's justice is necessarily manifest in life's circumstances, they essentially "define" God as unable to do otherwise. God requests that the friends offer Job's face to Him (rather than their own) in seeking reparation for their injustice. Job does intercede for his friends, and God is "turned at the penance of Job," such that he and his wife have more children, his wealth is restored to him twofold, and he lives to an old age, happily just as Job would have it be all along.[94] God chooses to reward Job in this life for his virtue, despite His being completely "free" to do otherwise.

The book of Job is replete with moral lessons. The most obvious is that, although suffering remains a mystery, not all misfortune is consequential to transgression (which allows for Job's righteousness despite his great misery) and that suffering potentially may also lead to conversion and a return to virtue.[95] Another, more suited to the theme of this book, is that man is not allowed to create his own truth — as in the case of Job's friends contorting the truth of Job's innocence (by ignoring it) to fit their narrative that the circumstantial events of one's life necessarily correlate with one's guilt or innocence, thereby "limiting" God to act in this way. Similarly, one is not free to decide his own morality; Job initially scrutinized God in his attempts to defend his own innocence. Man is not free to justify himself at the price of questioning God, who is the highest standard of justice. Man does not "get" to decide what is right behavior of God, nor of himself. Finally, reparation must be made for these grave offenses to the majesty of God.

---

[92] Job 40:1–2 (RSVCE). The Lord said to Job: "Shall a faultfinder contend with the Almighty? He who argues with God, let him answer it."

[93] Gregory the Great, *Morals on the Book of Job*, ed. Paul A. Boer, Sr. (Edmond, OK: Veritatis Splendor Publications, 2012), 3:624.

[94] Job 42:8–16.

[95] Barragán, "Christian Understanding."

Because he did atone for his own sin of accusing God of smiting an innocent man and because he was, in fact, otherwise innocent, Job was more worthy to offer sacrifices than his friends in seeking the required reparation for their injustice. God chose to give Job an essential role in the salvation of his friends.

The Book of Job as Prefiguring the Holy Face Devotion

The role Job played in the salvation of his friends may be interpreted as prefiguring both the Church and Christ. The friends, according to St. Gregory the Great, are "heretics," while Job is a type of the Church, "whose faith they used to impugn with their false assumptions." The heretics, therefore, must obtain their salvation by way of the Church's prayers.[96]

Interrelated, yet somehow more poignant than Job representing the Church while his friends represent heretics, is Job's vicarious, redemptive, Christlike suffering, which seems to be indicated by Job's face being more acceptable to God than that of his friends. Pope St. John Paul II, among others, saw the innocent suffering of Job in the Old Testament as prefiguring the Lord's Passion.[97] In this case, Job's face being offered is analogous to Christ's innocent suffering in atoning for the sins of man.

Considering the nineteenth-century revelations given by Christ requesting reparation to the Holy Face, there is a modern-day synthesis of these two notions of prefiguring in the book of Job — that of Job's face being offered to God, symbolizing prayers of the Church for heretics, and that of Job's face being offered to God, symbolizing Christ's great act of Redemption. This synthesis is that Job's face being offered to God in intercession for his friends *may also* prefigure man's offering of the wounded Face of Christ to the Father in reparation for modern sins against the majesty of God to draw mercy for sinners, as called for in the Holy Face devotion.

In the revelations, the Face of Christ symbolizes not only Christ's Redemption but also both the Godhead itself[98] and the doctrine of the Church. The doctrine is the "Face of the Church,"[99] which is wounded anew by the heretical

---

[96] Gregory the Great, *Morals on the Book of Job*, 3:624.
[97] Barragán, "Christian Understanding."
[98] Sister Mary St. Peter, *Life of Sister Mary St. Peter*, 253.
[99] Ibid., 245.

words and actions of modern blasphemous and atheistic thought. The suffering Face of Christ is offered anew as an extension of the Most Holy Sacrament of the Altar,[100] to atone for current affronts against the first three commandments. This act of reparation by man is an offering of Christ's Face — His merits and love — which is infinitely more pleasing to God than is the face of man (just as Job's face was more pleasing to God than that of his friends).

The offering of the wounded Face of Christ appeases the Father, and in His delight at the most beloved, suffering Face of the Son, He has pity on man's face, disfigured by sin (just as God was moved to pity for Job's friends out of love for Job).

> Man is invited to repair the outrages committed against God, and by a return of love, God promises to repair his image in man's soul [by] virtue of his adorable Face.... It seems that in ... the virtue and power of his Holy Face, he has grand designs of mercy over the souls of mankind.[101]

Just as Job's face was offered to the Father in place of his friends to appease their affronts to the majesty of God, drawing down mercy for them, so now the Face of Christ is offered to the Godhead to appease modern affronts to the majesty of God to draw down mercy for the masses. Christ has given via the Holy Face devotion a modern model for man's role in co-redemption. He has chosen to give man no less than an essential and necessary role to play in reclaiming the Church and times for Christ by aiding in the reorientation of man to God by repairing the affronts to His majesty, His sovereignty, His truth.

In addition to these parallels, the devotion is well explained by way of multiple analogies found within the book of Job: Satan wishing to tempt Job to blaspheme; Satan using Job's wife to tempt Job to "curse God, and die"; Satan being allowed to tempt Job; Job's leprosy; Job's resistance and great humility; God's acceptance of Job's face in place of that of his friends; and Job's reward of twice all his previous possessions for having interceded for his friends. All afford striking parallels to the essential fundamentals of the devotion, which make for a comprehensive outline in recounting the divine revelations given in the Holy Face devotion, echoing the lessons conveyed in the book of Job.

[100] Ibid., 311–312.
[101] Ibid., 255–256.

SATAN TEMPTS JOB TO BLASPHEME

The first of these analogous similarities — namely, the hope of Satan that Job will be driven to blasphemy — represents a major parallel to the grave transgression of blasphemy as seen in the Holy Face devotion. Therein, it is *the* sin for which to make reparation in that it is the opposite of fear of the Lord. Why else, of all the horrific crimes that the devil could hope to induce Job to undertake, would he choose to tempt him to blaspheme? Satan knows what man "forgets": that blasphemy is a sin against the dignity of God and that "this dreadful sin pierce[s] and wound[s] his Heart ... more than all other crimes."[102] Our Lord said in the revelations to Sister St. Pierre, "You cannot comprehend the abomination of this sin. If my justice were not restrained by my mercy, the guilty would be destroyed in an instant; even inanimate beings would feel my vengeance, but I have an eternity in which to punish the wicked."[103] Most Christians today willfully disregard the magnitude of this sin, a dark triumph for Satan.

To understand the importance of reparation to the Holy Face, it is necessary to be convinced of this unparalleled offense of blasphemy and the way in which it extends to include all of the first three commandments. The second commandment forbids us to blaspheme by taking the name of Our Lord in vain, which is not only irreverent but ultimately idolatrous in that there is an implication in so doing that one has the power to "conjure" God at one's bidding, "forming" the God of one's desire.[104] Our Lord made Sister St. Pierre understand that "the intelligence of man cannot conceive of the heinousness of the affronts offered God by the sin of blasphemy."[105] In addition, Sister St. Pierre understood through the revelations that the non-observance of the Lord's Day is similarly an

> outrage committed against the sovereignty of God, and an injury done to the sanctification of his Holy Name, a crime ... identical with that of blasphemy: in fact, when the day is no longer sanctified by the suspension of labor [and the worship of God], the Holy Name of the Lord is not adored, blessed, known, or glorified as it should be.[106]

---

[102] Ibid., 127.
[103] Ibid., 198.
[104] Randall Smith, "Take Not the Name of the Church in Vain," The Catholic Thing, December 13, 2022, https://www.thecatholicthing.org/2022/12/13/take-not-the-name-of-the-church-in-vain.
[105] Sister Mary St. Peter, *Life of Sister Mary St. Peter*, 204.
[106] Ibid., 183.

Likewise, if one contradicts the first commandment — by upholding another as God, or in effect worshipping some object or aspiration as God, or by believing that there is no God — one is also blaspheming by taking from the name of God the praise and glory due to it. Logically, the first three commandments, which outline right behavior toward God, are intrinsically connected as blasphemy in all its forms, which is the antithesis of the proper fear and respect due Our Lord and His name.

Mgr. Morlot, observing nineteenth-century France, wrote about the then newly universal, commonplace, and contagious character of these sins, which lead to intemperance and increased immorality:

> Have the workshops been closed? Has manual labor been suspended on the Lord's Day? Show me the street or the thoroughfare of the city in which the noise of commerce has for one instant been interrupted! Everywhere the same clamor resounds, the same agitation, the same commotion sways the multitude as on weekdays. The children of men pursue their avocations with the same ardor as on the days assigned to labor. Here we behold them erecting stupendous edifices which the hand of God refuses to bless; there, exposing the produce of their industry, pursuing their speculations, their negotiations, their insatiable craving for wealth, for power, for honor.
>
> Look at our villages, pass on to our hamlets, what do we behold? The forgetfulness of God which necessarily follows in the train of profanation, and the countless other disorders, none the less deplorable. Yet the most diabolical of all these outrages committed against the majesty of God, is the shameful desecration of the Sundays and holy days: one part of the day is consecrated to business; the other, to pleasure; forbidden labor being always followed by disorderly pleasure. Servile occupation is succeeded by intemperance and immorality.[107]

The magnitude of these iniquities is likewise and again clearly indicated in the revelations of Our Lord to Sister St. Pierre:

> The earth is covered with crime! The sins against the first three commandments have provoked the wrath of my Father; the Holy Name of God blasphemed, and the profanation of the Lord's Day fill to overflowing the measure of iniquity; this sin has mounted even to the throne of

---

[107] Sister Mary St. Peter, *Life of Sister Mary St. Peter*, 193–194.

the Most High, and has aroused his wrath, which will burst forth over mankind in an impetuous torrent, if his justice be not appeased.[108]

Satan is going to the heart of the matter by inducing man to contradict the first three commandments. Blasphemy, after all, is the hallmark of Satan's own deadly sin: pride. Fittingly, according to the revelations, Satan willingly delegates other categories of sin, but he keeps those of blasphemy to himself.[109]

Like all sin, blasphemy harms the sinner, for as Sister St. Pierre understood from Our Lord:

> Blasphemy and the violation of the Lord's Day are sins which attack God directly, in violation of the first three commandments; they confer no benefit on man but are sadly prejudicial alike to his temporal and spiritual happiness. They are diabolical in character: the unhappy transgressor labors not for himself but for the devil, who not only degrades, but enslaves his victim.[110]

Mankind has tragic evidence of both the diabolical character of blasphemy and the enslavement of Satan in the most meticulously documented exorcism to date in the United States, which was the basis of the 1973 movie *The Exorcist*.

The exorcist priest and his assistant suffered unspeakable insults, blasphemies, filthy language, and physical violence from a possessed boy[111] over a period of weeks. The devils left only when, instead of hearing guttural voices of demons coming from the boy, those surrounding the boy heard that of St. Michael, demanding that the evil spirits leave the body in the name of *Dominus* [the Lord]. The spirits had previously communicated that there was only one word that would drive them out and that the boy would never be allowed to say it.[112] Here one is reminded of the Scripture passage, "Whosoever shall call upon the name of the Lord, shall be saved" (Acts 2:21).

---

[108] Ibid., 158–159.
[109] Ibid., 257. Sister St. Pierre: "[The] flock of blasphemers was in a special manner under the guidance of the Prince of Darkness. The Lord gave me to understand, that Lucifer willingly abandoned to his subordinates the charge of the other troops of sinners, as for instance, the lewd, the intemperate, the avaricious, but the blasphemers, he kept as his favorite flock."
[110] Ibid., 184.
[111] The real-life case of exorcism involved a boy, who was, however, portrayed as a girl in the movie.
[112] Norman Fulkerson, "This Is How Saint Michael Cast Out Satan from Robbie Mannheim," Return to Order, March 3, 2019, www.returntoorder.org/2019/03/this-is-how-saint-michael-cast-out-satan-from-robbie-mannheim/.

This terrifying phenomenon indicates both the power of the name of God properly reverenced and the danger of its antithesis, blasphemy. (If blasphemy were not an emblem of godlessness, why would Satan use it?) Unaware though man chooses to be, sins of blasphemy are the mark of Satan's enslavement, producing their deadly effect upon man. St. Alphonsus de Liguori, in fact, describes blasphemy as "the deadliest of all sins and as ordinarily unpardonable, for it is a crime of the highest magnitude that can be committed against the Divinity in that it attacks God openly and directly.... Blasphemy is the cause of maledictions on ... earth."[113]

"Curse God and Die"

This notion that blasphemy is the deadliest of all sins is a second analogous likeness with the book of Job. Job's friends accuse him of having sinned, since they are convinced that such a turn of fate could not be explained by a just God otherwise. Job's wife, the only blessing not taken from Job at this point, believes that he has done no wrong but, in despair, wavers in her own trust in God, whom she accuses of punishing Job unjustly. She advises Job, "Curse God and die."[114]

Job's wife is a type of Eve[115] — as well as a representation of modern culture — in that she plays a part in Job's temptation and basically implies that Job should give up, since there is no longer reason for him to live. The larger point in helping to draw out a comparison to the devotion, however, is that there is an implication that blasphemy leads to death of soul. Our Lord related as much to Sister St. Pierre: "By blasphemy, the sinner outrages him to his face, attacks him openly, and pronounces upon himself his own judgment and condemnation."[116] Modern culture is somehow ignorant of what the epochs before have understood regarding the right order of things: there is no life of the soul without proper fear of God, and there is no proper fear of God without proper humility before Him in adhering to His commands, the foremost being the first three. This numbing of conscience, this topsy-turvy morality that can no longer call out outrages against the Divinity due to a sort of collective compliance to relativism, is a degeneration, making man's offenses even more heinous than those of the time when the revelations were first revealed to Sister St. Pierre.

---

[113] Sister Mary St. Peter, *Life of Sister Mary St. Peter*, 204.
[114] Laux, *Introduction to the Bible*, 63.
[115] Gregory the Great, *Morals on the Book of Job*, 1:116.
[116] Sister Mary St. Peter, *Life of Sister Mary St. Peter*, 127.

Writing in the 1950s, a biographer of Sister St. Pierre recognized the peril of this universal transgression, which is surely even more apparent today:

> We consider that to the blasphemies and to the multiplied individual transgressions there has succeeded a kind of collective sin, much more dangerous than the other because it is less apparent, and because, therefore, it provokes hardly a reaction. To the hostility and revolt of some, even a great number, a state of mind has succeeded, an atmosphere which one breathes without knowing it, and today's Christians, poisoned unaware, have a tendency to minimize the gravity of the outrages against God's very divinity, and no longer to notice their presence in the world. Fascinated no doubt by the more and more audacious freedom of habits and morals, do they not forget too much that the real origin of this laxity is to be found in certain refusal, or at least a certain forgetting, of God's rights? The three first Commandments will always remain the first, as also the three first demands of the Father will remain the most important. And there will never be Christian life — not only in theory but in fact, a life involving not knowledge and science alone, but above all a right will — without an initial active and effective avowal of God's Majesty, of His Universal Causality, of the Holiness of His Name.[117]

Satan seems to have succeeded in making man unaware of the dangers of denying God His rights, *which amounts to a categorical difference from the offenses of previous eras.*

Mankind is in a new age, one in which offenses against the Godhead are not even recognized as being wrong by the norms of society, nor by most Christians themselves, nay, even by some Church leaders. Ven. Fulton Sheen, writing in the 1940s, states that mediocrity and compromise characterize the lives of many Christians, such that there is no longer the conflict and opposition that is supposed to characterize us: "[Man is] influencing the world less than the world influences us. There is no apartness."[118] Our Lord revealed to Sister St. Pierre that "from the ignorance and contempt of which He is thus the object, results a social evil, so much the more pernicious and fatal to society at large and to individuals in

---

[117] Louis Van den Bossche, *The Message of Sister Mary of St. Peter*, trans. Mary G. Durham (France: Carmel of Tours, 1953), 200.

[118] Joseph Pronechen, "Did Fulton Sheen Prophecy about These Times?," *National Catholic Register,* January 28, 2019, www.ncregister.com/blog/joseph-pronechen/did-fulton-sheen-prophecy-about-these-times.

particular, as it daily tends to become more general and more prevalent."[119] Desensitized, man is the proverbial frog in a pot of water that has been slowly heated; he is being boiled unaware by way of his complacency and willful ignorance regarding the dangers of society's new norms.

How is it that man has arrived at this time "conspicuous for an evaporation of moral certitudes by which good and bad are judged"?[120] History is full of examples of bad popes and cardinals, bishops and priests, religious and laity, but these are times in which these "baddies" are not necessarily seen as bad. Before, there were scandals and heresies, but there was adequate response within the Church to at least see them as such and to voice truth until there was a return to the orthodox Faith and living. Yet now:

> Where are we to find a fourth-century Basil, or Gregory of Nazianzus, and Gregory of Nyssa? Where Athanasius of Egypt...? Where Hilary of Poitiers and Martin of Tours, or John Chrysostom (the golden mouth)? Where Cyril of Jerusalem, or Augustine or Ambrose...? Bishops one and all. Today, where do we find such bishops?[121]

Relativism has reached such a climax as to induce silence by those who should not be silent.

This silence is a way of affirming the upside-down morality that sees bad as good and good as bad. The warning of Isaiah seems fit to the times: "Woe to [those who] call evil good, and good evil: that put darkness for light, and light for darkness: that put bitter for sweet, and sweet for bitter" (5:20). Cardinal Müller warns in his "Manifesto of Faith":

> To keep silent about ... the truths of the Faith and to teach people accordingly is the greatest deception against which the Catechism vigorously warns. It represents the last trial of the Church and leads man to a religious delusion, "the price of their apostasy" (CCC 675); it is the fraud of Antichrist. "He will deceive those who are lost by all means of

---

[119] Sister Mary St. Peter, *Life of Sister Mary St. Peter*, 183.
[120] George Rutler, "Satan Kills Babies, Shatters Families, Corrupts Priests and Mocks the Church," *National Catholic Register*, February 19, 2019, www.ncregister.com/blog/fatherrutler/satan-kills-babies-shatters-families-corrupts-priests-and-mocks-the-church.
[121] Peter D. Beaulieu, "Quo Vadis: Where Are the Bishops and Laity of Old?," *The Catholic World Report*, February 19, 2019.

injustice; for they have closed themselves to the love of the truth by which they should be saved" (2 Thess. 2:10).[122]

Is this the "why" of man's current moral decline? Is God allowing the Church to be tested during these times in a unique way? Is this the time of the last tribulation of the Church, described in the *Catechism of the Catholic Church* as "a final trial that will shake the faith of many believers..., a 'mystery of iniquity,'... a religious deception,... an apostasy from the truth"?[123] If so, this would be a remarkable parallel between the book of Job and these times in which the Holy Face devotion was given to man: that God has permitted both Job in the Old Testament and, arguably, the Church today to undergo unbridled testing by Satan.

Unfettered Testing by Satan

Regarding this proposed unfettered testing by Satan during modern times, there is the well-known, albeit persistently chilling, evidence found in the vision Pope Leo XIII received October 13, 1884, just two months prior to the same pope signing the first brief of the Confraternity of the Holy Face and one year prior to his approving the Archconfraternity of the Holy Face immediately for the whole world. (Pope Leo XIII broke with tradition by not approving it incrementally, as it would usually have been only first approved for France, its place of origin; this signaled his belief in its utmost importance. His decree was *"non tam pro Galia, quam ubique"* — not only for France but for everywhere!)

Witnesses observed that after Pope Leo had celebrated Mass, he turned pale and collapsed as if dead. He had had a vision of Satan boasting to God that he could destroy the Church. Satan asked for, and was granted by God, one century and more power over those who would serve him. Satan remained determined, despite God reminding him that His Church could not be destroyed. The Lord then revealed the events of the twentieth century to Leo XIII. "He saw wars, immorality, genocide and apostasy on a large scale."[124] Pope Leo immediately composed the St. Michael Prayer, which was said as part of the Leonine Prayers after every Low Mass until Vatican II.

---

[122] Edward Pentin, "Cardinal Müller Issues 'Manifesto of Faith,'" *National Catholic Register*, February 8, 2019, https://www.ncregister.com/blog/cardinal-mueller-issues-manifesto-of-faith.
[123] *CCC*, 675.
[124] Joe Tremblay, "The 100 Year Test," *Catholic News Agency*, February 1, 2013, https://www.catholicnewsagency.com/column/the-100-year-test-2454.

What was foreseen by Pope Leo XIII on October 13, 1884—exactly 33 years before the miracle of the sun at Fatima—has been confirmed, not only by subsequent events, but by other credible sources. The work of iniquity which had gained much momentum outside the Church in the late 19th century and early 20th century, was about to make its way into the institutions of the Church. In fact, on June 29, 1972, Pope Paul VI confirmed just that when he addressed his audience. He said, "It is as if from some mysterious crack, no, it is not mysterious, from some crack the smoke of Satan has entered the temple of God." About a year later, on October 13, 1973, Our Lady of Akita, in an approved apparition in Japan, took this point further and gave us some idea how this "smoke" would take effect. She said, "The work of the devil will infiltrate even into the Church in such a way that one will see cardinals opposing cardinals, bishops against bishops.... The Church will be full of those who accept compromises, and the demon will press many priests and consecrated souls to leave the service of the Lord."[125]

Akita was not the first, nor the last, approved Marian apparition to forewarn of this great crisis of faith, this great tribulation for the Church.[126] In many respects, the anchor of these forewarnings is found in the revelations received by Sister St. Pierre in that Our Lord Himself therein is demanding reparation for offenses against the Godhead, while offenses against Our Lady are an *effect* of these sins against the Divinity, taking the form of heresies against the Face of the Church, as pertaining to her. Additionally, Christ announces this categorically different trial of the Church by His words "in no other time has iniquity reached such a degree."[127]

Sores "Like Another Lazarus"

According to the revelations given to Sister St. Pierre, this primal iniquity, the affront offered God by the sin of blasphemy, pierces the Sacred Heart of Christ and covers Him with sores "like another Lazarus."[128] This is yet another parallel with the book of Job in that in addition to his other depravations, Job loses his own health to leprosy: "Satan ... struck Job with a very grievous ulcer, from the sole of the foot even to the top of his head" (2:7). According to St. Gregory the Great, who sees Job as a type of the Church, the sores reaching all the way from the sole to the crown indicate that

---

[125] Ibid.
[126] Chapter seven will be devoted to a lengthier discussion of these Church-approved Marian apparitions.
[127] Sister Mary St. Peter, *Life of Sister Mary St. Peter*, 159.
[128] Ibid., 204.

Satan begins with tempting mere men, but he ends with "the very Head of the Church."[129] To extend this method of analogy to Job's story as prefiguring the Holy Face devotion, the wounds of blasphemy begin with the laity but end with those within the Church hierarchy itself, wounding Christ's Heart with sores "like another Lazarus": the worst imaginable malady generated by the worst imaginable crime.

Pertaining to these sores of leprosy that cover Our Lord's Heart due to the sin of blasphemy, Sister St. Pierre was made to recall by Our Lord that there were compassionate dogs who consoled poor Lazarus by licking his wounds, and He invited her to render Him a similar service by every day glorifying the holy name of God. Our Lord also made her understand that "a multitude of souls will be saved if his designs be accomplished."[130] Earlier, Our Lord revealed to Sister St. Pierre that blasphemy is like a poisoned arrow that perpetually wounds His Divine Heart (more than any other crime). To console His Heart, He wishes for the faithful to offer a "golden arrow," which wounds Him with delight and love, healing the wounds of malice that sinners inflict upon Him, a form of reparation particularly adapted to the crime to be expiated, a formula of prayer to console his Sacred Heart and to appease his anger.

The following is the prayer Our Lord dictated to her for the reparation of blasphemy against His holy name. He offered it to her as a golden dagger or arrow, assuring her that every time it was said, it would wound His Heart most lovingly:

> May the most holy, most sacred, most adorable, most incomprehensible, and ineffable Name of God be forever praised, blessed, loved, adored, and glorified, in heaven, on earth, and in hell,[131] by all the creatures of God, and by the Sacred Heart of Our Lord Jesus Christ in the Most Holy Sacrament of the Altar. Amen.[132]

---

[129] Gregory the Great, *Morals on the Book of Job*, 1:128.

[130] Sister Mary St. Peter, *Life of Sister Mary St. Peter*, 205.

[131] Sister Mary St. Peter, *Life of Sister Mary St. Peter*, 128. Sister St. Pierre writes, "As I was not a little astonished when Our Lord said, 'and in hell,' He had the goodness to make me understand that His justice was there glorified. I beg to remark, that He did not only mean the place where the wicked are punished, but also purgatory, where He is loved and glorified by the suffering souls. The word 'hell' is not merely applied to the place where the damned are confined, for our faith teaches us that the Savior descended into hell or Limbo, where the souls of the just were detained until his Coming; and does not our holy mother the Church pray her divine Spouse to deliver the souls of her children from the gates of hell? *A porta inferi erue, Domine, animas eorum* (Office of the Dead)."

[132] Ibid., 127.

Our Lord, after having revealed this prayer to Sister St. Pierre, warned her that she should beware of how she appreciates this favor, for He will demand an account of it. At that moment, Sister St. Pierre beheld flowing from the Sacred Heart of Jesus, wounded by this golden dagger, torrents of grace for the conversion of sinners.[133]

One can infer the immense responsibility for "those who have been given much" in the way of knowledge of God's demand for reparation; man will answer for knowledge not put into action to obtain grace for sinners,[134] for this prayer in honor of the holy name of God was to be "communicated and spread among the faithful"[135] to obtain mercy for sinners.[136] The soul offering this Golden Arrow prayer draws down graces for himself and others to orient each away from pride, toward humility, and toward proper fear of God, bringing back an avowal of God's majesty, of the holiness of His name.

Humility and Proper Fear of the Lord

This proper alignment of man to God and its great consolation to Him, by way of humility and persistent fear of the Lord by man, is another point of similarity to the book of Job. God is pleased by Job on account of these very dispositions. After his immense depravation, and despite later cursing the day he was born, he said to his wife, "If we have received good things at the hand of God, why should we not receive evil?" and "Job did not sin with his lips" (2:10). Despite Job never speaking impiously, he at times spoke too much of his own afflictions and too little of God's goodness toward him in the manner of his speech, thus causing him to humble himself before God by saying that he had spoken "inconsiderately."[137] God shows His pleasure and acceptance of Job's persistent humility by comparison to that lacking in Job's friends, who had provoked God's wrath, "kindled against [them]" when they failed to speak the "thing that is right before [God]" as had Job. God sees the ways of Job as being so far above those of his friends that God tells the friends to ask Job to intercede — to make reparation — for them (42:7–9).

---

[133] Ibid., 128–129.
[134] Ibid., 293.
[135] Ibid., 129.
[136] Our Lord told Sister St. Pierre that if she would place an obstacle on His designs, she would be responsible for the salvation of a multitude of souls. If, however, she was faithful in communicating His objective of reparation, those very souls would be "an ornament in [her] crown." Ibid., 159.
[137] Thoughtlessly, discourteously, (Job 39:34).

Man, too, is being asked to intercede for his "friends" by way of reparation to the Holy Face, though by the merits of Christ, rather than his own. Our Lord said to Sister St. Pierre that He would show mercy to the guilty, and that His justice would be appeased, if He could find devoted souls to say the prayers in reparation for blasphemy. The archbishop of Tours in his pastoral the ensuing Lent of 1844, after an interview with Sister St. Pierre, wrote the following:

> On the one hand, we behold open revolts and scandalous outrages committed against the divinity of God; on the other lukewarmness, nay more, total indifference in the fulfilment of duty [of right reverence to God]. These provoke the wrath of the Most High, whose justice, though patient and long-suffering, is, nevertheless, inevitable; whose vengeance, though tardy, is certain, for God has no need to punish day by day; His power is eternal and not to be confounded with the justice of man, intimidated by the number of the guilty, and which beholding the multitude to be punished, lets the sword fall powerless from its hand. It is not thus when God wishes to punish[;] it is not the number of the guilty which arrests His hand. He then counts but the just, and when these have disappeared from the face of the earth, His arm falls mercilessly.[138]

Sister St. Pierre understood that "in favor of the souls who would apply themselves to the reparation of blasphemy and the contempt against the Majesty of God, [Our Lord] would appease His Justice and give grace to the guilty."[139] God demands an account of this immense gift bestowed, for knowledge of the devotion devolves responsibility upon devotees. Man is to imitate the just Job in interceding for others in this great work of reparation.

OFFERING OF JOB'S FACE AND HIS DELIVERANCE

The Douay-Rheims translation of the Bible regarding this intercession of Job is striking: "The Lord accepted the *face* of Job" (42:9, my emphasis). This wording did not escape the notice of Ven. Dupont, who immersed himself daily in Scripture. He also observed about Job that "God promises to hear the prayers of Job; he has promised this to no one else in the holy books.... Man does not lose time when he prays for others. It is when he prays for his friends that Job is delivered."[140]

---

[138] Sister Mary St. Peter, *Life of Sister Mary St. Peter*, 194.
[139] Ibid., 160.
[140] Pierre Désiré Janvier, *The Holy Man of Tours* (Baltimore: John Murphy, 1882), 207.

This summarizes the last two parallels between the Holy Face devotion and the book of Job: the offering of Job's face as prefiguring the offering of Christ's Face in the Holy Face devotion and the deliverance of Job while he prayed for his friends as prefiguring man's own collective deliverance when man intercedes for others by making reparation to the Holy Face.

Man is like Job's friends in offering Christ's Face to the Father in place of his own, in that God is infinitely more pleased by the Face of His most beloved Son than by man's own sinful faces (just as God was more pleased by Job's face than that of his friends). Job is to Christ as Job's friends are to man, yet man is like Job, too, in that he is to make reparation for others, albeit not by his own merits but by Christ's.

The *offering of Christ's wounded Face to the Father* was revealed to Sister St. Pierre as the *method* of reparation for the sins of blasphemy. Not only does the perfect offering of Christ's merits ("veiled" in His face) appease the Father's justice, but the acts of reparation soothe the renewed wounds of Christ's face.

> The Work of Reparation through the Holy Face was suddenly revealed to her. She was transported in spirit to the road leading to Calvary. "There ... Our Lord gave me to behold in a most vivid manner, the pious Veronica, who, with her veil, wiped His adorable Face covered with spittle, dust, sweat, and blood. My divine Savior gave me to understand that the wicked by their blasphemy renew all the outrages once offered to His divine Face; these blasphemies, poured forth against the Divinity, like ... vile spittle..., disfigure the Face of Our Lord, who offered Himself as a victim for sinners. Then He told me that I must imitate the zeal of the pious Veronica who so courageously passed through the crowd of rough soldiers to offer Him some relief, and whom He gave me for my protectress and model. By endeavoring to offer reparation for blasphemy, we render Christ the same service as this heroic woman, and He looks upon those who act thus, with the same complaisance as if they had performed this act during His Passion."[141]

Christ rewards "Veronicas" by "wiping" in return, the sin from their own souls and imprinting His own image upon them, to the degree of their efforts of reparation.

---

[141] Sister Mary St. Peter, *Life of Sister Mary St. Peter*, 138–139.

Sister St. Pierre was led to understand that the holy and august Face of Christ, offered to us for our adoration, is the mirror of the ineffable perfections comprised in the most holy name of God.[142] When man adores the Face of Christ, he is consoling Him anew by avowing God's majesty and the holiness of His name. St. Paul says in 1 Corinthians that "the head of Christ is God" (11:3), which Sister St. Pierre recognizes as the essence of what was communicated to her: the august head of Jesus Christ is the picture and the emblem of the divine majesty, and His Holy Face is the image and the glory of God.[143] The Face of Our Lord is the sensible object offered for the adoration of the faithful to repair the outrages of blasphemers who attack the Divinity, of which it is the figure, the mirror, and the image. "In virtue of this adorable Face, offered to the Eternal Father, man can appease His anger and obtain the conversion of blasphemers."[144] The Church, His spouse, is His Mystical Body, and the doctrine of the Church is (also representative of) the face of this body. The Face of the Church is the Face of Jesus Christ.[145]

In these times, the Face of Christ's Mystical Body, the Church, is the "butt of all the outrages of God's enemies."[146] Our Lord told Sister St. Pierre, "Behold if there be any sorrow like unto my sorrow! My Divine Father and my cherished spouse, the Holy Church, are despised, outraged by my enemies. Will no one rise up to revenge me by defending them against those enemies?"[147] Man's predicament of unprecedented decline in morals and the inability to recognize moral certitude revolves around an unwillingness to submit to—and even a scorning of—the teachings of Our Lord preserved within the doctrine of the Catholic Church, beginning with those pertaining to the honor and fear due God's holy name.

God is demanding a new effort, the object of which is to repair these most loathsome crimes of modern society, "deep rooted impiety and absolute incredulity"[148] toward His doctrine. For this reason, Our Lord described this work of reparation to be "the most beautiful work that has yet appeared on the face of the earth."[149] It is the most beautiful work because it is offered to the Father *through*

---

[142] Ibid., 242.
[143] Ibid., 243.
[144] Ibid., 244.
[145] Ibid., 244–245.
[146] Ibid., 246.
[147] Ibid., 185.
[148] Ibid., 311–312.
[149] Ibid., 311.

the merits of Christ's dolorous Face; it does not therefore "override" the beauty of Christ's Redemption, for it is an extension of it. Mankind is being given by God a more specific role in the Redemption, however, given that "in no other time has iniquity reached such a degree."[150]

The beauty of this work is that it is Christ who is giving us in mercy His Face to be offered by mankind to appease the wrath of God and to bring salvation to men. Pope St. John Paul II wrote in his *Salvifici Doloris*,

> The Redeemer suffered in place of man and for man. Every man *has his own share in the Redemption*. Each is also *called to share in that suffering* through which the Redemption was accomplished.... Christ *has also raised human suffering to the level of the Redemption*. Thus, each man, in his suffering, can also become a sharer in the redemptive suffering of Christ.[151]

John Paul II's Magisterium is joined by those of Pope St. Pius X and Pope St. Pius XI, as well as many saints, beginning with St. Paul and, in more recent times, St. Maximilian Kolbe, St. Teresa Benedicta of the Cross, St. Pio of Pietrelcina, and St. Teresa of Calcutta, all referring to the reality of co-redemption.[152] This co-redemption is man's privileged contribution in the salvation of souls. One should not be surprised, then, when this work of reparation, *which is an extension of the great work of Redemption*, calls him to put man's salvation in his own collective hands, not by his own merits but by offering in reparation those of the most holy and adorable Face of God's Son.

Our Lord wishes to make "an alliance between His Justice and His Mercy,"[153] allowing for the conversion of sinners. Christ describes His Holy Face as an immense gift to us, which is to be offered to the Father "as the sole means of appeasing Him."[154] It is the most noble and the most necessary work of our times.[155] Our Lord told Sister St. Pierre that the wounded Face of Christ "was the greatest grace he could have given after that of the sacraments"[156] and was to become the distinctive symbol of the projected work.

---

[150] Ibid., 159.
[151] *Apostolic Letter of John Paul II: On the Christian Meaning of Human Suffering* (Boston: Pauline Books, 1984), 30–31.
[152] Michael Giesler, *How Christ Saves Souls — with Us: The Mystery of Co-Redemption* (Steubenville, OH: Emmaus Road, 2022), xxvii.
[153] Sister Mary St. Peter, *Life of Sister Mary St. Peter*, 287.
[154] Ibid., 290.
[155] Ibid., 312.
[156] Ibid., 247.

Earlier Our Lord warns that man should beware of how he appreciates this favor, for He will demand an account of it. Here He makes clear that man has been given an unprecedented gift of grace, exceeded only by that of the sacraments. In addition, He states clearly that in no other time has iniquity reached such a degree and that this sin of blasphemy has mounted even to the throne of the Most High, arousing His wrath, which will burst forth over mankind in an impetuous torrent, if His justice be not appeased. What is one to conclude other than that man is urgently commended to make use of devotion to the Holy Face to aid in the salvation of himself and his brethren in reclaiming the Church and times for Christ? In fact, Our Lord gives Sister St. Pierre the ominous warning, "Woe to those who do not make reparation!"[157]

This call for solidarity in offering reparation for one's brethren is a reminder that lost souls are a real consequence of neglecting one's duty as members of the communion of saints in which each member contributes to the good and welfare of all. "As members of the Church, Christ's Mystical Body on earth, [man] can win many graces for [himself] and others if [his] soul [is] pleasing to God."[158] St. Paul speaks of this when he states that he rejoices in his sufferings for the sake of the Church and that in his flesh he completes what is lacking in Christ's afflictions for the sake of His body (Col. 1:24).[159]

> As [man] is necessarily united with Christ in His mission, since [mankind] form[s] His Mystical Body, so [man] must necessarily cooperate with Him in His sufferings or "Passion." Therefore, Saint Paul when explaining the necessity of our cooperating with Jesus in His work of Redemption, goes straight to the point and tells [Christians to] "fill up those things that are wanting," not in the *mission* of Christ, but in His *passion*.... The two unite, neither can exist alone. [Man] must make Reparation with Christ.[160]

Pope St. John Paul II speaks of each man's responsibility to act as the Good Samaritan to our neighbors:

---

[157] Ibid., 161.
[158] Giesler, *Christ Saves Souls*, xxii.
[159] Ibid.
[160] Raoul Plus, *The Ideal of Reparation*, trans. Madame Cecilia (London: Burns, Oates & Washbourne, 1921), 17.

> Christ's revelation of the salvific meaning of suffering *is in no way identified with an attitude of passivity....* The first and second parts of Christ's words about the Final Judgment unambiguously show how essential it is, for the eternal life of every individual, to "stop," as the Good Samaritan did, at the suffering of one's neighbor, to have "compassion" for that suffering, and to give some help.[161]

Our Lord told Sister St. Pierre, "Sinners, as clouds of dust borne on the wind, are whirled from this world and precipitated into hell. Have pity on your brethren and pray for them!"[162]

Man is held accountable for not helping those in need around him, and far from it somehow detracting from the good he may obtain for himself in prayer, like Job, he himself is saved when he intercedes for sinners. According to St. Gregory the Great, a penitent deserves to be heard the more quickly in his own behalf, the more devoutly he has interceded for his friends, for the sacrifice of prayer is more willingly received, which is favored with love for one's neighbor.[163] Job was given twice all his previous possessions when he prayed for his friends, for the Lord was "turned at the penance of Job" (42:10). Similarly, Our Lord offers unparalleled promises for the faithful who practice the Holy Face devotion:

> By my Holy Face you will work marvels.
> You will obtain from my Holy Face the salvation of a multitude of sinners.
> All those who honor My Face in a spirit of reparation will by doing perform the office of the pious Veronica.
> According to the care they take in making reparation to My Face, disfigured by blasphemers, so will I take care of their souls which have been disfigured by sin. My Face is the Seal of the Divinity, which has the virtue of reproducing in souls the image of God; I will imprint thereon my own image, and I will render it as beautiful as when it came forth from the baptismal font.
> Those who by words, prayers or writing defend My cause in the Work of Reparation, especially My priests, I will defend before My Father, and will give them My Kingdom.

---

[161] *Apostolic Letter of John Paul II*, 52–53.
[162] Sister Mary St. Peter, *Life of Sister Mary St. Peter*, 309.
[163] Gregory the Great, *Morals on the Book of Job*, 3:630.

> As in an earthly kingdom, the subjects can procure all they desire by being provided with a piece of money stamped with the effigy of the monarch, so also shall you be able to obtain all that you desire in the kingdom of Heaven, on presenting the impress of my sacred humanity, which is my Holy Face.
>
> Those who on earth contemplate the wounds of My Face shall in Heaven behold it radiant with glory.
>
> They will receive in their souls a bright and constant irradiation of My Divinity, that by their likeness to My Face they shall shine with particular splendor in Heaven.
>
> I will defend them, I will preserve them, and I assure them of Final Perseverance.[164]

These promises attached to the Holy Face devotion speak of the gift of God's Kingdom, the salvation of a multitude, the working of prodigies, and the shining with splendor in Heaven. They are unparalleled and supernaturally oriented,[165] which indicates the superior nature and the importance of the devotion. God wishes to reward man in a marvelous fashion for making reparation not just for himself but for others, as he did Job. He wishes to be "turned at the penance" of the faithful.

One may feel uneasy at some of the promises attached to the devotion, seeing them as too fantastic, too liberal on the part of Our Lord, such that, perhaps, one may question whether they should be taken literally. One may question especially whether prodigies and marvels, as in miracles, could really flow from this devotion in the here and now. Remarkably, man has bountiful evidence of their literal truth.

In 1851, less than a decade after these revelations began, Ven. Leo Dupont realized the first miracle to be tied to the devotion. It was the first of *thousands* — six thousand of which are certified, spanned over a period of thirty years, such that Pope Pius IX declared Dupont "perhaps the greatest miracle worker in Church history." The miracles were effected through the prayers of the devotion and oil from a lamp burning in front of a Holy Face image, which had been

---

[164] Sister Mary St. Peter, *Life of Sister Mary St. Peter*, preface, 124, 139, 205, 251, 254, 255, 256, 263, 291, 302.

[165] As will be explained in greater detail in chapter 7, the promises attached to the Sacred and Immaculate Hearts and to the Rosary, for example, are aligned generally more to personal salvation and temporal assistance versus the Holy Face promises, which pertain additionally to salvation of the masses, heavenly rewards, and supernatural assistance. The promises of Divine Mercy come closest by comparison, but even they are exceeded by the Holy Face.

touched to Veronica's veil in the Vatican. This original veil had become miraculously distinct and of a flesh-like hue — a marked contrast from its two-millenial-old, dark and blurred features — during a Christmas octave exposition in 1849, less than six months after the death of Sister St. Pierre. The Holy Face devotion and the "Holy Man of Tours" (Ven. Dupont) became household names throughout France and the world in consequence of these miracles, which were more numerous than even those of Lourdes.

A Modern-Day Job

Having discussed Job, the devotion revealed in the revelations to Sister St. Pierre, and briefly, Ven. Dupont, there is an anecdote that ties the three together, allowing for another sort of parallel between Job and, in this instance, Leo Dupont: Once while Sister St. Pierre was seeking the means of covering some expenses pertaining to another devotion, "The Little Gospel," to be printed by permission of her superiors, Our Lord directed her to address herself to His servant, "[Monsieur] Dupont," and say to him that the Infant Jesus requested of him this work of charity as the tithe of all the benefits He had bestowed upon him, for the work was most agreeable to Him. Sister St. Pierre then said to Our Lord, "If you would only promise me some recompense for him, or at least some grace for his family!" Our Lord replied, "His love for me is so pure that he will perform this service without [Me] offering him any inducement. For his disinterested love and devotion, I will recompense him magnificently in Heaven."[166]

If Job is among the most endearing of all characters in history, the same must be said for the person of Leo Dupont. Among other marked similarities, Ven. Dupont had in common with Job a heroically virtuous and pious life, despite great trials and sacrifices, his being marked by the extraordinary practice of, and zeal for, the Holy Face devotion. They shared a charm that flowed from profound humility and proper fear of the Lord. Ven. Dupont, in many respects, is the modern-day Job, a current champion of champions of reparation and right reverence due God's majesty and holy name.

> *For as the heavens are high above the earth, so great is*
> *his steadfast love toward those who fear him.*
>
> *— Psalm 103:11 (RSVCE)*

---

[166] Sister Mary St. Peter, *Life of Sister Mary St. Peter*, 221–222.

UNVEILING the SIXTH STATION of the CROSS

CHAPTER 1

St. Joan of Arc: Forerunner of Sister Marie de St. Pierre, Forebearer of the Holy Face Devotion

Devotion to the Holy Face is not new, nor is making reparation to God. Both may be rightly first attributed to the angels and especially St. Michael, who, according to Catholic tradition, countered Satan's challenge to the majesty of the Almighty by declaring, "Who is like unto God?" St. Michael is additionally credited with leading the good angels in victory over Lucifer and his rebel angels, such that according to St. Francis de Sales,[167] veneration to St. Michael is considered a remedy against offenses to the rights of God — a means of reparation. Indeed, St. Michael was the first to "repair" or make reparation for affronts to God, restoring proper reverence to His "Face." Fittingly, he is one of three patrons of the Holy Face devotion as well as one of three spiritual guides for St. Joan of Arc. In line with both tasks of the archangel, St. Gregory the Great noted that whenever some act of wondrous power must be performed, St. Michael is sent so that by his actions and name (which means "Who is like God?"), all may know that no one can do what God alone does by His superior power.

As for devotion to the Face of God and the act of reparation in the history of man, "seeking the Face of God" was continually referenced in the Old

---

[167] Cathal Ó hAimheirgin, *Consecration to St. Michael* (St. Mary's, KS: Angelus Press, 2021), 14.

Testament as expressing not only a longing on the part of the Israelites but a command from the Almighty. Certainly, "the psalms and the prophets have been only one long echo of this inexhaustible nostalgia of exiled man, of the prodigal child."[168] As a demand of God, this "seeking" referred to the need for reparation by His Chosen People for blasphemous affronts that they from time to time committed against Him, lest He withdraw His "Face" (His blessing), by turning His "Face" from them. The nostalgic longing for God, the seeking of His Face, on the part of the Israelites was a desire to be caught up (again) in His mercy and truth, justice and peace, which was, in fact, again achievable after the requisite reconciliation. It was as if the Face of God literally needed to be "turned" (back) toward them for the Israelites to be able to behold it once again — to be able to enjoy God's blessings once again. This is succinctly summarized in the familiar verse in Psalm 79:4, "Convert us, O God: and shew us thy face, and we shall be saved."

Fittingly, the Israelites were the first to see the Face of their long-awaited Messiah as the God incarnate, the Immanuel ("God with us"), which has been adored since Mary and Joseph first laid eyes upon the Christ Child. Certainly, "at every moment of the life of Jesus one saw the reflection of the divine face appear,"[169] for "the light of the knowledge of the glory of God [is] in the face of Jesus Christ" (2 Cor. 4:6). And Christ revealed Himself as *the* "way, and the truth, and the life" (John 14:6), referring in large part to His role as merciful mediator of the Father, performing Himself, in the place of the Israelites (and all sinners), the ultimate reparation by way of His Redemption. Certainly, the whole of Catholic history is since dappled with miracles and saints and art and writings illuminating the glory and beauty in Christ's Face — whether "radiant in the splendor of the Transfiguration [or] disfigured and veiled under the outrages of the praetorium"[170] — as well as the ongoing importance of reparation as a shared obligation of co-redemption for members of Christ's Mystical Body.[171]

---

[168] Louis Van den Bossche, *The Message of Sister Mary of St. Peter*, trans. Mary G. Durham (France: Carmel of Tours, 1953), 8.

[169] Ibid., 8.

[170] Ibid.

[171] "As we are necessarily united with Christ in His mission, since we form His Mystical Body, so we must necessarily cooperate with Him in His sufferings or 'Passion.' Therefore, St. Paul [explains] that we must 'fill up those things that are wanting,' not in the *mission* of Christ, but in His Passion (Col. 1:24). The two unite, neither can exist

"To unveil and soothe the Face of God"[172] — to seek and make reparation to God's Face — then, is not new. What *is* new is the uniting of the act of reparation with devotion to the Holy Face as *a directed and specific God-given means for man to utilize the power of Christ (as "hidden" in His wounded Countenance) to draw mercy for sinners.* It is the offering by man of the merits and love *encased in Christ's suffering Face*[173] to the Father as reparation for *current* offenses against the first three commandments — those concerning the rights of God — to draw graces for the salvation of the masses during this era of iniquity, which, according to Our Lord, has yet to be exceeded.[174] This modern, most efficacious means of co-redemption in making reparation to the Father via the offering of Christ's Face (rather than one's own) is the essence of the Holy Face devotion and is referred to by Christ as "the sole means of appeasing His Father":[175] a soothing of God's Face par excellence to repair the unprecedented offenses against His majesty in today's era. Indeed, this new work of reparation was requested by Christ (to specifically include the utilization of His wounded Countenance as a unique and powerful offering of reparation to the Father) as recently as the 1840s, designed to counter fresh affronts of irreverence to God that flowed from the blasphemous ideology surrounding the French Revolution (now sadly the norm). Nevertheless, the modern foundation of the Holy Face devotion in some sense began four hundred years before with the onset of St. Joan of Arc's most extraordinary role in the liberation of France from English invasion.

Also occurring in the 1840s, the historian and archivist Jules Quicherat unearthed the records of her trials. In them Joan is found to be a witch by a corrupt, English-sympathizing ecclesial court and then exonerated by "rehabilitation" proceedings in Rome twenty-five years later. Prior to this rediscovery, her story was viewed more "as a vaguely defined romance than as definite and authentic history."[176] The validity of the incredibly bizarre, miraculous events surrounding Joan's life, as well as her singularly virtuous

---

alone. We must make Reparation with Christ." Raoul Plus, *The Ideal of Reparation*, trans. Madame Cecilia (London: Burns, Oats & Washbourne, 1921), 17.

[172] Van den Bossche, *Message*, 9.

[173] Christ is the head, and the members of the Church are the body (as in the Mystical Body of Christ). In addition, Christ's merits and love are infinitely more pleasing than the merits and love encased in man's "face."

[174] Sister Mary of St. Peter, *Life of Sister Mary St. Peter*, ed. Rev. P. Janvier (France, 1994), 159.

[175] "Offer my Face to My Father, for it is the sole means of appeasing Him." Ibid., 290.

[176] Mark Twain, *Joan of Arc* (San Francisco: Ignatius, 2007), 441.

character, is confirmed under oath by eyewitnesses.[177] Indeed, the evidence from Joan's trials and rehabilitation records abundantly affirms the saintly quality of this maiden savior of France, who, in her preservation of France, also safeguarded Catholicism.

The victories of the Maid of Orléans essentially secured France as "Eldest Daughter of the Church" — referring to its status as the first Catholic monarchy, beginning with the entry of the Frankish kingdom into the Catholic Church upon the baptism of King Clovis I in 496. This allowed for the continuation of its crucial role in the stalwart defense of Catholicism throughout the world, as well. As the liberator of France, St. Joan of Arc is the forerunner to Sister Marie de St. Pierre, the French Carmelite who received revelations from Christ to initiate the Holy Face devotion and who would also be called to save France via spiritual combat. And in some important respects, she is the forebearer of the devotion itself. For St. Joan of Arc and Sister St. Pierre were each "unlikely" maiden saviors of France and, consequently, Catholicism in France (thus bolstering the Catholic Church herself); each was an astounding testament of God's ongoing activity in human life and history; and each played an essential role in the development of key Catholic devotions, including those to the Sacred Heart, the Immaculate Heart, and the Holy Face. Remarkably, these devotions are all arguably better understood in the hindsight of — as perhaps even ultimately intended for — the third millennium: a testament to their ongoing relevance and that of France's maiden deliverers.

✠ ✠ ✠

St. Joan of Arc, virgin, mystic, martyr, and prophetess, is regarded by her admirers, and indeed the Church, as a heroine deliverer of France for her role during the last phase of the bloody Hundred Years' War with England. She was given the nickname "Maid of Orléans" for her success in heading a relief army against a devastating seven-month siege in Orléans that collapsed only nine days later, on the feast of St. Michael. The victory for France held strategic and symbolic significance: for either side, occupancy of Orléans was necessary to win the war.

Within nine months, notwithstanding hating the sight of blood and never herself having killed anyone, Joan also led timely victories along the Loire River, including a crushing defeat at Patay. This afforded the French, who had been

---

[177] Ibid.

under the rule of the English king Henry VI, the ability to name the (contested-by-the-English) heir Charles VII as their legitimate king. The consecration of the king at Rheims (which had been captured by the English) was consequently a long-desired event by his countrymen, despite the corrupt influence of his court and his own flagrant ineptitude.[178] This restoring of France's lost sovereignty, along with the return of nearly all significant parcels of land previously riven from France by England — thanks in largest part to the victories led by Joan of Arc — boosted the exhausted morale of the French and forged the way for the 1453 liberation of Bordeaux. This Battle of Castillon marked the end to the Hundred Years' War, which had long ravaged the "French" underdogs.

Joan, a most improbable aspirant for these tasks, did not conceive of them herself. She began as a humble fifteenth-century peasant girl residing in a tiny, no-name northeast farm village of France. She lived there simply and contentedly with her family and friends. Though she had been taught prayers and the basics of her Faith by her pious family, she had nothing akin to formal education and, like most of her acquaintances, could not read or write. She had never seen a battle, had not ridden a (saddled) horse, nor had any idea how to lead men, much less how to conceive of or execute military tactics and strategies. Instead, she was often at Mass, had great compassion for the poor and wounded, and, like all the girls in her neck of late-medieval France, took pride in her spinning and sewing. Joan herself stated that there was nobody in all the world who could recover the kingdom for France if not for her, *though she would have rather remained spinning at her mother's side*, for it was not her "condition" to undertake the mission, despite her Lord willing it.[179] She was the improbable, young King David destined to slay Goliath.

Still, she began her holy quest by confidently and fearlessly presenting herself to the Dauphin, the then-as-yet-unanointed King Charles VII. Playing off a statement from Joan that she would be able to recognize him no matter his concealment, the king disguised himself from her upon their first meeting. She immediately spotted him among his courtiers, knelt before him instead of any of the more nobly dressed advisors, and announced to him in a humble yet matter-of-fact manner that God had sent her to save France.

---

[178] Twain, *Joan of Arc*, 70, 113, and Régine Pernoud, *Joan of Arc by Herself and Her Witnesses* (Lanham, MD: Scarborough House, 1994), 443.

[179] Pernoud, *Joan of Arc by Herself*, 35.

Having undertaken the journey to Chinon through lands held by England and the dukes of Burgundy who disputed Charles VII's pedigree, Joan unflinchingly told the Dauphin she had been commanded by God, Michael the Archangel, and the saints Catherine of Alexandria and Margaret of Antioch[180] to undertake three tasks — to save the city of Orleans from the nearly one-hundred-year English invasion, to see the Dauphin crowned and consecrated at Rheims, deep in enemy territory, and to force the English out of France.[181]

She told the king that she was unafraid, that *for this she was born.*

To determine whether Joan's commands came from Heaven or Hell, the king requested that she undergo an extensive three-week questioning at Poitiers by a committee of bishops and theologians. They reported back to him that they found nothing in her contrary to the Catholic Faith, "no evil, but only good, humility, virginity, devotion, honesty, simplicity,"[182] and that, considering the necessity, the king should make use of her to help him, "for at that time, there was no hope but in God."[183] In addition, they warned that to repel the assistance would be to offend the Holy Spirit and render him unworthy of the aid of God.[184] Despite these findings, the king did not initially show great respect for Joan and intended her only to be a figurehead.[185] Still, Joan managed fruitful requests of the king, including that he give his kingdom to the King of Heaven, who would in return restore him to his original estate.[186] (This request, that of the French kings being asked to acknowledge Christ as true king, has been echoed in France's history, most notably to Louis XIV, who was asked through St. Margaret Mary Alacoque to consecrate his nation to the Sacred Heart. The request was unfulfilled for one hundred years to the day, until, before he was

---

[180] St. Catherine and St. Margaret were among saints, known as the Fourteen Holy Helpers, who were popular during the Middle Ages for assisting in ailments such as the Plague and various troubles. Margaret had been a shepherdess and Catherine had debated pagan philosophers. Both died martyrs.

[181] Sean Fitzpatrick, "St. Joan of Arc: Girl Power or Godly Power?," *Crisis Magazine*, May 29, 2021, https://www.crisismagazine.com/2021/st-joan-of-arc-girl-power-or-godly-power.

[182] Pernoud, *Joan of Arc by Herself*, 58.

[183] Ibid., 51, 57.

[184] Twain, *Joan of Arc*, 140.

[185] Kathryn Neves, "Joan of Arc: A Hero or a Villian?," The Professional Theatre at Southern Utah University News/Blog, April 19, 2018, https://www.bard.org/news/joan-of-arc-a-hero-or-a-villian/.

[186] Pernoud, *Joan of Arc by Herself*, 50.

imprisoned, the king's grandson, Louis XVI, "made the consecration most piously of both his nation and himself to the Sacred Heart, but it was too late to save France or the king.")[187] Joan was ultimately able to convince Charles VII, among others, of the authenticity of her mission in part by various foretelling: disclosing to the king a fear that was previously known only by him — most probably having to do with whether he was the true heir descending from the House of France, which Joan affirmed;[188] the date when she herself would be wounded in battle; as well as specific future victories — including the precise nature, place, and time limit. And the conquests did come, one after the other, all led by the seventeen-year-old maiden clad in white armor, *la Pucelle*.

During her battles, Joan carried a banner patterned in fleurs-de-lis and bearing the names of Jesus and Mary, indicative of her stalwart devotion to God, the Church, and her homeland. She was in fact a highly determined warrior, never wanting to negotiate or be cautious.[189] When asked why her flag was displayed so prominently at the king's coronation, she replied simply and poignantly that it had borne the burden, it had earned the honor.[190] Joan was told by the king to choose her reward for her part in his long-overdue coronation. She selflessly asked only that her little village never be taxed again and expressed a desire to return home when France was freed.

Yet Joan would never see her homeland again, and her biggest challenges lay ahead of her. She would bear the ongoing and cowardly incompetence and disloyalty of the king, deception from within her own ranks, and the unabashed corruption of prominent French Church officials. She faced all with remarkably heroic courage and determination.

> Despite [her] unprecedented victor[ies], the apathetic Charles VII neglected to launch her against Paris while the army's morale was high. When an assault was finally launched, Joan failed to take the city. As efforts were underway to make further assay for Paris, Joan was captured by the Burgundians [French sympathizers of the English] and sold to the English as a prisoner. After several escape attempts from her

---

[187] Edouard Belaga, "My Dear France, the Tender Daughter of the Sacred Heart," Catholic Stand, accessed June 12, 2023, https://catholicstand.com/dear-france-tender-daughter-sacred-heart-3/.
[188] Pernoud, *Joan of Arc by Herself*, 53.
[189] Larissa Juliet Taylor, *The Virgin Warrior: The Life and Death of Joan of Arc* (New Haven: Yale University, 2009), 98.
[190] Twain, *Joan of Arc*, 446.

mocking captors, Joan was dragged before fifty clerical judges to stand trial as a heretic.

Determined to delegitimize the king Joan had put on the throne of France, her accusers had difficulty [however] in their illegal proceedings due to the sharp intelligence of their victim. Joan deftly answered questions of tremendous theological complexity and subtlety, giving her accusers little ground on which to base their accusation as they pressured her to confess to witchcraft, fabrications, and a plot to dress like a man.[191]

Seeking to pin Joan as a heretic and sorceress, her enemies, led by the bishop of Beauvais, ally of the Burgundians — via six public and nine private sessions of an ecclesial court — eventually ensnared her.

In the end, notwithstanding a remarkably capable self-defense in which she never wavered in her Catholic devotion, Joan was condemned to be burned at the stake. Abandoned by many of the French nobles and even the cowardly ingrate Charles VII — who had refused to help her upon her capture — she knelt praying for her French king and country in a last display of faith in God's ability to work through even the weakest of men and nations. As the flames of martyrdom rose, it was an Englishman who held a makeshift cross for her to kiss.[192]

The French Church sadly has held pockets that were not immune to political corruption. Albeit posthumously, Joan, however, received at length a fair trial. In 1456, approximately twenty-five years after her death, she was found by Rome to be a martyr. The court that had previously tried her was declared to have violated Church law, and the bishop of Beauvais, who headed the illegal proceedings against her, was excommunicated. Joan was beatified in 1909 and canonized in 1920.

Charles VII came to be a more competently decisive king after Joan's death and even supported her rehabilitation trial in Rome. (It has been argued, however, given Joan had placed him on the throne, that he wanted to help bolster the legitimacy of his pedigree in consideration of the initial condemnation of Joan as heretic.) He revamped his army and persuaded the duke of Burgundy to break his alliance with the English. Victories were won over Normandy and Bordeaux, the final English hold in southern France. Only the port city of Calais

---

[191] Fitzpatrick, "St. Joan of Arc."
[192] Pernoud, *Joan of Arc by Herself*, 231.

on the northern coast of France was left to the English, ending their decisive (though somewhat intermittent) grip going back to the days of William the Conqueror.[193]

✠ ✠ ✠

Eager to validate Joan's mission, the late-medieval French were fond of recalling the mythical prophecy of Merlin some eight hundred years prior that France would be lost by a woman and restored by a woman.[194] They believed the betrayer to be the calamitous Isabella of Bavaria, married to the insane Charles VI. She was infamous for her baseness and for her part in the signing of the Treaty of Troyes in 1420. The agreement recognized King Henry V of England as heir to the French crown rather than her own son Charles (afterward VII). The redeemer, of course, they believed to be the Maid of Orléans. It is the mere stuff of legend but for the hindsight of history.

In more modern times, a most compelling defense of Joan comes from a surprising source: Mark Twain. Devoting over a decade to meticulously researching every detail of her life, the literary realist and religious skeptic Twain was in part convinced by the stranger-than-fiction events of her life: her extraordinary military successes, her ability to lead and challenge men to heroism, her prophecies, and her brilliant self-defense in court. Perhaps even more convincing to him was the virtuous genius of her character seeming to come quite literally from "nowhere" — that is, if nowhere may be equated with Domrémy, an obscure, "humble little hamlet of [Joan's] remote time and region,"[195] which could not have possibly offered her any knowledge, much less experience, in preparation for her sensational military and court trial escapades. Moreover,

> for Twain, the documents of Joan's famous trial in 1431, and the "Rehabilitation" proceedings after her death represent a complete, legal, and trustworthy source for her biography. What emerges from these extensive trial documents, eyewitness accounts, and manuscripts is simply St. Joan of Arc, with all her holiness, her prophecies, and her visions. And the facts point unmistakably to God's power. It is as if Twain's commitment to Realism defeats his skepticism.... Twain

---

[193] Christopher Zehnder, *Light to the Nations, Part One: The History of Christian Civilization*, ed. Rollin Lasseter (San Francisco: Ignatius Press, 2014), 398.
[194] Pernoud, *Joan of Arc by Herself*, 44.
[195] Twain, *Joan of Arc*, 34.

writes in his prefatory note to the novel: "The details of the life of Joan of Arc form a biography which is unique among the world's biographies in one respect: it is the only story of a human life which comes to us under oath, the only one which comes to us from the witness-stand." Joan's well-documented life, then, becomes a kind of case study for God's activity in human life and history.[196]

The very trial that was designed to be the means to vilify Joan affords history the ability to judge her life from the crucible of irrefutable documentation, countering her modern, likely misinformed skeptics.

Yet one might still legitimately wonder: Why would God intervene so blatantly to oust the English from France, both Catholic peoples at the time — also necessitating that Charles VII, a very unimpressive heir, be crowned? And why did He ask a saint to lead this effort in a bloody, rather than more "Christian," manner? These modern contentions ironically go beyond what St. Joan of Arc's accusers themselves set to prove. Their aim was simply to establish Joan as a witch or heretic. They did not go so far as to imply that if she were not, God must have therefore supported an unjust, needlessly bloody war. The argument therefore poses an unhappy alternative: it posits that God would not ask for anyone to lead a "needless" war, and in such a bloody manner. Since Joan claimed she was led by God, she must therefore be either deceiving or deceived (by Satan). If she were truly following the commands of God, then God behaved "ungodly" in pitting Catholic against Catholic in the setting of horrific and unwarranted war.

It would seem safe to assume that Joan did indeed follow the commands of God in consideration of the rigorous requirements for Catholic canonization in conjunction with her miraculous life events being one of the best documented in history.[197] There remains the matter, then, of why God would conduct the liberation of France in such a "barbaric" manner and whether there was any true necessity in freeing France from English rule (and in doing so putting a lamentable Dauphin upon the throne). What must God have been thinking?

Regarding the manner of liberation, a Dominican priest asked Joan during her early questioning at Poitiers why God, given that He can do whatever He

---

[196] Kelly Scott Franklin, "Why Was 'Joan of Arc' Mark Twain's Favorite among All His Many Books?," *The Catholic World Report*, May 29, 2021, http://www.catholicworldreport.com/2021/05/20/why-was-joan-of-arc-mark-twains-favorite-among-all-his-many-books.
[197] Twain, *Joan of Arc*, 441.

wills, would need men at arms to deliver France. Joan responded that God helps those who help themselves and that the sons of France were to fight the battles, but God would give the victory.[198] Indeed, somewhat perplexing battles involving Heaven are not without precedent. There are numerous examples in the Old Testament of bloody wars being directed by God: Israel versus Jericho (Josh. 6); Israel versus Philistines (1 Sam. 7); Nebuchadnezzar versus Pharaoh (Jer. 46), and so on. A summary of the Crusades being too expansive for the confines of this chapter, there are others in the era of Christendom. For example, Constantine defeated Maxentius after receiving a vision in which he heard the words "In this sign you will conquer," referring to the Chi-Rho (serving in place of the Cross, which was forbidden by the Roman authorities). The victory allowed for the Edict of Milan, granting legal status to Christians in 313. There was also the naval Battle of Lepanto in 1571 between the Holy League and the Ottoman Empire. Pius V had requested that the faithful petition the intercession of the Blessed Virgin Mary through the recitation of the Rosary, so when word reached the pope of the victory, he issued a new feast of Our Lady of Victory (now Holy Rosary). The victory was necessary to safeguard both Europe and Christendom. In consideration of these examples, the bloody manner and mystery, then, of Joan's battles need not necessarily preclude intervention by God, especially if other means had been shown to be ineffective.

To this point, there is the fact that "every French king for 200 years had tried by war, confiscation *or treaty* to regain Aquitaine,"[199] the region of which the English kings were dukes, which, however, belonged to France. (The English believed this gave Edward III right to claim the crown of France in 1337, after the Capetian king died without a successor. This was a catalyst of the Hundred Years' War, since, according to French law, the heir could not pass through the mother, as in the case of Edward.) Diplomacy, then, in the form of treaties, was attempted at various times, indicating ongoing efforts toward war as a last resort. Yet given that both countries were Catholic at the time, there remains the question whether it was truly essential that France remain a sovereign nation. Leaving worldly politics aside, does it seem reasonable that God would have felt the need to intervene to liberate one Catholic nation from another?

---

[198] Pernoud, *Joan of Arc by Herself*, 55.
[199] Barbara W. Tuchman, *A Distant Mirror* (New York: Ballantine Books, 1978), 72. (My emphasis.)

To put human speculation upon the "necessity" of an all-knowing God orchestrating St. Joan of Arc's role in the saving of France from the then-Catholic England, perhaps one consideration could be the Protestant Reformation, occurring less than a century after the death of Joan. In other words, while England and France were both Catholic at the time of the Hundred Years' War, England would soon not be. King Henry VIII was the major force in England abandoning entirely its Catholicity in favor of Protestantism (although there had been some precursors to this distancing from Rome, notably the Wycliffe Rebellion in the fourteenth century). Had France not lifted the siege at Orléans, the mechanism for her reclaiming her lost land to England, she would have soon become totally under English control. And consequently, the "New Israel," according to Pope St. Pius X,[200] the Eldest Daughter of the Church, along with its influence upon the rest of Christendom, would no longer be.

Though the Catholicism of France would later greatly diminish due to ideology surrounding the Enlightenment and the French Revolution, and though its Catholicity today continues to wane, the argument could be made that God apparently determined a stronghold was needed at the time to provide a nurturing backdrop for the then future, formal promulgation of several important Catholic devotions. Among them are those to the Sacred Heart, the Immaculate Heart, and the Holy Face — all "originating" in France after the Hundred Years' War (albeit having gradually developed from the onset of Christianity). While an in-depth discussion of the significance of these is saved for future chapters, it should be noted the three are complementary and are considered by most devout as no less than essential to modern Catholic piety. Additionally, they are increasingly relevant due to the crucial mystical role they provide man in the mitigation of what the *Catholic Catechism* terms a "final trial that will shake the faith of many believers [in the Church],"[201] commonly referred to as the Great Tribulation, borrowing from the book of Revelation (2:22).

Related to this are the copious Marian apparitions occurring in France after the time of Joan of Arc. While France has the most approved Marian apparitions by nation (exhibiting widespread "liturgical veneration endorsed by the Holy

---

[200] Hickson Family, "Pope Pius X's 1908 Words on Joan of Arc, Courage, and Lukewarm Catholics," *Ordo Dei* (blog), accessed May 17, 2023, https://ordodei.net/2018/12/15/pope-pius-xs-1908-words-on-joan-of-arc-courage-and-lukewarm-catholics/.
[201] CCC, 675–677.

See"), England has none.[202] This is not to say that England lacks devoted Catholics — it is, on the contrary, renowned for its martyrs of the same era. Rather, it is to illustrate in measurable terms the importance of France's then-stalwart Catholicism in contributing to the modern spirituality of the faithful. For whatever reason, the Blessed Virgin appeared in areas that upheld the Faith and that, in turn, enjoyed increased piety via devotions springing from these apparitions. In practical terms, France's Catholicity would also help enable initial approval of these apparitions from local bishops, paving the way for Rome's approval. (Apparitions occurring in a hostile-to-Catholics period in England, for example, would have a very difficult time gaining Church approval, in that there would be no local bishop to whom one could appeal for such.) Among those in France that are recognized by the Vatican are Our Lady of the Miraculous Medal, La Salette, Lourdes, Laus, and Pontmain. They continue to speak to the times regarding the importance of hope, faith, grace, prayer, penance, conversion, and the love and protection of Our Holy Mother for her children.

Indeed, regarding France's role in the preservation of Christianity, Pope St. Pius X said, referring to France during the beatification of Joan of Arc:

> Just as [God] once preferred the tribe of Judah to the tribes of Jacob's other sons and gave them special blessings, so he chose [France] in preference to all the other nations of the earth for the protection of the Catholic faith and the defense of religious freedom.... Only France is great among nations in this regard, by this covenant God will protect it by making it free and glorious, on this condition it will be possible to apply to France what is said in the holy books about Israel, "that no one was 'found' to insult this people except when it 'departed from God,'" *et non fuit qui insuttaset, populo ipsi visi quando reeessit a cultu Domini Dei sui*.[203]

And in a later address to the French people, the same pope is quoted:

> A day will come, and we hope it will not be far away, when France, like Saul on the road to Damascus, will be surrounded by a heavenly light and will hear a voice repeating to her, "My daughter, why do you persecute

---

[202] "Centuries of Miracles," *National Geographic*, November 13, 2015, https://www.nationalgeographic.com/science/article/151113-virgin-mary-sightings-map. Based on the Catholic website Miracle Hunter. NB: Walsingham, for example, was before the time of Joan of Arc, and others may not have approval of the Holy See.

[203] Hickson, "Pope Pius X's 1908 Words."

me?" And to her response, "Who art Thou, Lord?" the voice will reply, "I am Jesus, whom you persecute. It is hard for you to kick against the goad because, in your obstinacy, you destroy yourself." And she, trembling and astonished, will say, "Lord, what wouldst Thou have me do?" And He will say, "Rise up, wash the filth that has disfigured you, awaken in your heart those dormant affections and the pact of our alliance and go, *eldest daughter of the Church, predestined nation, vessel of election, go, as in the past, and carry my name before all peoples and before the kings of the earth*."[204]

More recently, in his 1996 homily to the French people celebrating the 1,500th anniversary of the conversion to Christianity of the pagan king Clovis, Pope St. John Paul II appealed to Catholics of France to "rediscover the source" of their baptism, "to review the vast spiritual history of the soul of France, [despite having] clouded times of infidelity and confrontations, the consequences of sin, [and to recall] that every trial is an urgent call to conversion and sanctity."[205] These are examples of popes linking France's soul, as a favored nation, to that of the Church at large, adding to the apparent "measurability" of the importance of France's then-resolute Catholicism in terms of the copious approved Marian apparitions and Catholic devotions springing from that nation soon after the time of Joan of Arc.

Regardless of whether one is convinced of the importance of France's sovereignty as a Catholic nation, given the amazing and apparently miraculous life and mission of St. Joan of Arc, cemented for all time in the records of her trials and in the rigorous investigative processes surrounding her canonization, there seems a call to submit humbly to what one may not understand regarding the ways of God. In the book of Job, God explains to Job and his friends that since man cannot comprehend the greatness and wisdom of the Creator and Ruler of the universe, he should bend humbly and trustingly under the hand of the Almighty.[206] Wisdom, instead of scrutinizing the behavior of God, is rather practicing fear of the Lord (Job 28:28). "O man, who art thou that repliest

---

[204] Plinio Corrêa de Oliveira, "Prophetic Insights of Saint Pius X about the Conversion of France," *Tradition, Family, and Property*, accessed May 22, 2023, https://www.tfp.org/prophetic-insights-of-saint-pius-x-about-the-conversion-of-france/. (My emphasis.)

[205] "Pope Ends Grueling Trip to France," *UPI*, September 22, 1996, accessed June 12, 2023, https://www.upi.com/Archives/1996/09/22/Pope-ends-grueling-trip-to-France.

[206] John Laux, *Chief Truths of the Faith* (Charlotte, NC: Saint Benedict Press, 1990), 30.

against God?" (Rom. 9:20). One does well to remember that God is not subject to the moral "constraints" of man.

If God were under the law as given to men, there would arguably be no Noah's Flood, no Sodom and Gomorrah, no slaying by Joshua of Hazor and his people, nor even the Son of God being sacrificed for the sake of mere mortals — all involving the "messy" love and mercy and justice of the Almighty, which is hard for man to comprehend in his day-to-day living and dying and pondering. And perhaps there would be no salvation of France by a young maiden in the form of a bloody war between one Catholic nation and another.

St. Joan of Arc is a heroine for all time. Like all saints, she is an example of what men may be if they exchange their wills for God's, exemplifying proper fear of the Lord. She boosted the exhausted morale of the French and does the same for Catholics today — as well as for Mark Twain-like skeptics. Her virtue, genius, heroism, courage, and mission are all stranger-than-fiction truths preserved under the oath of the witness stand, attesting to God's ongoing involvement in man's life and history. She was as unlikely as she proved extraordinary, each attribute manifesting the majesty and mystery of God. In her saving of France, Joan safeguarded its Catholicism, which in turn provided for invaluable future Catholic devotions — including that of the Holy Face. As such, St. Joan of Arc was the forerunner of another unlikely maiden savior of France, Sister Marie de St. Pierre, who likewise bolstered Catholicism through her rescue of France, the "New Israel." Joan's battles were material, while Sister St. Pierre's were spiritual, yet the life and death and prayer of both was "Great God, save France!" And He did.

Chapter 2

A Fitting Birthplace of the Devotion and Sister St. Pierre's New Home: The Carmel of Tours

Zelo zelatus sum pro Domino Deo exercituum.

With zeal have I been zealous for the Lord God of Hosts.

— *Motto of the Carmelite Order (words of Elijah, 1 Kings 19:10)*

EARLY IN HER MILITARY escapades, St. Joan of Arc was led by St. Michael the Archangel, St. Catherine of Alexandria, and St. Margaret of Antioch[207] to an ancient sword buried behind the altar of Sainte-Catherine-de-Fierbois. (The chapel continues to be a stop along the "French Way" of the ancient pilgrimage route to Santiago de Compostela in Spain.) Though never having killed anyone, Joan carried the sword with her when heading the French to victory over the English in crucial battles leading to the end of the Hundred Years' War, thus securing the status of France as Eldest Daughter of the Church. (The victories allowed France

---

[207] St. Catherine and St. Margaret were among saints, known as the Fourteen Holy Helpers, who were popular during the Middle Ages for assisting in ailments such as the Plague and various troubles. Margaret had been a shepherdess and Catherine had debated pagan philosophers. Both died martyrs.

to remain Catholic during England's soon-after abandoning of Catholicism entirely in favor of Protestantism.) The chapel was in the prefecture of Tours, the same city in which divine revelations were given over four hundred years later to the young Carmelite, Sister Marie de St. Pierre, to initiate the Holy Face devotion. The city thereby afforded the material armament of St. Joan of Arc as well as the spiritual armament of Sister St. Pierre, both unlikely maiden saviors of France and, in many respects, Catholicism itself. Remarkably, this is but one of several phenomena that designate the Carmel of Tours as a fitting birthplace of the Holy Face devotion.

The Carmel of Tours is one of the oldest of the Teresian reform in France.[208] St. Teresa of Avila (Teresa of Jesus), for whom this reform is named, was active during the Catholic resurgence in response to the Protestant Reformation, known as the Counter-Reformation. "The salvation of France was one of Saint Teresa's great aims when she founded her Reform and Our Lord also pressed Blessed Anne of Saint Bartholomew to pray for this intention."[209] Teresa is one of the greatest saints of the Church, a renowned mystic, and one of only four female Doctors of the Church. She, in conjunction with St. John of the Cross, also Doctor and mystic of the Church, instituted the branch of the Carmelite Order known as "discalced" or "barefoot," which is distinguished from the other by greater austerity. She entered the order at the early age of twenty and glorified it with twenty-seven years of tireless establishment of the reform. She also composed works considered classics in the tradition of Carmelite spirituality, as did St. John of the Cross. She has been given the affectionate title among the faithful and especially fellow Carmelites as "the glory of Spain."[210]

The name *Carmelite* is taken from Mount Carmel, which lies in northwestern Palestine and upon which a chapel to the Blessed Virgin as Our Lady of Mount Carmel, patroness of the Carmelite Order, was built by Christian hermits living there during the twelfth and thirteenth centuries. The word *Carmel* itself means "Vineyard of the Lord," a fitting title for the order that has produced holy men and women from whom grace has radiated, whose virtues have and

---

[208] Louis Van den Bossche, *The Message of Sister Mary of St. Peter*, trans. Mary G. Durham (France: Carmel of Tours, 1953), 37.

[209] Ibid., 117.

[210] 1880s flyer from the Carmelites of New Orleans. And Oswald Sobrino, "The Glory of Spain," Catholic Exchange, March 1, 2005, https://www.catholicexchange.com/the-glory-of-spain.

continue to be a bulwark of protection for the world at large. Its name is noted in biblical history as the place in which Elijah confronted the prophets of Baal, who were engaged in the blasphemous act of idolatry in worship of him and who foolishly accepted Elijah's challenge, which pitted the power of their idol against that of the Almighty. According to tradition, there was, even before the time of Christ, a religious community established on Mount Carmel.

Directed toward both contemplation and action, Carmel is devoted to the needs of the Church, the glory of God, and the salvation of souls. Carmelites also have an apostolate and charism centered on becoming ardently united to Christ by love. They are one of the four great mendicant orders of the Catholic Church (meaning "concerned with the care of souls") that seek to imitate Christ crucified, following His example by voluntarily imposing upon themselves a life of abnegation and penance to offset the world's iniquity. For above any desire to secure their own salvation, they seek the spiritual good of the world, an exalted charity toward men. Indeed, they exemplify the beauty of the doctrine of the communion of the saints in which all are called to contribute to the spiritual solidarity and unity of the Church, which consists of three states: the Church Militant (those alive on earth), the Church Penitent (those in Purgatory), and the Church Triumphant (those in Heaven). In addition to special devotion to Christ crucified, they are foremost in their devotion to the Blessed Mother of God as well as St. Joseph. In fact, they count among their members St. Simon Stock, to whom Our Lady revealed the scapular of Mount Carmel, which formed part of the Carmelite habit after 1287, as a devotional sacramental, signifying consecration to Mary and her protection. It promises to those who die wearing it salvation and continues to be worn by the devout throughout the world today. Incredibly, the Holy Face devotion *caps* each of these historical characteristics of Carmel, for it is a devotion centered on consolation and love of Christ, given through Our Lady as protection for the world by making reparation for the greatest iniquities of sinners (those concerning blasphemy), is done in selfless charity toward others' salvation as part of the spiritual solidarity of the Church, and promises the devotee personal deliverance as well as aid during life toward spiritual union with God.

The Tours Carmel had as its patron St. Martin (of Tours) to whom St. Teresa of Avila had a great devotion, having received signal graces many times during the octave of his feasts.[211] St. Martin, famed thaumaturge of Gaul, is legendary — among other wonder-working extraordinaire — for having raised three people from the dead.[212] He shares patronage of the Holy Face devotion with St. Michael the Archangel and St. Louis IX, both also great defenders of God's majesty and holy name. Fittingly, it was through the Holy Face devotion that Ven. Leo Dupont likewise became a great thaumaturge of Tours (so much so that Pope Pious IX referred to him as "perhaps the greatest miracle worker in Church history"). He was known in France and by the devout throughout the world as simply "the Holy Man of Tours." St. Teresa, having reformed the Carmelite Order, is additionally an apt patron, since Our Lord requests that by use of the Holy Face devotion, the enemies of Catholicism (internal and external) will be converted, essentially "reforming" — as in embracing the orthodoxy inherent in — Christ's Mystical Body, the Church.

Moreover, the Carmel of Tours was distinctly known for its devotion to the Sacred Heart. "One day Our Lord appeared to the prioress, showing His adorable Heart, enclosed wherein she beheld the hearts of all the religious of the community."[213] This is significant in that Christ revealed the Holy Face devotion to be the complement of that to the Sacred Heart.[214] Christ related to Sister St. Pierre early in the revelations that the Tours community in particular "desires the accomplishment of the designs of [His] Heart, and prays for this intention, [so] it is but just that it should have the honor of giving birth to this Devotion."[215] Indeed, it is *in union with the Sacred Heart* that reparation to the Father is made in devotion to the Holy Face.

The foundation of the Carmel of Tours, originally under the patronage of Our Lady of Angels, and later that of the Incarnation or Holy Mother of God, dates to 1608, just after the time of St. Teresa of Avila. In fact, the first prioress of the Carmel at Tours, Bl. Mother Anne of St. Bartholomew, aforementioned, was the devoted friend of St. Teresa who assisted the saint — and even held her

---

[211] Sister St. Pierre, *Life of Sister St. Pierre*, ed. Rev. P. Janvier (Baltimore: John Murphy, 1884), 54.
[212] Susan Wills, "Saint Martin of Tours, Who Raised Three People from the Dead," *Aleteia*, accessed December 29, 2020, https://aleteia.org/2014/11/11/saint-martin-of-tours-who-raised-three-people-from-the-dead/.
[213] Sister St. Pierre, *Life of Sister St. Pierre*, 61.
[214] Sister Mary St. Peter, *Life of Sister Mary St. Peter*, ed. Rev. P. Janvier (France, 1884), 121, 149.
[215] Ibid., 153.

in her arms—as she died.[216] St. Teresa appeared after her death to her friend and consoled her on her difficult journey from Spain to Tours, as well as during inevitable trials associated with the foundation of the new convent. St. Teresa, the inspiration for Sister St. Pierre's own attraction to Carmel and to whom her pious father Pierre had also been devoted, would also later appear to her in the interior of her soul, offering herself as a most powerful protectress, as directed by God, and consoler in affliction regarding the then future work of reparation, devotion to the Holy Face of Christ.[217]

St. Teresa also related to Sister St. Pierre that this work would become "the honor of Carmel."[218] (Her biographies uniformly use the article *the*, rather than *a* or *an*, before the word *honor*, implying a pinnacle sense to the phrase, as in "the glory" or "the crown" of Carmel.) This seems arguably to be a play off her own title, given affectionately by Carmelites, as "the glory of Spain," perhaps implying that the work of reparation would be "the honor" or "the glory" not just of Spain (or France or any country) but of all Carmel. This title becomes even more remarkable in hindsight, given that the order now possesses three Doctors of the Church, St. Teresa of Avila herself, St. John of the Cross, and St. Thérèse of Lisieux, none of whom were named Doctors until the twentieth century. There are also additional saints after the time of this vision: Teresa Benedicta of the Cross, and Teresa of Jesus of Los Andes (as well as St. Elizabeth of the Trinity), all adding to the impressive saintly lineage of the order, going back to Elijah as founder, and including St. Simon Stock. *Yet St. Teresa referred to the Holy Face devotion, not any of these, as "the honor of Carmel."* As will be discussed in chapter 6, the statement "the honor of Carmel" may have also alluded to the work of reparation "crowning" the insights of the tradition of the great Carmelite mystics in some key respects, thus also becoming *the honor* of the order's characteristic spirituality.

At the time of the foundation of the Carmel of Tours, the city held numerous heretics, descendants of the Huguenots, who were the instigators of civil war in the preceding century.[219] According to local legend, when the Huguenots learned of the number of nuns who were coming to reside in their city by way of crossing the Loire, they exclaimed, "May they go to the bottom of the

---

[216] Sister St. Pierre, *Life of Sister St. Pierre*, 55.
[217] Sister Mary St. Peter, *Life of Sister Mary St. Peter*, 381–382.
[218] Ibid.
[219] Ibid., 56.

river before reaching the shore!"[220] The Carmelites, however, overcame their animosity to the extent that these descendants of the early (French) Protestants exclaimed, "These Teresians can make Catholics of us in spite of ourselves!"[221] There was peace between the Huguenots and Carmelites from that time onward — surely in no small part due to the ongoing prayers and sacrifices of the nuns for their conversion.[222] This in some sense was a foreshadowing in that the Carmel of Tours would one day become the axis of conversion for modern heretics the world over via the then-as-yet-unrevealed devotion to the Holy Face, for the devotion is to make reparation for affronts against the first three commandments, which are the most offensive to God and especially prevalent in the current age, according to the revelations. (While offenses against the last seven commandments are equally prevalent today, the axis of moral law is the first three, those pertaining to the rights of God. All sin pertaining to the rights of men, comprised in the last seven commandments, hinges on the first three. Heresies are inherently blasphemous, forbidden by the first three commandments.)

The Carmelites of Tours were first, however, a stronghold against the somewhat localized heresy of Jansenism, prominent in the latter seventeenth century and the eighteenth century, which countered the spirit of Christianity by promoting an unhealthy emphasis on God's justice and a de-emphasis on man's necessary consent to grace, leading faithful souls astray and even toward the idea of predestination. Several times the nuns from Tours were sent by their superiors to defend or reestablish sound doctrine in others who had been more swayed by the heresy.[223] Especially prevalent in France, and likewise stemming from the Reformation,[224] Jansenism was a relatively mild forerunner to outrages to the Faith ushered by revolutionary men of that country during the late eighteenth century. The blasphemous ideology of these freethinking revolutionaries would be the impetus of Heaven declaring the necessity of reparation for current affronts against the "Face of the Church," her doctrine represented by the Face of Christ, in the Holy Face devotion.

---

[220] Ibid., 65.
[221] Ibid., 57.
[222] Ibid.
[223] Ibid., 61.
[224] Jansenism saw itself as a movement, in line with the theologians of the Reformation, to reform the Church to the spirit of early Christianity.

Indeed, during the Revolution of 1789, the nineteen nuns of the Carmel house of Tours were asked to sign the "Oath of Liberty."[225] None would, declaring that they had already offered to God their vows, which no human could dispense, and that they knew of no liberty more glorious than the practice of their monastic duties.[226] They were eventually driven from their convent and arrested. They were at length released, after terrible treatment resulting in the death of one blind elderly nun. They had to live apart, however, at the charity of generous lay hosts, until 1798, when they were able to resume former conventual life upon reentering a temporary convent. They never broke, even in prison, the chain of their holy observances,[227] constantly practicing even their strict rule of abstinence. In 1822 they were able to return to the original convent, which although needing many repairs and renovations, happily held intact the rooms in which St. Teresa had appeared to the mother prioress.

Also preserved was a miraculous painting representing the mystery of the Incarnation for which the monastery had been named.[228] This painting of the Virgin, situated thirty feet high upon a wall three feet thick, began to weep when what would be unsuccessful arrangements were being made for the sale of the church to be used as a theater (prior to the nuns managing to resume occupancy). In fact, it was the eve of the sale when a clerk witnessed the phenomenon. The clerk alerted the owner as well as the nuns, several of whom witnessed the event themselves. Whether the miraculous picture swayed the owner is not known, but he did break the bargain.[229]

No doubt providentially, the convent at Tours was the only Carmel in the world in possession of a likeness of the Face of Our Lord as preserved at Genoa, from which copies were sent to Spain, one of them having been brought to France when Cardinal de Bérulle was soliciting in Spain for nuns for the first foundation of the order in France.[230] According to pious tradition and narrated by St. John Damascene, the true picture of Jesus Christ was miraculously recorded on linen and sent to King Abgar, ruler of Edessa in Syria. This monarch, having heard of the miracles worked by Our Lord and of the holiness of His life, had a strong desire to

---

[225] An oath in support of civil constitution, denying the authority of the pope and signifying apostasy.
[226] Sister Mary St. Peter, *Life of Sister Mary St. Peter*, 70.
[227] Ibid., 64.
[228] Van den Bossche, *Message*, 38.
[229] Sister St. Pierre, *Life of Sister St. Pierre*, 65.
[230] Ibid., 66.

see Him or at least possess His portrait. Christ sent him a linen cloth that had been applied to His Face, leaving His imprint upon it. The pious sovereign received the portrait by way of ambassadors and paid it the greatest honor, designating it as the glory of the town. Later it was removed to Genoa for fear of Muslim invasion. Though the authenticity of this legend has not been fully attested,[231] it is rather incredible that the singular Carmel in possession of this true likeness of Christ was chosen to "manifest therein the mystery of His sorrowful Face, making the spot the cradle of that reparative homage, so justly His due."[232]

Indeed, a mere seventeen years after the nuns' return to the original monastery, Our Lord revealed to Sister St. Pierre that when she entered religious life, He would give her a "cross." She writes, "I am convinced that the Work of Reparation, which later the Lord revealed to me, was the predicted cross, for I found it in the Sacred Heart of Jesus; in this furnace of love did He first speak to me of that work which was to cost me so many sighs, and prayers, and tears."[233] She henceforth magnified devotion to the Heart of Jesus, fittingly exemplifying the honorary characteristic of her new home, the Carmel of Tours. And pertaining to the Carmelite Order itself, Our Lord later related to Sister St. Pierre, "[To] whom should I address Myself, if not to a Carmelite, whose very vocation enjoins upon her duty of unceasingly glorifying My Name?"[234]

✠ ✠ ✠

On the feast day of St. Francis of Assisi, which was also the death anniversary of St. Teresa of Avila, for whom she and her saintly father had so much devotion, Sister Marie de St. Pierre of the Holy Family (known by her Carmelite sisters and blood relation as Sister St. Pierre and commonly referred to as Sister Mary of St. Peter in the United States) was born Perrine-Julienne Francoise Eluere in Rennes on October 4, 1816. She was the sixth of twelve children born to Pierre René Eluere, a master locksmith artisan, and Francoise Jeanne (Portier) Eluere,[235]

---

[231] Abbé Janvier, *The Devotion to the Holy Face at Saint Peter's of the Vatican and in Other Celebrated Places: Historical Notices*, trans. A. R. Bennett (Tours: Oratory of the Holy Face, 1888), 117–118.
[232] Sister St. Pierre, *Life of Sister St. Pierre*, 66.
[233] Van den Bossche, *Message*, 37.
[234] Sister St. Pierre, *Life of Sister Saint Pierre*, 145.
[235] Eluere siblings were Francoise Louise Félicité, Prosper Michel Louis Marie, Louis Francois, Étienne Francois Denis, Marie Louis, Joseph Francois, Josephine Perrine Sainte, Aimée Jeanne Francoise, Joseph Maire Mathurin Michel, Jean Baptiste, and Rose Francoise Toussainte.

Sister Marie de St. Pierre

both very pious and exemplary Catholics (my great-great-great-grandparents). Though of humble material origin, Perrine was of the medieval noble line of the House of Bousis on her mother's side[236] (though she herself may not have been aware of this fact) and was very blessed in her spiritual upbringing.

Living above his shop on the same block as his parish church, "the old square of Saint Germain," Perrine's father Pierre was described by his pastor as "the best of parishioners" and was a remarkably holy man in his own right, being described by Perrine as a "copy of Saint Joseph."[237] Besides his wife, eleven of his twelve children successively preceded him to the grave, leaving only his eldest son Prosper[238] (my

---

[236] Francoise Jeanne (Portier) Eluere's twelfth great-grandfather was Lord Leonard Bousis, 1500–1550. Earlier research (pre-1500) of this line has not yet been attempted.

[237] Sister St. Pierre, *Life of Sister Saint Pierre*, 32.

[238] While one biography lists two children survivors, and while I do not know the exact date of Pierre's death, the children's death dates (except Prosper's) all precede the last letters written to Prosper by Pierre in 1866. Prosper Eluere, eldest brother of Sister St. Pierre, became a naturalized citizen of the United States in 1841.

Baptismal Entry for Perrine-Julien Francoise Eluere, St. Germain, Rennes, France, October 5, 1816

great-great-grandfather who immigrated to "Vincennes of America" in 1839). Despite the hardships of caring for a large family on his own and managing his laborious trade, Pierre attended morning Mass and evening Benediction daily and never failed in observing abstinences and fasts. He was known to be patient in his many tribulations and was undoubtedly an endearing and steady force among the inhabitants of the colorful, artisan-owned wattle-and-daub homes in his parish neighborhood; his, in fact, was situated just steps from the Church of St. Germain.

As a small child, Perrine was often ill and somewhat ill-tempered, having nearly died from scarlet fever at the age of four. And her youth was not without the usual, somewhat comically wayward antics of the very young. Once,

> to a former wet nurse who had come to greet the family and who had previously been the accidental cause of a burn scar which remained on Perrine's cheek: this little scrap of a three-or-four-year-old girl remarked in welcome, "You have already burned one cheek, are you coming today to fry my other?"[239]

Her parents trained her to overcome her self-love and pride, however, and ensured that she was instructed in the Faith. She began to conquer her impatience and

---

[239] Van den Bossche, *Message*, 18.

St. Germain Church, Rennes, France

obstinacy and developed an abhorrence of sin, soon reproaching herself for even the slightest imperfection.

Like St. Teresa of Avila before her, and St. Thérèse of Lisieux after, Perrine lost her mother before adolescence, at the age of twelve; in imitation of this spiritual mentor, St. Teresa, she allowed the profound loss to be the spark for her first turning to Our Lady in her mother's stead. Even prior to her First Communion at age ten, she was dedicated to the Way of the Cross and found solace in mental prayer. She grew in mortification, humility, and obedience in the coming years.

She had excellent spiritual direction, arranged for by her father, which led her to a devotion to the Sacred Heart and the Blessed Virgin, as well as to early acts of reparation. These were for her natural extensions of her love of the Holy Family, which she acquired at quite an early age, and which would one day become the center of her interior life.[240] Perrine endured a period of the scruples that "prevented her from being able to finish examinations of consciences, caused confessions to neither reassure nor console her, and by which

---

[240] Ibid., 29.

prayer offered no attraction,"[241] a period that was finally brought to an end by a confessor who forbade her to think of her sins again. Obeying, Perrine then became "continually aware of the presence of God,"[242] enjoying spiritual consolations unusual for her (or any) age.

Perrine was employed at this time as a young lady at her aunts' large apparel shop. (These aunts were on her father's side, Ursule Julie Jeanne Eluere and Francoise Julienne Michelle Benoist, the latter also being her godmother who arranged for her a little workstation near herself.) She worked as a seamstress for her aunts, her formal education consisting of only two years and her mother's death leaving her in need of feminine guidance. Managing to live a deep spiritual life while yet in the world, she made frequent spiritual communions and was a member of the Congregation of the Blessed Virgin, founded to preserve piety among young women and through which she made an act of consecration to the Holy Mother. There she counseled other working girls in piety, especially in prayer, one of whom entered the convent before she did, as Perrine herself was fond of recounting.

At the age of seventeen, "consolations [in prayer] gave place to dryness and interior aridity,"[243] such that she briefly abandoned mental prayer and began to give herself up to amusements and small vanities. She additionally felt it difficult to submit to her older sister, Francoise, who had the daunting charge over all her younger siblings in the mother's absence (and who, on at least one occasion and probably with some provocation, would "confess" Perrine's sins to the parish priest before Perrine herself arrived!). Her conscience, however, led Perrine to make a novena to the Blessed Virgin, inspiring her to a general confession and to promise God thereafter "inviolable fidelity."[244] Perrine attended an eight-day retreat, withdrew from her worldliness, and came to be more devoted to Our Lady, asking her for the grace to become a religious. One day, after praying before the Virgin's altar, the assistant priest, Célestine de la Hailandière,[245] who

---

[241] Ibid., 19.
[242] Sister Mary of St. Peter, *The Golden Arrow: The Revelations of Sister Mary of St. Peter*, ed. Dorothy Scallan (Charlotte, NC: Saint Benedict Press, 2012), 8.
[243] Sister St. Pierre, *Life of Sister Saint Pierre*, 12.
[244] Ibid., 15.
[245] This same priest was later assigned to the Diocese of Vincennes "of America" and asked Prosper, Perrine's eldest brother, to travel with him, commissioning him to do artisan ironwork on the construction of a new cathedral there, now a minor basilica and affectionately called "the Old Cathedral." Prosper did, in fact, complete the ironwork,

became the second bishop of "Vincennes in America," and who had introduced Perrine to the concept of mental prayer during one of his sermons, heard her Confession and was the first to suggest to her that she should become a religious. Before entering a convent, she would first, however, come under the counsel of a new spiritual director.

Under this director, Perrine made steady progress in spirit and virtue, and especially humility. She also became increasingly dedicated to the Sacred Heart, particularly in Adoration. A cousin of Perrine, Jenny Benoist (of her same age and almost certainly the daughter of Perrine's godmother) gave testimony of her throughout this time in her life that no one ever saw her in a bad temper.[246] Realizing that pride impeded her spiritual union with God, she began, on her own initiative, to routinely seek out humiliations — even inventing them — "for which her soul was thirsting, but which crucified her nature."[247] Her stern director, giving a rare glimpse of his affection for Perrine, would say in response to her exclamation of how costly the road of humiliation was, "My daughter, if it be painful to you to be thus humbled, I assure you it is not less so to me, to be obliged to humble you; but have courage."[248] Perrine also intensified her love of sufferings, prayer, obedience, charity, and reparation, all under the guidance of her new spiritual director.[249] Her deep love of the Infant Jesus and the Holy Family extended to new neighbors who to her resembled Jesus, Mary, and Joseph in poverty and want; "she visit[ed] them, help[ed] them, [came] to their aid in every way, material and spiritual."[250] In short, she found every means to "give to Our Lord" and already lived and breathed devotion to Him, especially as the Child Jesus.

Perrine continued under the counsel of her new director, Abbé Panager (or Abbé Panough, as is sometimes referenced), parish priest of St. Etienne in Rennes. He was an excellent confessor chosen by her previous, the pastor of St. Germain, whom she would keep until entering religious life. Well versed in the interior paths of the soul and having a gift for recognizing and directing

---

interior and exterior, as well as the intricate woodwork of the dais, or ambo; all is still intact in the beautifully restored St. Francis Xavier Cathedral in Vincennes, Indiana.
[246] Van den Bossche, *Message*, 24.
[247] Ibid., 28.
[248] Ibid., 28.
[249] Sister St. Pierre, *Life of Sister St. Pierre*, 19. And Van den Bossche, *Message*, 25, 28.
[250] Van den Bossche, *Message*, 31.

vocations,[251] this confessor was slow to make decisions and extremely thorough in the destruction of pride, taking five years to give his consent to Perrine's readiness for religious life. He was quite determined to send to a convent only those whom he was certain would remain there, leaving Perrine to lead a profound spiritual life in the world for some time longer. For Perrine, this excruciating delay was evidently in some way providentially necessary for a future "envoy of Christ," the agent of His message, making her "pliable to His great designs"[252] through unwavering and humble obedience to them.

The material road to the convent was no less full of delays and obstacles. Prior to his emigration to America, Perrine's eldest brother Prosper[253] was drafted into the French army and was unable to pay for his replacement by another (an acceptable practice in France at the time).[254] His father Pierre and his sisters were obliged to raise 2,000 francs to defray this expense, leaving Perrine with a dowry of only 600 francs to enter a convent. Yet this had not been the only material obstacle for her entering the religious life.

When Perrine's mother Francoise died, she left the widower Pierre a household and business to operate with only the help of his children. The pastor of St. Germain in Rennes felt this life was too hard for his friend, Pierre. Approaching Pierre about this subject, he was told that he was too busy to seek and court a wife. The good priest replied that he himself would find a suitable wife for Pierre — wishing to benefit both the "best of parishioners" and Perrine, whom he knew aspired to be a religious. He did, in fact, find Pierre a new and "excellent" wife, as described by Perrine. She was received into the family with respect and courtesy — and doubtless with relief — by the children and especially the eldest daughters, who had been caring for the household. Perrine, the second-oldest daughter, who then was responsible for most of the household duties in lieu of her sickly elder sister Francoise, now felt free to leave the house to become a religious. On the issue of the dowry, Our Lord related to Perrine that if

---

[251] Ibid., 23.
[252] Ibid., 26.
[253] Sister St. Pierre, *Life of Sister St. Pierre*, 33. "[Pierre's] eldest son, Prosper, had left France. Being much attached to Mgr. de la Hailandière, he had followed him to America, and settled at Vincennes, in the United States, where he continued his trade of locksmithing [and gunsmithing]. Finding his business prospects favorable, he remained there, and since has had no other communication with his father and family, except through letters. His life [in Vincennes], as when at home, is still that of a pious, edifying Christian."
[254] Prosper's original document of the sale of his commission in 1833.

Prosper Eluere in front of his shop in Vincennes, Indiana

He could give her a vocation, He could certainly provide her with a dowry. Perrine credited the Blessed Virgin with help from a young lady whose name was Mary and who quite unexpectedly supplied generously most of the sum remaining prior to her own entry to religious.[255]

There was also some help from a rich vicar-general. He was some seventy years of age, yet his faculties were unimpaired. Perrine had had him as a spiritual director during her time of "lukewarmness" in which she "often gave him time for annoyance."[256] His apparent desire to put Perrine's vocation to the test by way of extreme humiliation became a favorite story of her future prioress in Carmel. Perrine relates:

> Respectfully kneeling at the feet of this venerable priest, I opened the subject of my vocation to him, but he at once began to humiliate me in a most unpredictable fashion and with gestures of trying to push me away. It happened that my kneeling posture made me fall on my side,

---

[255] Sister Mary of St. Peter, *Golden Arrow*, 43.
[256] Ibid., 39.

but Our Lord sustained me with His powerful grace. I remained in that tiresome position, respecting the Will of God in that of His minister. Then taking his breviary, the priest began to read his office.

A while later he gave me the order to rise, which I obeyed instantly. But there was yet another test awaiting me ... by far more terrible than the first. The details of the mortifying episode that now took place I prefer to pass over in silence at this time for I have already in the past on several different occasions repeated to our Mother in the cloister a full account of what transpired. This story, indeed, made [all the nuns] laugh very heartily, for in point of truth it was so ridiculous that it proved very amusing, except of course for me who was the principal actor in the drama.[257]

This self-deprecating anecdote, related in Perrine's own words, gives a glimpse of her cheerful and happy character, both by virtue and natural disposition.[258] One of Perrine's workshop companions, who herself entered the Carmel of Nevers in 1849, describes Perrine as being generally loved by all those who knew her and considered by her peers to have already been a saint.[259] One can imagine how easily she must have attracted the confidence of even her worldly and fun-loving seamstress companions, for hers was that "mysterious radiance of souls united to God,"[260] exuding indefatigable joy, unpretentiousness, and devotion.

It was only a day after this humiliating incident that Our Lord, who already communicated to Perrine through inner locutions by which she "beheld Him in the depths of his holy heart"[261] — no doubt an extension of her great devotion to the Sacred Heart — related to her during Holy Communion that it would be through the Blessed Virgin that she would be granted her petition of becoming a Carmelite. Still living at home and working at her aunts' dress shop, nine days earlier Perrine offered the instruments of her seamstress's trade, her scissors, and needles, at the Shrine of Notre Dame de la Peinière, some six leagues from her home, beginning a novena to the Blessed Virgin for this intention. She therein entreated Mary to not oblige her to work longer on the "clothes of vanity."

Previously she had also venerated relics of St. Martin and received Holy Communion in his honor to request his intercession in resolving some material

---

[257] Ibid., 40.
[258] Sister St. Pierre, *Life of Sister St. Pierre*, 52.
[259] Van den Bossche, *Message*, 68.
[260] Ibid., 24.
[261] Sister St. Pierre, *Life of Sister St. Pierre*, 31.

delays. Not knowing which part of "Gaul" St. Martin had evangelized, she asked him to receive her into his diocese "if there are any nuns [there]."[262] She was at last assured by Our Lord that she would become a Carmelite. Her confessor then suddenly informed her that he had obtained her admittance to the Carmelite convent in Tours, initiating from a request for young postulants from the prioress herself. It was a convent she did not even know existed. Perrine thus made the connection that St. Martin *of Tours* had evidently also had a hand in obtaining her request.[263] Leaving all she loved in the world and escorted by her virtuous father, Perrine left (providentially, the result of a delay) for Tours on the feast of St. Martin, November 11, 1839. She arrived on the vigil of the feast of All Carmelite Saints, an additional connection to those whom she had invoked. She was twenty-three years of age.

Prior to her departure, as was a touching custom of Catholic Brittany, Perrine's numerous relations gathered around in festivity for a last time, pouring affection and sentiments upon her. "Although deeply touched at parting from Perrine, none of them would have had her return, for they beheld in her perseverance, happiness for her and benedictions for themselves; and their hopes were to be more than realized."[264] As for Perrine, she writes, "Joyfully I bade farewell to my family and country; though I loved my family, and was beloved by them, my ardent desire to serve the Holy Family in Carmel, completely swallowed up those feelings of anguish consequent upon a separation so painful to nature."[265] When she said her goodbyes to her priest director, he said that he felt confident in her vocation but gave the prophetic caution, "Do quickly what you have to do; hasten to sanctify yourself, for I foresee that your career will not be long."[266]

Reaching the long-awaited threshold of Carmel, Perrine bade a poignant final farewell to a most beloved father who, when he kissed her for the last time, gave his blessing and said that the desire to conform to God's will was all that would induce him to such a sacrifice. Barely resigned to the grief of not seeing Perrine again in this life, Pierre felt a loss that would surely have been unbearable had he known that she would be yet another child to precede him in death — that the priest's ominous prediction would come to pass. (He

---

[262] Van den Bossche, *Message*, 32.
[263] Sister St. Pierre, *Life of Sister St. Pierre*, 36, 47.
[264] Ibid., 48.
[265] Ibid., 49.
[266] Ibid., 50.

outlived Perrine, in fact, by nearly twenty years.) Perrine writes, "If, at that moment, I made to God the sacrifice of a good father, He gave me in return a good mother, who was, in her great charity, to render to my soul services of inestimable value."[267] This mother was the Reverend Mother Mary of the Incarnation, prioress and mistress of novices. While still in the world, Christ made known to Perrine that the mother whom He had destined for her would have special grace to direct her in His ways. In fact, Mother Mary of the Incarnation was by degrees given to understand Perrine's interior.[268]

---

[267] Ibid., 51.
[268] Sister Mary of St. Peter, *Golden Arrow*, 47.

Chapter 3

The "Donkey" Ambassadress of Christ

Perrine continued in her interior attraction to the Holy Family, which she began as a child, leading her to desire to become a "servant" of the Holy Family at the time of entering Carmel. Devotion to the Holy Family was further inspired early on by reading that St. Teresa had a vision of the monastery she founded at Avila being guarded on one side by St. Joseph and on the other by the Blessed Virgin, while Jesus remained in the middle.[269] Already drawn to a devotion that she then learned was shared by St. Teresa, Perrine felt specifically called to enter a Carmelite convent. She indeed became very much at home in the Carmel of Tours.

Wishing to perpetually serve the Holy Family, she considered herself a domestic of the Child Jesus.

> [Sister St. Pierre was] also truly the Servant of the Holy Family which she [would continue] later, and until the end of her life ... because during her whole life she [kept] that marvelous gift of childhood which permit[ted] her to enter in the game, body and soul, and to contribute perfectly a natural disposition to the supernatural work of grace and gifts.[270]

This continuous method of contemplation, in which she lived virtually every moment of the day with only the humble and selfless intention of serving the

---

[269] Louis Van den Bossche, *The Message of Sister Mary of St. Peter*, trans. Mary G. Durham (France: Carmel of Tours, 1953), 41.
[270] Ibid., 31.

Holy Family and the Child Jesus — motivated by simple love of them — led to a profound devotion to the divine infancy of Jesus. Sister St. Pierre writes, "As I was being formed to the religious life of Carmel, and was then but a little child, our Lord attracted me in a very special manner to His Holy Infancy, making known to me to have great devotion to Him in that state."[271] Later, in fact, no doubt feeling that the role of the maidservant was too honorable, she modified her ambition to be that of becoming the personal donkey of Christ.[272]

Sister St. Pierre's devotion to the Infant Jesus as His servant was effectively the "little way of spiritual childhood," (which will be discussed in greater length in chapter 6). As St. Thérèse of Lisieux would say, she was working not to become a saint but to give joy to God.[273] She did this "work" in complete surrender to God's grace, doing even the smallest tasks with great love and offering especially her weakness, her "littleness," as a gift — in service to and in company with the Child Jesus. Writing before the death of Sister St. Pierre and some twenty-five years before the birth of St. Thérèse, Abbé Botrel, who knew Sister St. Pierre, writes:

> This new flower of Carmel [Sister St. Pierre] has a singular relation with [St. Teresa of Avila], in that the grit of her spirit is strong.... She differs [from Teresa, however] in that her way is simple like that of a little child, carried in arms and sometimes being allowed to fall to earth, without however denying the grace which she had received.... [She] was always simple and naïve like a little child toward her superiors, always submissive, always humble toward all and of a charity which covers everything.[274]

Abbé Botrel recognized in hindsight that this description of Sister St. Pierre was the way of childhood, such as St. Thérèse later taught.[275] Indeed, Sister St. Pierre *lived* the "little way" well before it was written by St. Thérèse.[276]

---

[271] Sister St. Pierre, *Life of Sister St. Pierre*, ed. Rev. P. Janvier (Baltimore: John Murphy, 1884), 77.
[272] Ibid., 45.
[273] Ida Friederike Görres, *The Hidden Face: A Study of St. Thérèse of Lisieux* (New York: Pantheon, 1959), 103.
[274] Van den Bossche, *Message*, 42–43.
[275] Ibid., 43.
[276] Ibid., 42–43. A longer discussion of this comparison with St. Thérèse will follow in chapter 6.

Embracing spiritual childhood, she was delighted to be the mere "donkey" of Christ and toiled joyfully under the harness of His grace.

Moreover, special attraction was given to her for this devotion by Christ. Our Lord, having made known to her what He desired of her, inspired her to honor Him each day of the month, a month of the Holy Infant Jesus, meditating on respective mysteries of His youth.[277] As His domestic, Sister St. Pierre considered herself performing all her actions in union with the Divine Infant.

> For her, the smallest details [of this meditation] were translated into a reality which was living in her soul, sustaining, and vivifying the multiplicity of those acts[. This] continual presence of God allowed Sister [St. Pierre] to remain united to God, and as she had avowed, "to never lose sight of Our Lord." During the whole time that her postulancy and novitiate lasted[,] her entire days "constituted only one prayer." What multiplicity of actions would have been capable of breaking this supernatural unity?[278]

This loving devotion to the Divine Infant and to the Holy Family was the origin and permanent foundation of the life of her soul.[279] She sought only to aid and console the Child Jesus and Holy Family, wishing to take the most obscure and humble role possible. In doing so, however, she, perhaps unwittingly, afforded herself a most efficacious path to holiness, for as is taught by St. John of the Cross, "In spiritual poverty, hope [as in not only trusting exclusively in, but also as in wishing to attain only, God] finds the purity that makes for its perfection.... It will be the more perfect the more it hopes in God solely, to the exclusion of any other motive than God Himself."[280] Sister St. Pierre was, in fact, singularly motivated by love of God, especially as the Child Jesus.

As an indication of the effectiveness of Sister St. Pierre's spiritual exercise of meditation on the early life of Christ for the purpose of applying each encounter of the day to service of Him, she felt it aroused the jealous ire of the devil. One evening, he manifested himself in the "emotions of [Sister St. Pierre's] soul" by a terrifying experience of her being smothered by Satan's claws in beastly form.

---

[277] Sister Mary St. Peter, *Life of Sister Mary St. Peter*, ed. Rev. P. Janvier (France, 1884), 87.
[278] Van den Bossche, *Message*, 47.
[279] Ibid., 41.
[280] P. Marie-Eugène, *A Practical Synthesis of Carmelite Spirituality*, trans. M. Verda Clare, vol. 2, *I Am a Daughter of the Church* (Allen, TX: Christian Classics, 1955), 382–383.

Sister St. Pierre called upon the Blessed Virgin, and at her name, "the devil took flight."[281] The experience only affirmed her resolve to dedicate herself to the Child Jesus in this manner of contemplation, especially now in preparation for her final vows.

She made her profession on June 8, 1841, taking the name of Sister Marie de St. Pierre (Sister Mary of St. Peter) *of the Holy Family*, also consecrating herself to Jesus, Mary, and Joseph. Love of the Holy Family and the infancy of Jesus prepared Sister St. Pierre for remarkable communications with the Blessed Virgin toward the end of her short life.[282] First, however, it led to a great desire to glorify, aid, and console God, keystones of the future work of reparation. Yet, even after the designs of this great work were given to her, which would be intrinsically intertwined with the most dolorous scenes of Christ's Passion and which was to be her life's work, she was always drawn back to this first consoling mystery of His youthful life.[283] She cherished it to the very end.

Once professed and having consecrated herself to the Infant Jesus as His servant on the same day, Sister St. Pierre was charged by Christ to "guard his flock in the pasture of his divine Infancy,"[284] such that she was inspired to arrange an additional spiritual exercise in honor of the twelve mysteries of the first twelve years of His life, to obtain graces for her fellow man. *It was the first practical work in what she would come to understand as her mission to save souls in particular ways as deputed by God.* These "flocks of Christ" were composed of

> the universality of mankind, the Pope, and the priests, religious, kings, freemasons, actors, infidels, nations, heretics, and schismatics, Jews, unbelievers, hardened sinners, the lukewarm. Finally, completing the circle: the just souls. Later, God will make her pass to other mysteries in the life of her Christ, but it will always be He alone who will lead her.[285]

Indeed, after this inspiration, she felt distinctly that Christ became the director and master of her soul such that she had only to follow spontaneously the light of His grace.

---

[281] Van den Bossche, *Message*, 84.
[282] Sister St. Pierre, *Life of Sister St. Pierre*, 84.
[283] Sister Mary St. Peter, *Life of Sister Mary St. Peter*, 94.
[284] Ibid., 100–101.
[285] Van den Bossche, *Message*, 52.

Sister St. Pierre continued to honor Christ's infancy and youth on respective days of the month and considered herself to labor through the day for the salvation of the flocks of the Infant Jesus via the Twelve Mysteries exercise, praying for a different "flock" each month. She then became additionally attracted to a perpetual meditation on the mysteries of Our Lord's entire life, assigning each hour to a mystery, by which she united herself to Him in an apparently effortless, loving contemplation.

> Beginning with His Holy Infancy, she successively followed His Hidden, Dolorous, and Glorious Life, from His Incarnation in Mary's womb, until His triumphant Ascension. She had divided the day in such a manner, that each hour recalled to her some circumstance of these mysteries, upon which she would concentrate with lively faith and loving contemplation.[286]

Likely unaware, by incorporating this dizzying (though effortless to her) regimen, rotating each hour and day and month in meditation of different aspects of the life of Christ and the "flocks" He wished to be guarded, Sister St. Pierre had adopted a method most approved by liturgists and spiritual masters, in imitation of "being united in spirit to Our Lord in the mysteries of His sacred life [as is done] during the psalmody and recitation of the office."[287] Meditation on the life of Christ, His sacred humanity, was also strongly advocated by St. Teresa of Avila as desirous in accompanying one even to spiritual union, for "Teresian spirituality [as lived by Sister St. Pierre] is essentially Christocentric,... to find Jesus and keep Him company."[288]

In return, it seemed to her that Our Lord gave Himself to her with all His merits. She writes, "He unites my soul to his, causing me to participate in the honor which he renders his Father as Victim."[289] She then would offer Christ as Victim to the Eternal Father through the hands of the Blessed Virgin, as a sacrifice of reparation and thanksgiving for all the perfections of the Holy Trinity, effecting in her soul sublime fear of the Lord. This was a preparation and a precursor of the offering of the merits of Christ, encased in His wounded Countenance, to the Father in reparation for current blasphemous affronts to

---

[286] Sister St. Pierre, *Life of Sister St. Pierre*, 91.
[287] Sister Mary St. Peter, *Life of Sister Mary St. Peter*, 103.
[288] P. Marie-Eugène, *I Am a Daughter*, 419–420.
[289] Sister Mary St. Peter, *Life of Sister Mary St. Peter*, 106.

the Trinity, receiving graces for sinners in return, all flowing through the Holy Virgin, which is the heart of the Holy Face devotion.

These acts produced in her fear of the Lord par excellence, such that humility was the essence of Sister St. Pierre. It was "the natural fruit of her continual application to the mysteries of the life of the Savior." Indeed, Sister St. Pierre's maxim was "God alone, his will and his glory,"[290] perfect spiritual poverty. She writes, "The Lord makes me feel how incapable I am of all good and how deep is my misery. The Child Jesus leads His ass by the bridle of His holy grace[;] I have only to obey and renounce my will."[291] She was in fact totally obedient to the slightest notions of this grace.

This exceedingly profound obedience to grace prepared her for the astounding mission of speaking to men on behalf of God. Louis Van den Bossche, secretary of state to Pope Pius XII, observes:

> There is no doubt that [Sister St. Pierre] was elevated very early to passive contemplation, without having ever neglected the struggles of asceticism. But if, in her relatively numerous writings, it is not possible to bring forward and follow the history of a soul which is progressing it must be that it was not her mission to show like [St. Teresa of Avila or St. Thérèse of Lisieux] or Saint John of the Cross, a harmony of mystic doctrine.... [Rather, there is] a close connection between the interior perfection of the little nun and her prophetic message.... [Sister St. Pierre's] great mission, that which ruled all the management of her interior and exterior life, was to serve as God's instrument to remind the world of certain aspects of His providential plan. She had to be the human instrument transmitting to earthly ears the great voice of the Father.[292]

Led by the bridle of His grace, Christ's "donkey" was, in fact, His messenger, His ambassadress, "the instrument of which God wished to make use to warn the world."[293]

While the mother prioress genuinely believed Sister St. Pierre to in fact be operating in grace, she never let up the test of trials: inflicting humiliations, reprimanding her, deliberately crossing her, and commanding her to follow the

---

[290] Ibid., 107.
[291] Sister St. Pierre, *Life of Sister St. Pierre*, 95.
[292] Van den Bossche, *Message*, 50.
[293] Ibid., 59.

ordinary course,[294] all to "guarantee" humility. This tireless mortification and humiliation of her was to confirm that Sister St. Pierre was motivated by the impulse of divine grace (and none other), always encouraging her to pursue a more ordinary spiritual course, as was the Carmelite preference.

In fact, she was assigned to the office of portress by the prioress Mother Mary, who — in her virtuous prudence, and stemming from her ability to join rigidity of her direction to the affectionate goodness of a real mother[295] — wished to check Sister St. Pierre in her habits of prayer and recollection. (Portress in Carmel was like a turn-sister,[296] a sort of middleman messenger with the outside world via a lay "out-sister.") She was the "intermediary placed between agitation and peace,"[297] a position she kept for the duration of her life in the convent.

She had previously been assured by a priest whom the mother prioress had selected, Father Vieillecases, director of the seminary of Tours, who was well versed in the interior life (and who would, incidentally, come to greatly esteem Sister St. Pierre),[298] that she should continue her contemplations without fear, in that her spiritual life was based on the solid ground of mortification. Consequently, prior to this new assignment, Sister St. Pierre's entire day was passed in uninterrupted prayer. Portress was therefore a duty quite contrary to her natural inclinations in that she feared it would inhibit the mental prayer so dear to her — and was in fact a perpetual source of penance and self-renunciation, evidently the means used by God to elevate her perfections. Her entire life became, interiorly and exteriorly, a continuous mortification, which freed her from the dominion of the senses.[299]

Yet she embraced the distractions joyfully, feeling that they matched well with the duties of a domestic of Christ. She writes,

> Notwithstanding my unworthiness, this Divine Child conferred upon me such especial graces that my employment in no way hindered my spirit of recollection; as heretofore during prayer, I was united to God.

---

[294] Sister St. Pierre, *Life of Sister St. Pierre*, 96.
[295] Van den Bossche, *Message*, 48.
[296] Sister St. Pierre, Life of Sister St. Pierre, 97. This was distinct from the position of out-sister, who directly communicated with persons in the world, performed by a Third Order Carmelite, rather than a cloistered Carmelite. Turn-sisters receive messages from the out-sister and transmit them within.
[297] Van den Bossche, *Message*, 48.
[298] Ibid., 48.
[299] Sister St. Pierre, *Life of Sister St. Pierre*, 98.

I labored during the day for the salvation of the flocks of the Infant Jesus, and at prayer, He repaid me a hundred-fold.[300]

Moreover, her assignment happily proved to be providential in the future reparatory work, for it put her in contact (though not face-to-face)[301] with pious secular persons, not least among whom was Ven. Leo Dupont, who may be described, opposite Sister St. Pierre, as instrumental in the "other half" of promulgating the Holy Face devotion.

☨ ☨ ☨

Briefly introduced earlier in the book, Ven. Dupont, a most eminently devout Catholic gentleman and benefactor of the Carmel of Tours, used his wealth and prestige to inform the public of reparation to the Holy Face, printing and distributing works on the Holy Face devotion, among other copious tasks of charity. His remarkable life was one of continual, selfless generosity — both material and spiritual — to others for the simple love of God and honor of His holy name and majesty. Incredibly, he became, like St. Martin of Tours before him, a great thaumaturge of Tours, as recognized by Pope Bl. Pius IX,[302] having performed thirty years of the Church's greatest miracle working in the parlor of his home. The miracles were effected through the prayers of the devotion and oil from a lamp burning in front of a Holy Face image, given to him by the prioress of the Tours Carmel, which had been touched to Veronica's veil in the Vatican. The features of Christ on this original veil had become miraculously clear and even animated, in stark contrast to their usual blurred and centuries-old fading, for three hours during a Christmas octave exposition in January 1849.

The Holy Face image linked to the devotion is from a hand-drawn copy of this "Miracle of the Vatican." The miraculous event occurred at a time when Pope Pius IX fled to Gaeta for safety due to a democratic insurgency in Italy, following the assassination of the minister Pellegrino Rossi. To obtain an end of

---

[300] Ibid.
[301] Van den Bossche, *Message*, 48. "One knows that in Carmel, this charge is carried out in the interior of the enclosure; but this does not prevent it from being fruitful with all kinds of distractions." Note: It was only for the approximately two-year interim in which the sisters lived at Le Place St. Gregorie, while they waited for the construction of their new monastery to be complete, that Sister St. Pierre was obliged to greet visitors to the convent "face-to-face," without the aid of a lay sister to be the go-between.
[302] Pope Pius IX declared Dupont "perhaps the greatest miracle worker in Church history." Pope St. John Paul II declared Dupont Venerable. The miracles began in 1851.

the evils ravaging the Church and Papal States, the pope hoped to appeal to God's mercy by displaying for public veneration at St. Peter's Basilica, from Christmas to Epiphany, the Holy Face image on Veronica's veil. This was in conjunction with ordering public prayers to be offered in all churches in Rome during the same period.

The canons of the basilica ordered the bells rung at sight of the miracle, which attracted crowds of people. The Holy Face, though covered with a thin veil, could be seen to become lifelike, changing expression and becoming enhanced in color. Numerous witnesses were now present, and the miracle was attested to by an apostolic notary during the incident, as well as documented in the daybook of the Vatican basilica. Detailed, hand-drawn copies of the Holy Face image were made immediately. They were touched to the original veil, a true relic of the Cross, and Longinus's spear, this being denoted by a red wax seal of the Vatican that was placed on each image before being disseminated to the devout. (In future years, more copies of the image on Veronica's veil were touched to these relics in the Vatican in the same manner and distributed as special relics of the Holy Face devotion.)

Ven. Dupont venerated the one given to him by Prioress Mother Mary, prominently placing it on his parlor mantel and always keeping it, along with his Bible, vigil with a lighted oil lamp. He never allowed base language or conversation in its presence and was a most stalwart defender of the holy name of God, promulgating tirelessly reparation to the Holy Face. The miracles at his hands, intrinsically linked to the dolorous Holy Face recorded on Veronica's veil image and prayers consistent with the devotion (the Archconfraternity of the Holy Face not yet having been approved), numbered some six thousand, in addition to thousands more undocumented, inexplicable healings. These wonders, along with his own quintessential devotion to the Holy Face, undoubtedly played a part in establishing the credibility of the revelations received from Christ by Sister St. Pierre.

Sister St. Pierre, who died not six months prior to the "Miracle of the Vatican," did not live to see these miracles manifest, nor the approval of the devotion for the whole world (though, happily, her only surviving sibling Prosper, then living in America, did). In a significant break with tradition (by not approving it more incrementally, beginning with the place of origin), Pope Leo XIII established the Archconfraternity of the Holy Face *immediately for the whole world* — "not only for France but for everywhere!" — in 1885.

✠ ✠ ✠

The full designs of the reparatory work for atheism, blasphemy, and the profanation of the holy days, as now encompassed in the Holy Face devotion, were only gradually revealed to Sister St. Pierre. First, less than a month into her life at Carmel, Sister St. Pierre was asked by Christ to accomplish in her soul what would be the work's foundation, the condition of her being given the mission of messenger of God, an act of perfect abandonment, to be given at her superior's consent.

> This act of [abandonment] was, in fact, the condition of the prophetic charisms which God wished to give in view of realizing a work. But for Mary of St. Peter, it was the act by which she made herself a victim in the place of a great many souls. And the first consideration which presented itself to her mind is clearly apostolic, the desire to save, by her abandon without reserve the souls who are falling or meriting to fall into hell at every moment.... [In the refusal of her superiors to make the act of abandonment,] she suffered the martyrdom of knowing the divine words reduced to silence, the merciful action of wisdom blocked by the scanty prudence of men.[303]

Yet, as far as "men" and prudence go, the character of Sister St. Pierre's superior could hardly be categorized as "scanty."

This superior, Mother Mary of the Incarnation, was a Breton like Sister St. Pierre. She played an important part in the communications of Sister St. Pierre and was herself a very capable and holy soul, having been entrusted by her own superiors to compile — *on the peril of her soul* — "The Carmelite's Treasure," preserving the traditions of the order and serving as the link between the ancient and modern times in Carmel.[304] She possessed the gift of discernment of spirits, and "obedience was the infallible mark by which she judged between the operations of grace and those of nature"; she administered humiliations without hesitation and showed (by design) an apparent indifference for any purported spiritual communications confided to her.[305] Yet, while

---

[303] Van den Bossche, *Message*, 63.
[304] Sister Mary St. Peter, *Life of Sister Mary St. Peter*, 81.
[305] Ibid., 81–86.

the Prioress ... never departed from her prudent firmness, she did not resist long the supernatural charm which came from [Sister St. Pierre, who had] a childlike gaze and a heart burning with love. Even when her reason obliged her to systematic doubt, she believed in the depth of her soul in the supernatural origin of Sister Saint [Pierre's] mystical experiences. Very soon, there was formed a tie of religious affection between the great prioress and she who [became] her little portress, a tie which [was] never to be broken and where one and the other [found] exactly what [was] necessary [to] accomplish their respective missions.[306]

The measured judgment of the prioress would prove to be an invaluable instrument in establishing credibility for the revelations given to Sister St. Pierre and, consequently, in their promulgation.

And so Sister St. Pierre related to Mother Mary of the Incarnation that Christ wished her to make to Him a perfect act of abandonment. She had been visited by Christ after receiving Communion, accompanied by the Archangel Raphael. Our Lord showed her the multitudes that were falling daily into Hell and expressed His wish that she should offer herself completely without reserve to His good pleasure in the rescue of these souls. He asked that she should abandon Him even the smallest merits that she might acquire in her new career for the accomplishment of His designs. Christ would in return take care of her interests and make her a partaker of His own merits. Christ further revealed to Sister St. Pierre that He Himself would be the director of her soul.

St. Raphael the Archangel assured her that if she consented, the angels would surround her deathbed and defend her against assaults of the devil.[307] The archangel also helped her to appreciate that it was possible for her to suffer and acquire merit, whereas for him, an angel, it was not, and that these were most desirable (human) traits that she should welcome.[308] She later understood this act of abandonment was in fact the foundation of her receiving the future revelations regarding the work of reparation.

Indeed, Sister St. Pierre would become a chosen soul whom Christ proposed to make an instrument of mercy,[309] called to a mission whose purpose

---

[306] Van den Bossche, *Message*, 39.
[307] Sister Mary St. Peter, *Life of Sister Mary St. Peter*, 79–80.
[308] Sister Mary of St. Peter, *The Golden Arrow: The Revelations of Sister Mary of St. Peter*, ed. Dorothy Scallan (Charlotte, NC: Saint Benedict Press, 2012), 50.
[309] Sister Mary St. Peter, *Life of Sister Mary St. Peter*, 81.

was the salvation of souls, yet she understood that obedience alone could keep her from all danger of illusion and self-deception.[310] As she was still a postulant (not yet bound by her profession) when Christ made this request of her, it was some time before she was granted permission by the prioress to willfully forsake all for Christ.

Prior to this request of self-sacrifice, the communications from Christ to Sister St. Pierre primarily had the purpose of the sanctification of her own soul. Now, like Carmel, which is devoted to the needs of the Church, the glory of God, and the salvation of souls, her communications inspired in her a spirit of sacrifice for the salvation of others. She writes:

> The Lord wished to teach me this attachment, this spirit of sacrifice, this zeal for [my neighbor's] salvation, sublime and disinterested virtue which I did not as yet know.... I have always considered this first appeal from the Lord as the foundation and base of Reparation which was bound to be communicated to me. It remains engraved in my soul.[311]

But before speaking openly to her about the reparation work, Christ waited for her superiors to give their permission for her to abandon all — her person and merits — for the accomplishments of His designs.[312]

Reflecting the wisdom of Mother Prioress, this took some time. The prioress began by forbidding Sister St. Pierre to pay attention to these supernatural aspirations so that her superiors could ascertain the credibility of the communications. And, as if to cement the importance of holy obedience, Sister St. Pierre "hardly heard interior words during this interim" — experiencing temporary and intermittent silence.[313] Christ, in some sense, submitted Himself with Sister St. Pierre in obedience until permission by the prioress was given.[314] Yet Sister St. Pierre continued with her spiritual exercises surrounding the Holy Family, the Infant Jesus, and the life of Christ, dying to everything that pleased her senses, while Christ continued to lead her by the bridle of grace; together they salvaged a perfect "rule" in the spirit of Carmel, such that her spiritual life ever deepened.

---

[310] Van den Bossche, *Message*, 44.
[311] Ibid., 52–53.
[312] Sister Mary of St. Peter, *Golden Arrow*, 49.
[313] Van den Bossche, *Message*, 53.
[314] Sister Mary St. Peter, *Life of Sister Mary St. Peter*, 81.

In 1843, Our Lord engaged Sister St. Pierre to pray intensely for Spain, which was undergoing a revolution. She was troubled knowing that religious there may be persecuted and given that Spain was such a great Catholic nation, no less than the very homeland of the reform of the Carmelites, which had taken place at the hands of St. Teresa of Avila and St. John of the Cross. She writes:

> I have never felt my soul so united to Our Lord as during that period. This Divine Master operated in me something which I can neither explain nor understand. It seemed that I heard Him ask mercy from His Father for that kingdom, and in a manner so pressing that I was astonished thereat; He made me [beg mercy] in His name; but I perceive that in endeavoring to explain this mystery of love, I only succeed in changing its nature, so I abandon it to the Hand of God.[315]

This mystical experience was a precursor to one even more astounding that involved Sister St. Pierre, though utilizing the merits of Christ, *being made "responsible for" the sins of France in their entirety*, per request of Christ Himself (which will be discussed more fully in chapter 5). For the moment, the experience surrounding Spain inclined Sister St. Pierre to feel more and more urged to make the act of complete abandonment. Though her superiors had always refused, she now realized an unexpected opportunity to renew her request.

☩ ☩ ☩

The convent at Tours had been for some time an obstacle to improvements by the city. Moreover, a neighbor's new buildings now overlooked the convent. Though not wanting to abandon the house that was blessed by the virtues of their first convent mothers, a ground they considered sacred and that they had restored and reinhabited at the cost of much labor and sacrifice,[316] the nuns now felt inclined to sell the property and build new before plans of city officials were put into execution.[317] The new ground under consideration seemed perfectly situated, isolated and quiet and near the archbishopric. Though monies were in part secured by a woman who was only a little acquainted with the community — through the intercession of St. Yves, patron of the poor — capital was still lacking. The task was an ongoing source of great anxiety to the mother prioress.

---

[315] Sister St. Pierre, *Life of Sister St. Pierre*, 99.
[316] Sister Mary St. Peter, *Life of Sister Mary St. Peter*, 112.
[317] Sister St. Pierre, *Life of Sister St. Pierre*, 100.

The prioress recommended to Sister St. Pierre the matter (with which she was probably already somewhat familiar due to her charge of portress), entreating her to pray to the Infant Jesus. In request for the property, Sister St. Pierre understood the Infant to reply, "Give me the property of your soul!"[318] She knew this to refer to the complete act of abandonment for which she still had not obtained permission to offer Him. She related to the prioress that if she would "sell" her to the Infant Jesus, He would give her money to build the house. Sister St. Pierre told the mother prioress, "When one has no money and when one has need of it, one sells one's donkey."[319] She implored the Infant to "purchase" her, as He would a domestic donkey, that she might then be at His disposal. After she "wove a little crown," comprised of the Twelve Years Mysteries that she had earlier been inspired to contemplate, Christ related to her to tell the prioress that if she were to write to a certain person, that person would assist in building the house and that, while the prioress would have much to overcome in the building, He would supply the "stones." Writing to the lady without giving any particulars, the prioress received back 500 francs. Mother Mary of the Incarnation for the moment, however, still withheld her consent of Sister St. Pierre's complete abandonment.[320] Yet Sister St. Pierre was nonetheless joyful in that Christ had shown that He desired to "buy His donkey."

Sister St. Pierre repeated thousands of times the prayer for the feast of the Holy Name of Jesus: "The name of Jesus is admirable above all names; come let us adore." She also engaged the other sisters to repeat it, forming invocations that she likened to bank notes on Divine Providence. At last, Sister St. Pierre understood that so long as the mother prioress built according to the rule of St. Teresa, Christ would pay for all, utilizing various sources.[321] When Sister St. Pierre related this to the prioress, the prioress recounted that she had been greatly troubled the night prior because the plan proposed by the architect was not in accordance with the usual mode of a convent of Carmel. She then began procuring another plan that was in conformity with the customs of the great Carmel reformer, St. Teresa. She took the message given to Sister St. Pierre as confirmation that obtaining new plans was the correct path.

---

[318] Van den Bossche, *Message*, 57.
[319] Ibid., 57.
[320] Sister St. Pierre, *Life of Sister St. Pierre*, 115–116.
[321] Ibid., 117.

Sister St. Pierre later understood that she herself was to furnish the building "stones," which would form a foundation of great benedictions upon the house. Yet

> as she will soon realize, this will not be without great suffering for her. The hour was going to sound when God would make [Sister St. Pierre] understand that the blessings which she must attract upon the enterprise would be obtained by the work of Reparation for blasphemies of which she was going to be made the messenger.... Very great interior sufferings [were preparing] her for her mission.[322]

Indeed, the work of reparation would soon be revealed to her. But first Our Lord sought to further prepare her soul.

One day Sister St. Pierre was speaking to the mother prioress of the abundance of grace that she had enjoyed prior to her entrance to Carmel (and prior to her being refused permission to make a total act of abandonment). The prioress suggested that the reason for this spiritual dryness must be that she had been unfaithful to God and that she should therefore offer prayers of amendment in reparation for faults as well as entreaties that her soul would be restored to the same condition in which it was when Christ communicated Himself so lavishly.

The next day, Sister St. Pierre heard an interior voice say, "Return to the house of thy Father, which is no other than my Heart."[323] She also understood that she should apply herself to honor Christ's Sacred Heart and that of His Mother, that they should not be separated.[324] (Thus, from the beginning, the Blessed Virgin was integral to this devotion, as will be made more clear in future revelations.) Christ, pleased with her offering, promised to bestow more graces than before since she was now united to Him through her vows. Yet "the Divine Master, in the order of His designs over His faithful servant, willed that she should reach the inmost depths of His Sacred Heart, were being initiated in the Reparative Mystery of His Dolorous Face."[325] She consequently entered a great spiritual darkness. She offered her suffering to the Lord for the salvation of souls and the accomplishments of His designs. Her soul, at length of some two years purified by the fire of suffering and relieved only after entreating St. Teresa of

---

[322] Louis Van den Bossche, *Message*, 57.
[323] Sister Mary St. Peter, *Life of Sister Mary St. Peter*, 119.
[324] Ibid.
[325] Sister St. Pierre, *Life of Sister St. Pierre*, 109.

Avila during a novena to her, was finally ready for the mission for which God intended her. The wounded Countenance of Christ was awaiting her discovery in the depths of His Heart.

Indeed, she would come to understand via the revelations of Christ that His dolorous Face is in fact the complement of His Sacred Heart. Ven. Dupont observed that "if the Heart of Jesus be the emblem of love, His Adorable Face is the expression of sufferings endured for us."[326] Father Cros, S.J., similarly observed that

> it was thus [Christ] showed Himself to Blessed Margaret Mary, and the Face of Jesus in that vision was surely the light, the life, and the expression of the Heart; that Face of Jesus at Paray-le-Monial [birthplace of the Sacred Heart devotion] was a dolorous Face, a *holy Face*. Behold, this Heart which has loved mankind so much, and which receives from them in return only ingratitude! — It was surely not joy that the Face of Jesus expressed.[327]

From this moment, Sister St. Pierre's interior life would become ever intimately immersed in the mysteries of Christ's wounded Countenance as the complement of devotion to the Sacred Heart — "the one is the manifestation and completion of the other."[328] Devotion to the Sacred Heart, the honorary characteristic of her beloved Carmel and the source of her own spiritual communications, would culminate in *"the honor of Carmel,"* reparation to the Holy Face, as foretold to Sister St. Pierre by St. Teresa of Avila herself.[329]

Yet for the donkey ambassadress, this task of prophetic messenger, relating requests of God concerning the work of reparation, culminating in the offering by man of the sorrowful Countenance of Christ to the Father to draw mercy for sinners, would reflect in her own face great sadness. "She was at the same time the silent victim offering herself for many others, and she who speaks in the

---

[326] Ibid.
[327] Ibid.
[328] Ibid. "M. Dupont, establishing a connection between the revelations of Blessed Margaret Mary and those of Sister St. Pierre says: 'If the Heart of Jesus be the emblem of love, His Adorable Face is the expression of suffering endured for us.' Rev. Cros writes that the Face of Jesus [in the vision of Margaret Mary] was a dolorous Face, a holy Face. 'Behold,' said he, 'This Heart which has loved mankind so much, and which receives from them in return only ingratitude!' — It was surely not joy that the Face of Jesus expressed."
[329] Ibid., 381.

name of God." *Hers was the mission of that of the prophets,*[330] for "to prophesy ... is to speak of God, not by proofs from outside, but by immediate interior impression."[331] And as such, she was perfectly in line with the Carmelite tradition of "holding oneself motionless before the living God"[332] in silent contemplation *and sharing its fruits for the spiritual good of the world.* For this work was not for Sister St. Pierre herself, but for everyone; it is an eternal truth for all times and all people.[333]

---

[330] Ibid., 109.
[331] Van den Bossche, *Message*, 62.
[332] Ibid., 62.
[333] Ibid., 60.

Chapter 4

The Mission

Holy and terrible is his name: the fear of the
Lord is the beginning of wisdom.

— Psalm 110:9–10

St. Louis IX, king of France, is one of the three patrons[334] of the Holy Face devotion. It is a fitting honor, for the Church has also named him protector of France, defender of the Roman Church, and avenger of the divine majesty outraged by blasphemy. It was the day after his feast,[335] August 26, 1843, that God revealed to Sister Marie de St. Pierre that which wounds His Sacred Heart and unleashes His wrath more than all other crimes: blasphemy.

A most terrible storm fell over the city of Tours, such that Sister St. Pierre felt that she had never realized the justice of an irritated God as at that moment. She unceasingly offered Jesus Christ to His heavenly Father for the necessities of Holy Mother Church as she lay prostrate praying, for she recalled that "according to the doctrine of the Apostles, the phenomena of nature are the visible signs of things invisible and supernatural."[336] She writes,

---

[334] The others were added later, St. Martin and St. Michael.
[335] Carmelites place great importance on correlations to the eight days following a feast, known as a feast's octave.
[336] Sister Mary St. Peter, *Life of Sister Mary St. Peter*, ed. Rev. P. Janvier (France, 1884), 126.

Then He opened His Heart to me, and gathering there the powers of my soul, He addressed me in these words: "*My Name is everywhere blasphemed, even children blaspheme.*" And He made me understand that this frightful sin more than any other, grievously wounds His Divine Heart; by blasphemy, the sinner curses Him to His Face, attacks Him openly, annuls Redemption, and pronounces his own condemnation and judgment. Blasphemy is a poisoned arrow, ever wounding His Heart. He told me that He wished to give me a "Golden Arrow," wherewith to wound His Heart delightfully, and heal these wounds inflicted by sinner's malice.[337]

Christ revealed to Sister St. Pierre that His Heart would be wounded most lovingly every time this "Golden Arrow" is said:

> May the most holy, the most sacred, most adorable, most incomprehensible, and ineffable Name of God be forever praised, blessed, loved, adored, and glorified, in heaven, on earth, and in hell, by all creatures of God, and by the Sacred Heart of our Lord Jesus Christ in the most Holy Sacrament of the Altar. Amen.[338]

As also explained in footnote 131, Sister St. Pierre writes, "As I was not a little astonished when Our Lord said, 'and in hell,' He had the goodness to make me understand that His justice was there glorified. I beg to remark, that He did not only mean the place where the wicked are punished, but also purgatory, where He is loved and glorified by the suffering souls. The word 'hell' is not merely applied to the place where the damned are confined, for our faith teaches us that the Savior descended into hell or Limbo, where the souls of the just were detained until his Coming; and does not our holy mother the Church pray her divine

---

[337] Sister St. Pierre, *Life of Sister St. Pierre*, ed. Rev. P. Janvier (Baltimore: John Murphy, 1884), 113–114.

[338] There are slight variations of this prayer, according to the source biography used. This is the one ultimately adopted by the Archconfraternity of the Holy Face, as listed in its *Manual*. Also, Sister St. Pierre, *Life of Sister St. Pierre*, 115: The translators of the biography made the following footnote: "Our Lord used the plural expression, '*dans les enfers*,' which literally translated would be 'in the hells,' or 'infernal regions'; but the latter does not strike us as the exact expression applicable here, and the former, 'the hells' good usage does not sanction in English, so using the singular number, 'in hell,' we have given 'The Golden Arrow' as it generally appears in our language."

Spouse to deliver the souls of her children from the gates of hell? *A porta inferi erue, Domine, animas eorum* (Office of the Dead)."[339]

Finally, Our Lord indicated that Sister St. Pierre (and all who recite the Golden Arrow) should be careful how the favor of this powerful reparatory prayer is appreciated, for He shall demand an account of it. At that moment, she also beheld flowing from the Sacred Heart, wounded by this golden dagger, "torrents of grace for the conversion of sinners."[340] Sister St. Pierre asked Christ whether He held her responsible for the sins of blasphemers. Though He did not immediately answer her, future revelations made clear that she, and all who know about this great grace,[341] *are urgently commended to make use of it* for the many sinners who, as also revealed at Fatima, will go to Hell if no one prays for them — makes reparation for them. Finally, because of the gravity of this request from God, Our Lord revealed that Satan will work tirelessly for its annihilation (though he will not ultimately succeed).[342]

Reverend Mother Mary did not disappoint in her characteristically cautious judgment regarding the messages given to Sister St. Pierre. She showed apparent indifference to Sister St. Pierre when presented with the Golden Arrow prayer. And when the young Carmelite had been inspired on the feast of St. Michael to compose an exercise of reparation, to follow the recitation of the Golden Arrow, which commenced with the Magnificat and was succeeded by twenty-four verses — making reparation for the blasphemies that are uttered at every hour of the day — the prioress refused her request to say the prayers. Sister St. Pierre writes that Christ made known to her, however, that the praises were very pleasing to Him, and that He desires that this devotion should be spread. She adds:

> Our Lord ... made me participate in the desire which He has to see the name of His Divine Father glorified; and it [appeared] to me that like the angels who ceaselessly chant the Sanctus, I must apply myself to glorify His Holy Name; that in doing this exercise, I would accomplish the order which He had given to me to [honor] His Divine Heart and

---

[339] Sister Mary St. Peter, *Life of Sister Mary St. Peter*, 128.
[340] Ibid., 129.
[341] Sister St. Pierre, *Life of Sister St. Pierre*, 116. Christ had ordered Sister St. Pierre to make it known, to spread it abroad — the formula of praise of the holy name of God was not for her alone.
[342] Sister Mary St. Peter, *Life of Sister Mary St. Peter*, 130.

that of His Holy Mother [which He had elsewhere requested never be separated] because they were equally wounded by blasphemy.[343]

The prayers contained "nothing but what was in conformity with the spirit of the Church,"[344] but the prioress remained firm in not allowing Sister St. Pierre to recite them.

Moreover, when Sister St. Pierre related that she had been more generally, entirely occupied in repairing the outrages committed against God by blasphemers, Reverend Mother forbade her to continue, reproaching her for presuming to make reparation for others, "whilst perhaps she herself had blasphemed God in her heart." She said, "Would you not do better to meditate on these words which may be addressed to you some day: 'Go ye cursed into everlasting fire?'"[345] In addition to wanting to test Sister St. Pierre as to whether the messages were truly from God, the prioress, perhaps unwittingly, anticipated the objection of some today: that it is presumptuous for one, perhaps sinful himself, to believe and act as if he could possibly aid in the redemption of other souls. Yet considering that this is what is asked in numerous devotions to Christ (and Marian apparitions) surrounding and succeeding the revelations given to Sister St. Pierre, the real obligation, the heavenly plea, the universal request to pray and sacrifice for others, *as also outlined in the doctrine of the communion of saints*, is not so shocking, nor presumptuous, for *all* are in a very true sense reliant on the prayers of others.

Regardless, for Sister St. Pierre, this constant testing and humiliation by her superiors was part of her predicted cross in transmitting the heavenly messages she received, yet she always abided in humble obedience to their direction, even above that to which she had been given by Christ Himself. For in keeping with the Carmelite fashion and believing that her superiors did nothing without the permission of Our Lord, she knew that unwavering obedience was the truest test of authenticity of the messages. Christ confirmed this when He told her that it was more necessary to obey her superiors than to credit what she believed to have heard from Him.[346]

---

[343] Louis Van den Bossche, *The Message of Sister Mary of St. Peter*, trans. Mary G. Durham (France: Carmel of Tours, 1953), 75.
[344] Sister Mary St. Peter, *Life of Sister Mary St. Peter*, 131.
[345] Ibid., 132.
[346] Ibid., 132.

✠ ✠ ✠

One day Sister St. Pierre unexpectedly received some consolation from her doubting superiors. While Sister St. Pierre knelt before the prioress, relating to her the cross that the revelations had brought her, Mother Mary of the Incarnation replied that she could do nothing for her, that she must "bring forth this work by [her] own sufferings."[347] Then, as Reverend Mother stood there holding a book, a leaflet fell from it on which was printed an appeal to the French nation to appease the anger of God, irritated by blasphemy, by means of reparation (a striking resemblance to the communications given to Sister St. Pierre). The prioress was astonished, as the book had likely remained on its shelf some twenty years, and not only had she herself never seen the leaflet before, but no one in the house knew anything of it either. The writing also mentioned that blasphemy drew the anger of God on France and that prayers and supplications, like those given to Sister St. Pierre, were needed to avert punishment. Reverend Mother said that if she did not know the good sister, she would believe her a sorceress (revealing a crack in her seemingly inexorably severe exterior). Sister St. Pierre related to the prioress that she felt the angels had had a hand, for she had invoked them before entering her office. When the prioress investigated further, she discovered that the publisher of the leaflet was Abbé Soyer, who later became bishop of Luçon. "To his first title, 'A Warning to the French People,' was added 'A Reparation to Appease the Wrath of God.'"[348] He had been solicited by a Carmelite of Poitiers, Sister Adelaide, who was in communication with Our Lord and was the most humble and saintly soul the Abbé had ever met. She died just twenty-six days before Sister St. Pierre had been led to the work of reparation for blasphemy.

Another remarkable coincidence was that on the same day mentioned, when Sister St. Pierre received the Golden Arrow prayer, August 26, 1843, the Carmel of Tours received from Leo Dupont (now Venerable) the formula of prayer known as the Quarantine of St. Louis. The convent was by some oversight neglected in receiving them in time to say as requested, from July 16 to August 25 (completed on the feast of St. Louis IX, king of France, entreating his intercession). The rest of the Tours religious communities did, however, receive them prior, being able to recite the prayers to honor the holy name of God and in reparation for blasphemy, as indicated. It seemed in hindsight that the prayers of many faithful religious of

---

[347] Ibid., 134.
[348] Sister St. Pierre, *Life of Sister St. Pierre*, 121.

various communities had been answered in the revelations given to Sister St. Pierre, which began the first day of the octave of the feast of St. Louis, revered for his defense of the honor of God and His holy name.

In addition to these occurrences, Pope Gregory XVI signed a brief for a confraternity under the patronage of St. Louis for the reparation of blasphemy against the name of God on August 8 of the same year, 1843. And occurring about the same time, the bishop of Nantes had approved an association to make reparation for blasphemy, to which an indulgence of forty days was attached, apparently helping the small country village of Nantes to squelch its strange addiction to blasphemy. Altogether, the above served to relax Sister St. Pierre's superiors, such that she was allowed to occupy herself with the work that had been given to her by God. The reprieve did not last for long, however, for when Our Lord requested that Sister St. Pierre have the prayers printed, this renewed the mother prioress's desire to ascertain if it were truly God who guided her. Christ comforted Sister St. Pierre, however, telling her, "As long as you continue to be humble and obedient, rest assured that you are under no illusion."[349]

Shortly after, Reverend Mother became very ill. Christ revealed on the feast of St. Michael that if the community would make a novena before the Blessed Sacrament in reparation for blasphemy against the holy name of God and say the prayers of the twenty-four-verse exercise, for which He had inspired Sister St. Pierre, He would lavish grace upon the community in return for this consolation to His Sacred Heart as well as ease the suffering of the prioress. Asking the protection of the Blessed Mother, Sister St. Pierre communicated the above to Reverend Mother. She consented, so long as the sisters should not know that the prayers came from Sister St. Pierre. (They believed them to be from their confessor because he had written them out for them.) Christ requested that the prioress should begin to promulgate these prayers of reparation and promised the restoration of her health (as an indication that she should do so). He assured Sister St. Pierre that there was nothing in the devotion contrary to the spirit of the Church, "which has been established to glorify the Holy Name of God."[350] Reverend Mother was, in fact, restored to health on the ninth day of the novena and soon after fulfilled Christ's request that she transmit the prayers of reparation.

---

[349] Sister Mary St. Peter, *Life of Sister Mary St. Peter*, 139.
[350] Ibid., 141.

Reverend Mother began to be more convinced not only of the validity of the messages entrusted to Sister St. Pierre but also of their magnitude, especially in that Christ was requesting that they be communicated to the world. She consequently placed Sister St. Pierre in direct communication with Father Vieillecases, director of the seminary of Tours, while "only those deemed indispensable in carrying out the designs of God, were told of these supernatural operations."[351] Two priests of the diocese became successive directors of Sister St. Pierre. The first was Father Alleron, dean of Notre Dame de la Riche, who had been superior of the Carmelites for twenty-four years, always preferring the ordinary way; the second was Father Jean Solomon. Father Alleron began by making the revelations the subject of jest, "as if they were of no importance whatever,"[352] but by degrees, he became convinced of the revelations and was even the first to request permission to establish in his parish the work of reparation as specified by Sister St. Pierre (though permission was refused). He was friends with Leo Dupont as well as Father Solomon, who became confessor of the Carmelites in 1839 and was the constant confessor of Sister St. Pierre for six years. Solomon had advised Dupont to publish the pamphlet on the "Association in Reparation of Blasphemy," approved by Monsignor Morlot, who would later become bishop of Tours. Yet despite his copious admirable qualities, Solomon was "of a timorous conscience, sometimes amounting to scrupulosity, which caused him to suspect the devil in the simplest circumstances."[353] This, combined with incurable deafness, led him to indecision and distrust of the communications made to Sister St. Pierre, suspecting them a product of her imagination or even a snare of the devil. Notwithstanding, he, too, by degrees, recognized the "action of God in this pure and humble soul; and from the moment he became convinced, he rendered her every assistance in his power, defending her cause on every occasion."[354] Now that Reverend Mother recognized the work was to become public, consultation from these two men of God was invaluable.

✠ ✠ ✠

As to the nature of the communications given to Sister St. Pierre, she described them as "Our Lord [having] either concentrated all the powers of her soul in his

---

[351] Ibid., 142.
[352] Sister St. Pierre, *Life of Sister St. Pierre*, 131.
[353] Sister Mary St. Peter, *Life of Sister Mary St. Peter*, 146.
[354] Ibid.

Sacred Heart, as she herself expressed it, or seemed to come himself to reside in her heart, and there reveal his intentions."[355] In both manners, the messages took place in the "superior part of her soul," and a perfect union seems to have been the result, her aspirations being perfectly in line with the will of the Lord.[356] She writes,

> I am often fixed on this kind of prayer, which is not entirely supernatural, only I feel that the powers of my soul are sheltered by the Sacred Heart of Jesus; then Our Lord acts in me and I in Him; distractions are rare because the imagination is captive. But when I am thus close beside Our Lord and He wishes to communicate something [about the] work of Reparation to me, He Himself causes a second working in my soul; I feel that I cannot act any more. It appears to me that my own spirit humbles itself to make way for that of Our Lord. Then my soul hears His interior word. In this state the soul finds itself in God without knowing how she entered there....
>
> It is impossible for me to meditate for a long time ... because I have not the mind for it[;] in the end this attraction which comes from the Heart of Jesus draws my soul into Him and I find myself in this divine sanctuary, enclosed like a little child is in the womb of his mother. Then ... my poor soul finds itself released from the struggle. It is Our Lord who has called me to this method of prayer. At the beginning I used not to dare to follow this attraction, in the fear of not making my prayer well, at not following my method. But Our Lord who desired that I might follow His, suggested this thought to my mind one day, that, if the King invited me to his table, it would be ridiculous that I should want to carry in my dinner with me.[357]

Her messages did not involve the senses in any respect — no visions or voices heard. She experienced the highest form of communication with Our Lord, a sort of infused understanding, for "the depth of the soul where the divine work [was] taking place, where she [perceived] the divine thought, [was] not the region of illusory perceptions nor even that of the constructions of natural reason. It [was] to the pinnacle of the spirit that God [communicated] His Spirit."[358] This presupposes that she had been raised to a very high degree of union with God.[359]

---

[355] Ibid., 147.
[356] Ibid., 148.
[357] Van den Bossche, *Message*, 64–65.
[358] Ibid., 65.
[359] Sister St. Pierre, *Life of Sister St. Pierre*, 135.

One day, while adoring the Blessed Sacrament, her soul "in the Heart of Jesus" was "as in a burning furnace." She felt her soul "delightfully lost, annihilated in Jesus."[360] She felt God was her beginning and her end.[361] Then Christ revealed to her that the reason He chose her to manifest His designs was that she was the "most unworthy" and that she had offered herself to Him for the accomplishments of these designs. He said that she had won His Heart by this offering and that she should be humble and simple and make known her imperfections, for this will "redound to [His] glory."[362] He asked that the sisters make a novena in reparation of blasphemy and disclosed that He had a burning desire for this work, *that it might invoke His mercy on mankind*. He therefore urgently requested that the prayers be printed.

Sensing anxiety in Sister St. Pierre and feeling she had too great a desire to propagate the devotion, Reverend Mother refused to comply, explaining the enormity of Sister St. Pierre's pride in asking, "since there were so many other beautiful prayers composed by the Holy Fathers of the Church."[363] She forbade Sister St. Pierre to think further about the matter and even imposed a penance on her. Remarkably and surely by the grace of God, Sister St. Pierre felt great interior joy at the humiliations, such that "all the compliments in the world could not have produced."[364] She thereby felt further resolved to humble herself before God and sacrificed her desire of asking for the establishment of the devotion. She promised to think no more of it to become more obedient. She did, however, continue to practice interior acts of reparation, since she believed it her duty and was not forbidden to do so.

✠ ✠ ✠

Sister St. Pierre only grew in her desire to offer compassion to Our Lord for the sorrows of His Heart instigated from the continual blasphemy of God's holy name. She imagined how it would please Him "if the faithful children of the Church would lovingly unite themselves with him in the Holy Sacrament of the altar, and with the holy angels and saints, to love and bless the Name of his heavenly Father,"[365] which was her custom, "finding in such holy company,

---

[360] Sister Mary St. Peter, *Life of Sister Mary St. Peter*, 149.
[361] Sister St. Pierre, *Life of Sister St. Pierre*, 136.
[362] Sister Mary St. Peter, *Life of Sister Mary St. Peter*, 151.
[363] Ibid., 152.
[364] Ibid.
[365] Ibid., 153.

an adequate supplement for [her] unworthiness."[366] For, she writes, "If this Divine Savior can experience bitterness of soul, he must indeed be sorrowful unto death in beholding mankind, ever blaspheming His [Father's] Holy Name and thus uniting themselves to Lucifer and the reprobates, instead of to Himself, which would supply their deficiencies and enable them to love and glorify His heavenly Father."[367] She placed her prayers in the Sacred Heart, by the hands of Mary and Joseph, begging the Savior to multiply them, "like the loaves in the desert." She then was inspired to compose the "Crown to the Holy Name of God for the Reparation of Blasphemers," a chaplet that may be said on rosary beads. She felt that it was most odious to Satan, such that she placed it under the protection of Our Lady. (This is distinct from the "Crown in Honor of the Holy Name of Jesus," a chaplet to glorify the name of Jesus; it and the Little Gospel sachet are concerned more with the name of Jesus, as opposed to that of the Father, which is the primary focus of the Holy Face devotion, per se.)

Sister St. Pierre was one day warned by Our Lord of the rage of Satan because of the work of reparation, but He assured her that He gave His Name to be her light and strength in battle. "Satan will make use of every means in his power to annihilate this work from the very onset: but the most Holy Name of God will triumph, and the angels will gain the victory."[368] She also felt inspired to seek the aid of Our Lady of Perpetual Help for the future of this work (on which she had still been forbidden to think), for there was a statue in the convent of Our Lady under this title, which had a miraculous transfer of sorts from the attic to the main living quarters.[369] She felt tranquil afterword and tried to be very obedient to the prioress.

☩ ☩ ☩

The mother prioress had still not consented to Sister St. Pierre's act of perfect abandonment as requested by Christ going back to just after her entry to Carmel, yet she writes, "[Christ] urged me to offer him the donation of myself."[370] She felt this meant to offer God the sacrifice of her entire person, and of all the merits she might be able to acquire in Carmel. In the meanwhile, and throughout the

---

[366] Ibid.
[367] Sister St. Pierre, *Life of Sister St. Pierre*, 139.
[368] Sister Mary St. Peter, *Life of Sister Mary St. Peter*, 155.
[369] Ibid., 156–157 for full discussion.
[370] Ibid.

remainder of her life, understanding that this work of reparation *can be worthily done only in union with the Sacred Heart*,[371] she would receive Communion in reparation for the outrages committed against the majesty of God, *annihilating herself in His Sacred Heart*, so that He might perform in her the "office of mediation between God and man."[372]

When Sister St. Pierre made this offering on the feast of St. John of the Cross, father of the reformed Carmel, Christ revealed that He had yet made known but a part of the designs of His Heart. He wished to reveal them to her in their full extent:

> The earth is covered with crime! The sins against the three first commandments have provoked the wrath of My Father; the Holy Name of God blasphemed, and the profanation of the Lord's Day fill to overflowing the measure of iniquity; this sin has mounted even to the throne of the Most High, and has aroused His wrath, which will burst forth over mankind in an impetuous torrent, if His justice be not appeased; in no other time has iniquity reached such a degree. I most ardently desire the formation of a society well approved and properly organized, to honor the Name of My Father. Your superior is right in remaining inactive until this work can be established on a solid and permanent foundation, for otherwise, my designs would not be accomplished.[373]

Christ warned her not to place obstacles to His designs, for she would render herself responsible for the salvation of a multitude of souls, but if she were faithful, these very souls would become an ornament in her crown. He desired that this work of reparation would be a means of mercy to sinners. Indeed, she understood that, like Abraham's plea, begging that God spare the guilty if only ten just men were found, she felt that justice would be appeased, and that God would show mercy to the guilty, if He could find devoted souls to say the prayers in reparation for blasphemy.[374]

Our Lord told her thirteen days later that His anger was manifested against France, and that He suffers patiently all the affronts against Himself, but the outrages committed against His Divine Father provoke His just indignation. He

---

[371] Ibid., 158. And Sister St. Pierre, *Life of Sister St. Pierre*, 144.
[372] Sister Mary St. Peter, *Life of Sister Mary St. Peter*, 158.
[373] Ibid., 158–159.
[374] Ibid., 160.

declared, "France has suckled the breasts of mercy even unto blood, for this reason shall mercy cede to justice."[375] For this reason, Christ threatened to remove Himself from that nation. Sister St. Pierre then asked whether France may be pardoned once more if the prayers of reparation are offered, to which He replied:

> I shall pardon her, but remember, only once more. As this sin of blasphemy is publicly committed everywhere in the kingdom of France, the reparation must likewise be made throughout the nation in every village and in every hamlet; woe to those who do not make reparation![376]

From the testimony of another sister, Sister St. Pierre left the choir "as pale as death, covered with tears and bearing an expression of sorrow that was long discernible; these outward signs were always visible whenever she received any revelation of this nature; she appeared as if crushed under the weight of Divine wrath."[377]

France, her beloved nation, was justly singled out, for it was a chosen nation of God, much like Israel of old, as would later be observed by Pope St. Pius X.

> Blasphemy, rife within her borders, wrests from her grasp the␣scepter of that providential character she held among nations and causes her to lay at the feet of impiety all that influence and ascendency, which the marvelous resources of her natural genius and [Catholic] temperament have given her over the whole world. By the revolutionary spirit, of which she has become in Europe the principal center, and most active furnace, by the practical atheism she professes in her government and laws, does she exercise, in regard to blasphemy, a kind of universal proselytism, not less baneful to individuals than to society. Is it then astonishing that she should be especially menaced by the shafts of Divine Justice?[378]

Indeed, then (as now again throughout the world), blasphemy issues forth from every part of society, attacking the Godhead openly, and "to the vile blasphemy of the common people is added the doctrinal blasphemy of the free-thinker."[379]

---

[375] Sister St. Pierre, *Life of Sister St. Pierre*, 147.
[376] Sister Mary St. Peter, *Life of Sister Mary St. Peter*, 161.
[377] Ibid., 162.
[378] Sister St. Pierre, *Life of Sister St. Pierre*, 149.
[379] Sister Mary St. Peter, *Life of Sister Mary St. Peter*, 163.

It attacks, first, the dignitaries of the Church, those most worthy of respect and the most elevated, then dogmatic teachings, aye, the very existence of Christianity itself; yet more, it hesitates not to attack God Himself, to deny His nature, His rights, nay His very existence.... That it is that "fills the measure of iniquity to overflowing," and cries to heaven for vengeance.[380]

Designated Eldest Daughter of the Church for being the first Catholic nation from the time of King Clovis I's baptism, France is the most favored by Heaven, the beloved of Christ. Blasphemy impedes its providential role, however, and offers its impious example to other nations.[381] This was the cause for France being threatened with the wrath of God. Yet hope for this nation was in the work of reparation.

☩ ☩ ☩

Perplexed why Our Lord should need her total abandonment to His designs, as expressly allowed by her superiors, Sister St. Pierre was at length given not only permission but the understanding that the superiors would themselves have a large share in the work of reparation and would face many obstacles so that Christ, "in a manner, respected their free will."[382] The act of total abandonment would in some way free the voice of God.[383] She made the following perfect act of abandonment to the Child Jesus on Christmas Day, 1843:

> Act of perfect donation to the most Holy Infant Jesus, according to the extent of His will upon me, for the accomplishment of His designs for the glory of the Holy Name of God.
>
> O most Holy and most amiable Infant Jesus! That day so ardently desired has at last arrived, when without fear of failing in obedience, I may freely offer myself to Thee, according to the extent of Thy power and Thy Will over my soul, for the accomplishment of Thy designs. I am most unworthy, it is true, of making Thee this offering, but O Divine Child! since it appears that Thou dost desire it, vouchsafe to purify Thy victim by the tears of Thy Holy Infancy, and Thy Precious Blood. Yes, my divine Spouse, on this ever memorable night of Thy august

---

[380] Ibid.
[381] Ibid., 164.
[382] Ibid., 169.
[383] Van den Bossche, *Message*, 59.

Nativity, prostrate before Thee in the crib, with full permission to do so, I offer myself entirely to Thee, through the blessed hands of Mary and Joseph, upon the flaming altar of Thy Sacred Heart consumed with love; under the protection of the Angels and Saints, I there make Thee the entire sacrifice of myself for the fulfilment of Thy designs to the glory of God's Holy Name. O Divine Child! Who didst say to Thy holy Mother when she found Thee in the temple of Jerusalem, "Why did ye seek me? Did ye not know that I must be about My Father's business?" deign to receive me, this day, as Thy disciple. Grant, that in union with Thee, I may henceforth be occupied only with such things as regard the service of Thy Divine Father, and the glory of His Holy Name. O most Holy Infant Jesus! God and Man; I renounce myself, and I give myself entirely to Thee. Do with me, and in me what will be pleasing to Thee, for the accomplishment of Thy designs; I am Thy property, take sovereign possession of me. Yes, Divine Child, most gladly for the love of Thee, do I divest myself of all things forever. Deign then, in Thy great mercy, to clothe me with the garment of Thy sacred merits which is perfumed with the good odor of Thy virtues, that on the day of judgment, I may receive the blessing of Thy celestial Father. Amen.[384]

It was thus that Sister St. Pierre fulfilled the request of Christ to give herself entirely to Him, without fear of failing in obedience to her superiors.

Having now made the long-awaited act of abandonment and knowing that Our Lord wished to have the prayers of reparation for blasphemy propagated over the whole world, Sister St. Pierre again approached Reverend Mother about having the prayers printed. She met with the response that she was self-willed and obstinate to continue to think of this work of reparation. Yet in addition to having the authenticity of the prayers validated by the numerous favors granted to the sisters who said the novenas of reparation (who, since they were unaware from whence the prayers originated, freely related the favors), Christ assured her that the prayers would be printed and distributed throughout the world.

Then her superiors, to discern whether it was truly God who led her, demanded an account of her interior life. They concluded that she had by degrees been led to "the most sublime heights of the contemplative life," progressing no less than in the unitive life. Her superiors no longer doubted, convinced that "grace had taken entire possession of this holy soul, to mold it according to its

---

[384] Sister St. Pierre, *Life of Sister St. Pierre*, 154–155.

designs, to make of it a privileged instrument in the great work so necessary to France and to the Church."[385]

Our Lord lost no time in making His requests more explicit: not only was an ordinary association of reparation necessary, but an archconfraternity was necessary, from which confraternities of the same work would converge "as the rays of a disk to its center."[386] This 1847 association differed from that of (the previously approved 1843 one from) Rome in adding to reparation for blasphemy the violation of the Lord's Day and holy days, which is an outrage committed against the sovereignty of God and an injury done to the sanctification of His holy name, for when the day is no longer sanctified by the suspension of labor, the holy name of the Lord is not adored, blessed, known, or glorified as it should be.[387] (France was, in fact, the first nation, even among those of Islam and Judaism, that did not reserve a day of public prayer.) The 1847 archconfraternity[388] differs from the most recent Archconfraternity of the Holy Face as approved by Pope Leo XIII in 1885; the latter attaches the wounded Countenance of Christ as the sensible object of adoration for the archconfraternity, as well as some slight differences in obligations.

Our Lord again warned that the devil would make use of every means in his power to crush this work from the beginning.[389] As for Sister St. Pierre, she felt that she could bear the burden no longer without falling under its weight, having such

---

[385] Sister Mary St. Peter, *Life of Sister Mary St. Peter*, 178.
[386] Ibid.
[387] Ibid., 183.
[388] Ibid., 180–181. "To the rules and regulations prescribed by the association at Rome [by decree of Gregory XVI, August 8, 1843], others were [to be] added to the one established in France; for instance, that the members should perform no manual labor, nor allow others to labor.... Our Lord desires first, that this association be placed under the patronage of St. Martin, St. Louis, and St. Michael; second, that each member recite daily a Pater, Ave, and Gloria, followed by the act of praise which he gave me under the title of 'The Golden Arrow,' with an invocation to the holy patrons; but on Sunday and Holydays, they should recite all the prayers of Reparation, in expiation for the outrages committed against God on these holy days and to obtain mercy for the guilty. [Sister St. Pierre] beheld this association under the figure of an army of valiant soldiers ... that should bear the title of 'Defenders of the Holy Name of God.' He also gave [her] to understand that each member should wear a badge in the form of a cross, bearing on one side *Sit nomen Domini benedictum* [blessed be the name of the Lord], and on the other *Vade retro, Satana* [Be gone, Satan]. That he would give to this heavenly device a secret virtue to combat against the demon of blasphemy; that every time a member heard a blasphemy uttered, He should repeat the words written on this cross, and in this manner to wage war against Satan, thus glorifying God."
[389] Ibid., 181.

interior pain because of her desire to see this work established that she was unable to take any nourishment whatsoever. She felt she must do all that was within her power by asking permission to address the archbishop about the association that Our Lord requested.[390] In consideration of this, Reverend Mother felt the need to inform Monsignor Morlot, archbishop of Tours, of all that had transpired in the soul of Sister St. Pierre. He was highly reputed and known for his prudence, but "when a point of any difficulty arose, he allowed himself to be swayed by the opinion of his counsellors, who were often the cause of turning him from a decision prompted by his natural good sense,"[391] as had even been observed by Leo Dupont. The archbishop requested that all the writings of the sister be brought to him after he had read the minute account given by Father Alleron and Mother Mary of the Incarnation. He was impressed with the sincerity of the writing and especially the communications themselves, even initiating in his own diocese the association already founded at Notre Dame de la Riche for the reparation of blasphemy. Yet while permission had been granted for Sister St. Pierre to write to the archbishop, he had still made no effort to establish the association of reparation as specified "according to the demand of Our Lord."[392]

Christ related to her that during the interim (until the archbishop would approve the association), He desired to make reparation in her own soul.

> Our Lord inspired me to present myself before Him in the name of France, to receive Him in the kingdom of my heart, and to offer Him my communion in a spirit of reparation for the crimes of which our nation is guilty.... He communicated himself to my soul, *telling me that He charged me with the salvation of France, and constituted me His ambassadress to treat of peace with Him*; also, that I should remain humbly prostrate before Him in the most Blessed Sacrament of the altar, praying for France and for the establishment of the Work of Reparation.[393]

She continued to "apply herself" for several days to adore Jesus in the Blessed Sacrament, keeping in His divine presence wherever she need be, remaining in spirit "there at his feet, praying in the name of France."[394]

---

[390] Ibid., 187.
[391] Ibid., 190.
[392] Ibid., 195.
[393] Ibid., 196–197.
[394] Ibid., 197.

Christ, in turn, related to her that she could not comprehend the abomination of the sin of blasphemy, nor could the intelligence of mankind in general conceive the heinousness of the affronts offered God by this sin:[395] "If my justice were not restrained by my mercy, the guilty would be destroyed in an instant; even inanimate beings would feel my vengeance, but I have an eternity in which to punish the wicked."[396] Then He revealed to Sister St. Pierre "the excellence of this Work of Reparation, how far it surpassed all other devotions, and how agreeable it was to God, to the Angels, the Saints and how salutary to the Church. Oh! [if souls but knew] the glory they acquire in saying only once in the spirit of Reparation for blasphemy: *Mirabile Nomen Dei* [Admirable is the name of God]!"[397] Given, as Christ related, that the sin of blasphemy "pierces his Sacred Heart, and covers him with wounds like another Lazarus,"[398] He invited her to render Him consolation similar to the "compassionate dogs who consoled poor Lazarus by licking his wounds,"[399] by every day glorifying the holy name of God. For Christ told her that "whatever one does for My Glory is to me a delicious repast."[400] Selflessly, Sister St. Pierre complied, thinking only of offering Christ some consolation (and not whether it would afford her herself any ease in suffering). In fact, Christ warned her that Satan would give her a distaste for the work of reparation for a time.[401] Undeterred, she writes:

> [Christ] made me understand that I would render Him a great service by using my tongue every day in glorifying the Holy Name of God, despised and blasphemed by sinners, without considering whether this exercise was giving me interior consolations, but to think [only that] it was healing His Divine Wounds and giving Him great satisfaction.[402]

---

[395] Ibid., 204. "On this subject St. Alphonsus de Liguori says, 'Blasphemy, so widespread in our days, is an abomination to the Lord. It is the [deadliest] of all sins, and is ordinarily unpardonable, for it is a crime of the highest magnitude that can be committed against the Divinity; a crime which attacks God openly and directly; a crime therefore which God rarely pardons.'"
[396] Ibid., 198.
[397] Sister St. Pierre, *Life of Sister St. Pierre*, 180.
[398] Sister Mary St. Peter, *Life of Sister Mary St. Peter*, 204.
[399] Ibid., 204.
[400] Sister St. Pierre, *Life of Sister St. Pierre*, 182.
[401] Van den Bossche, *Message*, 89.
[402] Ibid., 93.

Sister St. Pierre understood that Our Lord desired a "mediator between himself and France, in order that he might extend to it his mercy"[403] and that "a multitude of souls [would] be saved if his designs be accomplished."[404]

Indeed, Sister St. Pierre would become that mediator, but in the interim, to prepare her for this work, she was not spared additional interior suffering. Overwhelmed with darkness and her own weakness and incapacity in the face of her daunting mission, she described her assignment as "a burning fire which [caused her] to suffer more or less, according to the good pleasure of God."[405] She never let up her ceaseless begging of God to spare France and to establish in all its cities the work of reparation. Our Lord consoled her by impressing upon her that she must have "courage and confidence" in this work and in her partaking of "His chalice" but that He would also send consolations. Thus Sister St. Pierre "is at the same time the messenger of God for the Work of Reparation, and herself a reparatrix [co-redeemer in Christ, not equal]. She is the passive instrument and voluntary victim; under this double title, she must continue to undergo the sufferings of purifications in order that the instrument may be supple and the victim perfectly pure."[406] The future would behold that the object of the mission given to Sister St. Pierre, the salvation of France — "that nation formerly the glory of Christian Europe, [then] gangrened even to the heart with godlessness and impiety" — would in fact be granted so that her country (if only for a time) could once again be restored to "all her glorious privileges."[407]

---

[403] Sister Mary St. Peter, *Life of Sister Mary St. Peter*, 199.
[404] Ibid., 205.
[405] Sister St. Pierre, *Life of Sister St. Pierre*, 181.
[406] Van den Bossche, *Message*, 91.
[407] Sister Mary St. Peter, *Life of Sister Mary St. Peter*, 229.

Chapter 5

The Holy Face and the Salvation of France

For the zeal of thy house hath eaten me up: and the reproaches of them that reproached thee are fallen upon me.

— Psalm 68:10

Here in Carmel, there is nothing, nothing but God. He is all, He suffices, and one lives for Him alone and for His glory ... in this life of prayer and contemplation, interceding always for His people before the Face of God.

— St. Elizabeth of the Trinity

As stated in the introductory writing of the book, the most distinctive feature of the Holy Face devotion as revealed to Sister St. Pierre is the utilization of the merits veiled within the wounded Face of Christ as both a powerful means of reparation offered to God the Father to invoke His mercy for sinners and as an instrument to reproduce, in souls who honor it, the likeness of God, together described by Christ as "the greatest source of grace second to the sacraments."[408] "Man is invited to repair the outrages committed against God and by a return of

---

[408] Sister St. Pierre, *Life of Sister St. Pierre*, ed. Rev. P. Janvier (Baltimore: John Murphy, 1884), 226.

love, God promises to repair His Image in man's soul in virtue of His Holy Face."[409] (Again, like St. Veronica, man offers consolation to Christ through reparation, and in return, like the image of Christ placed upon Veronica's veil, Christ imprints the divine likeness upon the devotee.) Yet this was not immediately revealed to Sister St. Pierre. By November 1844, in fact, *the sins that demand reparation* had been fully revealed, but *the nature of the means of reparation* became the object of a new group of communications.[410] The means of reparation, as well as reciprocal graces for devotees, is so attached to the image of the live, suffering Face of the Savior, as consoled by St. Veronica and preserved by Christ upon her veil, that the Holy Face devotion as revealed to Sister St. Pierre becomes essentially nonsensical without the association.

Between this first set of revelations and what would follow concerning the significance of Christ's Holy Face regarding the devotion, during the interim, Christ urged Sister St. Pierre to address the archbishop in person (a progression from the letter she wrote to him, as discussed in the previous chapter). She writes, "What an interior martyrdom I then suffered, God alone knows: I could not eat, I could not live."[411] Our Lord assured her, however, that He would accompany her and would suggest what she should say. While the archbishop truly appreciated the rare virtues of Sister St. Pierre and did personally desire to establish the work of reparation by giving it the necessary publicity, he responded that it was a very difficult undertaking, having obstacles of which she was unaware. He ended by asking her to pray about the obstacles and for him, too, and to make him aware of any new lights on the subject that Our Lord may give. He added,

> My child, your revelations do not bear the stamp of illusion, on the contrary, I recognize thereon the *seal of God*. We have made inquiries and find that others have had the same inspirations as yourself concerning this Work of Reparation; it exists in Italy, and there is a movement toward it in several dioceses of France. It is my desire that pious souls practice this devotion; and do you especially, my child, offer yourself to God as a *victim* — offer your penances, and all your works in the spirit of Reparation, for the Church and for France; unite yourself to our Lord in the Most

---

[409] Ibid., 255–256.
[410] Louis Van den Bossche, *The Message of Sister Mary of St. Peter*, trans. Mary G. Durham (France: Carmel of Tours, 1953), 94.
[411] Sister St. Pierre, *Life of Sister St. Pierre*, 210.

Blessed Sacrament of the Altar, to render with Him honor, praise and glory to the Three Divine Persons of the Adorable Trinity; let us endeavor to arrest the arm of the Lord about to descend upon us; let us address ourselves to the holy heart of Mary, offering the Eternal Father, through the hands of this august Mother, the Blood, sufferings and all the merits of His Son, that thus, such is my hope, we may appease the anger of God.... I find nothing whatever objectionable in this; pray the Lord to enlighten me and let us act solely for the advancement of His glory.[412]

Despite Sister St. Pierre's disappointment that the archbishop was not more proactive in approving the association, she was consoled that he found nothing objectionable in the work, nor anything of illusion in the revelations. She felt more assured of the divine origin of her messages (which she, in humility, often doubted) and that God in His own time would remove any obstacles, for she placed more weight upon the words of her superiors than on the interior words, though she believed them to come from God.

In time, Archbishop Morlot did at least approve the prayers of reparation and granted permission to have them printed, but Sister St. Pierre lamented:

> This printing was not done immediately, and in the meantime, our Lord made me understand that the mere printing of these Prayers, without appending thereto some explanation of the Work to be established, would not suffice; that to excite the interest of the faithful in saying them, it was necessary to instruct them somewhat concerning the designs of His Will herein, and that when this had been done, we would see the pious feast upon these Prayers of the Reparation.... He also made known to me that *these Prayers would be very efficacious in the conversion of sinners.* [Here she is referring to the pamphlet on blasphemy entitled "Association of Prayers," compiled by Rev. Jean Salmon, which became widely distributed and for which Ven. Dupont defrayed the cost.][413]

The prayers were recited throughout France with great devotion, some twenty-five thousand copies being distributed, and while Christ made known to Sister St. Pierre that He was pleased, He still insisted that an association of reparation be established as He had requested.

---

[412] Ibid., 212–213.
[413] Ibid., 214–215.

Sister St. Pierre complied with the archbishop's request that she pray for more light regarding the establishment of the work. But at this time, also during the interim before the second set of revelations, she entered again the path of interior trials, feeling that her sins were the obstacles retarding the accomplishment of the work of reparation. The demon "assailed her by thousands and thousands of temptations, to which was added the deprivation of all sensible consolations; it seemed to her that her soul had lost even sanctifying grace; and finding only disgust and bitterness in devotions formerly most dear to her, she became reduced to a state of spiritual agony, and scarcely dared receive Holy Communion."[414] She could no longer make acts to glorify the holy name of God; attempts only stirred repugnance and resentment.[415] Indeed, she suffered three months of God's silence and inward sufferings. Yet remembering that it would wound Christ's Heart most delightfully, she at length had the courage to say ten times the "Golden Arrow" in addition to receiving Holy Communion in reparation for blasphemy. Consolation immediately came when Christ assured her that it was the demons who were filling her with sadness and disgust, wishing to annihilate the work. Then Our Lord granted her one of His most consoling and fruitful communications.[416] The Reparative Mystery of the Holy Face was at once revealed to her, freeing her from all former disgust for the work.

She felt herself carried spiritually before the charitable act of St. Veronica (a Jewish lady, as mentioned, who, according to Catholic tradition, with her veil had wiped the Holy Face of the Savior, covered with spittle, dust, sweat, and blood, despite needing to traverse the crowd of her enemies, the Roman soldiers). She understood that the impious, by their blasphemies, renew the outrages offered His Holy Face: "All the blasphemies now hurled against the Divinity, Whom they cannot reach, falling back, like the spittle of the Jews, upon the Face of our Lord, Who offered Himself a Victim for sinners."[417] He told her that He wished her to imitate the pious Veronica and that He presented her to Sister St. Pierre as her protectress and model. He made clear that all who promote the reparation for blasphemy render the same service as Veronica and that He regards those who do so with the "same complacent eyes as He gazed upon

---

[414] Ibid., 216.
[415] Van den Bossche, *Message*, 96.
[416] Sister St. Pierre, *Life of Sister St. Pierre*, 217.
[417] Ibid., 218.

her when on His road to Calvary."[418] He promised that He would grant graces to her community through the merits of Veronica's service to Him. He therefore entreated that Veronica be especially honored in the Carmelite convent at Tours. In this first communication regarding the Holy Face, Christ had presented "the marvelous economy of the Reparation for Blasphemy in its germ," still leaving the "blossom" for future revelations.[419]

Sister St. Pierre immediately asked Reverend Mother what favor she would like, by virtue of the promise of the Savior, to grant them through the merits of Veronica. She replied, "Ask of Him, that He may have the goodness to veil our faces, which will be exposed to the gaze of seculars, if that lot of land adjoining our garden be sold to strangers; ask Him, therefore, to give it to His daughters; and if He grants you this favor, your Superiors will consider it a sensible proof of the spirit which leads you."[420] Mother Mary of the Incarnation was quite occupied during this time completing the construction of the new convent and the purchase of necessary surroundings on the Rue des Ursulines, while dealing with the inconveniences of living during the interim on the Place Saint-Grégoire, a home somewhat inconvenient for Discalced Carmelites. On one side of the new property was a portion that would have overlooked their garden. Naturally, this was a serious concern for cloistered nuns, whose rule ordains that they be absolutely hidden from the people of the world. Sister St. Pierre immediately began a novena to the Holy Face for the request of Reverend Mother. The land was in fact purchased from a man who had previously been unbending in his refusal to sell the property, but not before another revelation was given to Sister St. Pierre, specifically concerning a way in which she could "purchase" the land.

In obedience to the archbishop, Sister St. Pierre renewed the request for new light on the work of reparation. Christ then "very profoundly collected the power of [her] soul within Himself, in the contemplation of His adorable Face."[421] He revealed to her that this august and Holy Face offered to our adoration "was the ineffable mirror of those Divine perfections, comprised and contained in the Holy Name of God."[422] She felt that the observance of St. Paul

---

[418] Ibid.
[419] Sister Mary St. Peter, *Life of Sister Mary St. Peter*, ed. Rev. P. Janvier (France, 1884), 239.
[420] Sister St. Pierre, *Life of Sister St. Pierre*, 219.
[421] Ibid., 221.
[422] Ibid.

that "the head of Christ is God" represented the idea of that which had been communicated to her. Further, she understood:

> As the Sacred Heart of Jesus was the sensible object offered to our adoration, to represent His boundless love in the Sacrament of the Altar, likewise, in the Work of the Reparation, is our Lord's Face the sensible object offered to the adoration of the Associates, to atone for the outrages of blasphemers, who attack the Divinity of which It is the figure, the mirror and expression. In virtue of this adorable Face presented to the Eternal Father, [one] can appease His wrath and obtain the conversion of the impious and blasphemers. Such a devotion is not only not contrary to the Work but must needs be advantageous to its propagation.[423]

Then Sister St. Pierre received another light:

> Our Lord... made me comprehend that the Church, His Spouse, is His Mystical Body, and [the doctrine of the Church is] the Face of that Body. [The Face of the Church is at the same time the Face of Christ and, in a mystical sense, is also the face of its doctrine.] Then, He showed me this Face, a butt to the enemies of His Holy Name, and I saw those blasphemers and sectarians, renewed upon our Lord's Holy Face, all the opprobrium of His Passion. I also saw, by means of this Divine light, that the impious, by wicked words and blaspheming God's Holy Name, spat in our Savior's Face, and covered it with mud; that all the blows Holy Church and [her doctrine] receive from sectarians, were a renewal of the numerous buffets upon our Lord's Holy Face, and that these wretches, in striving to annihilate the Infinite merits of Its sufferings, cause the sweat, as it were, of this Holy Face.[424]

Christ then entreated for "Veronicas" to wipe and honor His Divine Face, which has but few adorers. He said again that *all who would apply themselves to this work would be performing for Him the office of the pious Veronica.* Finally, Our Lord told

---

[423] Ibid., 222–223.
[424] Ibid., 224. Sister St. Pierre had used the word *Religion*, but the editors expounded that this was more accurately explained as the doctrine of the Church, the entirety of the Christian revelation — what to believe, what to practice, and what homage we must render God. The "Face of the Church," that which we use to distinguish and recognize it as by its countenance, is the "Face of Jesus Christ."

Sister St. Pierre that He gave her this gift of His Face in virtue of the Holy Ghost, in the presence of His Father, the angels, and the saints, through the hands of His Holy Mother and St. Veronica, and that "by My Holy Face you will work wonders."[425] Indeed, she understood that this gift was not for her alone but was to become "the distinctive sign and the great lever of the projected Work of Reparation for Blasphemy, ... offered to the adoration of His children, as the especial and befitting object of devotion for the Associates of the Confraternity for the Reparation for Blasphemy."[426] Moreover, He related that *it was the greatest gift He could make, after that of the sacraments.*[427] He concluded by saying, "Now, those who will not recognize my work therein, it is because they will close their eyes."[428]

Two days later, on the feast of the holy apostles St. Simon and St. Jude, having taken the betrayal of Judas for the subject of her meditation during evening prayer, Sister St. Pierre considered the outrage inflicted upon the Face of Jesus by Judas's kiss of betrayal. It seemed to her that Christ invited her "to kiss most [lovingly] in a spirit of reparation, the image of His Holy Face." He then offered the comparison, "As in an earthly kingdom, a coin stamped with the king's effigy is the currency enabling one to purchase at will, so in the Kingdom of Heaven, is the precious coin of my Holy Humanity, which is my Adorable Countenance."[429] This revelation inspired Sister St. Pierre to "purchase" the land that Reverend Mother wished, using the "coin" of infinite value, the wounded Countenance of Christ, offered to God the Father in reparation for modern sins of blasphemy. The Lord assured her that the community would be in possession of the land within the year, which was in fact the case, realized in the most favorable conditions offered voluntarily by the landowner, though all had given the matter up as hopeless.[430] Despite being distraught by the death of the proprietor, Baron de Nom, an honorable and practical Catholic,[431] quite unexpectedly three days after the sale of the property, Sister St. Pierre felt the favor was a visible sign of what is received in the gift of the Holy Face. She writes, "I tremble in thinking of the account God will demand of me, if I strive not to render this precious talent fruitful for His

---

[425] Ibid., 225.
[426] Ibid., 226.
[427] Ibid.
[428] Van den Bossche, *Message*, 102.
[429] Sister St. Pierre, *Life of Sister St. Pierre*, 229.
[430] Ibid., 230.
[431] Ibid.

greater glory and the salvation of souls."[432] Then she received an additional light concerning the Holy Face.

She was led to understand:

> The Divine Head represents the Eternal Father Who is unbegotten, that the mouth of this Holy Face represents the Divine Word, begotten of the Father; the two eyes, the reciprocal love of the Father and the Son, for these two eyes have but one light, one identical knowledge, and produce the one same love, which typifies the Holy Ghost. Contemplate in His locks of hair the infinitude of the adorable perfections of the Most Blessed Trinity. Behold in this majestic head, precious portion of the Savior's Holy Humanity, the image of the Unity of God [the Holy Trinity]. It is this adorable and mysterious Face of the Savior which blasphemers cover with opprobrium, thus renewing the cruel sufferings of the Sacred Passion, by assailing the Divinity of which It is the image![433]

Our Lord again reiterated that He gave Sister St. Pierre His Holy Face as the principal object of the reparative adoration "to be wiped with her homages and perfumed with her praises."[434] He then promised,

> In proportion to your care in repairing the injuries My Face receives from blasphemers, will I take care of yours, which has been disfigured by sin; I will restore it to My likeness, and render it as beautiful as when it had just left the Baptismal font. Abandon yourself then into My hands, to suffer all things necessary for the renewal of that image on your soul.... There are men skilled in restoring bodily health; but I alone am the Healer of souls, I alone have the power of renewing in them the image of God. I have revealed to you this Work of Reparation, I have shown you its excellence, and now I promise you the reward. Oh! if you could behold the beauty of My face![435]

In November 1845, Christ then revealed that He uses the soul of His faithful servant as a means of reaching numberless others, as a "channel through which to reach souls of men redeemed by his Precious Blood."[436] He wanted her to make

---

[432] Ibid.
[433] Ibid., 231.
[434] Ibid.
[435] Ibid., 232.
[436] Sister Mary St. Peter, *Life of Sister Mary St. Peter*, 255.

known the virtue of His adorable Face, thereby to restore to souls God's image, effaced by sin. She writes, "Interiorly enlightened from on High, I behold that *this adorable Face is as the seal of the Divinity and possesses the power of reproducing in souls who honor It, the likeness of God.*"[437] She understood that if man, through his atoning for the outrages offered His God, "wipes" the Face of the Savior, covered with the spittle and buffets of blasphemers, He will wipe man's, which is defiled by his own sin. "Man is invited to repair the outrages committed against God, and by a return of love, God promises to repair His Image in man's soul in virtue of His Holy Face."[438] Furthermore, *the precious gift of the virtue of Christ's Holy Face is an infallible means of appeasing the anger of the Eternal Father, irritated against blasphemers.*[439] Sister St. Pierre was inspired to pray, "O God, our Protector, look upon us and cast Thine eyes on the Face of Thy Christ."[440]

Christ warned Sister St. Pierre that she would have much to suffer from Satan in advocating for blasphemers, for they are "in an especial manner, under the leadership of the Prince of Darkness, Lucifer willingly resigning to the other demons the chief command of other kinds of sinners ... but not of blasphemers, they being his flock of predilection."[441] He assured her, however, that St. Michael and the holy angels would protect her and that He gives His Cross as a crook, thus allowing her (all devotees) to become "a terror to Hell."[442] He commanded her to have confidence in His mercy, for "He had great designs of mercy towards this class of sinners and desired to use [her] as an instrument thereof."[443] He further explained that the work of reparation atones not only for what is generally termed blasphemy but also for attacks against religion (or Catholic doctrine) and the Holy Church and is intended especially for such blasphemies as are uttered against the Holy Name of God (as in God the Father).[444]

✠ ✠ ✠

---

[437] Sister St. Pierre, *Life of Sister St. Pierre*, 232–233.
[438] Sister Mary St. Peter, *Life of Sister Mary St. Peter*, 255–256.
[439] Sister St. Pierre, *Life of Sister St. Pierre*, 233.
[440] Sister Mary St. Peter, *Life of Sister Mary St. Peter*, 256.
[441] Sister St. Pierre, *Life of Sister St. Pierre*, 234.
[442] Sister Mary St. Peter, *Life of Sister Mary St. Peter*, 257.
[443] Sister St. Pierre, *Life of Sister St. Pierre*, 235.
[444] Sister Mary St. Peter, *Life of Sister Mary St. Peter*, 228. Also, Van den Bossche, *Message*, 106: "[Christ's] Adorable Face [suffers] the outrages committed by blasphemers against the Name of His Father."

In November 1846, continuing with His "design for mercy," Christ asked Sister St. Pierre to offer God the Father the Face of His Son to obtain mercy for the whole of France, which had become hideous in His eyes and provokes His justice. He explained that if she did not comply, France would feel the wrath of well-merited chastisements. He told Sister St. Pierre that "[France's] salvation lies in the Face of the Savior,... the proof of My goodness toward France that repays Me with ingratitude!"[445] She felt inspired to continually repeat the prayer, "Eternal Father, I offer Thee the adorable Face of Thy Well-beloved Son, for the honor and glory of Thy Holy Name, and for the salvation of France."[446] Subject to the grief of hearing these sets of revelations and continuing interior sufferings, Sister St. Pierre writes:

> My poor heart is pierced by a sword of grief; our Lord, this morning, again concentrated the powers of my soul upon His precious Head crowned with thorns, and His adorable Face, which is a butt for the outrages of the enemies of God and the Church. Again did I hear His dolorous plaints, "that *He sought in our convent souls who would repair the outrages inflicted on Him, and would heal His Divine Wounds, by applying to them the wine of compassion and the oil of charity*" — also, that if the Community embraced this exercise of the Reparation, *He would give it a kiss of love which would be the pledge of the eternal kiss* [eternal union].[447]

This is a most consoling promise to devotees (which will be discussed further in chapter 6). Sister St. Pierre's mission, like that of those who embrace her example, is a mission of ultimate charity, consolation for God and mercy for man, yet Christ in His goodness returns this generosity with a cascading of merciful love, a foreshadowing of union with Him.

Concerning this compassion that Christ seeks, He made known to Sister St. Pierre that two people had shown Him "signal services" during His Passion. The first was St. Veronica, commemorated in the Sixth Station of the Cross for her kindly act of wiping Christ's suffering Face on the road to Calvary. Her veil remains at St. Peter's Basilica in the Vatican and is considered one of the most precious relics of the Passion and exterior symbol of the work of reparation for blasphemy. The second was the penitent thief, St. Dismas, who from the cross

---

[445] Sister St. Pierre, *Life of Sister St. Pierre*, 236.
[446] Ibid.
[447] Ibid., 237.

openly defended Christ's cause and confessed His Divinity, which had been blasphemed by the other thief and the Jews, who were mocking Christ and saying that if He be the Son of God, let Him come down from the Cross, and they would believe in Him. Christ wished that both would be taken as models in the work of reparation: Veronica as a model for women, who are called to "wipe" Christ's Holy Face with the veil of their prayer, praise, and adoration, in atonement for the blasphemies of sinners, and Dismas as a model for men, especially ministers, who are called to boldly and publicly defend Him.[448] He reminded Sister St. Pierre of the immediate rewards given to each, that of the impression of His Divine Face and the promise of Paradise, respectively, such were their actions so pleasing to Him. "He then promised that all who by words, prayers or writings, defended His cause in this Work of Reparation for Blasphemy, [He] would defend before His Father, and He would give them His Kingdom."[449] To His ministers, who would preach His work, and to His spouses, who would strive to wipe and honor His Holy Face in atoning for these sins, He promises that at the hour of their death He will purify the face of their souls, by effacing the disfigurement of sin, and will restore them to their primitive beauty.[450] By the virtuous examples of St. Veronica and St. Dismas, as well as by the promises offered to the devotees who follow their example, Christ gives special instruction as to the means of accomplishing the work of reparation.

☩ ☩ ☩

Just two weeks after the apparitions of La Salette (which will be discussed in chapter 7), while Sister St. Pierre was still ignorant of the occurrence, and after months of interior suffering and silence from Christ, Sister St. Pierre received messages of a most disturbing nature. Christ related that His justice was irritated by the profanation of Sunday and that He sought a "victim." She reiterated her act of abandonment in her soul, and it seemed that Christ intended to take

---

[448] Ibid., 240. Also 243. "In the opinion of St. John Chrysostom, [St. Dismas's] faith excels that of Abraham, Moses, and Isaias. 'These,' says he, 'beheld Christ upon a throne, in the midst of glory, and they believed; but the "Good Thief" sees Him in torments on a cross, and he adores Him even as if radiant with glory; he looks up to Him on the cross and prays to Him as if He were seated in the highest Heavens; he beholds Him a condemned criminal, and he invokes Him as a King…, becoming at once an "evangelist" and a "prophet."'"

[449] Ibid., 241.

[450] Sister St. Pierre, *Life of Sister St. Pierre*, 241. And Sister Mary St. Peter, *Life of Sister Mary St. Peter*, 264.

possession of her whole soul anew, "thereby to suffer in [her] Himself, and thus to appease His justice."[451] He then asked her to receive Holy Communion every Sunday: first, in atonement for all unnecessary works on the holy day; second, with the intention of appeasing divine justice and to implore the conversion of sinners; and third, to obtain the cessation of Sunday labor. He additionally invited her to continually offer His Holy Face to His Father as the means of attaining His Father's mercy. Sister St. Pierre felt anxious to appease God in this way, that His impending chastisements might be averted.

Soon, there was no doubt that the chastisements had begun, as the children at La Salette had also been warned. There was flooding along the Loire, jeopardizing the entire city of Tours, which had not been witnessed in centuries.[452] "One could but acknowledge," observes Sister St. Pierre, "that Tours was saved only by a miracle. But alas!" she added, "the principal cause of so terrible a visitation — the profanation of Sunday, was and is still ignored."[453] Of equal concern was a famine, especially among the poor, as well as the fear of revolution. In fact, Our Lord made known to Sister St. Pierre that other chastisements were being prepared, and this time "He would use as the instruments of His wrath, not the elements, 'but the malice of revolutionary men!'"[454]

Our Lord soon revealed the method of mitigation: "Not satisfied to slight entirely the rights of Justice," He wished, according to Sister St. Pierre, "to make an alliance between His Justice and His Mercy, and for this end, He asked the establishment of the Work of the Reparation for the glory of His Holy Name. Yes," said Sister St. Pierre, "He will disarm the anger of God, His Father, by offering Him [on behalf of man], the Work of the Reparation!"[455] She then felt inspired to compose this prayer: "Eternal Father, look upon the Divine Heart of Jesus, which I offer Thee to receive the wine of Thy Justice, that it may be changed for us into the wine of Mercy."[456] And He made her understand that each time this petition was offered, it would obtain a drop of the wine of divine wrath, which, falling into the vase of the Sacred Heart of Jesus, would be

---

[451] Sister St. Pierre, *Life of Sister St. Pierre*, 261.
[452] Sister Mary St. Peter, *Life of Sister Mary St. Peter*, 285.
[453] Sister St. Pierre, *Life of Sister St. Pierre*, 262.
[454] Ibid., 263.
[455] Ibid., 264.
[456] Ibid., 263–264.

changed into a wine of mercy.[457] "The Sacred Heart of Jesus will drink this bitter chalice, and His sweet and Holy Face will appease God's wrath."[458]

Finally, Christ again related to Sister St. Pierre, "*Even as I have assumed all the sins of the world, do I wish you to assume those of France. I will suffer in you to appease the anger of My Father, and I will give you all My merits to cancel your debts.*"[459] She then felt herself as though covered with crimes and asked pardon of Him with the same confusion as if she had really committed them herself.[460] When she doubted that God would use so vile an instrument as herself for so great a mission, He related that just as He gives a king to a certain country in the order of His grace, could He not assign a nation to an individual to take charge of its spiritual needs? He added,

> Wherefore, I commit France to your keeping; pray for her and immolate yourself for her. I give you anew My Head [the chief and most important member of My Sacred Person];[461] offer It to My Father to appease the Divine Justice. Oh! if you knew the power, the virtue residing therein; and wherefore? Because I have taken upon My Head all the sins of mankind, that My Members may be spared. Therefore, offer My Face to My Father, for this is the [sole][462] means of appeasing Him.[463]

Sister St. Pierre abandoned herself to the Savior as His victim, ready to give all to whatever He may ask, even accepting the charge of the spiritual care of France, so long as Christ would be its Sovereign, feeling that the Father's wrath would be arrested, beholding His Son upon its throne. She supplicated Christ as King, begging Him not to abandon a nation that "multiplies its alms to make known His Name among idolatrous nations."[464] Archbishop Morlot, having requested that information be sent to him regarding all that was revealed to Sister St. Pierre, was informed by the prioress the duty placed upon the sister and the real danger to which France was subject. He replied that there was no doubt but that the calamities of France were the chastisements of its sins and

---

[457] Ibid., 265.
[458] Van den Bossche, *Message*, 116.
[459] Sister St. Pierre, *Life of Sister St. Pierre*, 265.
[460] Ibid., 266.
[461] Sister Mary St. Peter, *Life of Sister Mary St. Peter*, 290.
[462] Ibid.
[463] Sister St. Pierre, *Life of Sister St. Pierre*, 266.
[464] Ibid., 247.

infidelities and asked that this "chosen soul [of Sister St. Pierre] use all her efforts to stay the torrent of evil."[465]

Thus, the salvation of France was inseparably associated with the work of reparation, Our Lord offering for both the same exterior sign and efficacious means, namely, His adorable, wounded Face. Assigning Sister St. Pierre as steward of France, He again placed His Holy Face in her hands, in order that she may unceasingly offer it to the Father for the salvation of France: "For by it you obtain the conversion of many sinners; nothing that you ask in virtue of this offering will be refused you. Ah! If you did but know how pleasing is the sight of My Face to My Father!"[466] "Make use of this divine talent. You have in this that which can settle all the needs of My household. By this Holy Face you will obtain the salvation of many sinners. Nothing will be refused you by means of this offering."[467] The ideas of reparation, the salvation of France, and the Holy Face were never separated in the mind of Sister St. Pierre. She offered ceaselessly the Face of the Savior to the Eternal Father for the salvation of France and to obtain through this the establishment of the work of reparation.[468]

She also received understanding regarding Christ's infinite mercy: "He began by impressing upon my mind the sense of His sovereign justice, showing me the waters of His ire, but, at the same time, commanding me to drain them with His Divine Heart, that they might be lost in this Abyss of Mercy."[469] Another day, "Our Lord showing me the multitude of souls falling into Hell, invited me, in the most touching manner, to help rescue these poor sinners, blindly rushing into the eternal abyss, making me understand that His Mercy would open their eyes, were [the devout, fulfilling the real obligation of the Christian toward these unfortunate] to … [pray] most fervently for the conversion of these misguided ones,"[470] whose eyes would have been opened "if charitable souls had interceded in their behalf."[471] He added, "My daughter, I give you My Face and My Heart, I give you My Blood, I give you My Wounds; draw from them and pour out upon others! Buy freely, for My Blood is the price of souls! Oh! that sorrow for My Heart to behold despised by men, remedies which have

---

[465] Sister Mary St. Peter, *Life of Sister Mary St. Peter*, 288.
[466] Ibid., 268.
[467] Van den Bossche, *Message*, 118.
[468] Sister Mary St. Peter, *Life of Sister Mary St. Peter*, 292.
[469] Sister St. Pierre, *Life of Sister St. Pierre*, 269.
[470] Ibid.
[471] Sister Mary St. Peter, *Life of Sister Mary St. Peter*, 293.

cost Me so dearly!"[472] On another occasion, Christ placed her at the "gate of Time," that she might help those passing from time to eternity: "Oh! when we reflect that whilst Divine Justice is always impending over the guilty, yet we may plead their cause, how … Divine Mercy, constrained by fervent and piercing supplications, may at last touch their hearts, and snatch them from perdition!"[473] Finally, Our Lord related to Sister St. Pierre that her daily devotion on behalf of France had resulted in a "mysterious wall protecting France against the shafts of the Divine Justice."[474] Her method was to present the Face of Christ to His Father, one hundred times a day, in honor of all the mysteries of the life and death of the Divine Savior, for the salvation of France.

In January 1847, Christ not only desired that Sister St. Pierre pray for France, but He confided other souls to her, to join His Mother in the spiritual assistance of the dying. As the servant of the Blessed Virgin, she accompanied her, standing beside these travelers "from Time to Eternity." Christ bestowed the Carmelite to His Mother for this great mission. She writes, "O, the blindness of men! Ardently pursuing the perishable treasure of Earth, whose united value could not purchase a single soul, yet ignoring and despising the Gift of God, the veritable treasure of the Christian, these infinite merits, which, presented at the band of Divine Mercy, can purchase millions of immortal souls!"[475] She explains that *no one* ought to pray, or to present himself before the Eternal Father, "unprovided with a portion of the precious merits of His Son," in that one's merits may be lacking. Uniting one's prayers with Christ, Sister St. Pierre understands that man should offer to the Eternal Father Christ's Sacred Heart, His adorable Face, and His divine wounds; His tears, His blood, and His sweat; His journey, His labors, His words, and His silence: all that He has suffered in each of the mysteries of His life. She concludes that in the Lord's committing souls to her care, He has at the same time revealed *how* she (and all devout) must save them.[476]

☩ ☩ ☩

Meanwhile, though Sister St. Pierre's superiors were convinced of her mission, it took some time for them to agree to at least publish anonymously a concise

---

[472] Sister St. Pierre, *Life of Sister St. Pierre*, 270.
[473] Ibid., 271.
[474] Ibid., 271.
[475] Ibid., 273.
[476] Ibid., 275.

account of the revelations, which took the form of "An Abridgment of Facts concerning the Establishment of the Work of the Reparation for Blasphemy." It was a pamphlet in handwritten form, mainly intended for a few Carmelite convents and devout individuals, a total of only fifty being copied. The archbishop approved, referring to the work as "most necessary,"[477] also giving permission for printing a small book, *Association of Prayers against Blasphemy*, as well as a "Litany of the Holy Face," which Sister St. Pierre had composed under divine inspiration. Sister St. Pierre was relieved, believing for a time that God's requests had been fulfilled.

Expanding upon the revelations regarding the Holy Face, Our Lord related to her that His love is most unappreciated in the Most Holy Sacrament of the Altar, a lack of faith among Christians being so prevalent. She understood that His Holy Face is hidden under the eucharistic veil and that it is by this august Sacrament that Jesus wishes to communicate to souls the virtue of His Holy Face, which is "more dazzling than the sun."[478] He again promised to imprint His divine likeness upon the souls of those who honor it.[479] She better understood the connection between Our Lord's holy name and His Face. "He has made me understand that the impious, by their blasphemies, attack His Adorable Face, and the faithful glorify It, by homage and praise to His Name and His Sacred Person. The merit is in the person, but the accompanying glory is in the name which recalls this glory each time it is pronounced; the merit or demerit of a person is ever attached to His name."[480] "The Holy Name of God expresses the Divinity and contains all the perfections of the Creator; it follows, therefore, that the blasphemies of this Sacred Name insult God directly.... Jesus became man by the Incarnation; it is He who has suffered in His adorable Face all the outrages committed by the blasphemers of the Name of His Father."[481] In the work of reparation, "the glory which [devotees] render His Name encircles His august brow, and is portrayed on His most Holy Face in the adorable Sacrament of the altar."[482] Indeed, the work of reparation is an extension of the offering of the Holy Sacrifice of the Mass.

---

[477] Sister Mary St. Peter, *Life of Sister Mary St. Peter*, 301.
[478] Sister St. Pierre, *Life of Sister St. Pierre*, 278.
[479] Ibid.
[480] Ibid., 279.
[481] Sister Mary St. Peter, *Life of Sister Mary St. Peter*, 303.
[482] Ibid., 304.

Our Lord related to Sister St. Pierre in a most poignant fashion that He is not known, is not loved, and His commandments are despised. Then He entreated her yet again: "Sinners are snatched from this world and precipitated into Hell like dust swept away by a whirlwind! Have pity on your fellow creatures, pray for them; with your love, wipe the Blood which flows from My wounds; love me, and fear not; when you raise your heart to Me in love, I will receive it in My Hands, and there it is safe."[483] In March 1847, He encouraged her that the work would be established and that He permitted the demon to cross His works, thereby to test the confidence of His servants. "Today," He said, "Rejoice, my daughter, for there is about to dawn upon the earth ... the most beautiful [Work][484] under the sun; offer My Heart to obtain it." He was referring to the work of the reparation for blasphemy, by the merits of His sorrowful Face. Certainly the Redemption of humanity, continually renewed in the Sacrament of the Altar, is *the* most beautiful work that may be conceived, but since that universal sacrifice by Our Savior, He has made clear that iniquity has never reached such a degree, manifesting especially in radical impiety and absolute incredulity, "the two most loathsome wounds of modern society,"[485] represented by blasphemy in all its forms. In the face of such evil, the sole mediator, God incarnate, has offered His Divine Face, a new work for the atonement necessitated by novel offenses. "The Work of the Reparation is so intimately connected with the Redemption of man, so identified with the expiation on Calvary, that [it may be considered] a renewal and continuation of the same; and, hence, notwithstanding the feeble, unworthy instruments employed, it may justly be termed the 'most beautiful of works,' as it is, in reality, the most necessary [and noble][486] for the needs of the present age."[487]

The pamphlet "The Abridgment of Facts" had produced an earnest desire to see the work of reparation established. However, "the contents ... had excited

---

[483] Sister St. Pierre, *Life of Sister St. Pierre*, 285.
[484] Ibid., 286. While this specific quote says, "one of the most beautiful Works," the other original source biography clearly states, "the most beautiful Work," and this source says in a few paragraphs that it may be justly termed the "most beautiful of works," as it is the most necessary for the needs of the present age. Sister Mary St. Peter, *Life of Sister Mary St. Peter*, 311: "Rejoice, My daughter, the hour approaches, for the birth of the most beautiful work that has yet appeared on the face of the earth."
[485] Sister Mary St. Peter, *Life of Sister Mary St. Peter*, 311.
[486] Ibid.
[487] Sister St. Pierre, *Life of Sister St. Pierre*, 287. And Sister Mary St. Peter, *Life of Sister Mary St. Peter*, 312.

some undesirable attention by reason of the political events of the times ... [such that] the archbishop finally imposed silence, as well on the Carmelite convent, as on M. Dupont."[488] The distribution of the pamphlet was discontinued and all work of reparation outside the convent was effectively halted. Inside the convent, however, Sister St. Pierre continued to receive revelations pertaining to the work, though all connected with her, save her superiors and one secretary, remained unaware of these messages. Christ insisted that the work would need the formality of a papal brief so that its foundation would be secure. He also warned that if the work was not established, France was in great danger, for the disasters with which it had been struck were only the forerunner of what divine justice was preparing if "His mercy has given ... a means of salvation ... [that] be not established."[489]

Our Lord here mentions Communists for the first time, which He said had made but one outbreak, but "Oh! if you knew their secret and diabolical machinations, their anti-Christian principles! They await but the favorable moment to inflame all France. Hence, to obtain mercy, ask, then, for the Work of Reparation from Him who has the right to establish it."[490] Sister St. Pierre consequently requested once again to write the archbishop, but the prioress refused. Christ charged Sister St. Pierre to pray without ceasing for the establishment of the work, nonetheless, and "to offer herself entirely to Him, ready to suffer in body and soul, all that He wills for the accomplishment of His designs."[491] Sister St. Pierre felt that from that moment, she had been "upon the cross." Yet she considered herself most unworthy to suffer for so noble a cause: "the glory of God and the salvation of souls!"[492]

✣ ✣ ✣

Considering the extensive revelations given to Sister St. Pierre concerning the wounded Holy Face, as well as sorrowful Holy Face connections to the spirituality of St. Thérèse and the Carmelite tradition (to be discussed in chapter 6), and as is made clear in the *Manual of the Archconfraternity of the Holy Face*, the Veronica veil image is the logical object of adoration of the Holy Face devotion. Some associate

---

[488] Sister St. Pierre, *Life of Sister St. Pierre*, 288.
[489] Ibid., 290.
[490] Ibid.
[491] Ibid., 292.
[492] Sister Mary St. Peter, *Life of Sister Mary St. Peter*, 317.

other images of Christ with the devotion, and while they are beautiful and often have compelling origins of their own, the revelations *as given to Sister St. Pierre* and the thousands of miracles associated with the Holy Face devotion involving the Veronica Veil relic image (which itself is the result of Christ's miraculous imprint upon it as well as the object of the "Miracle of the Vatican") indicate that the dolorous (sorrowful) Face of Christ, as recorded on the veil of Veronica, is key to the devotion. Offered to the Father in reparation for sins against the first three commandments, it is the sorrowful Face that is so pleasing to the Father, moved by the suffering Face of His Son to have pity for man's face, disfigured by iniquity. Seeking "Veronicas" to console His Face injured by modern offenses, Christ revealed that "in proportion to [man's] care in repairing the injuries [His] Face receives from blasphemies, [He will] take care of his, which has been disfigured by sin."[493] Again, it is specifically the wounded Face of Christ as object of adoration in the Holy Face devotion and offered in reparation to the Father for affronts to Him as Godhead, having the power to reproduce the image of God in man (not unlike the image of Christ left upon Veronica's veil), which Our Lord revealed to Sister St. Pierre as "the greatest source of grace, second only to the sacraments."

(The authenticity of the veil of Veronica as preserved at the Vatican, and even the historic person now known as Veronica, has been the subject of debate in recent years. An in-depth defense of the veil at the Vatican will be in part the topic of a second book, as will be the life and miracles of Ven. Dupont.)

---

[493] Sister Mary St. Peter, *Life of Sister Mary St. Peter*, 232.

St. Thérèse of the Child Jesus and the Holy Face

Chapter 6

Sister St. Pierre, St. Thérèse, and the Holy Face

1. Complementary Spiritualities

Mercy and judgment I will sing to thee, O Lord.

— Psalm 100:1

JUST FORTY YEARS AFTER the death of Sister St. Pierre, another *petite* French soul, the "Little Flower," entered Carmel. She, too, embraced the wounded Countenance of Christ in a most prodigious way, further enhancing the understanding of its efficacious, hidden beauty for the faithful, focusing especially on the "prize" of devotion to the Holy Face: mercy. The spiritualities of St. Thérèse and Sister St. Pierre are remarkably complementary, and there is striking — albeit seemingly forgotten — evidence that the collection of revelations from Christ given to initiate the Holy Face devotion (taking as its scriptural foundation Isaiah 53), along with Sister St. Pierre's prayers, mystical favors, and insights, greatly contributed to the underlying basis of St. Thérèse of Lisieux's devotion.[494] Specifically, "*contemplation of the Holy Face* holds ... a

---

[494] *The Prayers of St. Thérèse of Lisieux*, trans. Aletheia Kane (Washington, D.C.: ICS Publications, 2020), 94. "The Carmelite of Lisieux owes much to the Carmelite of Tours, Mary of Saint Peter: the latter's *Life* and the various manuals, short works, or leaflets of the Confraternity of Tours.... It is not surprising, then, that several expressions would have passed into ...

considerable place in the spiritual life of Saint Thérèse."[495] Indeed, Thérèse herself designates the treasures veiled in the suffering Face of Christ as "the foundation of all [her] piety."[496]

Shortly after her entry into Carmel, St. Thérèse began to delve more deeply into the riches of Christ's Passion. The timing coincided with what she referred to as her father's three years of martyrdom in which he endured a series of strokes, resulting in his entry into a mental institution only a month after Thérèse received her religious habit. She felt that he became the living personification of Christ as the Man of Sorrows: "His [face] was as it were hidden" (Isa. 53:3). During this time of intense grief and sorrow for the Little Flower, "spiritual aridity was [her] daily bread."[497] A few months prior, St. Thérèse apparently began to discover the "secrets" of the Holy Face.[498] She writes, "Until then I had not appreciated the beauties of the [wounded] Holy Face. It was my dear mother, Agnes of Jesus, who unveiled them to me."[499] Even more so during the end of her life, St. Thérèse came to worship Christ as depicted in Isaiah 53:1–5, sorrowful and acquainted with infirmity:

> "a worm and no man," as "a leper and as one struck by God and afflicted," as "one hidden and despised"; and the inspiration of this worship [was] her deep devotion to the bruised and Wounded Face of Jesus [as] the symbol of "his saturation with reproaches." ... Here she [was] at one with Sister Marie de [St.] Pierre, whose very life was the Reparative worship of the Holy Face.[500]

Thérèse's ... writings." See page for examples. And Sister Mary Emmanuel, *Life of Sister Marie de St. Pierre of the Holy Family, Carmelite of Tours, 1816–1848: A Forerunner of St. Thérèse of Lisieux* (London: Burns, Oates & Washbourne, 1938), 14. And, Ibid., 6: "We have full proof, in documents recently made know to us, that the devotion to the Holy Face at Lisieux originated in the revelations to Sister Marie de St. Pierre." And, Ibid., 6–14 (for full discussion).

[495] P. Marie-Eugène, *A Practical Synthesis of Carmelite Spirituality*, trans. M. Verda Clare, vol 2, *I Am a Daughter of the Church* (Allen, TX: Christian Classics, 1997), 436.

[496] Ibid. "A few weeks before she died, she wrote that her devotion to the Holy Face, or rather all her spirituality, was based upon Isaias 53:1–3."

[497] Thérèse of Lisieux, *Story of a Soul: The Autobiography of St. Thérèse of Lisieux*, 3rd ed., trans. John Clarke (Washington, D.C.: ICS Publications, 1996), 157.

[498] P. Marie-Eugène, *I Am a Daughter*, 434.

[499] Thérèse of Lisieux, *Story of a Soul*, 73.

[500] Sister Mary Emmanuel, *Life of Sister Marie*, 6. "Theresa says that the 53rd chapter of Isaias was 'the foundation of all her piety,' and the symbols, to her, of this chapter was the Holy Face."

Thérèse first signed her name "of the Child Jesus *and the Holy Face*" the day she received the habit, January 10, 1889;[501] "from that time on, the suffering Face of Our Lord was to be forever before her loving gaze."[502] Yet not only did both Sister St. Pierre and St. Thérèse place the hidden beauty of Christ's wounded Countenance at the center of their own spiritual lives, but each additionally relied upon the wounded Face of Christ in her quest to assist in the redemption of her brethren.

Christ Himself commanded of Sister St. Pierre this recourse to His wounded Countenance by way of a most shocking request. In continuation of chapter 5, she was literally appointed by Christ with the deliverance of her country from chastisements that were manifesting in both the elements and in the actions of revolutionary men.[503] Vast flooding along the Loire, unequaled in centuries, and famine among the lower classes[504] had already broken out when, on February 13, 1848, Our Lord related to Sister St. Pierre additional impending woes by telling her that the Church was threatened with a horrific catastrophe and to pray unceasingly. The prediction was fulfilled by way of the terrible "Days of February," a (second) revolution that threw Louis Philippe from his throne and made France a republic once again. The quake shook Europe in a series of revolutions. This included Rome, where the mobs stoned the pontifical palace and desecrated churches and convents, demanding that the civil power of the pontiff be replaced by a "Roman Republic," necessitating that the pope flee to Gaeta for safety. Yet France remained the epicenter, for Christ relayed that "the torrents of divine justice were not yet entirely exhausted toward France."[505] The Eldest Daughter of the Church was being singled out by God for punishment justly merited due to its primacy in sins relating to the blasphemy and the profanation of Sunday, which had become normalized during and after the revolution. The punishment fit the crime, for France undoubtedly hastened modern evils of blasphemy, current offenses against the rights of God, which Christ describes as never before having been exceeded.[506]

---

[501] Thérèse of Lisieux, *Story of a Soul*, 152.
[502] P. Marie-Eugène, *I Am a Daughter*, 435.
[503] For full discussion of this event in the life of Sister St. Pierre, see chapter 5.
[504] Sister Mary St. Peter, *Life of Sister Mary St. Peter*, ed. Rev. P. Janvier (France, 1884), 285.
[505] Ibid., 287.
[506] Ibid., 159.

Our Lord told Sister St. Pierre that while *He had taken on the sins of the world, He charged her with the salvation of France*,[507] though He encouraged her by saying:

> I will suffer in you, [to] appease the wrath of My Father, and I will cede to you all My merits that you may acquit yourself of your assumed debts.... I appoint you today as My agent, and I ... remit My Holy Face into your hands, to offer it unceasingly to My Father for the salvation of France.... By this Holy Face, you will obtain the salvation of a multitude of sinners.[508]

In Sister St. Pierre, the Father desired to make an "alliance" between His justice and His mercy, and also for this purpose, He asked for the establishment of reparation in honor of His holy name, with the wounded Countenance of Christ as the efficacious object of adoration in this work, that His anger might be disarmed.[509] In her salvation of France, Sister St. Pierre was a type of St. Joan of Arc, though Joan's battles were material while those of the Carmelite were spiritual.

Additionally, Sister St. Pierre was to be the model for the faithful to follow in drawing mercy from the Father through appeasement of His justice by offering the "chief and most important member of [Christ's] sacred person,"[510] the Divine Face of the Savior, to the Father in reparation as specified in the Holy Face devotion. At length, the Lord told her that in consequence of the newly established work of reparation (which had received some initial approval during this time), France would not be entirely consumed in His Father's wrath, which it otherwise would have been, and that the priests would be spared.[511] France and the Church were secured for the moment. All who were privy to the sister's communications, including her archbishop, attributed to the work of reparation France's temporary deliverance from the tyranny of revolutionary men.[512]

Sister St. Pierre demonstrated the selfless cooperation of man with the might of God in achieving the salvation of the masses (and thereby, mitigation

---

[507] Ibid., 289.
[508] Ibid.
[509] Ibid., 287.
[510] Ibid., 290.
[511] Ibid., 385.
[512] Ibid., 288.

of chastisements). For as Christ likewise related to St. Margaret Mary in revealing to her devotion to His Sacred Heart, "One just soul can obtain the pardon of a thousand sinners.... In this way, without infringing on the rights of justice, God [can] exercise His mercy superabundantly. He frequently asks [man] to co-operate with Him..., [to] provide opportunities for Him to show His infinite mercy."[513] Yet the Holy Face offering stipulates that man is to utilize not his own but the merits, the love *of Christ*, enveloped in His wounded Face, in his supplications to the Father to draw mercy for his brethren. Again, this cooperation between the efficacious power residing in Christ's wounded Countenance as offered by man in reparation to God to draw graces for the multitudes — allowing also in the process for the divine likeness to be impressed upon the devotee himself — is, according to Christ, "the greatest source of grace second to the sacraments"[514] and "the sole means of appeasing [His Father's justice]."[515]

Recourse to the wounded Face of Christ thereby won for Sister St. Pierre the salvation of France from chastisements justly merited due to its unprecedented iniquities committed against God's primal commands,[516] providing a modern model for man's role in co-redemption. Recourse to the wounded Face of Christ won for St. Thérèse an interior battle with the same forces of evil,[517] manifested for her, however, in the shadow of the dark night of the soul.[518] In this darkness, which commenced Easter 1896, St. Thérèse *felt* (though she would not let herself believe[519]) what is now the predominant sentiment, that there is no Heaven, that God does not exist — atheism, a loss of faith (which is, paradoxically, the essence of the blasphemy and infidelity against God for which one is to make reparation in the Holy Face devotion). Thérèse writes, "[Christ] permitted my soul to be invaded by the thickest darkness, and ... the thought of

---

[513] Raoul Plus, *The Ideal of Reparation*, trans. Madame Cecilia (London: Burns, Oates & Washbourne, 1921), 63.
[514] Sister Mary St. Peter, *Life of Sister Mary St. Peter*, 246–247.
[515] Ibid., 290.
[516] Ibid., 159. Our Lord to Sister St. Pierre: "In no other time has iniquity reached such a degree."
[517] Dorothy Scallan, *The Whole World Will Love Me: The Life of St. Thérèse of the Child Jesus and of the Holy Face (1873–1897)*, ed. Emeric B. Scallan, S.T.B. (Rockford, IL: TAN Books, 2005), 306. "At once she recognized the foe assailing her. It was the spirit of blasphemy and infidelity. That he disguised himself as an intellectual and proposed disbelief in God as rational, did not for a moment deceive the sister."
[518] This is a term used by St. John of the Cross to indicate a passive stage of purification of a soul on the journey to mystical union with God.
[519] Thérèse of Lisieux, *Story of a Soul*, 214.

heaven, up until then so sweet to me, [was] no longer anything but the cause of struggle and torment."[520] This suffering was heretofore unimaginable to the saint, yet "during this period, interior darkness [did] not conceal the Holy Face [from Thérèse]. On the contrary, its beauty, [arose] before her during the night of trial: it [was] the divine Sun that [was] to dispel the painful darkness."[521] She ultimately understood Christ's suffering as synonymous with His love, such that she longed to return this love to Him, utilizing her suffering as a consoling offering, taking on that which is lacking in her fellow brethren as well.

St. Thérèse, like Sister St. Pierre, therefore, also presents a contemporary model for man's role in co-redemption, for she felt her experience of extreme spiritual dryness and temptation against faith, surrounding her in a total darkness, was a type of sharing in Christ's vicarious atonement or reparation, such that she desired to exchange places with unbelievers, offering herself for their conversion. She pleaded with Christ: "May all those who were not enlightened by the bright flame of faith one day see it shine. O Jesus! If it is needful that the table soiled by them be purified by a soul who loves You, then I desire to eat this bread of trial at this table until it pleases You to bring me into Your bright Kingdom."[522] ... [Even] if my suffering was ... unknown to You, which is impossible, I would still be happy to have it, if through it I could prevent or make reparation for one single sin against *faith*.[523]

Trusting in the merciful love encased within the wounded Face of Christ, which had taken upon itself the punishment of man, she offered the pains associated with her dark night to obtain the "light of faith" for those unbelievers. She "burned to snatch [souls of sinners] from the eternal flames."[524] In her interior dryness, she found, like Christ on His Cross, a thirst for souls, forgetting herself and living — or, in some very real sense, dying — for others.

Certainly, "it is almost impossible to comprehend that Thérèse was able to achieve such magnificent surrender in the midst of constant spiritual aridity."[525] Yet it was in this dryness that St. Thérèse identified with St. John of the Cross,

---

[520] Ibid., 211.
[521] P. Marie-Eugène, *I Am a Daughter*, 436.
[522] Thérèse of Lisieux, *Story of a Soul*, 212.
[523] Ibid., 214.
[524] Ibid., 99.
[525] Ida Friederike Görres, *The Hidden Face: A Study of St. Thérèse of Lisieux* (New York: Pantheon Books, 1959), 247.

who corroborated the intuitions she felt in her soul[526] and assured her that "the dark night of the [soul] brings with it [an] hour of supernatural hope."[527] Indeed, she was fond of quoting from the book of Job, "Even if God should slay me I would still trust in Him," surely the greatest of all expressions of hope.[528] Trust in God's goodness and mercy, a hope against hope, *embodied in the wounded Face of Christ*, which had borne all the sins of man for man's salvation, was the transformative key in St. Thérèse's own spiritual life — and also afforded her the ability to confidently plead on behalf of her brethren. Indeed, she extended even the smallest offerings of trust and hope in a desire to both console the suffering Face of her Lord and save sinners.

This was St. Thérèse's now famous offering of countless little sacrifices — always in a spirit of absolute trust and surrender — as selfless tokens of love, given as consolations to Christ and expecting mercy for sinners in return (which she terms her Little Way). In addition, she offered her greatest suffering of the dark night of the soul to exchange places with unbelievers in selfless atonement. These actions of co-redemption allowed St. Thérèse to make herself more and more a vessel in which to receive the unhoused merciful love of God, taking upon herself the love of God that had been rejected by others, becoming a victim of God's merciful love.

In 1895, two years prior to her death, St. Thérèse asked Our Lord whether His justice alone receives victims or rather, does not His merciful love also need them? She stated:

> On all sides [Your merciful love] is ignored, rejected.... The hearts on which You would pour it out turn to creatures, seeking happiness in miserable and fleeting affections instead of casting themselves into Your arms, into the ineffable furnace of Your infinite love.... If Your justice — the justice You exercise on earth — be satisfied to discharge itself on voluntary victims, how much the more must Your merciful love desire to enkindle souls, since Your mercy reaches even to the heavens.... O Jesus, that I may be that happy victim, consume Your holocaust in the fire of Divine Love.[529]

---

[526] P. Marie-Eugène, *Under the Torrent of His Love: Thérèse of Lisieux, a Spiritual Genius*, trans. Mary Thomas Noble (Philippines: St. Paul's, 2007), 19.
[527] P. Marie-Eugène, *I Am a Daughter*, 380.
[528] Görres, *Hidden Face*, 248.
[529] Thérèse of Lisieux, *Little Catechism of the Act of Oblation of St. Thérèse of the Child Jesus* (Manchester, NH: Sophia Institute Press, 2012), 2.

Her offering of love was intended both to soothe the Sacred Heart of Christ, returning love for love, and to be a vessel to collect the love He longed to give others, trusting in its power to inebriate her, giving her recourse to aid in the salvation of her brethren — in some sense, to dispense His love upon the world. Love's fire consumed her and made her its victim.

The Little Way of St. Thérèse, then, is the way or practice of offering everyday sacrifices to Christ to console Him while trusting in His transformative mercy for sinners in return. It is the showing and receiving from Him merciful love instead of ingratitude and neglect. Victimhood to merciful love is the natural culmination of the Little Way: Taking consolation a step further, souls receive from Christ *on behalf of others* the love and mercy that Christ longs to bestow by further trusting in and depending completely upon Him. In return, the soul is showered with the merciful love of Christ — the merciful love rejected by others, empowering one to sacrifice for even more souls. St. Thérèse took consolation to its logical end by offering to receive from God *all* His "unrequited" love, making herself a vessel of God's merciful love, confirming her victimhood by allowing Christ to love *in her*[530] all those who rejected Him.

In imitation of St. Veronica, Sister St. Pierre likewise offered countless little sacrifices in reparation for the sins of others *as consolations to the injuries of Christ's Face*. For Our Lord revealed to Sister St. Pierre that everything that is done for His glory is to Him a "delightful feast."[531] In addition, Christ taught her to offer again and again *His* merits and love, shrouded in His wounded Countenance, to the Father in reparation for poor sinners. Christ desired that through these selfless actions, she might become more and more a vessel of reparation — even, per Christ's request, taking upon herself the justice intended for France! Christ consequently asked that she immolate herself for France, constantly offering His wounded Countenance to the Father to appease Him.[532] At His request, she housed the unhoused justice of God, becoming a victim of justice, allowing Christ to mediate *in her* God's justice and mercy.[533]

The progression of these respective victimhoods is not unfamiliar in the realm of Catholic spirituality. One might say that man is first to live a Christian life, then become a co-redeemer in Christ, and finally, uniting himself to Christ

---

[530] Thérèse of Lisieux, *Story of a Soul*, 221.
[531] Sister Mary Emmanuel, *Life of Sister Marie*, vii.
[532] Sister Mary St. Peter, *Life of Sister Mary St. Peter*, 290.
[533] Ibid., 159, 199.

and in a spirit of total self-sacrifice, he is to become, in Him, a self-immolating victim.[534] The doctrine of victimhood is as old as the Gospel. It is the very foundation of the preaching of St. Paul, of the early Church Fathers, and of the Church in all ages. In Romans, for example, St. Paul entreats that Christians present their bodies as a living sacrifice, holy, pleasing unto God (12:1).[535] Paul also writes that he no longer lives, but rather Christ lives in him (Gal. 2:20), and refers to himself as "always being given up to death for Jesus' sake, so that the life of Jesus may be manifested in [his] mortal flesh" (2 Cor. 4:11, RSVCE). This annihilation of oneself *of all but that which is of Christ*, this joined victimhood with Christ, allows one to not only love God with one's whole heart and soul but to love one's neighbor as oneself: it epitomizes the great two-part commandment given to man by Christ.

☩ ☩ ☩

Despite both Sister St. Pierre and St. Thérèse exemplifying this united victimhood with Christ, it seems at first glance that they recognized very distinct paths or "ways" to God's mercy: one through reparation to satisfy God's justice to draw His mercy for sinners, and the other through love, expressed as trust in God to draw forth His mercy for sinners. It is true that Sister St. Pierre was chosen as a victim by divine justice to appease God's wrath, ignited by France's primal sins of blasphemy, housing the unhoused justice of God, while St. Thérèse offered herself as a victim not of God's justice but of His merciful love to console God by making "love loved,"[536] housing God's unhoused merciful love. "Manifestly, however, these were one and the same thing. [Christ reveals to Sister St. Pierre that blasphemy wounds His Heart more than any other sin, so] if Divine justice was being outraged by blasphemers and infidels as by no other crime, then also was Divine love spurned by these excesses [of modern times]."[537] God's justice is inextricably tied to His love, after all, for it is perfectly manifested in Christ's Passion, forming Jesus as the prototypical vessel of reparation (and merciful love), the ultimate mediator of God's justice and mercy.

Man is called to imitate this union in offering reparation and consolation to God's justice to draw mercy for sinners in the Holy Face devotion. Work of

---

[534] Plus, *Ideal of Reparation*, 17, 92.
[535] Ibid., 17.
[536] Sister Mary Emmanuel, *Life of Sister Marie*, 2–3.
[537] Scallan, *The Whole World*, 313.

reparation is therefore a pragmatic love of God and love of neighbor: it is consolation — appeasement — of God and mercy for man. In her own way, St. Thérèse followed this atonement, this reparation, to its natural end in her "martyrdom" of love:

> For what answer can there be for God, whose reality filled [St. Thérèse's] life, whom she encountered in the Scriptures, in the figure of the Child in the Crib, and in the Holy Face? What answer but this love, love and love alone? How oppressed Thérèse was by the dark, the terrifying mystery of malice: that man refuses God this love — the sole thing that God asks of him. The bloody, spat-upon face of Christ was the silent, fearful, never-to-be-forgotten embodiment of the response which had in fact been given to Our Lord's appeal, and which was still being given.
>
> "He came to what was His own, and they who were His own gave Him no welcome." There was only one thing to do: to "console" Him.
>
> To comfort Him means: to do [one's] best to compensate for the frightful thing which can no longer be undone; not only to bewail it, but to make up for it by all possible love, devotion, loyalty and even pain, so that He will no longer be able to say that He trod the winepress all alone. It means, finally, if possible, to convert the blasphemers and the blind into lovers and believers. That is atonement: love of God and love of sinners inseparably fused into one white-hot emotion. Thérèse wanted to save souls so that God would no longer be offended and would be loved again; she wanted to love God still more so that His fire might transform her and give her power to save her brothers. Here was the innermost core of the Carmelite vocation. Whoever seriously sets out along this stream surrenders to a vertiginous current which inexorably rushes toward a cataract: complete abandonment. Who can draw the line, saying: thus far and no farther? Whoever wishes for perfect love must at last be carried along into that greatest love which lays down life for friends. Thus, Christ will be followed to the end. Physical martyrdom, a bloody death, is only one form of this fate.[538]

As was true of Sister St. Pierre, love of God and man were united in St. Thérèse's victimhood, corresponding to her desire to atone and console to the point of "martyrdom." Indeed, both endured a non-bloody martyrdom, a victimhood, which was essentially the same.

---

[538] Görres, *Hidden Face*, 264–265.

Housing the unhoused justice of God, per Christ's request, Sister St. Pierre, as a vessel of mediation between God's justice and mercy, gave her whole self to Christ, even her very life, for the salvation of France. Renewing the act of abandonment to Christ that she had received permission from her superiors to make, she offered her life for sinners on Good Friday, 1848. She soon after contracted tuberculosis and died just over three months later on July 8. Besides tuberculosis, she suffered a terrible cancer-like ulcer in her throat. Her superiors believed this was yet one more means of atonement for the sins of blasphemy.

St. Thérèse also died of tuberculosis after offering herself as a sacrificial victim to the merciful love of God on Good Friday, contracting the disease nearly a year later. She arguably suffered more, however, from her dark night of the soul during the same last months of her life, constantly enduring the feelings of loss of faith. She never resisted, however, in offering her every trial and smallest of sacrifices for love of Christ. For her, too, to be a victim (even a victim of love) meant exposing oneself to all anguish, all torment, all bitterness, for as she was fond of saying, "Love lives only on sacrifice." As a vessel containing the unrequited merciful love of God, St. Thérèse offered to the end her extreme suffering for the salvation of blasphemers and nonbelievers.

Both, in their selfless atonement — one primarily through appeal to God's justice and one through appeal to God's mercy — in a very real sense laid down their lives for sinners. Justice and mercy: one relates complementary to the other in the context of God's love — as do the distinct paths to mercy of Sister St. Pierre and St. Thérèse.

2. But Isn't St. Thérèse's Path Understood to "Bypass" Justice?

It is not for our justifications that we present our prayers before thy face, but for the multitude of thy tender mercies.

—Daniel 9:18

One might contend, however, that St. Thérèse had such a preference for mercy that it seems unlikely that she herself would have seen her victimhood as relating complementary to one of justice. To this point, she stated (within a broader context) that she was not attracted to the thought of becoming a victim of justice.[539] Indeed, modern hermeneutics of the saint tout her completely "independent" and "immediate" path of mercy in attaining holiness as "bypassing" justice altogether.[540] St. Thérèse's victimhood, after all, is commonly understood as one of mercy, not justice, based upon love and not fear, a method by which even "little" souls attain great sanctity.[541] Indeed, this way is contrasted by her to that of those, perhaps, "larger" souls who offer themselves as victims of God's justice to stay the punishments reserved for sinners.

Bl. Marie-Eugène of the Child Jesus, O.C.D., renowned for devoting more than forty years to the study of the life and spirituality of St. Thérèse, among others, takes the saint's great espousal for mercy as evidence of her reacting to the prevailing heresy of Jansenism[542] of the time, which upheld an unhealthy, heretical notion of God's justice and victimhood to it, while de-emphasizing free will, espousing predestination, and generally placing an unhealthy emphasis on the importance of personal merit in attaining sanctity. St. Thérèse's purported response to Jansenism is not without evidence,[543] including the fact that the heresy still had some hold in France during her time.

---

[539] Thérèse of Lisieux, *Story of a Soul*, 180.

[540] Michael Gaitley, M.I.C., *33 Days to Merciful Love: A Do-It-Yourself Retreat in Preparation for Consecration to Divine Mercy* (Stockbridge, MA: Marian Press, 2016), 71. "Clearly, St. Thérèse's path is one of mercy and not justice." P. Marie-Eugène, *Under the Torrent*, 35, 25. "The God whom Thérèse discovered was no longer the God who is 'Justice,' so to speak, but the God who is 'Mercy.' She saw everything in the light of Mercy." And "Her confidence in the Mercy which exceeds Justice."

[541] Gaitley, *33 Days to Merciful Love*, 71.

[542] Ibid., 69–70. Father Gaitley holds that St. Thérèse's preference for mercy was a reaction against Jansenism. It was a reaction against those offering themselves as a victim soul to God's justice, whereby they make a "sort of deal with the Lord," such as exchanging the punishment that is due to sinners with the blessings normally received as a faithful religious. This became an unhealthy practice under the heretical influence of Jansenism, which upheld a distorted view of God's justice. NB: This was *not* at all the same as Sister St. Pierre *being chosen by God* as a victim of divine justice. In addition, the Holy Face devotion is making reparation — not by one's own merits but *by offering those infinite merits of Christ Himself in His wounded Holy Face to God the Father*. And, Sister Mary St. Peter, *Life of Sister Mary St. Peter*, 69. Sister St. Pierre would have been well versed on the dangers of Jansenism in that "on several occasions, the religious of this monastery [at Tours] were chosen by their superiors either to defend or to establish sound doctrine in other convents, in which the members had insensibly become imbued with the spirit of heresy [regarding Jansenism]."

[543] Gaitley, *33 Days to Merciful Love*, 69–70. It was likely just after St. Thérèse was read the obituary of a nun who apparently had a distorted notion of her own victimhood to divine justice that Thérèse was inspired to make her offering to merciful love.

> In this period — she was born in 1873 — [there was] a spirituality so different from [today] that it is almost incomprehensible [now].... The concept of God as a figure of Justice developed in the 17th century and continued through the 18th, to the point where the God of Love was almost lost from view. During this period mystics were rare, and suspect.... [Then] in the wake of the Revolution came a sense of sin, perhaps also of guilt, which [additionally] affected all of spirituality.[544]

Thérèse's doctrine of love stood in stark contrast to her milieu — to all that she heard and saw practiced around her.

Evidently in part as a response to Jansenism, then, but certainly also in consequence of her love and insights into spiritual childhood, as inspired by the writings of St. John of the Cross,[545] Thérèse developed the idea that it was not necessary to make heroic offerings of merit in attaining sanctity, like so many saints before her. Instead, she emphasized reliance upon God's mercy rather than personal merit. In light of this spiritual childhood, Thérèse contrasted the "larger" souls (of great saints) to her own, which she consciously desired to be always "weak" and "little."[546] In fact, she insisted that it was her weakness (and not any merit on her part) that made her dare to offer herself as a victim of Christ's love.[547] Thérèse's spiritual childhood is similar to St. John of the Cross's spiritual poverty wherein God pours His love on those who surrender themselves to Him in faith and hope, who are made pure because they are stripped of all else — a sort of ordinary and everyday "mystical asceticism"[548] that leads to humility and confidence in attitude before God. Borrowing from this notion, Thérèse's spirituality largely celebrates the helplessness, the "demerits," of the human soul in imitation of the simplicity and purity of a child.

Whether contrasting her "lack" of merits to the heroic ones of great saints, or her desire to remain "little" before God to the "larger" souls of these great saints, it is possible that St. Thérèse's evident preference for mercy was not so much an aversion to God's justice as it was to "man's." For she resisted the pride she felt

---

[544] P. Marie-Eugène, *Under the Torrent*, 7–8.
[545] P. Marie-Eugène, *I Am a Daughter*, 388–389. "The Saint of Lisieux is truly a daughter of Saint John of the Cross. There is no doubt her doctrine of spiritual childhood rests on the mystical doctor." And Thérèse of Lisieux, *Story of a Soul*, 179. "At the ages of seventeen and eighteen, I had no other spiritual nourishment."
[546] Thérèse of Lisieux, *Story of a Soul*, 208.
[547] P. Marie-Eugène, *I Am a Daughter*, 398.
[548] Ibid., 391.

"nineteenth century asceticism of extraordinary mortifications engendered"[549] as well as the notions that the Eternal Father would on the Day of Judgment look at one's list of merits, so to speak; in opposition, she was determined to not present any merits of her own, *but only those of Our Lord*. She writes: "In the evening of this brief day, I shall appear before You with empty hands, *for I do not ask You, O Lord, to count my works. In Your eyes all our justice is blemished. Therefore, I will robe myself in Your own justice* and receive from Your love the eternal possession of Yourself."[550] She preferred to "let God love [her] as much as He [wanted]..., and it [was] because of this that [she felt that she would] get such a good reception."[551] She did not want to "limit" His love to the "worth" of her merits. Indeed, Marie-Eugène held that Thérèse even saw personal merits as "paltry."[552] Regardless, she certainly de-emphasized the value of merits that consisted in doing or giving much in lieu of loving much.[553] Yet she at the same time cleaved to God's "own justice." It is therefore arguably not God's justice nor the appeasement of justice per se that she wished to bypass—for she even ties God's justice with His love—but rather the way in which appeasement of justice was usually attempted, namely by the offering of one's *own merits*. To this point, she states, "I was thinking about the souls who offer themselves as victims of God's Justice ... to turn away the punishments reserved for sinners, *drawing upon themselves*. This offering seemed great and very generous to me, but I was far from feeling attracted to making it."[554] It seems it was the "drawing upon themselves" for which St. Thérèse had an aversion. She sought to veer people away from the idea of a God who "served as a dispenser of rewards ..., counting up merits, [instead of a God delighting in the honoring of] His mercy,... to lead them, rather, in the way of absolute confidence."[555] Simply put, St. Thérèse espoused God's mercy over *man's* justice.

Though St. Thérèse was clearly inspired to offerings of personal trust, not merit, it does not necessarily follow, then, that she was trying to avert *God's* justice, nor ultimately even victimhood to it. Rather it seems that she saw the consoling of God's mercy as the complement to the appeasing of His justice. For she stated that she admired the generosity and goodness of those (orthodox)

---

[549] P. Marie-Eugène, *Under the Torrent*, 48.
[550] Görres, *Hidden Face*, 269. My emphasis.
[551] P. Marie-Eugène, *Under the Torrent*, 24.
[552] Ibid., 25.
[553] Ibid., 111.
[554] Thérèse of Lisieux, *Story of a Soul*, 180. (My emphasis.)
[555] P. Marie-Eugène, *Under the Torrent*, 26.

souls who offered themselves as victims to justice.[556] And again, she upheld God's justice as being clothed with love, *perhaps even more so than the other perfections*. Thérèse also expressed that she hoped as much in the justice of God as in His mercy in that it is *because God is just that He is merciful*, His justice "taking into account man's weaknesses,"[557] prompting His bestowing of mercy according to man's needs. Her statement that mercy flows from justice would certainly indicate an understanding of the two being complementary. And as previously mentioned, she herself wished to exchange places with unbelievers as a means of atoning for them, seeking to "prevent or make reparation for (even) one single sin against *faith*."[558] This may be interpreted as much an act on her part to satisfy justice as to console mercy (even more by her choice of the word *reparation*, which especially in her time, was associated with appeasing justice). She also joined "love and reparation" as well as referenced "merits" in one of her prayers: "I offer you every beat of my heart and so many acts of love and reparation and I unite them to your infinite merits."[559] Again, use of the words *reparation* and *merits*, especially by Thérèse, seems indicative of fulfilling the demands of justice. Additionally, the saint wrote, "*To satisfy Divine Justice*, perfect victims were necessary [in times past], but the law of Love has succeeded to the law of fear, and Love has chosen me as a holocaust, me, a weak and imperfect creature."[560] This quote validates her preference of love over merits, yet it also confirms that she saw her offerings to merciful love as complementary to those of justice — perhaps, even, as ultimately synonymous with satisfying justice.

Bl. Marie-Eugène notes that the Council of Trent declares mercy as surpassing all merit,[561] which would allow for the St. Thérèse "shortcut" to mercy to in some sense "bypass" or "trump" *merit*. Yet St. Thérèse surely embraced justice *itself* as the complement to mercy, as also declared in the same Council, in which

---

[556] Thérèse of Lisieux, *Story of a Soul*, 180.
[557] Ibid. (My emphasis.)
[558] Ibid., 214. Also, this mirrors Sister St. Pierre's understanding of the intrinsic interconnectedness of the one to the other in explaining that Our Lord wished to establish an "alliance" — a marriage or covenant — between His justice and mercy via the work of reparation.
[559] *Prayers of St. Thérèse*, p. 86.
[560] Ibid., 195. (My emphasis.)
[561] "Decree on Justification," in *The Canons and Decrees of the Council of Trent*, trans. H. J. Schroeder (Charlotte, NC: TAN Books, 1978). NB: I cannot find the exact quote referenced in P. Marie-Eugène, *Under the Torrent*, 23.

the two attributes of God are seen as "corresponding and equal."[562] As such, mercy does not "trump" the justice of God — only that of "man." St. Thérèse is used as an example in the *Catechism of the Catholic Church* as representing the understanding of the saints that the *charity of Christ is the source in man of all his merit*.[563] Thus, the merits of man's good works are gifts of divine goodness.[564] St. Thérèse extends this logically in her offering to merciful love by asking God *to be* her sanctity — that is, she wishes to rely only on *His* merits in attaining holiness.[565] And (as referenced in the previous paragraph), one of her prayers asks Christ to unite her acts of love and reparation to His infinite merits. These are a blurring of the "littleness" of her own offerings of love and trust to mercy with the offerings of merit — God's merit — to justice. This sheds light on her statement that the Holy Face was the "source of all her piety": She did not only mean that the "secrets" of the Holy Face helped her attain holiness, but rather that the merits and love residing in the wounded Countenance of Christ — residing in God — *was* her piety, *her* sanctity!

This understanding is *identical* to that given in the Holy Face devotion for which St. Thérèse had a profound regard. In fact, her purported "sidestepping" of justice would require that she saw her path to mercy as quite distinctive from the framework of the revelations surrounding reparation to the Holy Face in which the necessary appeasement of divine justice is made through an appeal *to the Father's compassion* for the suffering Countenance of His Son. Therein, it is the *merits of Christ Himself* that satiate justice *and provide for mercy*, allowing for an alliance[566] of justice and mercy in the broader context of God's love. Echoing this is the recurring theme of St. Thérèse of the offering to the Father of the "tears" of Christ's wounded Countenance, as she puts it, to draw mercy for sinners.[567] Moreover, the devotion's offering promotes Thérèse's idea of spiritual childhood in that one realizes that his merits and love are nothing to that encased in the suffering Face of the Savior. Like Job's friends, one understands that there is a "face" more

---

[562] "Fifth Petition of the Lord's Prayer: Debts," in *The Catechism of the Council of Trent*, trans. John A. McHugh and Charles J. Callan (1923), 329.
[563] *CCC*, 2011.
[564] Council of Trent: DS 1548. *CCC*, 2009.
[565] Gaitley, *33 Days to Merciful Love*, 85.
[566] Sister Mary St. Peter, *Life of Sister Mary St. Peter*, 158, 199, 287.
[567] *Prayers of St. Thérèse*, 92. One example: "The *Tears* that veil your *divine look* seem to us like *precious Diamonds* which we want to collect to buy the souls of our brothers and sisters with their infinite value."

worthy — more mercy-invoking — than his own in attempting appeasement of God's justice.[568] One becomes totally reliant on the merits of Christ (rather than his own). And per the promises of the devotion, the imprint of the divine likeness is, remarkably, impressed upon the devotee himself. Like St. Thérèse's request of God in her offering to merciful love, this all allows for Christ's sanctity *to become that of the devotee* — allowing for God's sanctity to become his: the making of perfect victimhood to both mercy and justice.

✠ ✠ ✠

Curiously, most post-1950s hagiographies of St. Thérèse rarely mention the love she had for the revelations given to Sister St. Pierre, nor even for Sister St. Pierre herself. Even her constant recourse to the wounded Holy Face in her own later spirituality is sometimes omitted, which is perhaps one reason why her approach to justice and mercy has been interpreted as so binary in recent times. To this point, with few exceptions, references to her almost always truncate her full name, "Thérèse of the Child Jesus and Holy Face," to exclude the "Holy Face."[569] To not consider Thérèse's great regard for Sister St. Pierre and the mystical implications of the Holy Face devotion in the context of framing her own spirituality seems an injustice to St. Thérèse, however, given her own intensely profound devotion to the Holy Face (initially introduced to her through the Holy Face devotion), that which she proclaimed as being *the basis of all her piety*. In fact, it is known that after reading and studying the life of Sister St. Pierre and making it known to her novices, St. Thérèse thereafter *always wore a picture of the Holy Face of Tours as well as a relic of Sister St. Pierre near her heart*.[570] She also always carried a picture of the Holy Face in her breviary and kept one in front of her place in choir for meditation, and during her long illness, she had one pinned to her bed-curtain "and studied it constantly in order to bear her pain."[571] Her coat of arms also included the sorrowful Holy Face.[572] This is not to mention the notable dedication

---

[568] God had requested that Job, with whom He was pleased, offer "his face" (in place of those of his friends) when seeking reparation for their injustice.

[569] References to the Holy Face devotion in the spiritual life of St. Thérèse largely cease after the 1950s. *Prayers of St. Thérèse*, 18. Regarding Thérèse's consecration to the Holy Face: "The importance of which has perhaps not been emphasized enough by Theresian exegetes."

[570] Sister Mary Emmanuel, *Life of Sister Marie*, 9. Also, *Prayers of St. Thérèse*, 89.

[571] Görres, *Hidden Face*, 261.

[572] *Prayers of St. Thérèse*, 97.

to the Holy Face devotion within her parental family[573] (including that of her blood sisters, who also became her sisters in Carmel).[574] Nor is it to mention the almost universal backdrop of the spirituality of the devotion at that time,[575] pervasive especially within French Carmelite monasteries like Lisieux. (The devotion sprang from neighboring Tours and was approved for the whole world by Pope Leo XIII approximately only three years prior to St. Thérèse's entry to Carmel.) It could be argued, regarding the common spirituality within those convents during St. Thérèse's short life, that the context of the Holy Face was such a celebrated "given" as to literally go without saying. (And happily, though it was a devotion centered on the appeasement of justice, it was in stark contrast to Jansenism, for it de-emphasized the offering of personal merits in lieu of those of Christ Himself to invoke the compassion of the Father.) The devotion's popularity at the time even rivaled that of the Sacred Heart.

Additionally, in as much as reparation to the Holy Face was understood as "the most noble and necessary work of the time,"[576] coupled with St. Thérèse's understanding that mercy flows *from* justice,[577] it is not an "option" likely to have

---

[573] Dominicans of the Holy Face of Tours proudly display a photo of the enrollment of the Martin family members in the Archconfraternity of the Holy Face prior to Thérèse's entry to Carmel.

[574] *Prayers of St. Thérèse*, 93–94. "Sister Genevieve ... composed 33 notes 'of Reparation' that the sisters drew by lot on [August 6] during exposition of the Blessed Sacrament in the Oratory; they kept up this custom for some 60 years more.... Marie Agnes of the Holy Face ... was equally very drawn to the Holy Face since her childhood."

[575] As previously discussed, Ven. Dupont, who had wrought over six thousand documented miracles — and many more undocumented — using oil from a lamp burning in front of a Veronica veil relic touched to Veronica's veil in the Vatican, the lance of Longinus, and a true relic of the Cross as well as prayers compatible with the devotion (the official prayers of the Archconfraternity of the Holy Face having not yet been established), brought knowledge of the Holy Face devotion to the whole world. In fact, letters coming from every corner of the world were simply addressed to "The Holy Man of Tours" yet would successfully reach him, such was his — and the devotion's — fame in the late nineteenth century (and especially in France).

[576] Sister Mary St. Peter, *Life of Sister Mary St. Peter*, 311–312. "The Redemption of Christ is the noblest and most sublime Work that has ever been accomplished." And, Ibid. "In our time, the spirit of evil, armed with pride and sensuality, has inflicted on society two wounds of such magnitude as have hitherto been unknown[:] deep-rooted impiety and absolute incredulity..., which corrode all that is most sacred." And, Ibid. "To combat this, Christ demands ... a new work whose object is to repair these crimes of modern society. The Reparation is intimately allied to the great Work of the Redemption and is ... *the most noble* and the most necessary work for our times."

[577] Thérèse of Lisieux, *Letters of St. Thérèse to Her Sister Celine* (1897), https://www.pathsoflove.com/pdf/ThereseLetters.pdf, 29.

been overlooked, much less consciously circumvented, by St. Thérèse. Testimony indicates that upon first entering Carmel, St. Thérèse was immersed in devotion to the Holy Face,[578] such that she undoubtedly understood it to be a most generous grace given by God for the times, *as a most efficacious means to mercy through offerings of consolation* (in imitation of St. Veronica).[579] Moreover, the devotion is intimately allied to — even *an extension of* — the Redemption of Our Lord, as continually renewed in the Most Holy Sacrament of the Altar.[580] In union with the Sacred Heart of Jesus, as offered in the Mass,[581] *the soul unites itself to something infinitely more meritorious and efficacious than itself.* It offers the wounded Face of the most beloved Son — incomparably more pleasing than anything that may be offered of oneself — to the Father, the Godhead, in this "mother of all devotions."[582]

Undoubtedly, St. Thérèse would have at least subconsciously taken into consideration the divine revelations given to Sister St. Pierre in forming her own spirituality in that it "debuted" the veiled beauty in the wounded Holy Face as depicted in Isaiah 53. Many of her prayers and poems clearly draw inspiration from them, for example: the "Canticle to the Holy Face," her "Consecration to the Holy Face," "My Heaven on Earth," "O Hidden God," "I Am the Jesus of Thérèse," "Eternal Father, Since You Have Given Me," and "Make Me Resemble You."[583] Evidenced in these writings is that she embraced the revelations and prayers given to Sister St. Pierre as the *complement* to her own victimhood to merciful love. In fact, the consecration to the Holy Face for members of the archconfraternity (to which Thérèse belonged prior to her entry to Carmel)

---

[578] Sister Mary Emmanuel, *Life of Sister Marie*, 9.
[579] Sister Mary St. Peter, *Life of Sister Mary St. Peter*, 393.
[580] Ibid., 311–312.
[581] Ibid., 153.
[582] Sister St. Pierre, *Life of Sister St. Pierre*, ed. Since the Holy Face devotion is practiced *in union with* the Sacred Heart in the Most Holy Sacrament of the Altar and since it is designed to both appease and console the Godhead, it surpasses other devotions having to do with reparation to various aspects of the sacred humanity (versus divinity) of Christ — e.g., heart, blood, Passion of Christ, etc., while also complementing them. Rev. P. Janvier (Baltimore: John Murphy, 1884), 180. "He made me understand the excellence of the Work of the Reparation, how *it surpassed the various other devotions*, how agreeable it was to God, to the Angels, the Saints, and how salutary to the Church." (My emphasis.)
[583] *Prayers of St. Thérèse*. And *The Poetry of St. Thérèse of Lisieux*, trans. Donald Kinney (Washington, D.C.: ICS Publications, 2020). There are many more examples, especially echoing the promises of the Holy Face devotion, such as God bestowing mercy and imprinting His divine likeness in return for acts of consolation, etc.

opens with a resolution to *join with the merciful love with which Christ's Holy Face is animated toward poor sinners*, to repair the outrages that the crimes of the present day inflict upon His Face. There is a seamlessness of the offerings of consolation (reparation) to the Holy Face to that of merciful love, as evidenced by Thérèse asking those companions who had already offered themselves to merciful love in 1895 to solemnly consecrate themselves to the "Adorable Face of Jesus" in 1896 "as if one consecration prolonged the other."[584] Now-mostly-forgotten assessments of the influence of Sister St. Pierre upon St. Thérèse assert that St. Thérèse is the instrument chosen by God to continue and to spread the mission of Sister St. Pierre,[585] such that the distinct paths to mercy of Sister St. Pierre and St. Thérèse are arguably not only complementary but synergistic — better together than are the sum of their parts. As evidence, each practiced essential elements of both paths as a unified whole, even having an apparently greater fondness for the "other's" devotion.

Though Sister St. Pierre lived and breathed reparation to the Holy Face, she might well have added to her name "of the Infant Jesus" such was her love for Christ under this devotion.[586] In fact, when the time came for her to fulfill the act of total abandonment that Christ had requested of her since her first entering Carmel, she formulated one that was a consecration to the Child Jesus (rather than any other aspect of Christ's sacred humanity). Even near death, her devotion to the Infant Jesus remained her favorite: "She felt that the stable of Bethlehem was ever the home of her soul."[587] This is reflected in the life of Sister St. Pierre in which she perfectly lived the spiritual childhood so luminously taught by her successor, St. Thérèse. Moreover, the quality of her characteristic virtues were those of the holy infancy of Christ — simplicity, innocence, candor, humility, childlike docility, obedience, and gracious gaiety.[588] According to Abbé Botrel, who knew Sister St. Pierre, "She was always simple and naive like a little child toward her superiors, always humble toward all and of a charity which covers everything."[589] As mentioned in chapter 3, writing before her death in 1848, and twenty-five years before the birth of St. Thérèse, Botrel could not have in hindsight questioned "that in

---

[584] *Prayers of St. Thérèse*, 94.
[585] Sister Mary Emmanuel, *Life of Sister Marie*, 2.
[586] Ibid., 4.
[587] Sister Mary St. Peter, *Life of Sister Mary St. Peter*, 399.
[588] Sister Mary Emmanuel, *Life of Sister Marie*, 2.
[589] Louis Van den Bossche, *The Message of Sister Mary of St. Peter*, trans. Mary G. Durham (France: Carmel of Tours, 1953), 43.

resuming the simple way in which Sister Saint Pierre had walked, he was condensing in a few words the doctrine of the way of childhood.... [It was the way] Theresa of the Child Jesus [would one day show], 'a simple way like that of a little child carried in arms,' and who yet [knew] how to recognize the merciful grace when God lets him fall."[590] Moreover, Sister St. Pierre understood that the offering of Christ's merits and love to the Father, rather than her own, in reparation for current offenses against the first three commandments, was a guarantee that she would become more childlike, poorer in spirit. For it is an act of meekness to do so (inherently acknowledging that one's own merits are as nothing to Christ's). And according to the promises attached to the devotion, whoever makes this reparation performs the office of the pious Veronica, and Christ, in turn, reproduces His image in them, making them as beautiful as when they "came forth from the baptismal font,"[591] surely restoring to them again the singular longing for and confidence in God, which is the very state of spiritual childhood. As discussed in detail in chapter 3, she further exemplified the Little Way of her successor, St. Thérèse, in that she was a master at making constant small acts of sacrifice throughout her days and months in honor of the Child Jesus and in consolation of the Holy Face. Hers was a seemingly dizzying regimen of reflecting on the various events of Christ's life, holding a special meditation on the infancy of Christ, rotating each hour and day and month in dedication of different aspects of His sacred humanity, joining the reflections with her sacrifices. She was simply motivated by love, always wishing to honor and console Our Lord. She wrote that God had reduced her soul to the state of a *little child* yet that Christ desired for her to become even more childlike as she approached death.[592] She spent the final time remaining to her on earth in a very close union, an identification with the Child Jesus on His Mother's breast, practicing virtues of His earliest infancy.[593]

Conversely, St. Thérèse is known throughout the world as the champion of littleness, of spiritual childhood, yet her blood sister and superior in Carmel, Sister Agnes of Jesus, stated that however tender was the devotion St. Thérèse had for the Child Jesus, it could not be compared to the devotion she had for the Holy Face.[594] During her entire hidden life at Carmel, St. Thérèse constantly applied

---

[590] Ibid., 42–43.
[591] Sister Mary St. Peter, *Life of Sister Mary St. Peter*, 254, 291.
[592] Sister Mary Emmanuel, *Life of Sister Marie*, 5.
[593] Ibid.
[594] Ibid., 10.

herself to penetrate the secrets contained in the wounded Face of Christ, pondering His unspeakable mental anguish. As mentioned, St. Thérèse composed a consecration to the Holy Face (rather than to the Infant Jesus) for her novices, which included inspirations from the Litanies of the Holy Face, written by Sister St. Pierre.[595] And in one of St. Thérèse's prayers to the Eternal Father, since He has given to her for her inheritance the adorable Face of His Divine Son, she offers that Face to Him and begs Him, in exchange for this coin of infinite value, to forget the ingratitude of souls dedicated to Him and to pardon all poor sinners.[596] As previously discussed, another asks that God imprint the image of His Holy Face upon her, making her holy.[597] These prayers are an almost word-for-word quotation of some of the prayers and revelations given to Sister St. Pierre and are no less than the very essence of the Holy Face devotion. As stated, from the time of first learning the secrets hidden in the wounded Face of Christ, the wounded Countenance as depicted in Isaiah 53 became, as St. Thérèse herself states, "the source of all her piety."[598] Mother Agnes attested that devotion to the suffering Face of Our Savior was *the* leading attraction of St. Thérèse, and her sister Celine states that the Holy Face of Our Lord was Thérèse's "Book of Imitation of Christ," from which she drew her science of love.[599]

☩ ☩ ☩

In conclusion, St. Thérèse saw divine justice as being clothed with love, even more so than God's other perfections, but since her concept of spiritual childhood was not consistent with offerings of her own merits to justice, she made instead gifts to God's mercy of her trust in His goodness. Still, among other instances, she blurred the two offerings of merit and trust in clinging happily to the sanctity *of God* — His merits, rather than her own — in attaining holiness, as expressed in her offering to merciful love. Related is her statement of the Holy Face being the source of all her piety, surely an indication in part that she had in fact embraced the merits and love encased in the Holy Face of Christ as providing for her own sanctity, to in turn be offered for her brethren. This was first requested by Christ of Sister St. Pierre in making reparation to the Father — that the faithful should offer not their own merits

---

[595] *Prayers of St. Thérèse*, 96.
[596] "Eternal Father, Since You Have Given Me." Ibid., 103.
[597] "My Heaven on Earth," in *Poetry of St. Thérèse*, 110.
[598] P. Marie-Eugène, *I Am a Daughter*, 436.
[599] Sister Mary Emmanuel, *Life of Sister Marie*, 11.

but those of Christ to the Father in atoning for modern sins against the first three commandments, "assuming" Christ's sanctity. St. Thérèse was a student and devotee of the Holy Face par excellence. She herself espoused divine justice as the source of mercy and even stated that love had chosen her weakness *to satisfy justice*. The sublime dynamic in which the appeasement of divine justice and the consoling of mercy — corresponding to the offerings of reparation and trust — relate interdependently was manifest in her prayers and writings. It seems far more likely that St. Thérèse was not so much "bypassing" justice on her path to merciful love as she was *embracing* it. For she offered the faithful, who had perhaps been steeped in the errors of Jansenism (as well as modern man who basically totally rejects God's attribute of justice), an understanding of the "total package" regarding God's love, as revealed to Sister St. Pierre, in which *both* justice and mercy are "desirable" perfections of the Almighty. Indeed, for Sister St. Pierre and St. Thérèse, appeasement of God's justice was synonymous with consoling His merciful love, the complementary nature of their spiritualities becoming even more evident in their mutual understanding of the "secrets" of the Holy Face.

3. Veiled Treasures of the Suffering Face of the Savior

Lord, hide us in the secret of Your Face!
Your beauty, which you know how to veil, discloses for me all its mystery.

— *St. Thérèse*

The "secrets" of the suffering Face of Christ revealed to Sister St. Pierre in the revelations surrounding the Holy Face devotion and those that St. Thérèse discovered, particularly within the depths of her own sorrow, not only correspond with one another but ultimately serve to cap essential insights of the great Carmelite mystical tradition. For the essence of Carmelite spirituality is to seek and experience God, not for any self-seeking gain, but rather to love Him, to think of and hope in Him alone (the contemplative life, however, always overflowing into the active care of souls). And the "veiled treasures" of the Holy Face are ultimately a means of assistance in this goal of contemplating God, ever building upon total dependence on Him and purity of heart. They include the wounded Holy Face as

1. fulcrum of merciful love;
2. "the greatest source of grace second to the sacraments";

3. a means to spiritual childhood;

4. the most distinguished feature of Christ's sacred humanity in which to "bring with" oneself on the way to union with God;

5. efficacious object of contemplation, the return gaze of Christ, and having the power to imprint its divine likeness upon the souls of men.

Each is a tool in striving toward living a truly divine life by embracing the suffering Savior as mediator and guide (as well as in Our Lady), such that they promote the raison d'être of Carmel: union with God.

The Holy Face as Fulcrum of Merciful Love

O Jesus, who, in Thy cruel Passion didst become the "reproach of men and the Man of Sorrows," I worship Thy divine Face. Once it shone with the beauty and sweetness of the Divinity; but now, for my sake, it is become as "the face of a leper." Yet, in that disfigured Countenance, I recognize Thy infinite love, and I am consumed with the desire of making Thee loved by all mankind. The tears that flowed so abundantly from Thy Eyes are to me as precious pearls that I delight to gather, that with their worth I may ransom the souls of poor sinners. O Jesus, whose Face is the sole beauty that ravishes my heart, I may not see here below the sweetness of Thy glance, nor feel the ineffable tenderness of Thy kiss, I bow to Thy Will — but I pray Thee to imprint in me Thy divine likeness, and I implore Thee so to inflame me with Thy love, that it may quickly consume me, and that I may soon reach the vision of Thy glorious Face in heaven. Amen.

— St. Thérèse's Consecration to the Holy Face

Suffering is at the core of the Christian Faith, championed by the Man of Sorrows in His Redemption. Poetry of St. John of the Cross movingly describes Christ in His redemptive act as the Shepherd who "spread His arms.... His heart an open wound with love."[600] Through His selfless sacrifice to save sinners, Christ revealed that *suffering is love*. Understanding and poignantly living this truth, St. Thérèse was fond of saying that love lives only on sacrifice. Indeed, her concept

---

[600] Paul-Marie, *Carmelite Spirituality in the Teresian Tradition*, trans. Kathryn Sullivan (Washington, D.C.: ICS Publications, 1998), 47.

of suffering progressed from seeing it as an inescapable facet of life, to a redemptive force to be used on behalf of sinners, and finally, as *the way* of loving.[601] She writes in a letter to Celine, "Let us not believe we can love without suffering, without suffering much."[602] (That is, one may suffer without loving, but one may not love without suffering.) The image she held of God as Father in fact became overshadowed by God as the Man of Sorrows, "His Face [being] as though hidden" (Isa. 53:3).[603] And she greatly preferred this image of Him. Its hidden beauty delighted her and made her joyously determined to return His love with love, to embrace suffering for love of Christ and neighbor. She writes, "What a mystery! If one sigh can save a soul, what can sufferings like ours not do? Let us refuse Jesus nothing."[604] For Thérèse, "suffering was a way of being like Jesus, mirroring His sorrowful Face, and especially a way of loving Him;"[605] it was also a way to remain "hidden," like Him. She writes, "I too want to hide my face. I want my beloved alone to see it, that He be the only one to count my tears."[606] She felt very strongly that it was through these tears of suffering that Jesus wanted her to save souls.[607] As such, suffering was central to her understanding of merciful love; it was an offering of love she could give Christ while utilizing it as a means of "atonement" for sinners. Giving and receiving Christ's love in place of sinners, it was a way to love Love itself, as well as her neighbor, a goal in Carmel described as the "double and single movement of love."[608]

As Sister St. Pierre before her, St. Thérèse recognized that the *wounded* Holy Face of Christ as preserved on Veronica's veil is nothing if not a fulcrum of merciful love: indeed, it is the *ultimate manifestation of merciful love*, for it is the very figure, mirror, and image of the Divine Trinity itself,[609] as well as the symbol of Christ's Redemption. As previously mentioned, the Veronica's veil relic image attached to the devotion is a miracle twice over commemorating the mercy shown by Veronica to mercy itself, first as a miraculous image left by Christ on

---

[601] Vincent O'Hara, "'His Face Was as Though Hidden': St. Thérèse's Understanding of Suffering," *Mount Carmel* 48, no. 4 (January–March 2001): 25–33.
[602] *Letters of St. Thérèse of Lisieux, General Correspondence*, 2 vols., trans. John Clarke (Washington, D.C.: ICS Publications, 1988), 89.
[603] O'Hara, "His Face," 25–33.
[604] *Letters of St. Thérèse*, 85.
[605] O'Hara, "His Face," 25–33.
[606] *Letters of St. Thérèse*, 137.
[607] Thérèse of Lisieux, *Story of a Soul*, 79.
[608] Paul-Marie, *Carmelite Spirituality*, 36.
[609] Thérèse of Lisieux, *Story of a Soul*, 244.

the road to Calvary, then as the object of the "Miracle of the Vatican" in which the veil became inexplicably "enlivened."[610] (It was also integral in the thousands of miracles performed at the hands of Ven. Dupont.) Veronica's veil is consequently a testament to merciful love given and received.

As discussed earlier, this image of the wounded Face of Christ was very precious to St. Thérèse; she always kept one near her heart, in her breviary, and pinned to her bed-curtains during her last illness. And her later spirituality was entirely based upon it (as representing the Man of Sorrows in Isaiah 53). St. Thérèse wrote to Celine, "I send you a picture of the Holy Face. The subject well suits the little sister of my soul. Oh, let her be another Veronica, let her wipe away the blood and the Tears of Jesus, her One Beloved, let her give Him souls!"[611] This is an echo of the words of Our Lord to Sister St. Pierre — "I seek Veronicas to worship My Holy Face, which has few adorers"[612] — and the promise Christ made that making reparation to His Face (which is a consolation to Him) would draw graces for the conversion of the masses. St. Thérèse composed a consecration to the Holy Face that states that under the disfigured features of Christ's wounded Face, she recognizes His infinite love and is consumed with the desire to love Him and make Him loved by men.[613] For St. Thérèse had

> meditated upon the Mystery of God's demanding men to love Him — and men's rejections of Him ... [and wondered,] "Suppose a human soul opened itself like a vessel, no, like an abyss, and offered to receive the disdained love of God? Suppose a mortal heart offered a shelter to the unhoused love of God in this world? Would that not be one response of

---

[610] As detailed in earlier parts of the book, Ven. Leo Dupont is known for his profound devotion to the Holy Face. It was at his hands that thirty years of the Church's greatest miracle working were manifested. The miracles were effected through the prayers of the devotion and oil from a lamp burning in front of a Holy Face image, which had been touched to Veronica's veil in the Vatican. This original veil had become miraculously "enlivened" for three hours during a Christmas octave exposition in 1849. The Holy Face image linked to the devotion is from a hand-drawn copy of this "Miracle of the Vatican." This comprises the second miracle; the first, as according to Catholic tradition, is the miraculous image left by Christ on Veronica's veil, after she sought to console Him during His Passion.

[611] Sister Mary Emmanuel, *Life of Sister Marie*, 11.

[612] Sister Mary Emmanuel, *Life of Sister Marie*, 11.

[613] Thérèse of Lisieux, "Prayers of St. Thérèse to the Holy Face of Jesus," Our Catholic Prayers, accessed Dec. 4, 2019, https://www.ourcatholicprayers.com/st-therese-holy-face-prayers.html.

the kind God sought in souls?" To be sure, the one who submitted to the wild lightnings of divine love, yielded fearlessly and defenselessly to them, would be destroyed by them — she realized this at once. What heart could withstand the onslaught of such an excess of love?[614]

The love "which gives itself freely and to which she surrendered herself without reserve was the outstanding characteristic of the saint, the special mark of her grace and mission in the Church."[615] Indeed, love consumed her in illness and the dark night of the soul. Wanting only to console and please Christ suffering, to let Him love as He wished,[616] she had conceived of becoming a "martyr" of this onslaught of love, a victim to merciful love. And she poured this love of God onto others.

Desiring love of man in the form of reparation, to console His renewed wounds of blasphemy in this era, to soothe Love, which was spurned by the distained love of blasphemers, Christ formed Sister St. Pierre into a victim of justice. She became a vessel to receive the justice meant for these sinners, in which it was turned to mercy for them — wherein Christ could perform His office of mediation between God's justice and mercy.[617] At Christ's request, Sister St. Pierre housed the unhoused justice of God in sacrificial imitation of the merciful love of Christ crucified. As victims, both Carmelite hearts became "like unto Christ," annihilated into His Heart, destroyed but for that which was Him, becoming themselves vessels of reparation and love — merciful love.

The Holy Face as the "Greatest Source of Grace Second to the Sacraments"

Your Face is my only wealth. I ask for nothing more. Hiding myself in it unceasingly, I will resemble You, Jesus.... Leave in me the Divine Impress of Your Features filled with sweetness, and soon I'll become holy. I shall draw hearts to You.

— *St. Thérèse of Lisieux*

This *selfless* giving and receiving of merciful love, performed, first, for love of God and, second, for love of neighbor, utilizing the wounded Countenance of

---

[614] Görres, *Hidden Face*, 265–266.
[615] P. Marie-Eugène, *Under the Torrent*, xxix.
[616] Ibid., 25.
[617] Sister Mary St. Peter, *Life of Sister Mary St. Peter*, 199.

Christ as a most efficacious offering of reparation to the Father, comprises, according to revelations given by Him to Sister St. Pierre, the "greatest source of grace second to the Sacraments."[618] The wounded Face of Christ, "containing," as it were, the sufferings of the Savior, pleases the Father immeasurably precisely because it is the offering of Christ's love (in that love is synonymous with suffering) — His being the ultimate. Though a God-centered offering, in return for this giving of the love of the Son to the Father in reparation for modern sins against the rights of God, *torrents of graces* are poured forth for the conversion of sinners, as was revealed to Sister St. Pierre. And great grace is reserved for devotees, as well. A central theme in this book is that, according to the care one takes in soothing Christ's Countenance, the devotee, like Veronica, receives an imprint of the divine likeness — only upon his immortal soul (rather than upon the veil).[619] Thus, in return for the selfless cooperation of man with the power of God (as residing in Christ's wounded Face), God bestows graces upon the multitudes[620] as well as those devoted to Him in this way.

The offering of the Holy Face in reparation is designed to be *the most* efficacious way to extend God love, as well as to expect love in return, save participation in the "source and summit of Christian Faith," the Holy Sacrifice of the Mass, *of which this cooperation between God and man*, however, *is an extension*.[621] It is so efficacious because Christ's Face — His merits, His love — is infinitely more pleasing to the Father than man's and, moreover, is offered to the Father as a *complement* to the offering of the Sacred Heart in the Most Holy Sacrament of the Altar. This act of adoration and love, in fact, is only properly made *through the Sacred Heart* (in that only Christ, the God-Man, is entirely holy, thereby being made singularly capable of truly glorifying and praising the Name of the Father).[622] Consequently, man appropriately offers this reparation of love *in* Christ, as He is the head and the faithful are the Mystical Body. (It mirrors the offering of the priest on behalf of the faithful *of God to God* in the Holy Sacrifice of the Mass.) And offering reparation in union with the Sacred

---

[618] Ibid., 246–247.
[619] Ibid., 254.
[620] Ibid., 293.
[621] Ibid., 254.
[622] Ibid., 304. See also Dietrich von Hildebrand, "The True Meaning of Sabbath Worship," in *Liturgy and Personality* (Steubenville, OH: Hildebrand Project, 2016).

Heart not only acts as *its complement*,[623] but it affords the Sacred Heart, according to Christ Himself, *its greatest consolation.*[624]

As extending the union of her whole being with Christ in Holy Communion, Sister St. Pierre's practice after receiving Holy Communion reflects man's proper mindset in also joining in Him regarding this reparatory work: as mentioned previously, she "annihilated" herself in the Sacred Heart so that Christ could perform in her "the office of mediator between God and man."[625] (Christ offered Sister St. Pierre a practical means of "exchanging" her heart with His: "Prepare your soul by recollection; purify it by contrition; then fill it with God.")[626] By consciously sacrificing all but that which was Christ in her, assuming humility and total trust and confidence in Christ, she made herself, in Christ, a premier vessel of reparation — and love.

Indeed, though the Holy Face devotion is centered on reparation, it is ultimately an offering of compassion and love. Our Lord related to Sister St. Pierre that He sought souls to repair the outrages inflicted on Him and to heal His wounds by applying to them "the wine of compassion and the oil of charity [through the reparatory work]."[627] (Yet consolation and compassion and charity toward Christ are surely the very hallmarks of victimhood to merciful love.) In reciprocity, Christ related that if souls dedicated themselves to this exercise of reparation, He would bestow upon them "*a kiss of love*, which would be *a pledge of the eternal union.*"[628] Our Lord appears to indicate that reparation to the Holy Face is *above all* an act of profound love, an act of the heart, for which He is prepared to return to the generous soul a most tender and lavish devotion, *a cascading of grace* and love.

St. Thérèse also understood the powerful grace "hidden" in the wounded Face of Christ to be drawn as mercy for sinners by offering Him consolation. In her consecration to the Holy Face, composed for herself, Sister Geneviève, and Sister Marie of the Trinity, she writes:

---

[623] Sister Mary St. Peter, *Life of Sister Mary St. Peter*, 121.
[624] Ibid., 261, 263, 264, 228. It is the greatest because it is a consolation to the Godhead (versus the humanity of Christ or Mary), and the reparation glorifies the holy name of God the Father.
[625] Ibid., 158.
[626] Ibid., 175.
[627] Ibid., 260.
[628] Ibid.

> Our souls understand Your language of *love*; we want to dry Your *gentle Face* and to console You for the forgetfulness of the wicked.... *O Face* more beautiful than the lilies and roses of springtime! You are not hidden from our eyes.... The *Tears* that veil Your *divine look* seem to us like *precious Diamonds* which we want to collect to buy the souls of our brothers and sisters with their infinite value.[629]

St. Thérèse lived this powerful exchange, consolation for God and merciful grace for sinners, within the mysterious depths of her suffering and in every detail of her life. "Thérèse's life thus unfolded as a growing discovery of this Mercy, given her in the midst of the anguish characteristic of great souls such as Saint John of the Cross, commissioned by God through the centuries to bring a message of renewal to the Church and the world."[630] And allowing herself to be consumed in this merciful love, she exemplified the very *heart* of reparation as requested in the Holy Face devotion — fittingly exhibiting an eminently Carmelite character for its God-centeredness and zeal for the conversion of sinners, made possible through this "the greatest grace second to the sacraments."

The Holy Face as A Means to Spiritual Childhood

> *Hope in God, for I will still give praise to him: the salvation of my countenance, and my God.*
>
> — Psalm 42:6

The Little Way, the "way of spiritual childhood" of St. Thérèse, is a summary of her doctrine of perfection, containing all the essential features of "imitation of the childhood of Christ."[631] It requires total dependence upon God:

> The soul that practices Spiritual Childhood leans upon God, as children do on their parents. All is from God, its loving Father, nothing from self. Love is expressed by humility and boundless childlike confidence. The soul recognizes to the full its own incapacity of all good, its unworthiness of all grace, but just because of its own helplessness, it expects all from God, it does not try to be good or great or strong, of

---

[629] *Prayers of St. Thérèse*, 92.
[630] P. Marie-Eugène, *Under the Torrent*, 3.
[631] Görres, *Hidden Face*, 259.

itself.... The truly loving soul is God's own child. She teaches all how this can be done in the simplest details of life, in everyday things within the reach of all.[632]

In the Little Way, it is important to recognize, through spiritual childhood, the darkness of one's littleness and brokenness, which is the object of God's mercy. If one is poor in spirit, without desires or virtues, he is more suitable for the merciful love of God.[633] Moreover, one needs to trust in God's promise of mercy, His merciful love, precisely because he is childlike — imperfect, weak, and sinful; if one is so helpless, he has only recourse to God.[634] St. Thérèse is often quoted as comparing the arms of Jesus to an elevator by which she would ascend to Heaven, such that it was not necessary for her to grow "larger," but rather that she should remain "small" (so as to remain in need of Christ's assistance). This amounts to a theological understanding that to be sanctified, one need only "correspond to grace with perfect docility ... the ideal of this correspondence [being] the way of spiritual infancy."[635] In spiritual childhood, one has sole recourse in divine fatherhood.

Yet this is not to be confused with inactivity or a complacent mediocrity; rather, taking on the spiritual simplicity of a child requires a decided fortitude, a sort of smiling, everyday asceticism, gleaned from mortification and purity of heart that prepare for the spiritual poverty that God Himself works in the soul. As St. Paul says, "Tribulation works out endurance, and endurance tried virtue, and tried virtue hope. And hope does not disappoint, because the charity of God is poured forth in our hearts by the Holy Spirit who had been given to us."[636] Virtues still need to be tried, and love is shown by acts, but one attributes all goodness in himself to God having placed these attributes upon him, to be used when necessary (though they remain God's). One should not worry or be unsettled, therefore, for God is directing all. It is a receptiveness of God's love by trusting in Him completely. Self-sufficiency and pride are the antithesis of spiritual childhood.

---

[632] Sister Mary Emmanuel, *Life of Sister Marie*, 5.
[633] Gaitley, *33 Days to Merciful Love*, 118.
[634] Ibid., 119.
[635] Raymond de Thomas de Saint-Laurent, *St. Thérèse of the Child Jesus* (Spring Grove, PA: The American Society for the Defense of Tradition, Family, and Property, 2018), 32.
[636] Rom. 5:3–5, in P. Marie-Eugène, *I Am a Daughter*, 387.

The practice of spiritual childhood, the practice of abandonment and trust, then, requires spiritual rigor, forming a disposition of the heart that is quite heroic. Abandonment is a disposal that surrenders to God completely. If one is without desires or virtues of his own, he will have more confidence in a God who loves him. Rather than having recourse to oneself or another, hope is in God alone — and especially in His mercy. "These virtues only reach their perfection in the complementary disposition of spiritual poverty,"[637] where one achieves detachment from all that is not God. According to St. John of the Cross, whose teaching became that of St. Thérèse,[638] just as one "clothes a poor man if one sees him naked, just so God clothes with His purity, with His joy and His love the soul that is stripped of its desires and is utterly indifferent to its own will."[639] He held that hope is purified through this poverty. Spiritual poverty became the most precious treasure of St. Thérèse, wishing only to please God, wishing to be oriented only toward God, wishing to hope only in God: it was a way of giving God joy, allowing Him in return to love as He wished. Only through absolute poverty — a "nothingness," according to St. John of the Cross — can one achieve a transforming union with God, the "light" of God's love and of one's own poverty in constant play.[640] She expressed this hope in God alone through the eyes of a child with "simplicity and depth: qualities of the great masters, [such that] through them little Thérèse enters fully into the family of great spiritual masters of all time."[641]

This mindset of littleness and poverty is also inherent in the spirituality underlying devotion to the Holy Face. What could be a greater testament to one's imperfect, weak, and sinful nature — of one's spiritual infancy — than the acknowledgment, in confident humility, that one's own merits and love are as nothing compared to the offering of Christ's to the Father? This is the "way" of reparation to the Holy Face. Another central theme of this book is the sure bet, born of trust and meekness, that, as Job's face was more pleasing to God than those of his friends, Christ's face is infinitely more pleasing to the Father than man's. Like St. Thérèse, one is assured that God will reward according to His own works, rather than his own. By acknowledging one's

---

[637] P. Marie-Eugène, *Under the Torrent*, 112.
[638] Ibid., 94, 113.
[639] P. Marie-Eugène, *I Am a Daughter*, 387.
[640] P. Marie-Eugène, *Under the Torrent*, 27.
[641] Ibid., 101.

unworthiness before God in this way, one exemplifies the object of the first three commandments, proper fear of the Lord. It is a most efficacious way to littleness, of being poor in spirit, for it is by default confidence in God and an admission of profound humility, a "nothingness," for which one may expect in return the "fullness" of limitless mercy for oneself and others, as promised in the Holy Face devotion, an immense grace tailored for these times by God.

Moreover, spirituality of the Holy Face devotion follows the directives of St. Thérèse when she says:

> One must do all in one's power, give without counting, constantly renounce oneself, in a word prove one's love by all the works in one's power. But in truth, since that is very little, it is urgent to put one's confidence in Him who alone sanctifies the works, and to confess oneself to be a useless servant.[642]

Like St. Thérèse, the devotee understands both his helplessness in making reparation to draw graces for sinners and his need to put forth selfless effort to entreat God's intervention. While the devotee is responsible for initiating the process, he is *assuming* the merits of love of Christ, transferring, so to speak, the sanctity of Christ onto oneself, such that as St. Thérèse proposes, one has no merits or virtues of his own, only those of God, allowing one to become united with Him. With St. Thérèse, one can say, "I under[stand] what real glory [is]. He whose Kingdom is not of this world showed me that true wisdom consists in 'desiring to be unknown and counted as nothing,' in 'placing one's joy in the contempt of self' Ah! I desire that, like the Face of Jesus, 'my face would be truly hidden, that no one on earth would know me.'"[643] It requires a spiritual rigor of both complete surrender to God in the desire to only please Him and the additionally selfless effort of making atonement for another. The Holy Face devotion, which makes accessible the treasures veiled in the Face of Christ, is another "little way," to spiritual poverty. For like the spiritual childhood of St. Thérèse, the devotion promotes a "littleness" that is transformed into profound spiritual strength: the strength, the sanctity, of God.

---

[642] P. Marie-Eugène, *I Am a Daughter*, 409.
[643] P. Marie-Eugène, *Under the Torrent*, 136.

St. Thérèse lived this strength as well as deep spiritual experience,[644] despite her statement that "she never had any special revelations about anything"[645] and her description of her spiritual life as the gloom of "a subterranean passage where it is neither cold or hot, where the sun does not shine, and in which the rain or the wind does not exist."[646] For she was "pierced" by the "wound of Love" following her oblation to merciful love in which she submitted to "the transformation of Love in its overflowing fullness." (This is only known to the world through a chance conversation with Mother Agnes, which shows how little Thérèse cared for extraordinary graces.)[647] On the other side of the spectrum of mystical experience, she endured the "interior drama of Gethsemane and Calvary, a fight to the death between Love and sin's hatred."[648] Regardless, she is remembered more for her profound obedience and discipline, rather than for any extraordinary spiritual experiences. This was shown in her very ordinary prayer and penances, which she referred to as "flowers" of small daily sacrifices.

It seems that St. Thérèse herself would have wished to be considered extraordinary "in love alone," though this "ordinary" St. Thérèse is now a saint and Doctor of the Church,[649] as well as co-patron saint of missionaries in recognition of her spreading God's mercy to the whole world through prayer.[650] (St. Thérèse never left the convent in Lisieux, yet paradoxically, she became a missionary to the world via the millions of copies read of her *Story of a Soul*.) The "little flowers" that St. Thérèse espoused consisted not necessarily in great actions, but rather in "simple surrender and gratitude."[651] For love that desires to give itself to man in an all-consuming fashion asks in return only confidence and abandonment. These qualities also promote true humility before God, proper fear of the Lord: the very goal of making reparation for offenses against the Godhead in the

---

[644] Raymond de Thomas, *St. Thérèse*, 26. "It is necessary to vindicate St. Thérèse in face of certain fumbling admirers who, under the mistaken pretext of making her more 'accessible,' minimize the gifts she received."
[645] Sister Mary Emmanuel, *Life of Sister Marie*, 4.
[646] P. Marie-Eugène, *Under the Torrent*, 137.
[647] Ibid., 138. This is how it was learned that she had experienced what St. Teresa of Avila called lights of the spirit.
[648] Ibid., 107.
[649] St. Thérèse (1873–1897) was canonized in 1925 and declared Doctor of the Church in 1997.
[650] St. Thérèse was declared patroness of missionaries by Pope Pius XI in 1927.
[651] Gaitley, *33 Days to Merciful Love*, 40.

Holy Face devotion. God desires "simple surrender in a faith and hope that are pure because they are stripped of all else,"[652] a spiritual poverty that is attainable by all and within the duties of ordinary life, in all walks of life, yet produces "the highest mystical life [which] can be lived in any setting and in all situations, beneath the veil which simplicity casts over its riches"[653] — a simplicity creating an attitude of the soul, always poor and without strength, of one truly poor in spirit, in which it is not necessary to strive for valiant deeds but rather to be hidden, like Christ veiled by His wounded Face.

The Holy Face as the Most Distinguished Feature of Christ's Sacred Humanity to "Bring with" Oneself on the Way to Union with God

According to Bl. Marie-Eugène, there is a central theme running through the life of St. Thérèse: to live in union with God. Yet this is to be done "not only from the contemplative point of view but also from that of our state in life, which she calls 'our divine duty.'" He also notes the theme of charity, with all the purifications it implies, in that it is the virtue of God, who is love.[654] These are certainly the themes of the Holy Face devotion as well. In charity and as part of one's divine duty, one is called to love God, to console Him through acts of reparation and to perform these acts so that God, in His delightful return, pours graces for the conversion of sinners. He implores this of the faithful,[655] yet rewards the devotee for his selflessness. Per the promises of Our Lord for devotion to His Holy Face, the divine likeness is stamped upon him, surely helping him progress toward spiritual union. But there is another "help," another "secret" of the wounded Countenance that aids in this union, as well: the Holy Face, as the most distinguished feature of Christ's sacred humanity, is most effective to "take with one" on the way to union with God.

The deeply contemplative spirituality of the great reformer of the Carmelite Order, St. Teresa of Avila, is essentially Christocentric. Along with Mary as Mediatrix and Mother of Grace, Jesus acts as Mediator at all phases of the spiritual life, according to St. Teresa, such that for her, prayer is unthinkable without

---

[652] P. Marie-Eugène, *I Am a Daughter*, 391.
[653] P. Marie-Eugène, *Under the Torrent*, 145. And P. Marie-Eugène, *I Am a Daughter*, 405.
[654] P. Marie-Eugène, *Under the Torrent*, 57.
[655] Christ warned, "Woe to those [cities] that do not make reparation" and revealed to Sister St. Pierre that she would be held accountable for not making use of this means of helping her brethren who were being cast into Hell.

doing so with Christ. "The prayer of recollection, the Teresian prayer par excellence, is actually nothing else than a collecting of the faculties in the interior of the soul, there to find Christ Jesus and keep Him company."[656] Observing that the transformations wrought by the redemptive blood of Christ are responsible for every spiritual renewal and at all stages, Teresa held that the soul has not only the right but the duty to have recourse explicitly to Jesus Christ, allowing for a more efficacious route to union with God.[657] She held this view despite contradictors of her time feeling that since the later stages of union with the Godhead are entirely spiritual, recourse to Christ's sacred humanity would be a "corporal" distraction in the embrace of God Himself.

Countering this thinking, Teresa composed a doctrine in her *Interior Castle* in which she most emphatically insists that even souls who have attained great progress in the interior life, if they "lose their Guide, the good Jesus, will be unable to find their way."[658] Therefore, the highest summits of the spiritual life are closed to those who would abandon the company of Christ's sacred humanity along the journey. She sees contrarians as lacking in humility, for "God is well pleased to see a soul humbly taking His Son as Mediator, [for] even if His Majesty is pleased to raise it to the highest contemplation, ... it realizes its unworthiness."[659] She adds:

> The last thing [one] should do is withdraw of set purpose from [his] greatest help and blessing, which is the most sacred Humanity of Our Lord Jesus Christ.... For life is long and there are many trials in it, and we have need to look at Christ our Pattern ... so that we may bear them perfectly. The good Jesus is too good company for us to forsake Him [as is] His most sacred Mother.[660]

While there are many aspects of Christ's sacred humanity that one may choose to "take with him" on the way to union with God, the Face of Christ is surely the most precious ornament as the most distinguishable feature of the sacred humanity, the chief and most important member of Christ's sacred person.[661] Following the example of St. Thérèse, one will find the sorrowful Face of Christ

---

[656] P. Marie-Eugène, *I Am a Daughter*, 420.
[657] Ibid., 422–423.
[658] Ibid., 425.
[659] Ibid., 426.
[660] Ibid., 429.
[661] Sister Mary St. Peter, *Life of Sister Mary St. Peter*, 290.

to be especially efficacious as recourse during the dark night, which resembles the Passion of Christ in a soul's journey to union.

This dark night of the soul, according to St. John of the Cross, is caused by the clash of two contraries: God's invading love and sin rooted in the depths of the soul. Though suffering for Christ is purely redemptive, sinners must endure it to be purified in preparation for perfect union with God. It is sustained only by intimate contact with the divine victim.

> It is through this contact, which a prolonged and penetrating gaze of the soul must maintain, that the soul draws from the sorrowful Face of Christ Jesus the science of divine love. Thus, it not only learns the meaning and value of the trial but grows in sympathy with the Master and in resemblance to Him.... Christian perfection lies in this resemblance and this compassion.... To withdraw from this divine model in the decisive period of purification and transformation is to wander off into by-roads, sacrificing to a natural sublimation of [one's] faculties the realization of that Christian perfection of which Jesus is the type.[662]

As stated in the process of St. Thérèse's beatification, "the Holy Face was the mirror in which Thérèse saw the soul and the heart of her beloved. This Holy Face was the meditation book from which she drew her signs of love."[663] As discussed previously, her later spiritual life almost entirely revolved around contemplation of the sorrowful Face of her Savior.

Indeed, the living reality of Christ's wounded Face was the essence of Thérèse's mature spiritual life.[664] It was not something to which she was only occasionally devoted. "Imprinted in the depths of her soul both by mystical experience and by trial, it [was] an interior reality always present, of human aspect with veiled features, eyes lowered, indistinct in its lines yet so living, a face that love perceived in the dark night more than does vision."[665] Taking the sorrowful Face of Christ with her during her dark night of the soul, St. Thérèse confirms the teaching of St. Teresa of Avila and St. John of the Cross, that the sacred humanity of Christ remains with one through the dark night as well as to union with God. "A source of life, a model to be imitated, the Holy Face is the great

---

[662] P. Marie-Eugène, *I Am a Daughter*, 431.
[663] Sister Mary Emmanuel, *Sister Marie*, 11.
[664] Ibid., 444.
[665] Ibid.

treasure of Thérèse, the kingdom that Jesus gave her as a dowry on the day of their divine espousals, so that all its divine traits might be reproduced in her soul."[666] As previously discussed, this treasure is made available for all in the Holy Face devotion, wherein Christ bestows the power in His Face to be embraced in the conversion of sinners as "the greatest source of grace second to the sacraments." Its likeness is generously imprinted on the souls of devotees, allowing for its divine traits to be reproduced in all who would seriously undertake this act of reparatory love.

The Holy Face as Efficacious Object of Contemplation

O Jesus! Your Veiled Gaze is our Heaven!
Make me resemble You, Jesus!

— St. Thérèse of Lisieux

Being in the presence of the Face of Christ has a transformative effect. Indeed, for St. Thérèse, "contemplation consists primarily in being with God and gazing upon him.... [For her,] devotion to the Holy Face meant looking at God, which was quite accurate and contemplative.... She saw God through His human form because there she found the reflection of divinity together with the traces of His suffering."[667] Contemplation is a form of selflessly "looking at" God, which may be done by adoring the Holy Eucharist, by studying a likeness of Christ, or by studying Him in Scripture, among other ways. The selfless part is key. Thérèse regarded Him in diverse ways not for her own fulfillment but always to give Him pleasure, to love Him. For her encounter with God gave her "nothing" in return, only dryness, "neither hot nor cold," as she described it. Yet according to St. Teresa of Avila, one may cling to God by sheer faith, as did St. Thérèse, without experiencing anything; indeed, this was Thérèse's entire life of prayer in Carmel.[668] There was only her constant gaze. St. John of the Cross says that perfect contemplation consists precisely in such fundamental starkness — even making the void

---

[666] Ibid., 437.
[667] P. Marie-Eugène, *Under the Torrent*, 39.
[668] Ibid., 41.

of spiritual experience more desirable than an excess, for "a soul's contemplation is perfect and excellent only in so far as it is pure and simple."[669]

> We find in Saint Thérèse ... both the absence of extraordinary graces and a habitual impression of the powerlessness and obscurity. Thus, the two indications which Saint John of the Cross gives, lofty divine communications and purity of soul, converge here and reveal an exceedingly lofty mystical life.[670]

Gazing at Christ with simple faith and love, even in the greatest dryness, is the only essential element of contemplation, its foundation and nourishment.[671] It was under the silent, sorrowful Face of her Savior that Thérèse formed her doctrine of merciful love. For the return glance of the Savior is transfixing and transforming.

St. John of the Cross wrote in his "Spiritual Canticle": "When you looked at me / Your eyes imprinted Your grace in me. / Since You have looked / And left in me grace and beauty ... / Let us rejoice, Beloved, / and let us go forth to behold ourselves in your beauty."[672] This was likely an inspiration to Thérèse's prayer, "I am the Jesus of Thérèse," where she asks the Child Jesus to "Imprint in me your childish virtues and graces so that on the day of my birth into Heaven, the angels and saints may recognize your little bride."[673] She also prayed, "I beg you to cast Your divine glance upon a great number of little souls. I beg You to choose a legion of little Victims worthy of your *love*."[674] The gaze of Christ is known to produce this victimhood. Christ's look from the Cross transformed St. Dismas into a soul of such great faith that St. John Chrysostom held that his faith exceeded even that of Abraham, Moses, and Isaiah.[675] There was the divine glance from Christ to St. Peter after he denied the Lord three times, which wounded him with sorrow and love, changing his cowardice and despair to fortitude and trust in God's mercy, fitting to his role of first pope. And there

---

[669] Ibid., 43.
[670] Ibid., 142–143.
[671] Ibid., 122, 123, 129.
[672] *Prayers of St. Thérèse*, 102.
[673] Ibid., 101. Thérèse is simply the French spelling of Teresa.
[674] P. Marie-Eugène, *Under the Torrent*, 110.
[675] Sister Mary St. Peter, *Life of Sister Mary St. Peter*, 266. "These have beheld Christ seated on the throne of his magnificence, surrounded with glory, and they believed; whereas the Good Thief beholds him in agony and on an infamous gibbet, yet he adores him as if he beheld him in the realms of his glory."

is a little-known letter from St. Ignatius to St. Polycarp of Smyrna, wherein despite Ignatius just having had the privilege of learning from Polycarp while visiting with him, Ignatius holds most precious the holy face of the man, a friend and disciple of John the Evangelist. "While I was impressed with your godly mind, which is fixed, as it were, on an immovable rock, I am more than grateful that I was granted the sight of your holy face. God grant I may never forget it!"[676] Polycarp had looked upon the face of Ignatius, who had looked upon the face of John the Evangelist, who had in turn looked upon the Face of the Lord Himself. The transfixed gaze of Christ transferred, as it were, from one to another who beheld it, produced a domino effect of almost palpable transformation in each, not unlike Moses needing to veil his face, which had become noticeably (physically) radiant after ascending Mount Sinai to converse with the Lord.[677]

Father Luigi Giussani refers to the piercing glance of Christ in his *At the Origin of the Christian Claim*, regarding the life of the disciples in the presence of Jesus:

> The greatest miracle of all was that truly human gaze which revealed man to himself and was impossible to evade. Nothing is more convincing to man than a gaze which takes hold of him and recognizes what he is, which reveals man to himself. Jesus saw inside man. No one could hide in front of him, and before him the depths of conscience had no secrets.... The ability to take hold of the heart of a man is the greatest, most persuasive miracle of all.[678]

To take hold of the heart of man, to transform it into the likeness of God, is surely the gaze of the veiled Face of Christ in the Most Holy Sacrament of the Altar as well. Related is the promise of Christ in the revelations given to Sister St. Pierre that the imprint of Christ will be placed upon the souls who make reparation, relative to the care with which they do so.

Distinct from this promise is the even more apt revelation from Christ that His Face "is the *seal of the Divinity, having the power to imprint itself on the souls of those who apply it to their persons.*"[679] This is surely nothing if not an aid to spiritual

---

[676] "St. Ignatius of Antioch Letter to Polycarp," trans. Cyril Richardson, https://www.orderofstignatius.org/files/Letters/Ignatius_to_Polycarp.pdf.

[677] Exod. 34:29–35.

[678] Luigi Giussani, *At the Origin of the Christian Claim*, trans. Viane Hewitt (Montreal: McGill-Queen's University, 1998), 53.

[679] Sister St. Pierre, *Life of Sister Saint Pierre*, 232-233.

union with Him. It is a desire to be like Christ on the part of the devotee and a gifted means to aid in doing so. It is like the effects of gazing at the veiled Face of Christ in the Most Holy Sacrament of the Altar, only with the explicit promise that by doing so and desiring to "apply" this divine likeness upon oneself, that it will be done. St. Elizabeth of the Trinity prayed to assume the image of Chist: "I don't want to live my own life, but to be transformed into Jesus Christ so that my life is more divine than human and the Father, bending low over me, may recognize in me the image of His Beloved Son."[680] This brings to full circle St. Thérèse's statement that the Holy Face was the source of all her piety (when taken literally): God has given devotees a means of taking on *His* piety, *His* sanctity, *His* likeness. God has given the means to obliging souls of a most advantageous step toward union with Him, a grace heretofore virtually unknown![681]

✠ ✠ ✠

The veiled treasures of the suffering Face of Christ ultimately concern themselves with the essence of the great Carmelite mystical tradition, going back to Elijah himself. He, as spiritual father of Carmel, was a contemplative in the core of his being, led by Yahweh to search for Him in deep solitude and contemplation of Him.

> Indeed, what is contemplation if not this eager search for God and this ongoing discovery of his presence? The prophet's mastery of the elements, his tranquil audacity, his familiarity with God, allow us to perceive the quality of his contemplation, while his demands on Mount Horeb reveal its purity and penetration. The Lord having announced his passage, Elijah rejects, one after another, the manifestations reminiscent of Mount Sinai — the hurricane which strikes the mountains, the earthquake, and the fire. He is not satisfied until, in a light, murmuring sound, God gives him a substantial vision of himself.[682]

The suffering Face of Christ, "unveiled," reveals the power residing therein, like the simple and unassuming murmuring sound heard by Elijah being the very voice of God. Elijah proclaimed that he was full of jealous zeal for the Lord God of Hosts because the Israelites had abandoned their covenant with

---

[680] Giovanna Della Croce, *Elizabeth of the Trinity: A Life of Praise to God*, trans. Julie Enzler (Manchester: Sophia, 2016), 51.
[681] Sister Mary Emmanuel, *Sister Marie*, 2.
[682] P. Marie-Eugène, *Under the Torrent*, 73.

Him, torn down His altars, and put His prophets to the sword.[683] How is Elijah's consuming desire to defend God's justice and to "make" Israel love Him again unlike Sister St. Pierre's victimhood to justice or St. Thérèse's victimhood to merciful love? For the sin of Israel weighs devastatingly upon Elijah as a defender of the God he loves.

There is within Carmel — from Elijah, to John the Baptist, to St. Teresa of Avila and St. John of the Cross, to Sister St. Pierre and St. Thérèse, and others — the duty to conserve and transmit a tradition and spirit that longs to defend and love God as He ought to be. It is built upon Elijah's zeal for God's justice and a desire to undo the wounds inflicted on Love by the disdain and malice of men. St. Anne of Jesus, friend of both St. Teresa of Avila and St. John of the Cross, once came in a dream to St. Thérèse, assuring her that "the way of spiritual childhood was the blessed continuation of the perfection traced out by the Reformers."[684] And St. Teresa of Avila herself — who had renewed her order precisely by being faithful to its rediscovery — once came to Sister St. Pierre "in the depths of her heart," telling her that the Holy Face devotion would be "the honor of Carmel." There is a sense in hindsight, especially given the complementary spiritualities of Sister St. Pierre and St. Thérèse, that this may have alluded to the work of reparation "crowning" the insights of the tradition in some key respects — perhaps even concerning the order's characteristic spirituality. For the Holy Face devotion is not only the "mother of all devotions" — focused, like Carmel, on the protection of Holy Mother Church, the salvation of the masses, and due deference for God's rights and glory — but especially, it is a spirituality of zeal and selfless love for the God of Hosts in the Carmelite fashion. It is to search in contemplation the Face of the Almighty and to be transfixed by His merciful love in return: per Christ's promise, *it is to assume the very likeness of God.*

> *O Adorable Face of Jesus, the only Beauty that captivates my heart,*
> *deign to imprint in me Your Divine Likeness so that You may not*
> *behold the soul of Your little bride without seeing Yourself in her.*
>
> — *St. Thérèse*

---

[683] 1 Kings 19:13–14.
[684] P. Marie-Eugène, *Under the Torrent,* 96.

Chapter 7

Mother of Mercy and the Pinnacle Devotion

1. True Devotion to Mary and the Holy Face

O Glorious Lady! Throned on high
Above the star-illumined sky;
Thereto ordained, thy bosom lent
To thy Creator nourishment.

— "O Gloriosa Virginum," hymn to praise the
Blessed Virgin, in honor of her divine maternity[685]

According to the revelations from Christ given to Sister St. Pierre, "The Holy Face Devotion emanates from the Sacred Heart, the one being the complement of the other,"[686] such that by praising and blessing the name of God, one honors the Sacred Heart.[687] Christ also told Sister St. Pierre that the two hearts, His Sacred Heart and that of His Mother, *must not be separated*.[688] (For they are

---

[685] The Virgin appeared to Sister St. Pierre as Queen of Carmel, asking her to recite this hymn (in its entirety) as many times as there are convents of Carmel in France, promising protection of them by way of her virginal milk, emblem of mercy. Sister St. Pierre, *Life of Sister St. Pierre*, ed. Rev. P. Janvier (Baltimore: John Murphy, 1884), 396–397.

[686] Sister Mary St. Peter, *Life of Sister Mary St. Peter*, ed. Rev. P. Janvier (France, 1884), 121.

[687] Ibid., 130.

[688] Ibid., 119.

intrinsically united in God's designs for mercy.) Consequently, when one honors the Sacred Heart by reverencing God's majesty, he is also honoring the heart of Mary. The Holy Face devotion is therefore likewise a complement to devotion to the Immaculate Heart. It is fitting, then, that Christ specified that His Mother have the privilege of "giving this devotion to His kingdom," in that it is "fraught with so much necessity and glory for God ... as a new pledge of mercy,"[689] under the title "Our Lady of the Holy Name of God."[690] It is also fitting that this devotion spawned from Carmel in which Mary is seen as the contemplative soul par excellence, for "in Carmel God is the objective, but the soul will become more and more Mary."[691] Indeed, Carmel was established for Our Lady's honor.

It should not be surprising, therefore, that another major commonality between the nineteenth-century French Carmelites, Sister St. Pierre and St. Thérèse, was their profound devotion to Mary. Specifically, they were both devoted to Mary as Mediatrix of All Graces and Mercy to Mankind, flowing from her privilege of divine maternity, wherein Mary's humanity is understood as elevated to the "plane of the hypostatic union,"[692] according to St. Ephraim, raising her above any other creature. She did not transmit divinity to her Son, but rather, as St. Cajetan says, "Mary attains to the confines of divinity by her own operation, in that she conceives God, engenders Him, gives Him birth, and nourishes Him with her milk."[693] Divine maternity is "a quality that puts Mary in immediate relationship with the Divinity Itself, the sum of all perfections."[694] In consequence of Christ as true God and true man, her preservation from the stain of Original Sin, and the Holy Ghost being her heavenly spouse, Mary is named Mother of God, Theotokos, as was first dogmatically proclaimed by the Third Ecumenical Council, held at Ephesus in 431.

---

[689] Ibid., 327.

[690] Ibid., 333. Also, Louis Van den Bossche, *The Message of Sister Mary of St. Peter*, trans. Mary G. Durham (France: Carmel of Tours, 1953), 136. Sister St. Pierre also understood Mary to be "the honor and the glory of the Holy Name of God" because she is the masterpiece of His hands, having worked marvels in her.

[691] Paul-Marie, *Carmelite Spirituality in the Teresian Tradition*, trans. Kathryn Sullivan (Washington, D.C.: ICS Publications, 1997), 30–31.

[692] P. Marie-Eugène, *A Practical Synthesis of Carmelite Spirituality*, trans. M. Verda Clare, vol 2, *I Am a Daughter of the Church* (Allen, TX: Christian Classics, 1997), 447. Also, hypostatic union refers to the unity of Christ's humanity and divinity into one person.

[693] Ibid.

[694] Anselm Burke, *Mary in History, in Faith and in Devotion* (New York: Scapular Press, 1956), 73.

A specific devotion to Mary under this title was introduced to Sister St. Pierre by way of a somewhat startling grace, which crowned her message and spirituality toward the end of her life.[695] This mystical experience flowed from her initial preparation for heavenly gifts by her filial devotion to the Blessed Virgin (which had always included the recitation of a daily Rosary and an early act of consecration),[696] as well as her special attraction for the Infant Jesus,[697] and culminated in the grace given to her to share in the mysteries of the divine maternity. This blessing was a very unusual mystical gift given to the likes of St. Bernard of Clairvaux and St. Fulbert before her,[698] wherein Mary, as an aspect of her divine maternity, is understood to also be privileged as the nurse to the God-Man,[699] an unknown and hidden mystery[700] surrounding the Virgin and her Child. As such, she ultimately provided for the redemptive blood of her Son through her virginal milk, which she shares as grace to her spiritual children as well.

> [Sister St. Pierre had] seen at the same time the merciful power of Mary, and the voluntary humiliation of Jesus in this mystery. It is through this humiliation of the Word that the light on the divine Maternity attaches itself to the Work of the Reparation and crowns it. As [Sister St. Pierre had] already offered His Son's humiliated Face to the offended Father,

---

[695] Discussion of this mystical experience is omitted from most post-1950s biographies of Sister St. Pierre, probably due to the belief that her last mystical experiences were only for the purpose of crowning her own spiritual life, rather than for the purpose of adding to her mission. I believe that her last mystical experiences cap her whole message and are essential in the understanding of the faithful, all of which is discussed in these sections.

[696] Van den Bossche, *Message*, 136. And Sister Mary St. Peter, *Life of Sister Mary St. Peter*, 15.

[697] Sister Mary St. Peter, *Life of Sister Mary St. Peter*, 354.

[698] Ibid., 349.

[699] Sister St. Pierre, *Life of Sister St. Pierre*, 229–330. "A few days ago, after Holy Communion, the Infant Jesus strongly attracted me to consider the honor and homage of perfect praise He rendered to His celestial Father, during the time He was nourished by the virginal milk of His most Holy Mother, and He has made me understand, that it is His Will I should adore Him in this humble state, in union with the holy Angels, that thus His Mercy may fill me with innocence, purity, simplicity, and that I may gather the precious graces flowing from the ineffable Mystery of a Child-God. Then, this Divine [Savior] transported my soul to a sublime state; and, in great elevation of spirit, I contemplated this prodigy of love and humility: Him Who is eternally begotten in the Bosom of the Father, in the splendors of His glory, nourished upon the milk of His august Mother! The Holy Ghost has made me enter the depths of this Mystery, which heretofore was unknown to me."

[700] Van den Bossche, *Message*, 144.

she will present it to Him in homage, "His divine Son in the state of littleness and humility."[701]

In response to the first blasphemy of Lucifer, all the way to those who currently blaspheme by denying the absolute truth and morality of God in exchange for "their own," to those who deny even the majesty due God's name, the perfect reparatory praise is rendered to the Father by both Christ's humiliated Face and by the helplessness of the Christ Child on Mary's breast.

Sister St. Pierre's mystical experience highlighting Mary as Mother of God and Mother of Man was to reward her for her sufferings endured for the cause of reparation and to "prefigure the graces of mercy and salvation [for the world] which would result from the establishment of the Work of Reparation."[702] Moreover, Sister St. Pierre understood through this mystical gift that "this mercy [flowing from reparation] *was to come through the hands of Mary, our Mother, and the Mediatrix*[703] of all graces."[704] It crowns the work of reparation by making even more explicit the "prize" of mercy and salvation that would be effected from the devotion, to flow abundantly in a new age, "placed under the sign of the Virgin and her universal mediation."[705] This "new age" is better understood in hindsight, particularly in light of the writings of St. Louis de Montfort.

✠ ✠ ✠

Inspired by Sister St. Pierre, as introduced to her by her mistress of novices,[706] St. Thérèse's well-known devotion to Mary was likewise especially drawn to this

---

[701] Ibid., 140.
[702] Sister Mary Emmanuel, *Life of Sister Marie de St. Pierre of the Holy Family, Carmelite of Tours, 1816–1848: A Forerunner of St. Thérèse of Lisieux* (London: Burns, Oates & Washbourne, 1938), 149.
[703] Sister St. Pierre herself did not know to use the term *mediatrix*, but her understanding was the same. More discussion will follow in the text of this section.
[704] Ibid. (My emphasis.) Also: "This future effusion of grace, promised to the world, will be the result of the merits and of the intercession of the Blessed Virgin." Sister Mary St. Peter, *Life of Sister Mary St. Peter*, 349.
[705] Van den Bossche, *Message*, 142.
[706] *The Poetry of St. Thérèse of Lisieux*, trans. Donald Kinney (Washington, D.C.: ICS Publications, 2020), 35–37. "[The attraction felt by St. Thérèse for the Infant Jesus taking nourishment from His Mother was like that of] Sister Mary of Saint Peter from Tours.... [Sister Marie of the Angels, her novice mistress, was] also a fervent reader of Sister Mary of Saint Peter."

aspect of the divine maternity[707] in which Mary is nurse to the Infant Jesus. This privilege of Mary was, in fact, the subject of her first poem.[708] There, she saw Mary as the ultimate instrument to the grace and mercy of her Son, "[His] divine blood [flowing from] Virginal Milk," even equating "[the] white Host [to] Virginal Milk."[709] And her last poem, dedicated to Mary as Mother of God and Man, speaks of the treasures of a mother belonging to her child: "I am your child, O my dearest Mother. Aren't your virtues and your love mine too? So, when the white Host comes into my heart, Jesus, your Sweet Lamb, thinks He is resting in you!"[710] This indicates an understanding, shared by Sister St. Pierre, of Mary's virtues and love being "exchanged" for one's own in the journey toward perfection, a key element of what is now understood as "true" devotion to Mary.

For St. Thérèse and especially Sister St. Pierre, who died some forty years before the Little Flower entered Carmel, devotion to Mary as Mother of God, Mother of Man, and Mother of Mercy was "total" in a time in which devotion to Mary was not understood to be nearly so all-encompassing as what is virtually taken for granted in the spirituality of the Church today. Current understanding is largely thanks to the writings of St. Louis de Montfort, Pope Leo XIII, St. Maximilian Kolbe, and Pope St. John Paul II, among others. F. W. Faber, the faithful translator of St. Louis de Montfort's *True Devotion to Mary*, writes in 1862:

> Jesus is obscured because Mary is kept in the background. Thousands of souls perish because Mary is withheld from them. *It is the miserable unworthy shadow which we call our devotion to the Blessed Virgin that is the cause of all these wants and blights,* these evils and omissions and declines. Yet, if we are to believe the revelations of the Saints, God is

---

[707] Sister Mary Emmanuel, *Life of Sister Marie*, vi. "Mere Marie Des Agnes, we are told, had a special love for the writings of Sister St. Pierre, and among them, her doctrine on the Divine Maternity, which she made known to Thérèse. Thus, was inspired Thérèse's first poem." Also, "The Cult of Mary as Mediatrix of all graces ... is a leading element in the life of Sister Saint Pierre, and through her this special cult of Mary as Mother of God and of man and the channel of all grace to man, her child in the spiritual order, spread to Lisieux. Saint Thérèse's ardent devotion to Mary is well known, and it was to this aspect of the Divine Maternity that she was especially drawn, through the influence of Sister Saint Pierre."

[708] Ibid., 12: "Le Lait Virginal de Marie, ou La Rosee Divine."

[709] *Poetry of St. Thérèse*, 37–38.

[710] Ibid., 216.

pressing for a greater, a wider, a stronger, quite another devotion to His Blessed Mother.[711]

St. Louis de Montfort is revered for his promulgation of what he describes as *true* devotion to Mary through Marian consecration, in which one, for the purpose of uniting oneself to Christ, dedicates himself *totally* to Mary as the spiritual Mother of mankind. It is marked by joining one's mind and will with Mary in a desire to be united with God. In the sense of giving of oneself entirely unto Mary, one becomes a "slave" of Mary, "turning over" everything to her — the disposition of one's body and soul, one's temporal and spiritual goods, intentions, prayers, actions, and even merits — becoming entirely dependent on her as a slave to his master or as a child to his mother. She, in turn, uses all as would be most suitable in forming the devotee into the likeness of Christ. However, man belongs to Christ through Mary only for the honor of belonging to Him — that is, man is to desire nothing in return, becoming completely disinterested in motive, save for pleasing God by promoting His Kingdom in oneself and others.

Indeed, "Saint Louis-Marie Grignion de Montfort set forth a revolution of Christian spirituality when he first taught about Marian consecration and presented his thirty-three-day plan to prepare souls for this big step in their relationship with Jesus."[712] Consecration's total commitment of self is in imitation of Mary's fiat (by which she consented without reserve to the workings of the Holy Spirit toward the Incarnation of Jesus, ultimately collaborating in Christ's Redemption). This undertaking on the part of a soul demands constant effort and renewed commitment, such that St. Louis devised a preparation of at least three weeks to make ready a soul for the task. Though a selfless undertaking, one does not suffer by making this consecration; rather, it is pure profit, for it is the easiest way to union with Christ, the most perfect and secure way, in that Mary is the best likeness of Christ, and she is closest to Him, having shared her very flesh and nourishment with Him as a newborn babe. St. Louis explains that one does all actions by Mary, with Mary, in Mary, and for Mary so that he may do them more perfectly by Jesus, with Jesus, in Jesus, and for Jesus. She is one's true mother and mediatrix, for she returns the offering of all one has to her by

---

[711] Louis de Montfort, *True Devotion to Mary*, trans. Frederick William Faber (London: Catholic Way, 2013), 11–12.

[712] Boniface Hicks, *The Fruit of Her Womb: 33-Day Preparation for Total Consecration to Jesus* (Manchester: Sophia Institute Press, 2022), 3.

sharing all that she has, covering petitions and good works with her own merits, making them exponentially more efficacious.

St. Louis writes:

> All our perfection consists in being conformed, united, and consecrated to Jesus Christ; and therefore, the most perfect of all devotions is, without any doubt, that which the most perfectly conforms, unites, and consecrates us to Jesus Christ. Now, Mary being the most conformed of all creatures to Jesus Christ, it follows that, of all devotions, that which most consecrates and conforms the soul to our Lord is devotion to His holy Mother, and that the more a soul is consecrated to Mary, the more it is consecrated to Jesus. Hence it comes to pass, that the most perfect consecration to Jesus Christ is nothing else but a perfect and entire consecration of [oneself] to the Blessed Virgin, and this is the devotion which I teach; or in other words, a perfect renewal of the vows and promises of holy Baptism.[713]

St. Louis's consecration to Mary has received commendations from Popes Pius IX, Leo XIII, Pius X, Benedict XV, Pius XI, Pius XII, Paul VI, and John Paul II.[714] They all affirm his consecration to Mary as the foremost Marian devotion. In addition, there have been a marked increase in saints and theologians promoting this *true* devotion to Mary since the mid-nineteenth century, to say nothing of it being inferred from Church-approved Marian apparitions, affording Catholics today a much more prevalent understanding of this most efficacious means of belonging totally to Jesus through Mary, a powerful way for all to achieve sanctity.

Though Sister St. Pierre lived a century after St. Louis wrote and taught, total consecration to Mary was generally unknown when she beheld this understanding clearly in the light of God through her mystical experience. In fact, St. Louis's writings were almost certainly not read by Sister St. Pierre. St. Louis de Montfort wrote approximately one hundred years prior to her revelations, but his writings were mysteriously hidden for those one hundred years — something he himself prophesized would happen because of the devil's efforts to thwart the message.[715] Yet her mystical insights are identical

---

[713] Ibid., 82.

[714] Vox Populi, "The Fifth Marian Dogma," Eternal Word Television Network, accessed January 8, 2020, https://www.ewtn.com/catholicism/library/fifth-marian-dogma.

[715] "St. Louis Marie Grignion de Montfort wrote the Treatise on True Devotion to the Blessed Virgin at the beginning of the 1700's, but the manuscript remained practically

to those promulgated by St. Louis relating to the spiritual nourishment of Mary as Mother of Man, that one should have total reliance upon her, as a babe has to his mother, for she is treasurer of God's graces.[716] She writes:

> Man should have continual recourse to the most Blessed Virgin, his Mother, if he wishes to arrive at the perfect age of manhood in Eternity. Behold the two grand mysteries of the Maternity of Mary, which the Infant Jesus wishes to teach me: Mary, Mother of God, and Mary, Mother of man. For this reason, it is, that he keeps me in constant contemplation of himself as Infant in the arms of his Mother, being nourished with her virginal milk, to teach me by his example to have recourse to her, that I may be fed with the heavenly dew of her virtues.[717]

Elsewhere she writes, "As long as man is upon earth, he is in a state of infancy; only in Heaven will he be the perfect age. That is why he must constantly have recourse to the Mother like a little child."[718] All is remarkably like the writing of St. Louis:

> Mary received from God a unique dominion over souls enabling her to nourish them and make them more and more godlike. Saint Augustine went so far as to say that even in this world all the elect are enclosed in the womb of Mary, and that their real birthday is when this good mother brings them forth to eternal life. Consequently, just as an infant draws all its nourishment from its mother, who gives according to its needs, so the elect draw their spiritual nourishment and all their strength from Mary.[719]

---

unknown for more than a century. When, almost by chance, it was at last discovered in 1842 and published in 1843." Louis de Montfort, *True Devotion*, 3. St. Louis wrote: "I clearly foresee that raging brutes will come in fur to tear with their diabolical teeth this little writing, and him whom the Holy Ghost has made use of to write it; or at least to envelop it in the silence of a coffer, in order that it may not appear." And, Ibid., 10. "The author died in 1716, and the treatise was found by accident by one of the priests of his congregation at St. Laurent-sur-Sevre, in 1842. The exiting superior was able to attest the handwriting as being that of the venerable founder." And, Ibid., 10–11. Part of the writings were published as early as 1843 but all writing did not received ecclesiastical approval until 1853, five years after the death of Sister St. Pierre.

[716] Van den Bossche, *Message*, 139.
[717] Sister Mary St. Peter, *Life of Sister Mary St. Peter*, 376.
[718] Van den Bossche, *Message*, 152.
[719] Louis de Montfort, *The Secret of Mary*, http://www.monfortian.info/writings/the-secret-of-mary.html, no. 14. Hicks, *The Fruit*, 6.

Moreover, in her mystical favors concerning the divine maternity, Sister St. Pierre understood that Mary is *necessary* in the order of reparation and mercy: she is man's lifeline to eternity, chosen by God to be the "milk of grace and mercy" for all men.[720]

This "necessity" of Mary may be understood, as St. Louis explains, as the "treasurer of grace, all-powerful queen and spiritual Mother," flowing from her role in the plan of the Trinity for salvation, her work for the reign of Christ in the world, and her transcendence as Mother of Christ and intimacy in relationship with the Father and the Holy Spirit.[721] Sister St. Pierre likewise understood Mary as the "legatee" of all grace, spiritual Mother to mankind, and a sharer in Christ's Redemption, all flowing from her role as Mother of God, by which she consented to provide her flesh and nourishment to be that of the Savior, which was ultimately shed in mercy for mankind.

Sister St. Pierre appears to have received understanding from God of what remains the undeclared fifth Marian dogma, that of Mary as Co-Redemptrix ("co" meaning "with," not "equal to"), Mediatrix of Grace, and Advocate for (or Mother of) Man.[722] This is significant because, while these titles are already contained in the official and authoritative teachings of the Church's Magisterium — interpreted from "sources of divine revelation, Sacred Scripture and Apostolic Tradition and as it is presently understood and experienced in the dynamic ecclesial life of the Living, Pondering, and Praying Church, the People of God"[723] — the faithful await their being declared as official dogma. Indeed, Christ described these mysteries flowing from the privilege of Mary as nurse to

---

[720] Sister St. Pierre, *Life of Sister St. Pierre*, 353.
[721] *Jesus Living in Mary: Handbook of the Spirituality of St. Louis Marie de Montfort*, ed. Stephano De Fiores (Bay Shore, NY: Montfort Publications, 1994), 821. As in the spirit of St. Montfort, "necessity" does not mean that consecration to Mary is the only way to Christ, but rather it is presented as an easy and foolproof way.
[722] Van den Bossche, *Message*, 204: "The role of the Blessed Virgin as mediatrix appears from the earliest communications on the subject of Reparation, and one knows that they were concluded in a sequence of lofty Marial contemplations which place the accent on the universal Mediation of Mary, Mother of God. The active intervention of the Blessed Virgin ... her co-operation in Christ's redeeming work, her participation in the distribution of graces since Calvary until the end of time, are very clearly stated by Sister St. Peter. We know also that, since her Message, the apparitions of the Virgin have succeeded, and they confirm singularly the affirmations of the Carmelite of Tours."
[723] Mark Miravalle, *Mary: Coredemptrix, Mediatrix, Advocate* (Santa Barbara: Queenship Publishing, 1993), xi.

God as a "treasure hidden in the field of His Church."[724] That Sister St. Pierre's mystical understanding and the writings of St. Louis de Montfort inherently affirm one another pertaining to the proposed fifth dogma is surely another argument in their favor.

St. Louis's monumental writings on the subject were just surfacing around the time of Sister St. Pierre's mystical experiences, though they were not given ecclesiastical approval until after her death. Sister St. Pierre's arriving at these theological insights independently of, albeit in a sense, concurrently to, St. Louis de Montfort seems likely, in part, because she did not know to use Montfort's terminology. Sister St. Pierre never spoke of Mary as Co-Redemptrix, Mediatrix, or Advocate; instead, she speaks of the grace and mercy at the maternal bosom, in that Christ has made His Divine Mother "legatee of the immense riches He has acquired for us during His laborious life, and His dolorous Passion, that she might become the admirable channel through which all His infinite merits would flow to the Holy Church, His spouse."[725] She further explains:

> Jesus made me understand that He wished to return to [His Mother] all He had received from her, for the accomplishment of the world's Redemption. She had nourished Him with her most pure milk. In gratitude, Jesus gave her His Blood, and made her Its depositary.... She stands at the foot of the Cross, to receive this Sacred Treasure, in the precious vase of her maternal heart. Mary had given Jesus His Adorable Body, and Jesus at death returned It to her, adorned with His Glorious Wounds, that she might draw from those sacred fountains eternal life for the children His love had begotten for her, by His Death. Yes, Jesus, with all His treasures, belongs to Mary. And Mary, with all her tenderness, belongs to mankind![726]

The above certainly expresses an understanding of Mary as Co-Redemptrix, Mediatrix, and Advocate for Man, albeit making use of different terminology.

Beyond theological understanding and spiritual devotion to Mary through the aspect of divine maternity, however, Sister St. Pierre herself was literally

---

[724] Sister St. Pierre, *Life of Sister St. Pierre*, 352.
[725] Sister Mary St. Peter, *Life of Sister Mary St. Peter*, 374.
[726] Sister Mary Emmanuel, *Life of Sister Marie*, 158.

"deputed to draw forth at this fountain of mercy *for the salvation of sinners*,"[727] an incredibly rare mystical charge, indeed. She writes:

> It is He who conducts me to this source of graces and benedictions, telling me to draw the milk of the divine mercy in the spirit of charity with which He Himself had drawn it; because He took this milk for all men, and for all men, He had poured it out in shedding His blood on the Cross. After His example, I must adapt for myself this mysterious liquor from Mary's breast in the name of all my brothers and henceforth pour it out like a heavenly dew upon the whole world to refresh it and purify the earth which is devoured by the fire of concupiscence and full of corruption.[728]

Sister St. Pierre explains that some souls have been appointed to honor Christ in the mysteries of His Passion (to suffer *with Christ* for the salvation of sinners) by way of the sacred stigmata, but for her, Christ bade her to bear the state of His infancy, that she might draw nearer to His Virgin Mother. Christ related to her that few souls are capable of this holy attention, which demands a great purity of heart.[729] Though believing herself the most feeble and abject instrument of the Lord, she was graced with drawing forth the milk of divine mercy, flowing forth from Christ's Mother, in the same spirit of charity "as Himself when a babe — that milk He received for all men, and which He imparted to them in shedding His Blood upon the Cross."[730] She looked upon herself as a mere "vase in the hands of the Infant Jesus, to receive from this mysterious fountain and then to pour forth this divine liquor, without anything being kept back for self-interest.[731] In another astounding mystical phenomenon (even exceeding that of her being designated by Christ to be responsible for all the sins of France, that it should be saved by her offering the merits of Christ's wounded Countenance to the Father in reparation), the little Breton was now given the mission of drawing forth from the Virgin Mother mercy for the salvation of sinners, not only in France[732] but throughout the world!

---

[727] Ibid., 378.
[728] Van den Bossche, *Message*, 153.
[729] Ibid., 149.
[730] Ibid., 377. And Sister St. Pierre, *Life of Sister St. Pierre*, 352.
[731] Van den Bossche, *Message*, 155.
[732] Sister St. Pierre, *Life of Sister St. Pierre*, 357–538.

Pertaining to the delicacy of her celestial charge, Sister St. Pierre experienced only the highest level of mysticism, which never involved sensible or imaginative manifestations, but rather allowed her to understand in only in an angelic and intellectual manner.[733] It should also be noted that this virginal milk only took on the virtue of sanctifying souls after it became the Blood of Christ, for by the Redemption all were made children of the Eternal Father and brethren of Our Lord. Hence, the Mother of Jesus became the Mother of man, and the Divine Son established her as the depositary of the riches and infinite merits of His life and Passion. This is consistent with Catholic doctrine that refers to Mary as the "Refuge of Sinners" and the "Treasurer of her Divine Son."[734] Through His Mother as an active, willful instrument, Christ distributes His merits, virtues, and graces to mankind, Mary's spiritual children.

Sister St. Pierre herself states that she was very surprised by the Lord asking her to contemplate His divine infancy under this mysterious aspect, so she sought to ascertain if any of the saints had treated this subject in writing. She was greatly consoled to learn of the "doctrine of some of the saints," written about by Father d'Argentan of the Capuchin Friars Minor, regarding this grand privilege of Mary, including a conference upon "The Divine Maternity of the Blessed Virgin, Nurse of the Incarnate Word."[735] She writes:

> Convinced that this devotion was neither novel, nor visionary, since Saint Augustine, Saint Athanasius and Saint Bernard have spoken of it with so much piety and eloquence, I became established in perfect peace of mind, abandoning myself into the hands of the Infant Jesus that he might perform His most holy will in me.[736]

And while St. Louis does not explicitly mention virginal milk, his writing comparing an infant drawing all nourishment from his mother to the elect drawing their spiritual strength from Mary would have surely been a consolation to Sister St. Pierre had she known of it. Regardless, it is compelling in hindsight to witness the affirmation of St. Louis de Montfort's spirituality in the form of the more-or-less

---

[733] Sister Mary Emmanuel, *Life of Sister Marie*, 150.
[734] Sister St. Pierre, *Life of Sister St. Pierre*, 354–355.
[735] Sister Mary St. Peter, *Life of Sister Mary St. Peter*, 359. And Sister St. Pierre, *Life of Sister St. Pierre*, 332–333.
[736] Sister Mary St. Peter, *Life of Sister Mary St. Peter*, 360.

concurrent mystical experience of Sister St. Pierre — even more convincing, if, as it appears, it may be assumed that she was ignorant of his writings.

2. The Title "Mother of All Devotions" Takes on Dual Implication

St. Louis de Montfort's total consecration to Mary, though novel, was promptly considered the preeminent devotion to Mary by numerous popes and saints, beginning with Pope Bl. Pius IX. The taking on of Mary's virtues and merits in exchange for one's own through true devotion to her is a singular, efficacious way of attaining sanctity. Not only did Sister St. Pierre's mystical experiences surrounding divine maternity confirm true devotion to Mary as outlined by St. Louis, but they, with him, essentially affirmed the proposed fifth dogma: Mary as Co-Redemptrix, Mediatrix, and Advocate for Man. But why should this double advocacy take place in the mid-nineteenth century? What significance does it have for the present time?

The four existent Church dogmas relating to the Blessed Virgin are Mary as Mother of God, the perpetual virginity of Mary, Mary's glorious Assumption, and Mary as the Immaculate Conception. The first two were proclaimed by the Church in reaction to notorious heresies. The dogma of Mary as Mother of God (Theotokos, "God bearer") was declared in 431 in reaction to Nestorianism, the belief that Christ was of two persons, human and divine, rather than one person with two natures, stating that Mary was the mother of the human person of Christ but not the divine. Ebionism taught that Joseph was the natural father of Jesus, who had been conceived through him; Helvidianism taught that Mary was a virgin at Christ's birth but afterward engaged in marital relations and conceived several children by Joseph; and Valentinianism held that the Holy Spirit placed Christ in Mary's womb but that Mary was not His genetic mother. To counter these heresies, the Second Council of Constantinople in 553 proclaimed Mary *Aeiparthenos,* meaning perpetual virgin, and in 649 at the Lateran Synod, Pope Martin I emphasized the threefold character of the perpetual virginity as before, during, and after the birth of Christ.

The more recent dogmas of the Immaculate Conception (1854), which holds that Mary, while fully human, was conceived without sin, and the Assumption of Mary (1950), which holds that Mary was assumed into Heaven body and soul, are more "preemptive"[737] in their declaration. Both of these dogmas have to do with the physical body of Mary, clearly making the case for her — and man — being holy. "The conception of a human being was declared sacred [as was] the passage of the body from this life to the next of a human body.... [All life] was defined as something belonging to God and not for [man] to expropriate."[738] These dogmas remind the faithful of man's true worth and the sacred gift of life that he has been given. "In [Mary's] Immaculate Conception and Assumption, she reveals the grandeur of [man's] beginning and the glory of [his] end.... Mary stands against any attempt to demean or manipulate the human body. She stands for the beauty and sanctity of each of her children."[739] The declaration of these dogmas is needed more than ever to strengthen the faithful in their resolve to cling to the truth of the Church in fighting errors countering the intrinsic value of life and the sacred beauty of the human body made in God's image.

The case for the proposed fifth dogma of Mary is both reactive and preemptive. The "synthesis of all heresies" is *modernism*, according to Pope St. Pius X, who warned of its "atheism and annihilation of all religion" from within in his 1907 encyclical *Pascendi Dominici Gregis*. Modernism, a form of rationalism that aims at the rejection of dogma and the divine authority of the Church,[740] has given rise to various postmodernisms, which surface today as moral relativism and wokeism. These ideologies deny natural law and the transcendence of God in lieu of man making himself a "god," deciding his own "truth," and "justice." Communism is, in some respects, the manifestation of the effects of modernism as a socioeconomic system, for they share in their foundation unprecedented blasphemies against the Godhead. And borrowing from modernism's tactic of infiltration, Communism — when not outright "destroying" God, the family, and man — sets out to annihilate all things enduring from within, especially Catholicism.

Ven. Fulton Sheen alluded to the Church being to Christ as Communism is to the antichrist. Indeed, modernism, with its various ideological "offspring," epitomizes the pride of Satan against the Godhead, declaring man as "like unto

---

[737] Robert B. Grieving, "God's Preemptive Strikes," *Crisis Magazine*, August 15, 2023, https://crisismagazine.com/opinion/gods-preemptive-strikes.
[738] Ibid.
[739] Ibid.
[740] Roderick A. McEachen, *Complete Catechism of Christian Doctrine* (Wheeling, WV: Catholic Supply House, 1911), 59.

God." As such, it is the "mother of all heresies." Yet Mary is "destroyer of all heresies." She will triumph, "crushing the head of Satan." Surely, all graces coming through her for the conversion of sinners and the enhancement of man's holiness should play a part in her triumph. A declared Marian fifth dogma of Mary as Co-Redemptrix, Mediatrix of All Graces and Mercy, and Advocate for Man is needed to edify the faithful's understanding of the efficacious recourse residing in Mary, the "lifeline to eternity." In doing so, it would help make explicit true devotion to Mary as spiritual weaponry to release man from the grip of Satan's favorite heretical ideologies (modernism and Communism), fashioned after his own primordial sin: blasphemous pride.

It is logical that Mary should use mankind, her spiritual children, in this fight, as is at least implicitly called for in numerous approved Marian apparitions. St. Maximilian Kolbe likewise affirms the necessity of man's recourse to Mary as Co-Redemptrix, Mediatrix, and Advocate for Man in this celestial battle. This is seen in his own consecration to Mary, which goes even further than Montfort's by spelling out, somewhat more precisely, the purpose of man's "slavery" to Mary. It is the official consecration for the Militia of the Immaculata, which he founded:

> O Immaculata, Queen of heaven and earth, refuge of sinners and our most loving Mother, God has willed to entrust the entire order of mercy to you.
>
> I, (Name), a repentant sinner, cast myself at your feet humbly imploring you to take me with all that I am and have, wholly to yourself as your possession and property. Please make of me, of all my powers of soul and body, of my whole life, death, and eternity, whatever most pleases you.
>
> *If it pleases you, use all that I am and have without reserve, wholly to accomplish what was said of you: "She will crush your head," and, "You alone have destroyed all heresies in the whole world." Let me be a fit instrument in your immaculate and merciful hands for introducing and increasing your glory to the maximum in all the many strayed and indifferent souls, and thus help extend as far as possible the blessed kingdom of the most Sacred Heart of Jesus. For wherever you enter you obtain the grace of conversion and growth in holiness, since it is through your hands that all graces come to us from the most Sacred Heart of Jesus.*[741]

---

[741] Michael Gaitley, M.I.C., *33 Days to Morning Glory: A Do-It-Yourself Retreat in Preparation for Marian Consecration* (Stockbridge, MA: Marian Press, 2013), 62-63. (My emphasis.)

St. Maximilian Kolbe is asking Mary to use him as (no less than) an instrument to assist in crushing the head of Satan by extending the Kingdom of God.[742] *Yet the faithful are asked to do the same.* Thus, the proposed fifth dogma of Mary would be reactive to the already present heresy of modernism *and* preemptive in its underscoring of man's role in helping Mary crush Satan by assisting in the conversion of the entire world. It would help recount and update the dangers of modernism — and all fundamentally blasphemous ideologies and economic systems — while assigning anew the role of the faithful in assisting Mary in her fight against these dangers, the fight against Satan, making explicit true devotion to Mary — and the Holy Face — as spiritual armament.

This is consistent with St. Louis de Montfort's understanding. He wrote the following concerning his belief that demonic beasts would wish to destroy his writing on true devotion to Mary:

> This very foresight encourages me, and makes me hope for great success, that is to say, for a great squadron of brave and valiant soldiers of Jesus and Mary, of both sexes, to combat the world, the devil, and corrupted nature, in those more than ever perilous times which are about to come. The Most High with His holy Mother has to form for Himself great saints who shall surpass most of the other saints in sanctity as much as the cedars of Lebanon outgrow little shrubs.[743]

According to St. Louis, this forming of great saints would be done through the "secret" of true devotion to Mary. True devotion and total consecration to Mary would be nonsensical without her roles of Co-Redemptrix, Mediatrix, and Advocate for (or Mother of) Man. For as Mother of God and Man, she provided nourishment ultimately shed as blood in Christ's Redemption, transmitting the grace of His sacrifice to her spiritual children, mediating the grace and mercy Christ won for man. Mary is worthy of man's recourse to her, for God chose to entrust to her "the entire order of Mercy."[744]

Ven. Sheen recalls that Mary's name means "One who has received Mercy" (Hos. 2:1): the antithesis of Satan.[745] Indeed, God has put enmity between her

---

[742] Ibid., 63.
[743] Ibid., 22.
[744] Ibid., 59.
[745] Fulton J. Sheen, *The World's First Love: Mary, Mother of God* (New York: McGraw-Hill, 1952), 239.

and Satan; she shall crush his head, and he shalt lie in wait for her heel (Gen. 3:15). Nothing could defeat Satan's pride more than a "mere" handmaid of the Lord becoming his victor: the embodiment of humility destroying the epitome of pride. St. Louis writes: "God has never made or formed but one enmity; but it is an irreconcilable one, which shall endure and develop even to the end. It is between Mary, His worthy Mother, and the devil — between the children and the servants of the Blessed Virgin and the children and instruments of Lucifer."[746] The Body of Christ is properly called the Church Militant, for "the entire Church is marked by the war of Satan against [Mary], because the Church is Christ in His living Mystical Body and she is at the same time His Bride as Virgin and mother having her model in the Blessed Virgin Mary, Mother of God."[747] This spiritual combat is conveyed by St. Paul: "Our wrestling is not against flesh and blood; but against principalities and power, against the rulers of the world of this darkness, against the spirits of wickedness in the high places" (Eph. 6:11–12). While the wrestling of principalities and powers is ongoing, there has been a "ramping up" of the manifestation of this reality, beginning in the nineteenth century, apparently coinciding with Pope Leo XIII's well-known, though persistently disturbing, vision.

Pope Leo XIII wrote eleven encyclicals on St. Louis de Montfort's true devotion to Mary and eight that attributed to her the role of Mediatrix; the first was written in 1883, even before his infamous mystical experience. As recounted in the introduction, the vision took place on October 13, 1884, exactly thirty-three years before the Miracle of the Sun at Fatima. After celebrating Mass and while in conference with the cardinals, Leo "witnessed" Satan boasting to God that he could destroy the Church. Satan was granted by God one century and more power over those who would serve him to accomplish his proposed task. Leo saw "the ages to come, the seductive powers and ravings of the devils against the Church in every land. But Saint Michael appeared in the moment of greatest distress and cast Satan and his cohorts back into the abyss of hell."[748] Leo soon after composed the St. Michael Prayer to be said by the universal Church — and which was said as part of the Leonine Prayers after every Low Mass until Vatican II "in order to obtain the help of God needful in

---

[746] Louis de Montfort, *True Devotion*, 39 (no. 52).
[747] Kevin Symonds, *Pope Leo XIII and the Prayer to St. Michael*, 2nd ed. (Boonville, NY: Preserving Christian Publications, 2018), iv.
[748] Ibid., ix, 8.

times of such difficulty and trial."[749] Just two months after the vision, Leo signed the first brief of the Confraternity of the Holy Face, and within the year, he immediately approved the Archconfraternity of the Holy Face "not only for France, but for the universe," breaking with tradition by not approving it more incrementally. And in 1888, Pope Leo beatified St. Louis de Montfort. The pontiff seems to have had a deep awareness of the spiritual armament needed for the faithful, led by the Church, to assist in defeating Satan; this weaponry consisted of man's true devotion to Mary as Co-Redemptrix, Mediatrix, and Advocate for Man as well as his making reparation to the Godhead as outlined in the Holy Face devotion, the pope having cemented it for all times and places by the archconfraternity.

Sister St. Pierre writes, "[Behold] these two precious streams, the Blood of Jesus and Mary's milk, let us unite our tears, thus forming, as it were, a powerful trinity which may, even on earth, be a pledge of our salvation."[750] She goes on to make the connection between the mitigation of God's justice for France (through the merits of Christ's Face offered as reparation for the outrages of blasphemy against God) and His Mother as the channel of His graces, bestowing mercy[751] upon that nation. Man is an important part of this "trinity," for he is to approach Christ, clothed with Mary's merits and virtues in exchange for giving his own to her in total consecration, and approach God the Father, clothed with Christ's merits and virtue (with Mary), as requested in the Holy Face devotion, begging mercy on the part of his brethren. Grace then flows (in the "opposite direction") from God the Father to Christ, from Christ to the Virgin, and from the Virgin to man, as Pope Leo XIII states in his encyclical *Iucunda Semper Expectatione* of September 8, 1894. Yet as part of the mysterious solidarity of the members of Christ's Mystical Body, man must initiate the process on behalf of his brethren.

Sister St. Pierre gave thanks to God for bestowing the two gifts of His adorable Face and the bosom of His august Mother, whence she "might imbibe the mysterious milk of grace and mercy"[752] for her brethren. She writes, "I behold ... the Adorable Face of my Divine Savior, whence flows the Precious Blood that assures me of Eternal Life, and ... the Maternal bosom of

---

[749] Ibid., 1.
[750] Sister St. Pierre, *Life of Sister St. Pierre*, 368–369.
[751] Ibid., 370–371.
[752] Ibid., 374.

Mary yielding a mysterious milk, sweet to my taste as the manna of old, and filling my soul with confidence in the infinite mercies, of which the Immaculate Virgin is the channel."[753] She ends by placing the Archconfraternity of Reparation[754] in the Sacred and Immaculate Hearts as its ever-powerful protectors.[755] For it is the offering of the wounded Countenance of Christ to the Father in reparation for affronts against the Godhead, as outlined in the Holy Face devotion, which is to draw the compassion of the Father, for the sake of His Son, in the form of mercy for sinners, and it is through Our Lady of the Holy Name of God that this mercy is to flow. The faithful, like Sister St. Pierre, are "deputed to draw forth at the fountain of mercy for the salvation of sinners" by making the requested reparation to the Father, drawing from its boundless treasures, channeled through Mary, "to be poured freely upon souls."[756] God has given man a necessary role in the salvation of his brethren.

Assuming this role, again as outlined in the introduction, the devout are consequently like both Job and his friends. Man is like Job's friends in offering Christ's Face to the Father in place of his own, in that God is infinitely more pleased by the Face of His most beloved Son than by man's own sinful faces (just as God was more pleased by Job's face than that of his friends). So Job is to Christ as Job's friends are to man, yet man is like Job, too, in that he is to make reparation for others, albeit not by his own merits but Christ's. For the Holy Face devotion, much like the spirituality of St. Thérèse, emphasized the importance of Christ's merits (rather than one's own) in attaining mercy for the salvation of sinners, unveiling Christ's Face as a most efficacious offering, *a power effectively previously unknown*,[757] even becoming, according to Christ, the "greatest source of grace second to the sacraments."[758]

Yet, even in this act of offering the Son's wounded Countenance to the Father in reparation, man does acquire merits (in that God has freely chosen to associate man with the work of His grace, flowing first from His own initiative, then from the collaboration of the faithful[759]). Christ says that "everything that

---

[753] Ibid.
[754] This was an early (1847), less comprehensive version of the work of reparation than the Archconfraternity of the Holy Face, which was approved after her death (1885).
[755] Sister St. Pierre, *Life of Sister St. Pierre*, 374.
[756] Sister Mary Emmanuel, *Life of Sister Marie*, 2.
[757] Ibid., 2.
[758] Sister Mary St. Peter, *Life of Sister Mary St. Peter*, 246–247.
[759] *CCC*, 2008.

is done for His Glory is to Him a delightful feast," surely accounting for some merit on the part of man for his effort in appeasing the Godhead (though not strictly deserved but as gifts of God's goodness[760]). St. Thérèse "redefined" merits as acts of kindness and consolation toward Christ, but clearly, *when done selflessly*, merits (as merits) are no less than acts of kindness and consolation toward Christ — as He says, "like *a delightful feast.*" So what is man to do with these "paltry" merits, as St. Thérèse would say? *He is to give them over selflessly and confidently to the Blessed Virgin, so that she may cover them with her own, making them exponentially more powerful.*

Thus, a comprehensive, modern celestial battle plan is born. Man turns over all to the Blessed Virgin as her spiritual child so that she may exchange his virtues and merits with her own, allowing him to stand before Christ "clothed" with His Mother. Man (with Mary) then likewise utilizes the merits and virtues of Christ in making a worthy offering of reparation *on behalf of his brethren* to God the Father for the modern affronts to Him. (These current affronts, according to Him, have never been exceeded, necessitating modern reparation to satisfy justice.) Appeased by this offering, the Father bestows mercy through Christ, which in turn flows to Mary, and from her to man. But again, man must initiate the process! Yet the rewards are truly biblical — no less than his assisting the Virgin in crushing the head of Satan by aiding in the restoration of life and light to the masses, thereby allowing for the destruction of heresies and their ideological-socioeconomic counterparts through the conversion of all. Thus, the Holy Face devotion as *Mother of All* Devotions (a play on today's vernacular expression) also refers to Mary's role as *the Mother* of All Devotions — the title suggesting a double connotation.

3. The Pinnacle Devotion

The crucial link between Mary and mercy is not limited to the Holy Face devotion, for Mary, as Mother of Mercy, provides a common thread within each, thereby affording approved devotions to Christ, as well as the Marian apparitions, as complements to one another. Mary appeared to St. Faustina on the feast of Our Lady of Mercy in 1935, revealing the (same) link between her spiritual motherhood and

---

[760] Council of Trent (1547): DS 1548.

Divine Mercy: "I am Mother to you all, thanks to the unfathomable mercy of God."[761] Indeed, Mary *embodies* mercy. St. Maximilian Kolbe wrote, "Saint Bernard says that the Lord God kept for Himself Justice but gave Mercy to the Mother of God.... The Immaculate receives the Mercy from the Lord God, but she is the personification of this Divine Mercy and that is why a soul is converted and sanctified if it turns to her."[762] This significance is brought forth in the insights of St. Louis de Montfort and the mystical experiences of Sister St. Pierre in the understanding of Mary's *essential* role in dispersing graces upon men, the true need for *total* reliance upon her, as a child to his mother (as discussed in the previous section). For her role as Mother of Mercy flows from her privilege of being Mother of God and Mother of Man. In that Jesus is flesh from her flesh, Mary made Christ's Redemption possible; Christ has returned His body to her, His merciful Mother, that she might collect His blood in her Immaculate Heart to pour upon men as grace for their conversion. All devotions to Christ and the Virgin inherently center upon this embodiment of Mary as Co-Redemptrix, Mediatrix, and Mother of Man, utilizing her to assist in the salvation of mankind.

Yet this role of Mother of Mercy, establishing Mary as the underlying link in all devotions to Christ and Mary, was most clearly designated and honored in the revelations surrounding the Holy Face devotion. This, together with the devotion's singularity in making reparation to the Godhead for modern offenses against the first three commandments (concerning the rights of God), makes it foundational to all others. Offered in union with the Sacred Heart in the Most Holy Sacrament of the Altar, the Holy Face devotion complements both the Sacred Heart and the Immaculate Heart, while giving them their greatest honor and consolation.[763] Given by God to appease justice for unparalleled times of iniquity and as an extension of Christ's Redemption, it sets forth the pattern of reparation or atonement first, followed by mercy, which is to flow through Mary. Though the devotee is called to selflessly assist in his brother's salvation by participating in this work, his own soul is transformed in the process, even receiving the imprint of Christ's likeness. These indicators, in addition to the devotion's

---

[761] Donald Calloway, M.I.C., *Purest of All Lilies: The Virgin Mary in the Spirituality of St. Faustina* (Stockbridge, MA: Marian Press, 2008).

[762] Carrie Gress, "The Hidden Connection between Mary and Divine Mercy," *National Catholic Register*, April 19, 2020, https://www.ncregister.com/blog/cgress/the-hidden-connection-between-mary-and-divine-mercy.

[763] Sister Mary St. Peter, *Life of Sister Mary St. Peter*, 127–130.

unparalleled promises and miracles, and per the words of Christ Himself, reveal reparation to the Holy Face as no less than the pinnacle devotion, the devotions' devotion, the "Mother of All Devotions."[764]

Together with true devotion to Mary (as discussed in the previous section), the work of reparation is a most efficacious tool, requested by God, for man to do his part to reclaim the Church and times for Christ. Again, Our Lord revealed that His wounded Face, as offered to the Father in reparation for offenses against the Trinity, is "the greatest grace second only to the Sacraments."[765] Our Lord also said of the devotion that it was "the most beautiful work that has yet appeared on the face of the earth,"[766] not "outshining" the beauty of Christ's Redemption but, rather, becoming an extension of it. For it is evidently both pleasing and fitting in God's eyes that mankind should take a more specific role in the salvation of his brethren, given how grave his offenses to God have become in modern times, "iniquity never having reached such a degree,"[767] according to Christ.

As previously discussed, reparation to the Holy Face is "intimately allied to the great Work of [Christ's] Redemption"[768] and is the most worthy and essential work of the era,[769] for God is demanding a new effort whose object is to repair the most despicable crimes of modern society, "deep rooted impiety and absolute incredulity."[770]

> These are two loathsome wounds of modern society which corrode all that is most sacred. To combat this satanical scourge and to expiate the abominations which result, our only Mediator offers us his Holy Face, this portion of his sacred humanity in which he suffered the ignominies of his Passion. He demands a new work whose object is to repair these crimes of modern society.[771]

[764] Sister Mary St. Peter, *Life of Sister Mary St. Peter*, 198. Also, devotions are forms of popular piety outside the liturgy, which is, however, their origin and aim.
[765] Ibid., 246–247.
[766] Ibid., 311–312.
[767] Ibid., 159.
[768] Ibid., 312.
[769] Ibid.
[770] Ibid., 311–312.
[771] Ibid.

Man's redemption was purchased for him by Christ on the Cross and is continually renewed in the source and summit of the Faith, the Holy Sacrifice of the Altar; it is by its excellence the noblest and most sublime manifestation of the wisdom and love of God. But current times, rampant with pride and blasphemy, have inflicted on society iniquity heretofore unequalled, according to Christ. These modern affronts "renew the injuries to His Face,"[772] making reparation to the Holy Face, together allied to the work of the Redemption, and offered by the Sacred Heart in the Most Holy Sacrament of the Altar, "the most noble and most necessary work of the times."[773] As confirmation of its essential status, the Holy Face devotion moreover *complements* both the Sacred Heart and the Immaculate Heart, also giving them their greatest honor and consolation,[774] as well as being "the sole means of appeasing the Father"[775] in the face of chastisement.

Repeated numerous times in the revelations given to Sister St. Pierre, Christ revealed that "Satan will make use of every means in his power to annihilate this work from the very outset."[776] The special attention given to it by the devil is another indication of the degree of importance it has in the ultimate spiritual unfolding of things. Indeed, regarding the devotion's significance, Our Lord Himself explained within the revelations to Sister St. Pierre how this reparation to the divinity of the Triune God, versus those pertaining more to the sacred humanity of Christ, is the highest devotion, far surpassing all others[777] (though all are interrelated and essential). For according to Christ, man cannot comprehend the malice and abomination of blasphemy, which opposes the reverence and glory due to Him. He told Sister St. Pierre that were His justice not restrained by His mercy, it would instantly crush the guilty (the blasphemers), and "all creatures, even those that are inanimate, would avenge His outraged honor."[778] Christ compared devotion to His Holy Face to "the miraculous wine served at the end of the wedding feast of Cana"[779] (contrasted with the "common

---

[772] Ibid., 238, 253.
[773] Ibid., 311–312.
[774] Ibid., 121, 130, 153, 158, 244.
[775] Ibid., 256, 290.
[776] Ibid., 154, 200, 329. "From the outset, Jesus declared to me that He would permit the devil to counteract His designs, in order that the confidence of His servants might be proven." And, Ibid., 310.
[777] Ibid., 198, 329.
[778] Ibid., 198.
[779] Ibid., 329.

wine" of the other devotions) and explicitly emphasized to Sister St. Pierre the excellence of the work of reparation,[780] how agreeable it was to God, the angels, and the saints, and how salutary it was to the Church, lamenting that if men but knew the glory the soul acquires in saying only once in a spirit of reparation for blasphemy, "Admirable is the name of God!"[781]

As previously outlined, offenses against the Godhead as represented by the Holy Face are (at the same time) offenses against the "Face of the Church," or her doctrine.[782] The modern predicament of an unprecedented, marked decline in morals ultimately revolves around an unwillingness by the world to submit to the immutable teachings of Our Lord preserved within the doctrine of the Catholic Church. The Holy Face devotion is to make reparation for offenses against the first three commandments, concerning the rights of God, prohibiting idolatry, irreverence, and the profanation of Sunday and holy days — in short, all blasphemy. They are foundational to the practice of the last seven commandments, which concern the rights of man and which prohibit sins against one's neighbor. Yet it seems that most today *at best* feel that the last seven can stand on their own. Denial of the part that God and the Church play in morality is essentially the problem of relativism in which each person decides for himself his own morality, making of himself a god, manifesting, at best, a confused notion of objective sin and, at worst, a total disregard of it.

Again, relativism gives way to socialism, Communism, atheism, and satanism; they all deny to varying degrees the absolute truth of God, manifested in natural law, which allows man to deduce the universal, God-given values and rights of men. These systems of thought are grave offenses to the Triune God, and Communism, as particularly mentioned in the revelations, is an especial evil to defeat in that it is "the sworn enem[y] of the Church and of ... Christ,"[783]

---

[780] Ibid., 198. And Sister St. Pierre, *Life of Sister St. Pierre*, 180.
[781] Sister Mary St. Peter, *Life of Sister Mary St. Peter*, 198.
[782] Ibid., 244–245.
[783] Ibid., 319. These are Our Lord's words to Sister St. Pierre. He recommended a specific (additional) means of combating Communists: offering the Cross and all instruments of His Passion in reparation to the Godhead.

As outlined also in footnote 54, it may be confusing to the reader why a book published in 1884 should be referenced in referring to Communism; the *Communist Manifesto* was not published until the year Sister St. Pierre died (1848), the Russian and Chinese revolutions had not taken place, and there were no countries at that time referred to as Communist. France, however, was the center of the "revolutionary and anti-social" spirit that had spread over Europe, "assuming different names at different

in its overtly anti-God foundation (as will be discussed at length in chapter 8). Man is to "repair" its (and all) offenses against the majesty of God in this reparation to the Godhead. The Holy Face devotion is thus a most timely offering designed to reorient man to God, presented by man *in union with Christ* to the Father, by virtue of the merits of Christ's dolorous Face.

In addition to being a most efficacious and timely remedy to man's modern ills, it is the most beautiful work in that it is Christ who is giving us, in mercy, His Face to be offered by mankind to appease the wrath of God the Father and to bring salvation to men, a completion of the circle: man is to assist in the redemption of his neighbor by offering in reparation (with Mary) the wounded Countenance of Christ to the Father. Again, it is a most powerful offering, for it allows man to utilize the merits and love of Christ, encapsulated in His wounded Countenance, to invoke the compassion of the Father, drawing mercy for sinners to flow through Mary, thereby uniting the power of God with the cooperation of man. Moved by the most adorable and beloved Face of His Son, disfigured by current blasphemies, and His wrath being subdued by this offering,[784] the Father has pity on man's face, disfigured by sin. The Father thus imprints the image of Christ upon the devotee, making man like unto Him. Man is thereby formed into a vessel of reparation and love in which he, in union with Christ (and Mary), becomes a mediator between God's justice and mercy, aiding in the salvation of his brethren, while also allowing for his own spiritual transformation in the process.

While according to the care with which a soul performs the reparatory work, his own soul is restored to its original beauty,[785] *Christ heavily emphasized the selflessness with which devotees should make reparation to the Godhead in this devotion.*[786] Yet an indication of the pinnacle nature of the Holy Face devotion are the unparalleled promises[787] attached to them. Well-known, popular devotions, like

---

epochs to suit the caprice of the moment; at one time styling themselves Socialists, then Liberals, and again Nihilists.... Toward the end of the reign of Louis Philip, at the period of ... the life and communications of Sr. Mary St. Peter,... they bore the appellation of Communists." Ibid., 318–319.

[784] Ibid., 198, 329.
[785] Sister St. Pierre, *Life of Sister St. Pierre*, 232.
[786] Ibid., 186.
[787] The Holy Face devotion promises (as also listed in the introduction) are:
By my Holy Face you will work marvels.
You will obtain from my Holy Face the salvation of a multitude of sinners.
All those who honor My Face in a spirit of reparation will by doing perform the office of the pious Veronica.

the Rosary and the Sacred Heart, likewise attach beautiful promises, mostly centered upon personal salvation and temporal assistance. The Divine Mercy devotion shares with the Holy Face similar promises to these, of final perseverance and the obtaining of all that is necessary in the way of temporal assistance, yet both additionally promise the salvation of the masses and heavenly rewards. The Holy Face devotion, however, is the only one to specifically list the working of miracles and the power of the Face of Christ having the ability to imprint itself upon the devotee, as well as offering the greatest source of grace second to the sacraments and being the sole means of appeasing the Father's wrath (in the face of chastisement).

Miracles matter in affirming celestial endeavors, for they are clear proof of the divine origin of revelation. "It is God's positive testimony that the doctrine [of revelation] is true, and God cannot testify to a lie."[788] Indeed, the wonders worked at the hands of Dupont[789] leave little doubt of the superlative nature of

---

According to the care they take in making reparation to My Face, disfigured by blasphemers, so will I take care of their souls which have been disfigured by sin. My Face is the Seal of the Divinity, which has the virtue of reproducing in souls the image of God; I will imprint thereon my own image, and I will render it as beautiful as when it came forth from the baptismal font.

My adorable Face is the seal of the Divinity, having the power to imprint Itself on the souls of those who apply it to their persons.

Those who by words, prayers or writing defend My cause in the Work of Reparation, especially My priests, I will defend before My Father, and will give them My Kingdom.

As in an earthly kingdom, the subjects can procure all they desire by being provided with a piece of money stamped with the effigy of the monarch, so also shall you be able to obtain all that you desire in the kingdom of heaven, on presenting the impress of my sacred humanity, which is my Holy Face.

Those who on earth contemplate the wounds of My Face shall in Heaven behold it radiant with glory.

They will receive in their souls a bright and constant irradiation of My Divinity, that by their likeness to My Face they shall shine with particular splendor in Heaven.

I will defend them, I will preserve them, and I assure them of Final Perseverance.

[788] Michael Sheehan, *Catholic Doctrine and Apologetics: Part 2; Apologetics*, ed. Denis Bouchard (Dublin: Gill and Son, 1962), 56.

[789] If not for the Church approval of the revelations surrounding the Holy Face devotion, one may see them as too fantastic, too liberal on the part of Our Lord, such that, perhaps, one may question whether they should be taken literally, concerning especially whether prodigies and marvels, as in miracles, could really flow from this devotion in the here and now. Remarkably, there is bountiful evidence of their literal truth. In 1851, less than a decade after these revelations began, Ven. Leo Dupont realized the first miracle to be tied to the devotion. It was the first of *thousands*, spanned over a period of thirty years, such that Pope Pius IX declared Dupont "perhaps the greatest miracle worker in Church

the devotion attached to them, surely playing a part in the revelations surrounding the Holy Face devotion gaining such decided and immediate approval from Pope Leo XIII.[790]

✠ ✠ ✠

In conclusion: as far as devotions go, reparation to the Holy Face is foremost. The Holy Face devotion is allied to the Redemption, hewn for repairing the ills of a time in which, according to Christ, iniquity has never been exceeded. Complementing the Sacred Heart in the Most Holy Sacrament of the Altar, it also outlines the necessity of true devotion to the Immaculate Heart as Co-Redemptrix, Mediatrix, and Advocate for Man in crushing Satan (discussed in the previous section) by countering man-modified, primordial sins of pride in making reparation to the Godhead. It is the greatest consolation and honor to both the Sacred and Immaculate Hearts. Christ's wounded Face, as offered to the Father in reparation for offenses against the first three commandments, is the greatest source of grace second to the sacraments and has the power of imprinting the divine likeness upon the devotee, all while drawing graces — flowing from the Father to the Son to Mary to man — for the salvation of the masses toward the conversion of the whole world. It is also the sole means of appeasing the Father, specifically in approaching His just wrath for the modern sins of blasphemy, making it a most efficacious spiritual armament in defeating Communism and all blasphemous ideologies, affording man the opportunity to do his part in reclaiming the Church and times for Christ. In addition to these indicators, Christ unambiguously stated in the revelations to Sister St. Pierre that reparation to the Holy Face is the highest devotion, far exceeding all other devotions, in its focus upon the Divine Trinity.

history." The number of his documented miracles exceeded even those at Lourdes and designated Ven. Dupont for all time "the Holy Man of Tours." He performed the miracles using prayers consistent with the Holy Face devotion and oil from a lamp burning in front of an image drawn from the "Miracle of the Vatican," in which Veronica's veil at the Vatican became miraculously enlivened during a Christmas octave exhibition in 1849, ordered by Pius IX to entreat God's protection of the Vatican during the wave of the second French revolution. Copies were made and had been touched to the original Veronica's veil, a true relic of the Cross, and the lance that pierced Christ's side, and these copies, indicated by a red wax seal, were distributed at first mostly to convents and monasteries, then to devout laity. The Carmel of Tours gave one to Dupont.

[790] (As mentioned, Pope Leo saw fit to break from tradition by not approving the devotion incrementally, as it would have usually been first only approved for France, its place of origin; instead, he approved the Archconfraternity of the Holy Face *immediately for the whole world* by papal brief in 1885.)

He also described it as the most beautiful work yet to appear under the sun and compared it to the miraculous wine served at the end of the wedding feast of Cana. As the highest devotion, and given to mankind by Our Lady, through whom the merciful graces for conversion of sinners flow, the title "Mother of All Devotions" is befitting.

4. The Holy Face Devotion as Synthesis of and Foundational to All Devotions

While all devotions were given distinctly for a reason, and all are intrinsically necessary and complementary, all rest in essential ways upon the foundation of the Holy Face devotion as given to Sister St. Pierre (as discussed in the previous section). Adoration and reparation to the Godhead are most specifically requested in the Holy Face devotion, which is the highest and most exalted worship, versus that to various aspects of Christ's sacred humanity, for in the revelations, the Face of Christ mirrors the very attributes of the Trinity as well as His human perfections. It is likewise the only devotion centered on reparation for offenses against the first three commandments, those concerning the rights of God, as opposed to those sins against one's neighbor. It is the greatest source of grace second to the sacraments and has the power to imprint the divine likeness upon devotees. It is the devotion that designates and most honors Mary's role as Co-Redemptrix, Mediatrix, and Advocate for Man, Christ even having bestowed her the honor of giving it to mankind under a new title, "Our Lady of the Holy Name of God." Its promises and miracles surpass those of other devotions, assisting man in his specific role to help in reclaiming for Christ the Church and times in the face of modern evils, those which Christ describes as never having been exceeded, for it unites the cooperation of man with the power of God in assisting Mary in defeating Satan. Key elements of the other devotions were set forth first or foremost in the Holy Face, making it not only complementary and foundational to them but in some sense their synthesis.

The Sacred Heart Devotion

Central to the Holy Face devotion is its complement: the Sacred Heart. The Sacred Heart devotion is centered on worship of Christ through His Heart, which represents His love as manifested in the Incarnation, wherein He, while remaining God, took the form of man; His love was likewise manifested in His Passion and death as well as the institution of the Eucharist. St. Margaret Mary Alacoque (d. 1690) suffered greatly in her youth from her father's premature death, a paralyzing illness, and cruel treatment from relatives, before becoming a Visitation nun of Paray-le-Monial, in Burgundy, France. She was not especially esteemed by some of the nuns, who considered her slow and awkward, yet she was granted the following revelation of Christ, and many to follow, revealing the secrets of His Sacred Heart:

> My Divine Heart is so inflamed with love for men ... that, being unable any longer to contain within Itself the flames of Its burning Charity, It must needs spread them abroad by thy means, and manifest Itself to [mankind] in order to enrich them with the precious treasures which I discover to thee, and which contain graces of sanctification and salvation necessary to withdraw them from the abyss of perdition.[791]

As part of Christ's design for the salvation of men who ignore the treasures of His Sacred Heart, St. Margaret Mary by degrees offered herself to bear the weight of the divine wrath in the place of guilty souls.

The devotion is to make reparation to Christ for man's ingratitude, especially shown by indifference to the Holy Eucharist. St. Margaret Mary writes,

> Jesus Christ, my sweet Master, presented Himself to me all resplendent with glory, His Five Wounds shining like five suns. From His Sacred Humanity issued flames on all sides, but especially from His adorable Breast, which resembled a furnace, and which was open and disclosed to me His most amiable Heart, the living source of these flames. He revealed to me at the same time the ineffable marvels of His pure love, and the excess of His love towards men. He complained of their ingratitude and said that He felt this more sensibly than any other pain in His Passion.... [He told me,] "They entertain only coldness towards Me, and the only return they make to My advances is by rejecting Me."[792]

---

[791] Margaret Mary Alacoque, *The Autobiography of Saint Margaret Mary*, trans. Sisters of the Visitation (Charlotte, NC: TAN Books, 2012), 53.
[792] George Tickell, *The Life of Blessed Margaret Mary, with Some Account of the Devotion to the Sacred Heart* (New York: P. J. Kenedy, 1904), 170–171.

She continued to suffer, especially on evenings between Thursday and Friday, to appease the justice of God by also mitigating in some way the bitterness Christ felt at being abandoned by His apostles.[793]

At the request of Christ, as revealed to St. Margaret Mary, the Church instituted a feast of the Sacred Heart, commemorating the unrequited love of the Sacred Heart in the Eucharist, celebrated on the Friday after the feast of Corpus Christi. Christ related to her,

> Behold this Heart, Which has loved men so much, that It has spared nothing, even to exhausting and consuming Itself, in order to testify to them Its love; and in return I receive from the greater number nothing but ingratitude by reason of their irreverence and sacrileges, and by the coldness and contempt which they show Me in this Sacrament of Love. But what I feel the most keenly is that it is hearts which are consecrated to me, that treat Me thus. Therefore, I ask of thee that the Friday after the Octave of Corpus Christi be set apart for a special Feast to honor My Heart, by communicating on that day and making reparation to It by a solemn act, [to] make amends for the indignities which It has received during the time It has been exposed on the altars. I promise thee that My Heart shall expand Itself to shed in abundance the influence of Its divine love upon those who shall thus honor It and cause It to be honored.[794]

The Sacred Heart devotion has been recommended by many popes, especially Leo XIII and Pius XI,[795] and has been enormously popular among the faithful for some centuries.

The devotion is centered on the person of Jesus, manifested by His love for man in His Sacred Heart, an aspect of Christ's sacred humanity.

> Since Christ is a Divine Person, [man owes] Him not only as God but also as Man the supreme worship of adoration. Everything in His human nature is divine and adorable, because it belongs to Him, the Second Person of the Blessed Trinity; but [to excite man's devotion, he may adore Him] in relation to His Precious Blood, His Five Wounds, or

---

[793] Alacoque, *Autobiography*, 57.
[794] Ibid., 95–96.
[795] Michael Sheehan, *Catholic Doctrine and Apologetics: Part 1; Catholic Doctrine*, ed. Denis Bouchard (Dublin: Gill and Son, 1962), 88.

His Sacred Heart... not as distinct from him, but as... [an aspect of His being both God and Man.]⁷⁹⁶

Adoration of aspects of Christ's sacred humanity ultimately, then, lead to adoration of His divinity. This is why, according to the revelations given to Sister St. Pierre, all devotions centered upon the sacred humanity of Christ are in a different category than that to the Holy Face, in that Christ's wounded Countenance as object of adoration in the Holy Face devotion represents foremost the very divinity of the Godhead, the Holy Trinity itself. The wounded Countenance is also representative of the Face of the Church, or her doctrine, wounded anew by blasphemous heresies against the Mystical Body of Christ, as well as the Face of Christ's sacred humanity, which received the blows of blasphemy during the Passion. It is primarily centered, however, on the Trinity and current offenses of irreverence and idolatry against it, renewing the injuries to Christ's Face. It does not "lead to" adoration of the divinity of Christ, for it is already adoration of His divinity — as the Second Person of the Holy Trinity and as representing the Godhead.

Yet the Sacred Heart and Holy Face are intrinsically complementary, the Sacred Heart even having provided the mystical backdrop for the initiation of devotion to the Holy Face. Our Lord warned Sister St. Pierre that "the demon would do his utmost to annihilate this Work [of Reparation, which] sprung from His Sacred Heart."⁷⁹⁷ And according to the revelations given to her, *the Holy Face is the corollary of devotion to the Sacred Heart*; the one is the manifestation and complement to the other. Indeed, "the Divine Master, in the order of His designs over His faithful servant, willed that [Sister St. Pierre] should reach the inmost depths of His Sacred Heart, [before] being initiated in the Reparative Mystery of His Dolorous Face."⁷⁹⁸ Ven. Dupont, establishing a connection between the revelations of Bl. (now St.) Margaret Mary Alacoque, says: "If the Heart of Jesus be the emblem of love, His Adorable Face is the expression of sufferings endured for us [in love]."⁷⁹⁹ The Face is the living, speaking reflection of the Heart, according to Father Cros, which is why the Church prefers the images of the Heart of Jesus not to be isolated from the Face. He also states that the

---

[796] Ibid., 88.
[797] Sister St. Pierre, *Life of Sister St. Pierre*, 164.
[798] Ibid., 109.
[799] Ibid.

Face of Jesus at Paray-le-Monial was a dolorous Face, expressing a Heart that has loved man so much, yet receives from him in return only ingratitude: "It was surely not joy that the Face of Jesus expressed."[800]

Moreover, Sister St. Pierre was adamant that the work of reparation to counter offenses against the Godhead and His Church "can be worthily done only by the Sacred Heart." She adds, "Therefore, when I receive Christ [in the Holy Eucharist], I begin by giving myself to Him, and annihilating myself in His Heart; then, I allow this Divine [Savior] to fulfil in my soul the office of Mediator between God and man."[801] Christ told her, "Behold! If there be any sorrow like unto Mine! My Divine Father, and my Spouse, Holy Church, *cherished objects of My Heart* are despised and outraged by My enemies! Will none rise to console Me, by combating in Their defense? ... Behold! What torrents of tears flow from My eyes!"[802] She adds:

> He has made me understand ... that mankind is incapable of comprehending the gross insult offered to God by blasphemy; *that it pierces His Heart*, and makes Him like unto another Lazarus, covered with sores; He invited me to imitate the dogs that consoled poor Lazarus by licking his ulcers; and He told me I would render Him a great service in thus employing my tongue to daily glorify the Most Holy Name of God despised and blasphemed by sinners; that I must do so without regard to an interior consolation the devotion might yield me, it should be sufficient for me to know that I thus healed His Divine Wounds, and afforded Him a signal gratification.[803]

Elsewhere Christ states that to honor and praise the name of the Father is of greatest consolation of His Sacred Heart.[804]

Indeed, Sister St. Pierre stated that it was in the Sacred Heart of Jesus that she found the work of reparation.[805] Sister St. Pierre often prayed, "Eternal Father, look upon the Divine Heart of Jesus, which I offer Thee to receive the wine of Thy Justice, that it may be changed for us into the wine of Mercy."[806] She understood

---

[800] Ibid.
[801] Ibid., 144.
[802] Ibid., 168. (My emphasis.)
[803] Ibid., 186. (My emphasis.)
[804] Ibid., 280.
[805] Ibid.
[806] Ibid., 264.

that each time she offered this petition, she would obtain "a drop of Divine wrath, which, falling ... into the Vase of the Sacred Heart of Jesus, would be changed into a wine of mercy." Our Lord told Sister St. Pierre:

> My daughter, I give you My Face and My Heart, I give you My Blood, I give you My Wounds; draw from them and pour out upon others! Buy freely, for My Blood is the price of souls! Oh! what sorrow for My Heart to behold despised by men, remedies which have cost Me so dearly! Ask of My Father as many souls as I have shed drops of blood in My Passion![807]

The two devotions are inherently united, despite the Holy Face being concerned with the Divinity, while the Sacred Heart is essentially concerned with Christ's humanity.

The Sacred Heart is also corollary with the Holy Eucharist, devotion to each reciprocally increasing the other, yet both are also intrinsically linked to the Holy Face.

> If we have devotion to the Sacred Heart, we will wish to find It to adore It, to love It, and where shall we look for It but in the Blessed Eucharist where It is found, eternally living?... The devotion to the Divine Heart infallibly brings souls to the Blessed Eucharist; and faith in and devotion to the Blessed Eucharist necessarily lead souls to discover the mysteries of Infinite Love of which the Divine Heart is the organ and the symbol.[808]

Sister St. Pierre is known to have had a very strong devotion to the Sacred Heart and Holy Face as veiled in the Most Holy Sacrament of the Altar. She writes six months before her death,

> Now my interior occupation is to adore Our Lord in the Most Holy Sacrament of the altar, as the real Restorer of the outrages committed against the glory of God His Father [as the veiled Face of Christ]. Oh, what consolations my soul feels in offering this Host of benediction and

---

[807] Ibid., 270.
[808] John Croiset, *The Devotion to the Sacred Heart*, 2nd ed., trans. Patrick O'Connell (Rockford, IL: TAN Books, 1988), 57 (extract from *The Book of Infinite Love* by Mother Louise Margaret).

Reparation to God's Majesty, insulted by the wicked. Immense are the graces which I receive from our Divine Savior in the Holy Eucharist, I cannot explain these favors. His way of working in my soul is more secret; they cause faith and charity to grow in me. Thus, my union with our Lord is greatly augmented: I am happily bound to His Feet in the Most holy Sacrament, and there I keep Him company with the Holy Angels. The dew of grace, falling on the ground of my soul, and the burning Sun of Jesus' Sacred Heart warming this poor sterile soil, causes holy thought to blossom which I present as flowers to Jesus, my Spouse. I have written of some of them of which I often make use in visiting our Amiable Jesus in the abode of His Love. They bring grace to my soul; it is the fruit of the Holy Spirit with which my heart nourishes itself with delight. Oh, what a treasure we have in the Adorable Eucharist; I have never well understood it.[809]

The Eucharist is the unique base of the personal reparation of Sister St. Pierre upon which the Sacred Heart and the Holy Face are united, forming a simple means of reparation toward the end of her life, wholly established in that of Christ and in prayer.[810] Indeed, she stated that Our Lord in the Blessed Sacrament and the prayers of the just are continually holding back divine wrath[811] in the face of so much evil, especially in the form of blasphemy against the Godhead, which excites the direct outrage of God's majesty.

The Holy Face Devotion as Revealed to Bl. Pierina

The Holy Face devotion as revealed to Sister St. Pierre and that revealed in the early twentieth century to Bl. Mother Maria Pierina De Micheli of the Italian Daughters of the Immaculate Conception are complementary. Indeed, they are deeply corresponding with one other, as well as to the Sacred Heart. No one who reads an account of Bl. Pierina's life can help but be moved by the severe trials and sufferings she underwent, largely and literally at the hands of Satan in his attempt to destroy her efforts of spreading devotion to the Holy Face. Both she and Sister St. Pierre were victim souls for the promotion of devotion to the Holy Face, as was St. Margaret Mary Alacoque for the Sacred Heart, abandoning themselves totally to Christ for their respective causes.

---

[809] Van den Bossche, *Message*, 162.
[810] Ibid.
[811] Ibid., 163.

Our Lady visited Bl. Pierina. She presented Pierina with a scapular that bore the image of the Holy Face of Jesus on one side, along with the words "Let Thy Face shine upon us, O Lord," and on the other a Host surrounded by rays and the words "Remain with us, Lord." Our Lady told her:

> This scapular is an armor of defense, a shield of strength, a token of the love and mercy which Jesus wishes to give to the world in these times of lust and hatred against God and His Church. Diabolical nets are set, to rob men of their faith. Evil spreads. There are very few true apostles. A divine remedy is necessary, and this remedy is the Holy Face of Jesus. All who wear a Scapular like this [or medal] and make, if possible, every Tuesday a visit to the Blessed Sacrament, [to] repair the outrages which the Face of my Son Jesus received during His Passion and receives every day in the Holy Eucharist will be strengthened in Faith, prompt to defend it and to overcome all difficulties internal and external. Furthermore, they will have a peaceful death under the loving gaze of my Divine Son.[812]

The requests of reparation from Christ given to Bl. Pierina center upon the outrages the Holy Face received in His Passion and still receives daily as veiled in the Most Holy Sacrament of the Altar (via neglect and irreverence). The Holy Face of Jesus became an entrance to Christ's Heart and a book of love for Pierina.[813] Christ having asked her for reparation, Pierina became increasingly desirous of suffering and immolating herself for the salvation of souls in imitation and contemplation of the Holy Face of Jesus in pain and suffering.

Like Sister St. Pierre before her, who was invited by Christ to "kiss most [lovingly] in a spirit of reparation for the betrayal kiss of Judas, the image of the Holy Face,"[814] Jesus repeated verbatim to Pierina that she kiss His Face in reparation for Judas's kiss. Later Christ appeared to her with a wounded Countenance (something Sister St. Pierre never actually saw in that her experiences were infused understanding and not visions). He told her:

> I wish that My Face, which reflects the intimate sorrow of My Soul, the suffering and love of My Heart, be more honored. Who contemplates Me consoles Me.... My beloved, I renew to you the offering of My Holy Face, so that you may offer it incessantly to God the Father. Through

---

[812] Ibid., 6.
[813] Hilary Conti, *Seeking the Face of Jesus* (Clifton, NJ: Holy Face Monastery, 1990), 66.
[814] Sister St. Pierre, *Life of Sister St. Pierre*, 229.

this offering you will obtain the salvation of many souls. When you shall offer it for My priests, wonders will be worked.... Contemplate My Face and you will penetrate the depths of the sorrows of My Heart. Console Me and look for souls who will immolate themselves with Me, for the salvation of the world.... Every time My Face is contemplated, I will pour out My love into the heart of those persons and by the means of My Holy Face, the salvation of many souls will be obtained.... Perhaps some souls fear that the devotion to My Holy Face will diminish that to My Heart. On the contrary, it will be a completion and augmentation of that devotion. Souls contemplating My Face participate in My Sorrow. They feel the necessity of love and reparation. Is not this the true devotion to My Heart?[815]

Christ told Pierina that He was "renewing the offering of His Holy Face, that it may be offered incessantly to God the Father."[816] This is surely a reference to the request made to Sister St. Pierre, as well as the request that "souls immolate themselves with Him for the salvation of the world, the Divine remedy being His Holy Face."[817] In many respects, the devotion as given to Bl. Pierina is a continuation of the one given to Sister St. Pierre.

The revelations given to Bl. Pierina continue the deep devotion to the veiled Face of Christ in the Most Holy Sacrament of the Altar, which was so dear to Sister St. Pierre, especially toward the end of her short life. Christ had asked Sister St. Pierre to receive Holy Communion in reparation for blasphemy and for the fact that His love was most unappreciated in the Blessed Sacrament. She understood that the Holy Face is hidden under the eucharistic veil and that it is by this august sacrament that Jesus wishes to communicate to souls the virtue of His Holy Face, which is there "more dazzling than the sun."[818] He then promised to imprint His divine likeness on the souls of those who honor it.[819]

Moreover, both devotions are complementary to that of the Sacred Heart, even "completing" it, according to Christ's revelations to Pierina, focusing on consoling Him through love and reparation. Christ also told Bl. Pierina:

---

[815] *The Treasure of the Holy Face of Jesus* (Montreal: Holy Face Association, 1993), 4. And Conti, *Seeking the Face*, 59–60, 69–70, 73–74.
[816] Conti, *Seeking the Face of Jesus*, 73.
[817] Ibid., 74.
[818] Sister St. Pierre, *Life of Sister St. Pierre*, 278.
[819] Ibid.

Do you see how I suffer? Yet very few understand Me. Those who say they love Me are very ungrateful. I have given My Heart as the sensible object of My love to men, and I give My Face as the sensible object of My sorrow for all the sins of men. I wish that It be venerated by a special feast on Tuesday, the day before Ash Wednesday, preceded by a novena in which all the faithful make reparation with Me, uniting themselves in participating with Me in My sorrow.[820]

In the Holy Face devotion as given to Sister St. Pierre:

The principal feast of the Archconfraternity of the Holy Face, based upon the revelations given to Sister Saint Pierre, is that of Saint Peter, in whose Church at Rome the Veil of Saint Veronica is preserved, while its lesser feasts are those of the Crown of Thorns and the Transfiguration. Moreover, special homage is paid to the Holy Face on Good Friday, when the Church commemorates the insults our Blessed Lord endured for us and especially the outrages offered to His Sacred Face, and also on Easter Sunday when the Veil of Saint Veronica is publicly exhibited at Rome in presence of the Sovereign Pontiff.[821]

Indeed, it seems the Sacred Heart and the two devotions to the Holy Face form a kind of "trinity" of reparation and love designed for the faithful, building upon and reverting to one another.

Yet they are given as distinct by Heaven for a reason and do have important differences. There are distinctions in the object of reparation, for example. The revelations given to Pierina focused on real-time injuries to the Face of Christ during His Passion and current suffering due to ongoing irreverence to the Blessed Sacrament. The Face of Christ in the revelations given to Sister St. Pierre also represents the merciful love of Christ's Redemption, reflected in His suffering for men during the Passion as imprinted on the veil of Veronica, but the Face is meant to primarily represent *current injuries to the Face of Christ* as representative of heresies against the Church's doctrine and especially blasphemies against the Trinity (wherein renewed injuries are caused by offenses "aimed" against the Church or Godhead "falling upon" Christ's Face). The Holy Face devotion as given to Bl. Pierina, like the Sacred Heart, is centered on making reparation to the sacred

---

[820] Conti, *Seeking the Face*, 83.
[821] *Manual of the Archconfraternity of the Holy Face* (Tours: Oratory of the Holy Face, 1887), 53–54.

humanity of Christ, while the one given to Sister St. Pierre makes reparation for offenses to the Godhead. While the devotion as given to Bl. Pierina is centered upon reparation for offenses against Christ's Face during the Passion and now in the Holy Sacrament, it also includes more general crimes of lust, for example (prohibited as part of the last seven sacraments, versus the first three). The devotion given to Sister St. Pierre is centered exclusively on crimes against the rights of God as prohibited in the first three commandments.

And there are different images associated with each: Pierina's devotion utilizes the Shroud of Turin, a suffering Face that is, however, no longer still living, a sign of the Savior's supreme sacrifice of death. The devotion as given to Sister St. Pierre utilizes the veil of Veronica, which recorded a living, still-suffering Face in need of consolation — by which merciful love was given and received by Veronica. Though the act of consolation is central to both, the devotion given to Bl. Pierina required consolation in the form of a metaphorical kiss, signifying love and appreciation toward Christ, especially in the Eucharist, while the one given to Sister St. Pierre asks consolation primarily through praises for God's majesty and the offering in reparation to the Godhead, which consoles the suffering Face of Jesus (as Head of His mystical body). Christ gave His wounded Countenance to be offered to the Father in reparation as an unparalleled gift to Sister St. Pierre (and all who practice the devotion), its power and graces heretofore virtually — if not altogether — unknown. He renewed this gift to Bl. Pierina, that it also be offered in reparation, though more centered on offenses to the sacred humanity of Christ than to that of the Godhead. And the promises of each share that this selfless offering of the suffering Face of Christ to the Father would result in the salvation of many souls, that marvels will be worked (when offered for priests, as specified in the case of Bl. Pierina's devotion), and that help with temporal needs would be granted as well as final perseverance. As previously outlined, there are significant additional promises of the Holy Face devotion as given to Sister St. Pierre.

Though there are notable differences, the devotions share much in common, and in many ways, the Holy Face as given to Bl. Pierina is a continuation of the one given to Sister St. Pierre. Pope St. John Paul II stated in his apostolic letter *Rosarium Virginis Mariae* that "to contemplate the Face of Christ, and to contemplate it with Mary, is the 'program which I have set before the Church at the dawn of the third millennium,'" at least implicitly dedicating the millennium to the Holy Face, while emphasizing a Marian dimension in doing so.[822] He also developed a eucharistic aspect in his encyclical *Ecclesia de Eucharistia*, explaining that the eucharistic Face of Jesus presents in sacramental form all the historic Faces of Jesus.[823] And while this was surely meant to discourage one image, one Face of Christ, to be placed above others in contemplating the Countenance of Christ, in the pope's emphasis on the eucharistic Face of Christ, many likely most associated the Bl. Pierina devotion with the call for a millennium of the Holy Face (though the Holy Face as given to Sister St. Pierre unequivocally also incorporates the Blessed Sacrament in its devotion, even making clear that the devotion is designed to be in union with the Sacred Heart in the Most Holy Sacrament of the Altar). The result seems to be a merging of the two devotions by the faithful, though, in the process, a diminishment of the message of each, resulting somehow especially in the abatement of the revelations given to Sister St. Pierre (in that, perhaps, they are not as immediately associated with the Blessed Sacrament, especially since Sister St. Pierre's original, longer biographies, which emphasize this fact, are much less readily available). The time seems ripe for the faithful to be fully informed of, and dedicated to, both, as was set forth in the revelations given to, and the sacrificial lives of, Sister St. Pierre and Bl. Pierina, respectively.

THE DIVINE MERCY DEVOTION

One may wonder how the Holy Face devotion as given to Sister St. Pierre could be complementary, much less foundational, to the Divine Mercy devotion. For the Holy Face devotion is centered on appeasing justice to draw mercy, while the Divine Mercy devotion — though also utilized in satisfying justice — is centered foremost on love and mercy, showcasing these as God's greatest attributes according to the revelations given to St. Faustina, even exceeding that of justice.[824] The devotion was given to St. Faustina Kowalska in the 1930s, beginning with a vision in which the young Polish nun saw Jesus with rays of mercy streaming from the area of His Heart. Christ related to her His mercy is unlimited and available even to the greatest sinners. The devotion was given to accentuate, as a means of salvation to sinners,

---

[822] "A Millennium of the Holy Face?," *National Catholic Register*, accessed October 2, 2023, https://www.ncregister.com/blog/a-millennium-of-the-holy-face.

[823] Ibid.

[824] Maria Faustina Kowalska, *Diary: Divine Mercy in My Soul* (Stockbridge, MA: Marian Press, 2003), no. 180.

God's mercy and love, which are most often rejected and unappreciated, according to Christ, for sinners do not trust in God's mercy as a recourse in salvation.

The problem in seeing the devotions as complementary, then, is reminiscent of the likely objection of most to the notion of the spiritualities of Sister St. Pierre and St. Thérèse of Lisieux being corresponding, given their seemingly opposed, respective victimhood to justice and mercy. Yet, as previously discussed, the victimhood of each is manifestly one and the same: Christ revealed to Sister St. Pierre that blasphemy wounds His Heart more than any other sin, so if divine justice is being outraged by the blasphemies of modern time more than those of any other, so is divine love being scorned by the same outrages. And ultimately, appeasing justice and satiating the unrequited love of God are not only achieved in the same selfless desire to appease God but are synonymous. Selfless reparation *is* an act of trust in God's goodness, as well as an act of merciful love of God and man — effecting appeasement of God and mercy for man. The Holy Face devotion and Divine Mercy may be seen in a similar complementary light.

Much like the spirituality of St. Thérèse, trust in God's mercy as a necessary component of the Divine Mercy devotion requires a childlike intimacy, a complete self-surrender to God in love.[825] St. Faustina writes, "I feel I am [God's] child, I feel I am wholly God's property.... I am completely at peace about everything because I know it is [God's] business to look after me. I have forgotten about myself completely. My trust placed in His Most Merciful Heart has no limit."[826] This childlike (yet heroic) trust in God is the essence of St. Thérèse's spiritual childhood. St. Faustina states almost verbatim what St. Thérèse expressed: "Even if [God] kills me, still will I trust in [Him]."[827] Christ related to her, "Every soul believing and trusting in My mercy will obtain it."[828] And "When a soul approaches Me with trust, I fill it with such an abundance of graces that it cannot contain them within itself, but radiates them to other souls."[829] Similarly, Christ told Faustina, "Take the graces that others spurn; take as many as you can carry."[830] This correlates with St. Thérèse's notion that souls

---

[825] M. Elzbieta Siepak and M. Nazaria Dlubak, *The Spirituality of Saint Faustina: The Road to Union with God*, trans. M. Nazareta Maleta and M. Caterina Esselen (Cracow: Sisters of Our Lady of Mercy, 2000), 42.
[826] Kowalska, *Diary*, no. 244.
[827] Ibid., no. 77.
[828] Ibid., no. 420.
[829] Ibid., no. 1074.
[830] Ibid., no. 454.

may receive the love of God rejected by others. Fittingly, St. Thérèse once appeared to St. Faustina in a dream and encouraged her to trust in Jesus.[831]

While the spirituality of the Holy Face devotion and that of St. Thérèse are deeply complementary, the Holy Face and Divine Mercy are in some sense even more so. For unlike St. Thérèse, St. Faustina did not feel personal merits, nor the corresponding need to satisfy justice, were problematic (the latter being generally attributed to Thérèse primarily only in more modern interpretations, as discussed previously). Christ related to St. Faustina, "Tell souls that I am giving them My mercy as a defense. I Myself am fighting for them and am bearing the just anger of My Father."[832] She was instructed by Christ, "Unite yourself continually with My agonizing Heart and make reparation to My justice."[833] He added, "If you knew what great merit and reward is earned by one act of pure love for Me, you would die of joy."[834] Yet *reparation* and *merit* and *reward* are words associated with appeasing justice, such that there is not a sense that justice is somehow "overridden" in the bestowing of all this mercy, but rather that it must still be satisfied — by Christ in this particular quote, but in Divine Mercy generally, man's efforts to atone for other is also required. Ultimately, then, Divine Mercy, like the Holy Face devotion, does not "bypass" justice, for Christ — and the faithful, in union with Christ — is satisfying it *on behalf of others*.

In the Holy Face devotion, the merits and love encased in the wounded Countenance of Christ are being offered in reparation to the Father to appease His justice and draw mercy for the masses; the devotee himself is also transformed by these graces into the divine likeness, becoming a vessel of reparation and merciful love for others. Similarly in Divine Mercy, souls are asked to join their sufferings to Christ's Passion in making atonement to the Father on behalf of sinners[835] and to please the heavenly Father with special pleasure by bearing Christ's features, so to speak, "to be a marvel to Angels and men."[836] For every soul, and especially those of religious, should reflect Christ's mercy. "My Heart overflows with compassion and mercy for all. The heart of My beloved must resemble Mine; from her heart must spring the fountain of My mercy for souls;

---

[831] Ibid., no. 150.
[832] Ibid., no. 1516.
[833] Ibid., no. 873.
[834] Ibid., no. 576.
[835] Ibid., no. 1032.
[836] Ibid., no. 367b.

otherwise, I will not acknowledge her as Mine."[837] And "They are a defense for the world before the justice of the Heavenly Father and a means of obtaining mercy for the world. The love and sacrifice of these souls [in this instance, those in convents] sustain the world in existence."[838] In the Holy Face, a soul is expected to help his brethren attain mercy by offering Christ's Face to the Father in reparation, but through this process, he is transformed — "rewarded" with the likeness of the Divinity, resulting in his being even more merciful to his brethren. In Divine Mercy, there is more of an emphasis on man himself attaining the personal transformation by his exercise of mercy toward others, thereby taking on Christ's features (by imitation of Him).

In revelations of Divine Mercy, Christ lists three ways that a soul may exercise this mercy toward his neighbor: by deed, by word, and by prayer. He states, "In these three degrees is contained the fullness of mercy, and it is an unquestionable proof of love for Me."[839] Active love of neighbor becomes as important as trust in God. As in the Holy Face revelations, Divine Mercy encompasses love of God and love of neighbor. St. Faustina writes, "The glory of the Church and the progress of many a soul depend on ... a small deed of mine, accomplished in a divinized way."[840] And "The sanctity or the fall of each individual soul has an effect upon the whole Church."[841] She even writes that she feels as though she is responsible for all souls,[842] her love of God requiring total self-immolation for the benefit of immortal souls.[843] Finally, she expresses an obligation to plead for mercy for the world: "I unite myself closely with Jesus and stand before Him as an atoning sacrifice on behalf of the world."[844] As with Divine Mercy, there is an obligation in the Holy Face devotion for each member of the Mystical Body of Christ to work for the benefit of the whole, to join in Christ's redemptive work, such that each soul does in some real sense become responsible for his brethren members.

Furthermore, everyday suffering (which may be offered for the atonement of the sins of others) should be accepted with love, though its power rests on the will, such that repugnance, far from lowering the value of sacrifice in the eyes of

---

[837] Ibid., no. 1148.
[838] Ibid.
[839] Ibid., no. 742.
[840] Ibid., no. 508.
[841] Ibid., no. 1475.
[842] Ibid., no. 1505.
[843] Siepak and Dlubak, *Spirituality of Saint Faustina*, 66.
[844] Kowalska, *Diary*, no. 482.

Christ, will enhance it.[845] And Christ tells Faustina, "You will save more souls through prayer and suffering than will a missionary through his teaching and sermons alone. I want to see you as a sacrifice of living love, which only then carries weight before Me."[846] In Divine Mercy both Christ and man, in union with Him, atone for sinners to satisfy justice. God is all-just and all-merciful,[847] so both attributes must be satisfied, even if mercy in some sense takes precedence, as stated in the revelations of Divine Mercy. Indeed, both the Holy Face and the Divine Mercy devotions are methods of satisfying justice for the purpose of drawing down mercy. One is accomplished through reparation, utilizing foremost the merits of Christ, and the other through trust in God's mercy and exhibiting sacrificial mercy to one's neighbor united with Christ's merits; the respective methods of each devotion are synonymous when done selflessly. One is accomplished through utilizing the merits and love encased in the Holy Face, and the other through the merits and love of Christ's Passion joined with personal sacrifices, both offered to the Father to appease His justice. In each, man must initiate the process by making these offerings.

Not only are the prayers of offerings to the Father in the Holy Face and Divine Mercy complementary, but the centrality of the Sacred Heart in each is likewise so. The Holy Face makes an offering of Christ's wounded Countenance in reparation to the Father, while the Divine Mercy makes an offering of Christ's Body, Blood, Soul, and Divinity to the Father in atonement for the sins of the whole world.[848] Interestingly, except for the Heart, which is centrally integrated into the respective (Holy Face and Divine Mercy) offerings, the Divine Mercy offering singles out not the Face but the "rest" of Christ's person: a tidy indicator of their highly complementary design. Moreover, in the Holy Face, the gifts of reparation to the Father can only be made properly through the Sacred Heart, comprising its greatest consolation, and mercy gained for sinners is returned through it. Likewise, in Divine Mercy, the soul is to unite itself with Christ's "agonizing" Heart to make reparation for His justice.[849] Also like the Holy Face devotion, Christ's mercy then passes into souls through "the divine-human Heart of Jesus as a ray from the

---

[845] Ibid., no. 1767.
[846] Ibid.
[847] Roderick MacEachen, *Complete Catechism of Christian Doctrine* (Wheeling, WV: Catholic Supply House, 1911), 21.
[848] Kowalska, *Diary*, no. 476.
[849] Ibid., no. 873.

sun passes through crystal."[850] Christ explains that from all His wounds mercy flows for souls, "but the wound in [His] Heart is the fountain of unfathomable mercy [and] from this fountain spring all graces for souls,"[851] thus the prayer of the devotion, "O Blood and Water which gushed forth from the Heart of Jesus as a fount of mercy for us, I trust in You!" The Holy Face, Sacred Heart, and Divine Mercy devotions are highly integral to one another.

Indeed, the respective Face, Body, Blood, Soul, and Divinity of Christ unite with the offering of Christ's selfless Passion in the Eucharist. Christ said to St. Faustina, "I desire to unite Myself with human souls; My great delight is to unite Myself with souls.... When I come to a human heart in Holy Communion, My hands are full of all kinds of graces which I want to give to the soul. But souls do not even pay an attention to Me.... Oh, how sad I am that souls do not recognize Love! They treat Me as a dead object."[852] He reiterates, "How painful it is to Me that souls so seldom unite themselves to Me in Holy Communion. I wait for souls, and they are indifferent toward Me. I love them tenderly and sincerely, and they distrust Me."[853] These revelations are mindful of the spirituality of St. Thérèse, Bl. Pierina, and Sister St. Pierre in that Christ is being scorned by indifferent and neglectful souls, especially in the Most Holy Sacrament of the Altar. Christ desires a return of love in the form of trust in Him, which is tied to humility in the Divine Mercy devotion.

Trust is a necessary mindset of the soul to receive mercy and is synonymous with humility in the Divine Mercy revelations, as is true in the Holy Face, which has as its very aim the repairing of the injuries to God brought upon by man's blasphemous pride, initiated through total reliance upon God in humility — even utilizing Christ's merits rather than his own. Christ tells St. Faustina, "Tell souls that from this fount of mercy [present in Confession] souls draw graces solely with the vessel of trust. If their trust is great, there is no limit to My generosity. The torrents of grace inundate humble souls. The proud remain always in poverty and misery because My grace turns away from them to humble souls."[854] And "When you lower and empty yourself before My Majesty, I then

---

[850] Ibid., no. 528.
[851] Ibid., no. 1190.
[852] Ibid., no. 1392.
[853] Ibid., no. 1447.
[854] Ibid., no. 1602.

pursue you with My graces and make use of My omnipotence to exalt you."[855] Elsewhere Christ states, "I lift the humble even to my very throne, because I want it so."[856] Finally, "Only the humble soul is able to receive My grace. I favor humble souls with My confidence."[857] In both devotions, trust and humility are *the* attitude on the part of man toward God. The virtues work together in forming the soul as totally reliant upon God, while realizing that all good within one's soul is a gift from God. This amounts to an openness to receiving God's graces by always and everywhere fulfilling His will. Christ told St. Faustina, "I demand of you a perfect and whole-burnt offering: an offering of the will. No other sacrifice can compare with this one.... For the accomplishment of this offering, you will unite yourself with Me on the Cross."[858] God's will is one and the same as His mercy, for He always wants and is ready to give what is best for the soul when it is opened to His movements through trust and humility. These are the lessons of Divine Mercy, which were the lessons of St. Thérèse, which were the lessons of the Holy Face.

✠ ✠ ✠

What, then, one may ask, are the differences between the Divine Mercy and Holy Face devotions, given their profound complementary nature? One distinction is the object of adoration in each. Divine Mercy shows the whole person of Christ (Body, Blood, Soul, and Divinity), resurrected and offering the white and red rays of grace and mercy from His Heart. Christ asks for the veneration of this painted image on the feast of Divine Mercy, promising, "By means of this Image I shall grant many graces to souls. It is to be a reminder of the demands of My mercy, because even the strongest faith is of no avail without works."[859] There is some indication that the features of this image align precisely with those of the Shroud of Turin.[860] (Similar tests have not yet been performed on the veil of Veronica.) This is fitting in that the Holy Face devotion given to Bl. Pierina is to make reparation for the sufferings to Christ's Face during the Passion, as well as current ingratitude and

---

[855] Ibid., no. 576.
[856] Ibid., no. 282.
[857] Ibid., no. 1220.
[858] Ibid., no. 923.
[859] Ibid., no. 742.
[860] ChurchPOP editor, "Divine Mercy Image vs. Shroud of Turin: Are They Identical? The Intriguing Evidence," ChurchPOP, January 11, 2020, https://www.churchpop.com/divine-mercy-image-vs-shroud-of-turin-are-they-identical-the-intriguing-evidence/.

neglect of Him in the Blessed Sacrament — both themes recurring in the Divine Mercy devotion. The Veronica veil relic image of Christ used as object of adoration in the Holy Face devotion features a living, suffering Face of Christ, in need of consolation by St. Veronica and all souls. As mentioned in itself, it is a miracle three times over, for it is a miraculous image of Christ left on Veronica's veil in return for her act of solace; it became miraculously enlivened in 1849 during a Christmas octave exposition; and copies of it have been used in miraculous healings, most especially that given to Ven. Dupont, designating him as perhaps the greatest miracle worker in Church history (according to Bl. Pius IX). Ongoing is the promise that Christ's Face is as the seal of the Divinity and possesses the power of reproducing in souls who honor it not only great graces but the very likeness of God.[861]

There are also some differences in the promises attached to each devotion, though their similarities are greater than any other two devotions when compared. For Divine Mercy, they include:

1. By means of the Divine Mercy image, many graces will be granted to souls.

2. The soul that will go to Confession and receive Holy Communion on the feast of Divine Mercy shall obtain complete forgiveness of sins and punishment.[862]

3. Souls that recite the Divine Mercy chaplet will receive great graces.[863]

4. Souls that immerse themselves in Christ's Passion, if even for a moment, at the three o'clock hour, will be refused nothing at this hour, for one who makes his request in virtue of Christ's Passion.[864]

5. Souls that especially venerate and glorify Christ's mercy will shine with a special brightness in the next life.[865]

These are similar to some of the more extraordinary promises of the Holy Face devotion:

1. Christ will imprint His own image upon souls in proportion to their consoling His Face, making them as beautiful as when they came forth from the baptismal font.

---

[861] Sister St. Pierre, *Life of Sister St. Pierre*, 232–233.
[862] Kowalska, *Diary*, no. 699.
[863] Ibid., no. 848.
[864] Ibid., no. 1320.
[865] Ibid., no. 1224.

2. Souls saying the Golden Arrow in a spirit of reparation will draw graces for the salvation of the masses.

3. Devotees will obtain all they ask by offering to the Father the adorable Face of the Son in reparation, like a coin of infinite value.

4. Those who on earth contemplate the wounds of Christ's Face shall in Heaven behold it radiant with glory and will receive in their souls a bright and constant irradiation of Christ's divinity, that by their likeness to His Face they shall shine with particular splendor in Heaven.

Both also promise the appeasement of God's wrath — storms in the case of Divine Mercy, whereas the Holy Face combats, in addition to the elements of nature, "the malice of revolutionary men."[866] Indeed, they are strikingly similar, save for the specific promise of the working of marvels in the Holy Face devotion and the imprinting of the divine likeness via the Holy Face (compared to receiving "great graces" by means of the Divine Mercy image). In addition, though not always mentioned with the other promises, the Holy Face bestows the greatest grace second to the sacraments upon the devotee (which may be a "backup" source of grace if the sacraments are withheld) and the Face offered to the Father in reparation as the sole means of appeasing His wrath (in mitigating chastisement).

Yet these are important distinctions, as is the role of Mary, Mother of God, as Co-Redemptrix, Mediatrix, and Mother of Man, debuted so decidedly in the Holy Face devotion, though these aspects of the Virgin are reiterated in the revelations of Divine Mercy. St. Faustina writes, "Through [Mary], as through a pure crystal, [God's] mercy was passed on to us. Through Her, man became pleasing to God; Through Her, streams of grace flowed down upon us."[867] And again, Mary appeared to Faustina, saying, "I am Mother to you all, thanks to the unfathomable mercy of God."[868] Faustina offered to Mary her soul, body, life, and death, and all that would follow it, placing everything in her hands.[869] She felt that Mary was always with her, like a good Mother, watching over all her trials and efforts,[870] and asked that she arrange everything, that it would be pleasing to her Son.[871] This indicates an understanding by Faustina of total devotion to Mary, in the fashion of

---

[866] Ibid., nos. 476, 1036, and 1565. And Sister St. Pierre, *Life of Sister St. Pierre*, 263.
[867] Kowalska, *Diary*, no. 1746.
[868] Ibid., no. 449.
[869] Ibid., no. 79.
[870] Ibid., no. 789.
[871] Ibid., no. 844.

St. Louis de Montfort and Sister St. Pierre. Yet the link between Mary and mercy and man's necessary total reliance on her is most clearly designated and honored in the revelations surrounding the Holy Face devotion.

And there is the foremost raison d'être of each. In the revelations of Divine Mercy, Christ says, "I desire that My mercy be worshipped, and I am giving the last hope of salvation, that is recourse to My mercy."[872] He also says, "Before I come as a just Judge, I first open wide the door of My mercy. He who refuses to pass through the door of My mercy must pass through the door of My justice."[873] And "I have an eternity for punishing [crimes], and so I am prolonging the time of mercy for the sake of [sinners]. But woe to them if they do not recognize this time of My visitation.... [Beg for] this grace for them, so that they may glorify My mercy."[874] He adds:

> In the Old Covenant I sent prophets wielding thunderbolts to My people. Today I am sending you with My mercy to the people of the whole world. I do not want to punish aching mankind, but I desire to heal it, pressing it to My Merciful Heart. I use punishment when they themselves force Me to do so; My hand is reluctant to take hold of the sword of justice. Before the Day of Justice, I am sending the Day of Mercy.[875]

Christ further tells St. Faustina, "Speak to the world about My mercy; let all mankind recognize My unfathomable mercy. It is a sign for the end times; after it will come the day of justice. While there is still time, let them have recourse to the fount of My mercy; let them profit from the Blood and Water which gushed forth for them."[876] Christ requests:

> [Let] the greatest sinners place their trust in My mercy. They have the right before others to trust in the abyss of My mercy. My daughter, write about My mercy towards tormented souls. Souls that make an appeal to My mercy delight Me. To such souls I grant even more graces than they ask. I cannot punish even the greatest sinner if he makes an appeal to

---

[872] Ibid., no. 998.
[873] Ibid., no. 1146.
[874] Ibid., no. 1160.
[875] Ibid., no. 1588.
[876] Ibid., no. 848.

My compassion, but on the contrary, I justify him in My unfathomable and inscrutable mercy.[877]

These revelations are paralleled in Scripture: "They that are in health need not a physician, but they that are ill. Go then and learn what this meaneth, I will have mercy and not sacrifice. For I am not come to call the just, but sinners" (Matt. 9:12–13). More than this for the current era, however, Christ desires mankind to honor His mercy, even to cling to it, for He offers it as a day of mercy, a last recourse for sinners before the day of justice.

This time of mercy will not last forever, per the words of Christ Himself. Christ will no longer restrain the sword of justice on the day of justice. And if ever there were a time when "[men] themselves force [Christ's] hand, though reluctant to take hold the sword of justice," it is surely nigh. The Israelites forced God's hand in the Old Testament, the punishment often taking the form of God withdrawing their religion, since they had proven themselves unworthy by way of their idolatry, irreverence, and blasphemy against God.[878] The revelations given to Sister St. Pierre relate the same concerning the blasphemies perpetrated by the "New Israel," France, during the eighteenth and nineteenth centuries. Churches were desecrated and priests and nuns of that nation were persecuted mercilessly during its first revolution and were only spared during the second, according to Christ, because of the personal sacrifices and especially offerings of Christ's merits to the Father by Sister St. Pierre at that time, as well as her efforts to establish the work of reparation (discussed in chapter 5). The remedy in wake of all chastisement is reparation — the appeasement of justice. And the Holy Face devotion offers this most efficaciously, according to Christ, via the power of His Holy Face, "almost unknown in the Church before [the private revelations given to Sister Saint Pierre]."[879]

The Marian apparitions of La Salette, Quito, and Fatima (to be discussed in the next section), as well as the vision of Leo XIII, foretell similar times fast approaching, if not already here. As mentioned, Pope Leo approved the Holy Face revelations more or less immediately after his vision of Satan challenging Christ that he could destroy the Church (evidently convinced of the devotion's efficacy

---

[877] Ibid., no. 1146.
[878] Lawrence Daniel Carney III, *The Secret of the Holy Face: The Devotion Destined to Save Society* (Gastonia, NC: TAN Books, 2022), 11.
[879] Sister Mary Emmanuel, *Sister Marie*, 2.

in the face of such ensuing celestial clashing). He also greatly approved of the writings of St. Louis de Montfort on true devotion to Mary during the same time frame. The Divine Mercy revelations came roughly fifty years into the approximately one hundred years granted by Christ to Satan to formulate designs for his proposed destruction of the Faith. Indeed, both the Holy Face and Divine Mercy devotions (as well as true devotion to Mary) are essential and are highly complementary in the wake of such spiritual embattlement. Mercy is needed to save the masses, producing more soldiers for Christ, yet in that God is all-just and all-merciful, appeasement of justice must come before mercy (as outlined even in the Divine Mercy revelations, wherein Christ and the devout, in union with Him, are to atone for sins of the world). Indeed, mercy is the prize of both devotions.

Justice and mercy relate complementary to each other in the context of God's love. As St. Thérèse says, "It is because God is just that he is merciful." And she upheld God's justice as being clothed with love, perhaps even more so than His other perfections. She herself sought to satisfy justice, not by her own merits but by assuming the sanctity of God. Divine Mercy, in some sense, is as much about justice as mercy, utilizing not only the merits of Christ's Passion as an offering to obtain mercy for sinners, but the sacrifice and return of mercy to others on the part of man. In all devotions, there is a pattern of appeasing justice for the purpose of attaining mercy.

In conclusion, this pattern of satisfying justice to draw mercy for sinners was set forth most distinctly in the Holy Face devotion as given to Sister St. Pierre — utilizing the very power of God encased in Christ's Face to attain it. As integral also in the Sacred Heart and Divine Mercy, among other devotions, "reparation is the forerunner to mercy."[880] In times of mercy and times of justice, the pattern remains. For appeasement of justice is foremost an act of love, in that selfless reparation *is* an act of trust and confidence in God's mercy. Whether a soul considers himself pulling at the heartstrings of Christ or pulling the scales of His justice, selfless acts to console Him — to appease Him — result in mercy for sinners. Yet, per Christ, in times of God's just punishment upon the world, the remedy is singular: selfless reparation to the Godhead. This pattern was set forth in the Old Testament and is a primary message given in the revelations to Sister St. Pierre. Therein it is *the* means of satiating justice, "the sole means of

---

[880] Sister Mary Emmanuel, *Life of Sister Marie*, vi.

appeasing God," according to Christ. For only one devotion is to be specifically utilized to the defeat of the enemies of the Church, the "malice of revolutionary men," the form of punishment God has warned for the times, which according to Christ, have never been exceeded in iniquity. And while there are beautiful and necessary devotions centered upon the sacred humanity of Christ — Bl. Pierina's and St. Margaret Mary's and St. Faustina's included — there is only one devoted to the rights, the adoration of, and reparation to the Trinity (offended so heinously by modern man). Only one devotion formally debuts Mary's role as Co-Redemptrix, Mediatrix, and Mother of Man, revealing her necessity in the celestial battle plan to involve man in Satan's defeat. Only one offers man a means of obtaining a secondary source of grace, which, in the event of the sacraments being withheld from the faithful, may be a "fallback" means of attaining grace by way of the Holy Face devotion, through the offering of Christ's Face to the Father in reparation, effecting "the greatest source of grace second to the sacraments." And only one has the capability, heretofore, virtually — if not altogether — unknown, of imprinting the divine likeness upon those who would apply it to themselves, as well as the power to generate miracles. That one is the Holy Face devotion as revealed to Sister St. Pierre, making it foundational to the others and, in many respects, a synthesis most resplendent: regarded by Christ Himself as "the most beautiful work under the sun."[881]

> *Only the powerful force of prayer and reparative penance will be able to save the world from what the justice of God has prepared.*
>
> — *The Virgin Mary speaking to Father Stefano Gobbi*[882]

> *The sure means of softening [God's] anger, and consequently the great means of salvation — the one which God Himself, before reducing us to extremities, has deigned to recommend — is REPARATION.... For if God is for us, who shall be against us?*
>
> — *Reverend P. Janvier, director of the Priests of the Holy Face at Tours*[883]

---

[881] *Life of Sister Mary of St. Peter*, 311–312.

[882] Father Gobbi received messages from Mary for a period of twenty-five years, guiding him to initiate the Marian Movement of Priests, dedicated to the Immaculate Heart of Mary.

[883] P. Janvier, author's preface to *Sister St. Pierre and the Work of Reparation: A Brief History*, trans. Mary Hoffman (London: Burns & Oates, 1885).

5. The Holy Face Devotion and Marian Apparitions

As is the case with devotions to the sacred humanity of Christ, Marian apparitions prepare man for adoration of the Godhead, while the Holy Face devotion *is* adoration of the Godhead, the highest and most exalted form of worship, making it foundational to all apparitions. According to St. Louis de Montfort, "Jesus Christ our Savior, true God and true Man, ought to be the last end of all our other devotions, else they are false and delusive.... If then, we establish the solid devotion to Our Blessed Lady, it is only to establish more perfectly the devotion to Jesus Christ."[884] In her apparitions, Mary prepares man to properly honor the Triune God by calling for penance and a return to virtue as means of atonement toward the salvation of the masses and mitigation of God's merciful chastisements. Yet Mary adds to the efficacy of man's sacrifices through her intercession on his behalf before her Son, as understood by St. Louis as well as revealed in the revelations from Christ surrounding the Holy Face devotion. Therein Mary's divine maternity affords her the roles of Co-Redemptrix, Mediatrix, and Mother of Man, spiritual weaponry for the Church Militant in the battle with Satan, led by the Virgin on behalf of God.

The Holy Face devotion follows the same pattern of that outlined in the Marian apparitions: man satisfying God's justice for the purpose of drawing down graces of mercy for the salvation of sinners, while lessening just punishment for offenses against the rights of God. However, it presents a progression wherein man may utilize, rather than merely his own, the *power of God* as present in the merits of Christ's wounded Face, offered in reparation to the Father. It is an offering of the head (Christ) for the members[885] in the unity of Christ's Mystical Body, selflessly presented by man for his brethren as part of the mysterious solidarity of these members. Christ is mediator between the Father and His members in the Holy Face devotion, while Mary (as she also presents herself in her apparitions) is intercessor on behalf of the faithful to her Son. This correlates with the spirituality of St. Louis, who advocates that one should always stand with Mary before Christ and with Christ (and Mary) before the Godhead. The saint writes: "It is more perfect because it is [humbler], not to approach God of ourselves, without taking a mediator.... Our

---

[884] Louis de Montfort, *True Devotion*, 45–46.
[885] Sister Mary St. Peter, Life of Sister Mary St. Peter, 290. "I have taken upon my head the sins of mankind, that my members might be spared."

Lord is our Advocate and Mediator of redemption with God the Father.... [Yet] let us say boldly with Saint Bernard, that we have need of a mediator with the Mediator Himself, and that is the divine Mary who is the most capable of filling that charitable office."[886] Mary's role of "secondary" mediator as presented in the apparitions, accompanying the "primary" mediator of Christ as presented in the Holy Face devotion, is another way in which the devotion is foundational to Marian apparitions.

Implicit and sometimes explicit in the apparitions, Mary is not only intercessor before Christ but also the "return" river of grace and mercy, from the Father to Christ to Mary, obtained on the part of man *by reforming one's life and offering prayers and penance for sinners to appease God*, toward the salvation of all. St. Louis writes of Mary, "She is His mysterious canal; she is His aqueduct, through which He makes His mercies flow gently and abundantly."[887] She is the mother of mercy and mediatrix of graces. Yet these consistent attributes of the Virgin as understood in the apparitions, and articulated by Montfort as "general of [God's] army, treasurer of His treasures, dispenser of His graces, worker of His greatest marvels, restorer of the human race, mediatrix of men, the exterminator of the enemies of God, and the faithful companion of His grandeurs and His triumphs,"[888] were most decidedly indicated and reverenced in the Holy Face revelations and the corresponding mystical experiences of Sister St. Pierre (as previously discussed), making the revelations of the Holy Face devotion, in yet another sense, foundational to the Marian apparitions.

The apparitions of La Salette, Lourdes, Quito, and Fatima, among others, tidily complement the themes of the Holy Face devotion. Mary as Mother of Mercy and Mediatrix of All Graces, pleading with man to appease God's justice to draw mercy for sinners, manifests in "two parts" in the well-known apparitions of the nineteenth century, Lourdes and La Salette. "At La Salette, Justice is dominant, Justice warns and threatens. At Lourdes it is Mercy, inviting and consoling."[889] Lourdes would not have taken place without the words of La Salette being heeded. The warnings of La Salette were a repetition of those given to Sister St. Pierre, fittingly reflected in her personal tie to La Salette, for the apparitions followed her specific request of Our Lady to inform someone

---

[886] Louis de Montfort, *True Devotion*, 58–60.
[887] Ibid., 26.
[888] Ibid., 28–29.
[889] Ibid., 156.

else of the messages of reparation for fear that her bishop would not approve the devotion.[890] The apparitions of Quito, while occurring over two hundred years prior to the revelations given to Sister St. Pierre, also "repeat" and elaborate upon some of the dire warnings for current times, an effect of the iniquity of the age never having been exceeded,[891] as well as God's just chastisement for such wickedness. It likewise emphasizes the necessity of reparation to quell these just punishments — as was even requested of the nuns at Quito of that time *for man today* (a nearly four-hundred-year "advancement"!). Finally, Sister St. Pierre's understanding of the all-pervading evil of Communism not only was ahead of her time (in that the Russian and Chinese revolutions had not yet taken place) but was a precursor and complement to the messages of the Marian apparitions of Fatima in which Our Lady expressly warns that "Russia's errors" will be spread if her messages requesting prayer and penance — reparation — are not heeded. Mary as Mother of Mercy and Refuge of Sinners, as explicitly presented at Fatima and confirmed by the Miracle of the Sun, is a continuation of the messages of La Salette, Lourdes, and Quito, as well as the revelations given to Sister St. Pierre: the crown apparition[892] complementing and affirming what was revealed in the crown devotion, that of the Holy Face — a final way in which the devotion is foundational.

Indeed, while all apparitions ultimately lead to the proper adoration of God, as called for in the Holy Face devotion, these four link in special ways to the revelations given to Sister St. Pierre by their emphasis on man's role in reparation toward the salvation of sinners and the mitigation of chastisements to assist Mary in her Immaculate Heart's triumph over Satan. According to St. Louis, "The power of Mary over all the devils will especially break out in the latter times, when Satan will lay his snares against her heel; that is to say, her humble slaves and her poor children, whom she will raise up to make war against him.... But in return for this, they shall be rich in the grace of God, which Mary shall distribute to them abundantly."[893] St. Louis also writes, "[The enmity between Mary, God's] worthy Mother, and the devil, between the children of the servants of the Blessed Virgin and the children and instruments of

---

[890] Sister Mary St. Peter, *Life of Sister Mary St. Peter*, 277–278.
[891] *Life of Sister Mary St. Peter*, 159.
[892] A phrase coined by Marianna Bartold, author of *Fatima: The Signs and Secrets* (Lapeer, MI: KIC, 2014).
[893] Louis de Montfort, *True Devotion*, 41.

Lucifer [shall endure and develop even to the end]. The most terrible of all the enemies which God has set up against the devil is His holy Mother, Mary."[894] Mary leads man to proper adoration of God, intercedes for man before her Son, is the return river of grace and mercy for acts of sacrifice and penance, and heads men in the battle with Satan, all by virtue of her motherhood to God and man. These themes are underlying in the apparitions of La Salette, Lourdes, Quito, and Fatima. Yet again, their foundation was definitively "debuted" in the Holy Face devotion by Sister St. Pierre's experience of Mary as Co-Redemptrix, Mediatrix, and Mother of Man, flowing from her privilege of divine maternity.

LA SALETTE

My Mother has spoken to mankind of My wrath; she longs to appease it.

— Our Lord to Sister St. Pierre

Likewise pleading for mankind to exhibit proper fear of the Lord, the Marian apparition of La Salette picks up where the revelations of Christ to Sister St. Pierre leave off, as briefly mentioned in the preface. They are linked in content and in the person of Sister St. Pierre, for the apparition was apparently an answer to a direct appeal from her to Our Lady. She writes, "Ah! How I suffer at being the sole depositary of this weighty secret, which I am obliged to keep within the silence of the cloister! O Holy Virgin, appear to someone in the world, and reveal there the afflicting knowledge imparted to me concerning my native land!"[895] This apparition was not better known, even in its day, though approved only five years after it took place, due to the influence of blasphemous ideology that had already infiltrated the Church in France;[896] it was not until Pope St. John Paul II reintroduced the apparitions during their 150th anniversary in 1996 that more today are familiar with them. For Our Lady of La Salette conveys the extreme offense that sins of blasphemy and the profanation of Sunday give to Our Lord and how His

---

[894] Ibid., 39.
[895] Sister Mary St. Peter, *Life of Sister Mary St. Peter*, 253–254.
[896] La Salette was a very unpopular apparition among the corrupt clergy and hierarchy, since it brought to light their offenses as part of the messages themselves; it is pertinent for this reason today, as well. Also, Joan Carroll Cruz, *See How She Loves Us: 50 Approved Apparitions of Our Lady* (Charlotte, NC: TAN Books, 2012), 111. The messages were confirmed by many popes since the time of Pius IX, and in 1942, a Mass and office were authorized.

hand of justice will not be held back forever. The La Salette messages echo the revelations of Sister St. Pierre in which reparation for sins of blasphemy — the opposite of fear of God — is consequently demanded of the faithful for themselves and others: France, in this case.

Ven. Dupont was a witness to the connection of Sister St. Pierre with the apparitions of Mary granted to the children of La Salette. He, being well acquainted with the Carmel in Tours and with the mother prioress and Sister St. Pierre especially, was told by Mother Prioress, in early September 1846, that Sister St. Pierre had received from Christ what would be the prophetic announcement of the apparition of La Salette and of Mary's merciful intervention in favor of France (for which Sister St. Pierre had been ceaselessly praying).[897] Christ related to Sister St. Pierre at that time that "My Mother has spoken to mankind of my wrath, she longs to appease it; ... [she requests of Me that I allow her] to pour out blessings upon my other children.' Then, full of mercy, she descended to earth; have confidence in her."[898] Ven. Dupont felt the language was "mysterious, linking the past with the present and the future."[899] Then in October, he received word of the apparition of the Blessed Virgin at La Salette, which had occurred on September 19, the fulfillment of the prediction revealed to Sister St. Pierre in the earlier part of that same month. Mother Prioress wrote, "Evidently, the mission confided to the little shepherds of the mountain was identical with that of the daughter of the cloister."[900] She saw La Salette as confirmation of the work of reparation.

Sister St. Pierre had long since ardently solicited Mary by way of daily reciting the Rosary to obtain the salvation of France and the establishment of the reparation in all her cities: "All my prayers and Holy Communions, all my desires, all my thoughts, were directed towards this Work, so dear to my heart."[901] Proving herself the "refuge of sinners," the Virgin Mary did intercede between France and God's wrath by descending to earth and requesting two children of the French Alps, Maximin Giraud and Mélanie Calvat, to reproach "her people" for their blatant contempt for God's commandments, especially by the profanation of the Lord's Day and blasphemy. Mary told the children: "If my people do

---

[897] Sister St. Pierre, *Life of Sister St. Pierre*, 249–252.
[898] Ibid., 250.
[899] Ibid.
[900] Ibid., 253.
[901] Ibid., 253–254.

not return to God by penance, I shall be forced to let fall the Hand of my Son; it now presses so heavily that I can scarce hold it longer. Oh! if ye but knew how much I suffer for you!"[902] The two child shepherds witnessed tears flowing from the Virgin's eyes, and she wore a crucifix upon her heart, surrounded by the instruments of the Passion, the cruel hammer and sharp pincers, "the ornaments of her maternal bosom."[903] She had initiated the apparition by telling Mélanie and Maximin not to be afraid, to come close to her, referring to them as her children, and that she had good news. By the ornaments she bore, her tears and suffering, her holding back the hand of her Son, her motherly entreating of the children, and the promise of good news, Our Lady implicitly presented herself as Co-Redemptrix, Mediatrix, and Mother of Man.[904]

Our Lady of La Salette warned of a great famine that would come (and did in fact come),[905] resulting from a bad wheat crop, which followed a potato blight the preceding year. She also disclosed a secret to the children, which Mélanie wrote down as instructed by Our Lady and which was given to Pope Pius IX in 1851, the year he approved the apparitions. In small part, it reads:

> The heads, the leaders of the people of God have neglected prayer and penance, and the devil has darkened their minds; they have become those wandering stars which the ancient devil will drag with his tail to destruction. God will permit the ancient serpent to sow divisions among the rulers, in all societies and in all families; both physical and moral punishments will be suffered. God will abandon men to themselves and will send chastisements one after the other.... Many will abandon the faith and the number of priests and religious who will separate themselves from the true religion will be great; even bishops will be found among these persons.[906]

---

[902] Ibid., 255.

[903] Ibid.

[904] Bartold, *Fatima*, 213. The author does not use this terminology but makes the same connections.

[905] The message was given by Our Lady on September 19, 1846. The famine followed in mid-1847, after the '46 crop of wheat was disastrous. The price rose from 19 francs per hectoliter in 1845 to 38 francs by mid-1847, double that of two years prior. "France reeled in the face of this agricultural crisis. Among its immediate consequences were food riots, an increase in begging, and an acceleration in the existing pattern of urban in-migration among the poor." *Global Crises and Social Movements: Artisans, Peasants, Populists, and the World Economy*, ed. Edmund Burke III (Boulder: Westview Press, 1988), 14–15.

[906] Cruz, *50 Approved Apparitions*, 108.

Mary additionally told the children that "Rome will lose the Faith and become the seat of the anti-Christ." She did not specify that the Church itself would become the seat of the antichrist,[907] though she did prophecy that "the Church will be in eclipse,"[908] as in a great crisis. This reflects the revelations given to Sister St. Pierre: "The Church is threatened with a terrible tempest. Pray, pray!"[909]

This prophecy, like the chastisements the Israelites underwent for their offenses against God, is a punishment to fit the crime, for a period of trial for the Church is both an effect of blasphemies and heresies against the Church and an allowed chastisement by God for those offenses. When the Israelites failed to keep their covenant with God, He would "turn His Face" from them by taking away their religion.[910] In the revelations given to Sister St. Pierre, "the Church is the Face of the Mystical Body of Christ now covered with wounds by the impious."[911] Crimes against the Church are crimes against the rights and majesty of God, those prohibited by the first three commandments, which have, according to Christ's revelation to Sister St. Pierre, "risen to the Throne of God and provoked His wrath which will soon burst forth if His justice be not appeased [for] in no time have these crimes reached such a pitch."[912] These violations draw forth their own chastisement, for in wounding the Face of Christ, they are disfiguring the Face of His Mystical Body, the Church. It is not "just" a matter, then, of the Faith being "turned from" — taken away from — the offenders but is worse: it is a defacing of their Faith, the Face of the Mystical Body of Christ, the Face of Christ, making it unrecognizable. Man is suffering from his own transgressions, bringing about a crisis in the Church, making it but a shadow of its former self, its "eclipse." Reparation is the explicit remedy given in the Old Testament, in Marian apparitions, as well as the revelations of the Holy Face devotion. Our Lady of La Salette wore the instruments of Christ's Passion around her neck; in yet another connection, man is asked to offer these instruments in reparation to the Father in the Holy Face devotion to become, like Mary, "a terror to hell,"[913] and an instrument of mercy.

---

[907] Bartold, *Fatima*, 213.
[908] *Apparition of the Blessed Virgin on the Mountain of La Salette on the 19th of September 1846*, ed. Association of the Children of Our Lady of La Salette, reproduction of the original 1879 edition of Lecce (Béaupreau, 1976), 19.
[909] Sister St. Pierre, *Life of Sister St. Pierre*, 379.
[910] Bartold, *Fatima*, 11.
[911] Sister St. Pierre, *Life of Sister St. Pierre*, 393.
[912] Ibid., 145.
[913] Sister Mary of St. Peter, *Life of Sister Mary St. Peter*, 257.

Though Our Lady continued with speaking about false doctrine being preached, leading to even more perversion of man, she assured the children that God will take care of His faithful servants and men of good will, and all will have knowledge of the truth. And in the end, men's pride will be consumed, and everything will be renewed, for God will be served and glorified.[914] This was the good news Our Lady brought to the children and her people.

In no small part due to the apparition, "Catholic France, recognizing her crime and fearing its chastisements, [at long last] began to enter upon the way of Reparation."[915] Sister St. Pierre wrote the following in thanksgiving:

> I return thee thanks, O Blessed Virgin Mary, for having given me those two little shepherds as sounding trumpets, echoing from the mountain to the ears of France, what had been communicated to me in the solitude of the cloister. The voices of these, my two dear little associates, were soon heard throughout the world, and a wonderful impression was thereby made upon souls; also, the striking similarity between their communications and mine have induced my worthy Superiors to believe that it would be conducive to the glory of God and the advancement of His Work were such correlation made known.[916]

These three humblest of ambassadors were sent to announce to France the woes impending for her transgression of the Lord's first three commandments, while also proclaiming the reward of mercy, should man do penance in returning to God. France, "who was to have been reduced to ashes, [was] but scathed by the flames."[917] Yet the warning has not yet been fulfilled in its entirety; it remains for current times, as does the admonition by Christ, "Woe to those who will not make this reparation!"[918]

Lourdes

Lourdes appears to be a consolation, a pouring of mercy, for the requests of justice being heeded at La Salette. Still visited by more than one million people annually,

---

[914] Cruz, *50 Approved Apparitions*, 109.
[915] Ibid., 256.
[916] Ibid., 256–257.
[917] Ibid., 259.
[918] Ibid., 147.

Lourdes, situated in the foothills of the Pyrenees in southern France, is the site of countless miracles, exceeded only by those performed at the hands of Ven. Dupont. (Besides the miracles of the Holy Face somewhat exceeding those of Lourdes in number,[919] Dupont also witnessed on at least one occasion a "nod" by Our Lady of Lourdes to her Son by way of a man who was refused healing at Lourdes subsequently being cured from oil burning in front of the Holy Face Veronica veil relic image and the intercession of Dupont.)[920] The apparitions at Lourdes took place just ten years after the death of Sister St. Pierre, beginning February 1858. Our Lady had appeared to the young Bernadette Soubirous, silently counting her rosary beads along with the girl, participating only in the Glorias. (Mary would not have joined in her own praises with the Ave Marias, nor needed to pray the Pater, which is for "needy mortals," according to the foremost biographer of St. Bernadette, Abbé Trochu.)[921] During the sixth apparition, the fourteen-year-old Bernadette was told to pray for sinners. And during the eighth apparition, the Virgin said three times, "Penance! Penance! Penance!" These requests were an echo of both the revelations given to Sister St. Pierre and the apparition at La Salette in their asking for reparation for sinners. France had in fact responded dutifully to the requests made from each, however, and Lourdes was the reward.

Additionally, Mary as Mother of Mercy is affirmed by the countless merciful healings flowing from this apparition (by way of the miraculous spring of Lourdes, which Our Lady bestowed), encouraging man to see her as intercessory recourse in obtaining grace and mercy. It was during the ninth visit that Our Lady requested Bernadette to drink from the fountain and bathe in it, though there was as yet no fountain or spring at Massabielle, the hump-like formation in the grotto where the young girl was gathering firewood. She was instructed to scratch the ground until a small pool appeared (perhaps signifying humiliation in penance for sinners).[922] The next day the pool was overflowing

---

[919] Over six thousand documented miracles and as many as ten thousand total were performed in connection with the Holy Face devotion at the hands of Venerable Dupont. Countless more were performed by way of the vial of Holy Face oil that he distributed to those who asked throughout the world. The estimated number of miraculous healings at Lourdes is around seven thousand, with seventy being officially recognized by the Church.

[920] Janvier, *Holy Man*, 324–330.

[921] Bartold, *Fatima*, 223.

[922] Ibid., 226.

and has since supplied water in the form of a spring for cures of pilgrims throughout the world, ongoing now for nearly two centuries.

During the sixteenth apparition, Our Lady told Bernadette, "I am the Immaculate Conception." (It was unlikely that the young girl had any idea of what this meant, as she was of an uneducated class and the dogma of the Immaculate Conception had occurred only four years prior in 1854.) Apart from confirming the Marian dogma of the Immaculate Conception declared by Pius IX, this is significant in that it is implicitly a reference to the triumph of the Immaculate Heart of Mary. A poignant and efficacious deliverance prayer for the faithful, "Invocation of the Heavenly Court," opens with an entreaty to the Virgin Most Powerful: "Thou who hast the power to crush the head of the ancient serpent with thy heel, come and exercise this power *flowing from the grace of thine Immaculate Conception*. Shield us under the mantle of thy purity and love, draw us into the *sweet abode of thy heart* and annihilate and render impotent the forces bent on destroying us."[923] Mary's Immaculate Conception, freeing her from all stain of original sin since the moment of her conception, is what juxtaposes her against Eve's original sin — of which all other men must partake — and affords her enmity with, and power to defeat, Satan, through the grace of God and the merits of her Son, Jesus Christ. Along with being preordained by God, it is Mary's singularity in being conceived "full of grace" that also makes possible her divine motherhood (necessitating her being the most perfect human that God's omnipotence could create — the very limits of divinity, according to St. Thomas Aquinas, and bordering upon God, according to St. Cajetan). From her divine maternity flow her roles of Co-Redemptrix, Mediatrix, and Mother of Man, his refuge and the path that leads him to God.[924] Mary declaring herself as the Immaculate Conception at Lourdes is thus an affirmation of St. Louis de Montfort's Mariology, which was also that of Sister St. Pierre, flowing from her mystical experiences and the revelations surrounding the Holy Face devotion.

The apparitions received approval just four years after they occurred, and a feast was set for February 11, the anniversary of the first apparition. Bernadette lies incorrupt in Nevers, where she became a Sister of Charity, having died an agonizing death in 1879 from tuberculosis of the bone. She led a quiet life of suffering and sacrifice,

---

[923] *Deliverance Prayers for Use by the Laity*, compiled by Chad Ripperger (Sensus Traditionis Press, 2020), 14. (My emphasis.)
[924] Bartold, *Fatima*, 298. Recounted by Sister Lucia of Fatima.

that of a victim soul; Our Lord often told her that she would not die until she had sacrificed all to Him.[925] A basilica built at the request of Our Lady stands at Lourdes, as well as her statue and sanctuary near the spring of water, the site of ongoing pilgrimages and healings. St. Bernadette was canonized by Pius XI in 1933.

Our Lady of Good Success

Mother Mariana de Jesús Torres (1563–1635), even as a child, received visits of the Blessed Mother. She had a great devotion to Mary under the title of Our Lady of Good Success, which was, in her early life, associated foremost with the miraculous statue of Madrid, discovered by Spanish friars on their way to Rome. Mariana joined the Conceptionist Order of the Immaculate Conception and was sent from Spain to Quito, Ecuador, to found another house of the order, of which she became abbess. There the Blessed Mother requested that she have a statue made, honoring her as Our Lady of Good Success, like the one in Madrid, only at Quito, Our Lady was to carry Christ on her left arm (rather than her right) "to restrain the Hand of Divine Justice."[926] It was made to the Virgin's exact dimensions and appearance and was miraculously finished by the archangels in 1611.[927] She promised consolation and preservation of the convent and for the faithful who would pray to her.

Mariana was a victim soul like none other, dying three times, being imprisoned three times (within the convent), and undergoing unimaginable suffering. Her mystical-turned-physical immolation to appease divine justice for (future) heresy, blasphemy, and impurity of the (now) modern epoch caused her to die for the first time. After choosing to continue her appeasement of divine justice (by living), she eventually suffered the interior wounds of Our Lord, undergoing a terrible paralysis and the dark night of the soul, while also being tempted to abandon her faith by the devil, who was visible to her; this condition lasted a year, with only a brief respite, causing her to die a second time. She additionally suffered five years of the torments of Hell on behalf of a rebellious sister of the order, who eventually died and, though she had imprisoned Mariana, was saved from Hell by Mariana's pleas to Christ on her behalf. This is not to mention the additional ongoing sacrifices and penance she endured toward the end of her

---

[925] Ibid.
[926] Marian Therese Horvat, *Our Lady of Good Success: Prophecies for Our Times* (Los Angeles: Tradition in Action, 2015), 38.
[927] Ibid., 49.

life, in imitation of Christ's Passion, to atone for spiritual depravity of the current times — ironically, the very times beginning in which the name of her beloved order, the Immaculate Conception, would be declared Marian dogma, as well as affirmed as such in the apparitions at Lourdes.

In fact, Mariana was told by Our Lady that "the dogma of Faith of the Immaculate Conception ... will be proclaimed during a time when the Church would be strongly attacked."[928] She specified that the same pope who would declare this dogma would also proclaim pontifical infallibility as dogma and would be persecuted and imprisoned in the Vatican "by the unjust usurpation of the Pontifical States through the iniquity, envy and avarice of an earthly monarch."[929] These prophecies did come to pass: Pope Pius IX proclaimed the Immaculate Conception in 1854, then papal infallibility in 1870; he was persecuted in the Vatican by Victor Emmanuel, who seized the last of the Papal States in 1870.[930] Including these and other prophecies, Mariana's life was inundated by numerous miracles and mystical favors. She was given additional, extensive foretelling of later centuries, all approved by the Church. As aforementioned, some have already occurred, but the most disturbing, often involving the Church, are apparently still ongoing, forming "a clear confirmation and an extension of what Our Lady came to say in Fatima."[931]

Now Servant of God, Mother Mariana de Jesús Torres died (for the final time) on January 16, 1635. After three hundred years, her body was discovered perfectly intact and remains so today, along with the bodies of her convent sisters who had also at that time immolated themselves, likewise becoming expiatory victims for the offenses of man today. Mariana was told of her death one year prior by the Virgin as well as the fact that her prophecies and favors would remain hidden until the end of the twentieth century, the very time for which she had offered herself as a victim.

Her prophecies include: apostasy in the clergy; corruption of priests and religious; the abuse and removal of the sacraments; rampant heresies; the waning of vocations due to poor formation; impurity such that there would be almost no virgin souls and it would even manifest in children; immodesty and the nearly complete corruption of manners and customs; a conspiracy against

---

[928] Ibid., chap. 1. P.22
[929] Ibid., chap. 5. P.65.
[930] Ibid.
[931] Ibid., P.15.

the Church; an extinguishing of the light of faith as in a crisis in the Church; and the dominion of Satan to be led by Masons. Terrible chastisements will be upon entire nations for sins of people and especially priests and religious.[932] As was requested of Sister St. Pierre and the children of Fatima, Our Lady told Mariana to have pity on her imprudent brethren and pray for them.[933]

She emphasized the importance of the sacrament of Penance and the weighty role of priests. She also revealed that faithful cloisters and monasteries are responsible for "the salvation of souls, the conversion of great sinners, the deferral of great scourges, the production and fertility of the land, the end of pestilence and wars and the harmony among nations. All is due to the prayers that rise from [them]."[934] She said that until the end of time, at least one sacrificial soul will inhabit the convent at Quito, imitating Mariana, to appease divine justice. As Mother of Mercy, Mary is their model, powerful placatory of divine justice and reservoir of mercy and pardon for every sinner who comes to her with a contrite heart.[935]

La Salette, Quito, and Fatima (as will be discussed) thus form complementary harbingers of both terrifying prophecies and, if reparation is made, hope in better times to come.

> The invocation of Good Success ... speaks of the happy development of the gestation of the Word from Conception to Birth. The contemplation of the mysteries of the august relationship between the Word and the Virgin during the nine months that He resided in her womb is implicitly contained in the Conceptionist vocation. In this sense, one understands that our lady wanted to reveal to a Conceptionist religious part of the secrets regarding the future of the Mystical Body of Christ.[936]

In the apparitions of Quito, the invocation of "good success" reveals a new era for Mary's glory, an era that would come much later, speaking of the "broad Marian protection she would give to the Holy Church during this time and of the happy establishment of the new era that will come. It is an invocation that relates to the future."[937]

---

[932] Ibid., 64.
[933] Ibid.
[934] Ibid., 66.
[935] Ibid., 38.
[936] Ibid., 15.
[937] Ibid.

The prophecies of Our Lady of Good Success tie "back" to (though occurring in time before) Lourdes, La Salette, and the revelations surrounding the Holy Face devotion, as well as Fatima (as will be discussed), in a call for prayer and sacrifice to make reparation for current abuses *as well as* the promise of mercy and reward for such acts of atonement. Mary assures man most explicitly in both Quito and Fatima that she will intervene and triumph. Our Lady of Good Success reveals herself as a powerful placative of divine justice as Mother of Mercy and specifically promises consolation and preservation, like La Salette, to faithful souls who are devoted to her by heeding her requests. Our Lady tells the current era: "When everything will seem lost and paralyzed, that will be 'the happy beginning of the complete restoration. This will mark the arrival of my hour, when I, in a marvelous way, will dethrone the proud and cursed Satan, trampling him under my feet and fettering him in the infernal abyss.'"[938] Yet man is an essential part of this dethronement, for she also makes clear that "in all times [she has] need of valiant souls to save [her] Church and the prevaricating world."[939]

Fatima

Lucia de Jesus dos Santos, Francisco Marto, who was Lucia's cousin, and Jacinta, Francisco's younger sister, were young shepherd children aged ten, nine, and seven, respectively, at the time of the first apparition of Our Lady of Fatima on May 13, 1917. To prepare them for the apparitions of Our Lady, they were first visited by the Angel of Peace, who is believed to be St. Michael[940] (who is also a patron of the Holy Face devotion). He knelt, touching his forehead to the ground, and had the children repeat three times: "My God, I believe, I adore, I hope, and I love Thee! I ask pardon of Thee for those who do not believe, do not adore, do not hope, and do not love Thee." He spoke to them of the importance of praying and making sacrifices: "Make of everything you can a sacrifice and offer it to God as an act of reparation for the sins by which He is offended, and in supplication for the conversion of sinners."[941] He also gave the following prayer:

> Most Holy Trinity, Father, Son, and Holy Spirit, I adore Thee profoundly. I offer Thee the Most Precious Body, Blood, Soul, and Divinity

---

[938] Ibid., chap. 5. P.69.
[939] Ibid., 54.
[940] Bartold, *Fatima*, 3.
[941] Cruz, *50 Approved Apparitions*, 164.

of Jesus Christ, present in all the tabernacles of the world, in reparation for the outrages, sacrileges and indifferences by which He is mortally offended. Through the infinite merits of His Most Sacred Heart and the Immaculate Heart of Mary, I beg the conversion of poor sinners.[942]

Finally, he gave them Holy Communion: the Host to Lucia and the Blood to Francisco and Jacinta. He asked them to make reparation while receiving Communion for the outrages of ungrateful men, as was asked of Sister St. Pierre by Christ. "Make reparation for their crimes and console your God,"[943] likewise a repetition of the primary request of the Holy Face devotion.

The following year, Our Lady appeared to the children, requesting that they say the Rosary daily for peace in the world and the end of the war (World War I) as well as practice devotion to her Immaculate Heart "which is so terribly outraged and offended by the sins of men."[944] Our Lady requested that reparation be made for offenses committed against her Immaculate Heart, which are in five categories: blasphemies against the Immaculate Conception, her perpetual virginity, and her divine maternity (as well as a refusal to recognize her as Mother of Men); blasphemies of those who publicly seek to sow in hearts of children indifference, scorn, or hatred of Mary; and blasphemies by those committing outrages against her holy images. All blasphemies against the Virgin are an effect of blasphemy against God in that they are heresies of dogma, an offense of the first commandment. The children understood that God was likewise offended and desired reparation and a return to virtue be made by all men: again, the essence of the Holy Face devotion.

Later in the apparitions, the children were shown Hell. Our Lady told them: "You have seen Hell where the souls of poor sinners go. To save them, God wishes to establish in the world devotion to My Immaculate Heart. If what I say to you is done, many souls will be saved and there will be peace."[945] She also warned, however, that if her words were not heeded, there would be persecutions of the Church, famine, and chastisements. Our Lord had likewise shown Sister St. Pierre the multitudes of souls falling into Hell, giving her the Golden Arrow prayer as a way to obtain torrents of grace for their conversion,[946] warning

---

[942] Ibid.
[943] Bartold, *Fatima*, 14.
[944] Cruz, *50 Approved Apparitions*, 165.
[945] Ibid.
[946] Sister St. Pierre, *Life of Sister St. Pierre*, 116.

that souls would be accountable for not making reparation. Other prayers and methods of atonement were given to Sister St. Pierre, the foremost being the offering of the suffering Face of Christ, which is no less than the power of God, to be presented by man to the Father in reparation. Both Fatima and the Holy Face devotion are most essentially a pleading, and means bestowed, by Heaven for man to take part in the salvation of the masses.

Our Lord warned Sister St. Pierre of the dangers of Communism, as particularly mentioned in the revelations as the "enemies of the Church and her Christ."[947] Therein, a specific remedy is given to offer the instruments of the Passion to defeat them — and all ideologies that place man in lieu of God and His Church as the authority of truth and morality. If reparation is not made, Our Lord warned Sister St. Pierre of the "malice of revolutionary men" as a chastisement. Our Lady specifically requested, for its conversion, the consecration of Russia to her Immaculate Heart and Communion of Reparation on the First Saturday of five consecutive months — to include the sacrament of Penance, the recitation of a five-decade Rosary, and separate fifteen-minute meditation on the mysteries of the Rosary. She likewise warned that if the requests were not made, the errors of that nation would spread. In hindsight, these errors have included atheism under Communism, its opposition to natural law, its stamping out of religion, tradition, and private property, and its interring in gulags or killing of opponents. The errors also include socialism, Freemasonry, modernism, and postmodernisms, for all, *as part of their design*, explicitly deny to varying degrees the majesty and authority of God. (Man's sin and weakness have led to the greed, tyranny, and godlessness that have become part of a now deeply flawed capitalism, though at least it was not *designed* to be — nor generally manifests as *overtly* — *anti-God*, despite the infiltration of Marxist ideals also making its wide-ranging godlessness less and less distinguishable from blatant Communism.)

Our Lady additionally requested the wearing of her scapular and later appeared to Lucia as Our Lady of Mount Carmel, both connections to Carmel, foremost dedicated to Our Lady (and responsible for spawning the Holy Face devotion). She asked for the daily recitation of the Rosary, which she promised would obtain for men the grace needed to overcome sin, and added the practice of saying after each mystery: "O my Jesus, forgive us our sins, save us from the fires of Hell. Lead all souls to Heaven, especially those with the greatest

---

[947] Ibid., P.294.

need of Thy mercy." She also asked for sacrifices, to include one's daily duties. She told the children, "Pray, pray very much, and make sacrifices for sinners; for many souls go to hell, because there are none to sacrifice themselves and to pray for them."[948] The same request was made almost verbatim by Christ to Sister St. Pierre: "Sinners are snatched from this world and precipitated into Hell like dust swept away by a whirlwind! Have pity on your fellow creatures, pray for them."[949] (Our Lady of Good Success at Quito also told Mariana to have pity on her imprudent brethren and pray for them.) Again, reparation for one's brethren in the mysterious solidarity of the Mystical Body of Christ is a primary, recurring theme in both the apparitions and the Holy Face devotion.

Our Lady had promised a miracle to help men believe in her appearances. It was manifested as one of biblical proportions, unequivocally placing the divine seal upon the messages and crowning this apparition in importance. This was the famous Miracle of the Sun, which took place October 13, 1917, exactly thirty-three years after Pope Leo XIII's vision of Satan challenging Christ that he could destroy the Church. The miracle was declared of supernatural character thirteen years later. Some seventy thousand witnesses flocked to the Cova da Iria, the open field in which the apparitions took place. Though the crowd was soaked through with rain, as the miracle began, their clothes were dried completely, as was the ground. The sun emitted all the colors of the rainbow, moved rapidly, spinning and emitting lights, and appeared as if falling toward the earth. When the sun resumed its normal position, color, and stationary stance, the crowd was overcome with emotion and fear.[950] More than confirming and crowning the Fatima apparitions, such an outstanding and public miracle surely has a proportionately significant message to convey.

The miracle's extensive signs and symbolism are beyond the scope of this writing, but limiting discussion to the word *sun* in scriptural references with which most would be familiar, two seem apt: "a woman clothed with the sun," a verse from Revelation (12:1) referring to Mary, and "the Sun of justice," an allegorical reference to the Messiah in Malachi (4:2). According to Lucia, "Opening her hands, Our Lady made them reflect on the sun and, as she ascended, the reflection of her own light continued to be projected on the sun

---

[948] Bartold, *Fatima*, 29.
[949] Sister St. Pierre, *Life of Sister St. Pierre*, 284. Also 70, 269.
[950] Cruz, *50 Approved Apparitions*, 166.

itself."[951] And "at the precise moment, Our Lady cast her own light upon the sun, the drenching rain suddenly stopped, the brooding clouds dispersed, and the sky became clearer."[952] Our Lady of Fatima was both "clothed" with the "Sun of justice" yet emitted her own light onto it, causing the illumination of the sky and the dispersing of clouds, in preparation for the glorious display of the sun. It is reminiscent of the Mother of Mercy, clothed with the justice of her Son, yet also reflecting it back through herself, bringing the light of grace to the masses, while dispersing the cloud of sin, to draw man to the glory of her Son. It is the unified essence of Fatima and the Holy Face devotion: the appeasement of justice to draw mercy for the conversion of sinners, flowing from Christ through the hands of the Virgin, which she uses to bring men closer to Christ.

Just two years after the miracle, both Jacinta and Francisco died of influenza, their death having been foretold by Our Lady. Lucia first attended the convent school of the Sisters of St. Dorothy in Vilar, then became a postulant of the order in 1925. Later, she entered the Discalced Carmelites in Coimbra on May 13, 1949. She took the name Sister Mary of the Sorrowful Mother. The bishop of Leiria-Fatima officially declared the apparitions "worthy of credibility" in 1930. Popes Paul VI and John Paul II visited the shrine several times. John Paul attributed to Our Lady the saving of his life from an assassination attempt on the anniversary of the first apparition, May 13, 1981. Sister Lucia died February 13, 2005, and is entombed beside Francisco and Jacinta in the basilica of Fatima.[953] In 2017, Francisco and Jacinta were canonized, and Lucia (who lived much longer) was declared Servant of God.

In Conclusion: The Crown Apparition and the Mother of All Devotions

The Holy Face devotion, per Christ Himself, as revealed to Sister St. Pierre, is the pinnacle devotion, the devotions' devotion, the "mother of all devotions." For the Holy Face devotion is allied to the Redemption, designed by God to be the remedy of a time in which, according to Christ, iniquity has never been exceeded. It counters man-modified, primordial sins of pride in making reparation to the Godhead. Complementing and being the greatest honor of the

---

[951] Ibid., 82.
[952] Ibid.
[953] Sister St. Pierre, *Life of Sister St. Pierre*, 166–167.

Sacred Heart in the Most Holy Sacrament of the Altar, it also outlines the necessity of true devotion to the Immaculate Heart. As the highest devotion, and given to mankind by Our Lady, through whom the merciful graces for conversion of sinners flow, the title "Mother of All Devotions" is metaphorically indicative of both.

Indeed, Mary as mercy is the common link in all devotions and apparitions. Christ is mediator between the Father and His members in the Holy Face devotion, while Mary is intercessor on behalf of the faithful to her Son. Yet Mary is not only intercessor before Christ but also the "return" river of grace and mercy, from the Father to Christ to Mary, obtained on the part of man by reforming one's life and offering prayers and penance for sinners to appease God, toward the salvation of all. Mary is thus revealed in the revelations and mystical experiences surrounding the Holy Face devotion, as well as in her apparitions, as *the way* to Christ, flowing from her privilege of divine maternity. The understanding is identical to that of St. Louis de Montfort, which was also confirmed by Our Lady's words to Lucia during the Fatima apparitions, "My Immaculate Heart will be your refuge, and the path that leads you to God."[954] Reflected in this quote and flowing from Mary as Mother of God and Mother of Mercy is her role as Co-Redemptrix, Mediatrix, and Mother of Man: true devotion to Mary always leading to true devotion of God. This being made most explicit in the apparitions of Fatima, as well as having been revealed in the revelations of the Holy Face devotion, makes them, among other ways, the complementary crown apparition and pinnacle devotion, respectively.

Fatima presents a synthesis of the themes of all apparitions. This is apparently confirmed in the Miracle of the Sun, yet its themes are also those of the Holy Face devotion, synthesis of all devotions. The Holy Face devotion and the Marian apparition of Fatima are in fact so complementary as to be sister devotions. In addition to the Immaculate Heart as means of salvation for sinners in each, there is also a call for man to participate in particular ways toward this salvation through the appeasement of divine justice. This need to appease God's justice is affirmed in both by making known the reality of Hell and the fact that souls are going there because there is no one to pray or make reparation for them. Likewise warning of the reality of evil, the Holy Face devotion warns of the dangers of Communism in all its manifestations — the malice of revolutionary men — while Fatima warns that "Russia would spread her errors throughout the world, provoking wars and

---

[954] Sister Mary Lucia, *Memoirs* (1976), 163, quoted in Bartold, *Fatima*, 171.

persecutions against the Church" if requests of prayer and reparation are not met. Errors contained within Russia include all ideologies that deny the absolute truth and morality of God and His Church, the very sins for which man is called to make reparation in the Holy Face devotion.

As a remedy for such blasphemous ideologies, propitiatory sacrifice in the form of reparation is required; in the Holy Face devotion, reparation is made for sins against the Godhead, while in Fatima, reparation is made for blasphemies against the Immaculate Heart of Mary. Blasphemies concerning Mary are an effect of those concerning the Godhead, for they flow from false religions as doctrinal heresies, which are sins against the first commandment. In both, there is an implication that all other means of combat against these evils are useless without first making this propitiatory reparation, by which man is to become a "terror to Hell." For according to the revelations given to Sister St. Pierre, Satan willingly delegates other categories of sin but keeps those of blasphemy to himself (and desires at all costs to annihilate efforts to make reparation for them).

Both offer hope and a pragmatic means for man to aid in the fight with evil, promising conversion, peace, and a defeat of the enemies of the Church in return. Pius IX referred to the Holy Face devotion as "destined to save society,"[955] while Our Lady promises the conversion of Russia and a period of peace in the world for fulfilling the requests she made at Fatima. The Holy Face devotion was given to man by Our Lady of the Holy Name of God, and in Fatima, Our Lady promises the Immaculate Heart will triumph. Modernism is "the synthesis of all evils"[956] destined to be conquered by Fatima, the synthesis of all Marian apparitions, *along with* the Holy Face devotion, the synthesis of all devotions.

The Holy Face devotion and Fatima share emphasis on man's role in reparation toward the salvation of sinners and the mitigation of chastisements, all to assist Mary in her Immaculate Heart's triumph over Satan by a universal return to proper fear of the Lord. According to St. Louis de Montfort, "The power of Mary over all the devils will especially break out in the latter times, when Satan will lay his snares against her heel; that is to say, her humble slaves and her poor children, whom she will raise up to make war against him.... But in return for this, they shall be rich in the grace of God, which Mary shall distribute to them

---

[955] Pope Bl. Pius IX said this regarding the Holy Face devotion: Fr. Lawrence Carney, *The Secret of the Holy Face: The Devotion Destined to Save Society*, Gastonia: TAN, 2022, inside cover.

[956] As stated by Pope St. Pius X in his *Pascendi Dominici Gregis*.

abundantly."[957] Man is to assist the Virgin, his refuge, in crushing the head of Satan by aiding in the restoration of life and light to the masses, thereby allowing for the destruction of heresies and their ideological-socioeconomic counterparts through the conversion of all.

This assistance by man in the Virgin's triumph over Satan is a recurrent, underlying theme in the apparitions of La Salette, Lourdes, Quito, and Fatima. Yet it was definitively "debuted" in the Holy Face devotion by Sister St. Pierre's experience of Mary as Co-Redemptrix, Mediatrix, and Mother of Man, flowing from her privilege of divine maternity. The title "Mother of All Devotions" thus takes on unifying, dual significance. Indeed, the Holy Face devotion was "found" in the Sacred Heart, even as Fatima sprang from the Immaculate Heart. As Christ told Sister St. Pierre, the two Hearts must not be separated. The requests of Christ in the Holy Face devotion and Mary in the apparitions of Fatima are to be fulfilled *together*. "The 'Great Sign,' given on October 13, 1917, majestically summarizes the whole Fatima message of God's Divine Mercy and Justice, which are inseparable."[958] Yet this is the message, too, of the Holy Face devotion: the woman clothed with the Sun of justice absorbs its brilliance, emanating her own — its own — brightness back unto it, setting alight the now illumined, cloud-ridden sky with grace and mercy for the masses: all resplendent, the woman reveals "the most beautiful work under the sun" by returning to it its own healing rays.

The heavens declared his justice: and all people saw his glory.

— Psalm 96:6

---

[957] Louis de Montfort, *True Devotion*, 41.
[958] Bartold, *Fatima*, 79.

Chapter 8

The Holy Face "Face-Off" with Communism

Let God arise, and let his enemies be scattered: and let them that hate him flee from before his face.

— Psalm 67:2

Just as a primary reason for the categorical difference between the Holy Face devotion and those centered upon Christ's sacred humanity concerns the former's preeminence in undertaking the most noble adoration and reparation to the Godhead itself, the inverse is true: the overt stamping upon the rights of God as prohibited in the first three commandments constitutes the greatest evil. The pinnacle devotion is designed to make reparation for the highest crimes — those that are not "just" godless but anti-God. The editors of the autobiography of Sister St. Pierre write:

> Secret Societies, which at the present day are the bane of France, and openly wage war against the Church of God, had for a long time plotted in the religious sects, whose pernicious influence insidiously permeated the entire world. France, unhappily, has been the principal center, and the most active furnace of such machinations, for from her midst, from Paris especially, has the revolutionary and Anti-Social spirit, diffused

itself over the whole of Europe, assuming diverse names according to the country and times, such as Socialism, Liberalism, Nihilism. Toward the end of the reign of Louis-Philippe, the period we have now reached in the life of Sister Saint Pierre, it was called Communism. By degrees, the Communist party had invaded the irreligious press, and now counted organs [as in part of the larger organization] and writers of some celebrity in the schools of philosophy, and the current literature of the day. Several of them, in different places, had even tried to bring about the realization of their dangerous Utopian schemes. Especially by its occult maneuvers was the faction growing more powerful and dangerous. Having skillfully prepared its underground mines, the moment of the explosion was near, and the government, as is often the case in such circumstances with parties most interested, suspected nothing. France unconsciously slept upon a volcano. From the depths of her retreat, enlightened from On High, the humble daughter of Carmel, ever solicitous for the needs of her Fatherland, and the salvation of souls, was sounding the alarm to the sacred sentinels, and pointing out to them the means of averting these perils.[959]

These means for averting such perils were in fact specifically indicated to Sister St. Pierre by Christ. He commanded her to make war on the Communists, telling her that "they are the enemies of the Church and of her Christ," disclosing also that most of these members had been born in the Church, "whose bitter, open enemies they now are!"[960]

Indeed, the chastisement of "the malice of revolutionary men" of which Christ warned is foremost an attack upon the Church, resulting in even some of her members "turncoating" to become open enemies of their own shared Mystical Body. Infiltration of Freemasonry, modernism, and Communism has led to blasphemies in the form of heterodoxy and even apostasy within the Church, which was warned about by various popes in the nineteenth and twentieth centuries, including: Pope Leo XIII after his vision of 1884 in which Satan was given permission by God to attempt to destroy the Church (and which consequently led him to compose the St. Michael Prayer); Pope St. Pius X in his 1907 encyclical *Pascendi Dominici Gregis* in which he warns of modernists who "put their designs for [the Church's] ruin into operation not from without but from

---

[959] Sister St. Pierre, *Life of Sister St. Pierre*, ed. Rev. P. Janvier (Baltimore: John Murphy, 1884), 293–294.
[960] Ibid.

within"; and Pope St. Paul VI, who stated in 1972 that "the smoke of Satan had entered the Church," perhaps referring to "anti-communism documents of Vatican II not being published."[961] Among others,[962] there is also the well-known testimony of Bella Dodd, a former high-ranking Communist in the United States, who spoke extensively of the infiltration of the Church by Soviet agents, even in the highest places, all with the goal of subverting the Church from within. She (as a single agent) personally recruited more than eleven hundred Communist sympathizers to enter Catholic seminaries.[963]

The object of this infiltration was (and is) to destroy the faith of individual members by promoting a watered-down, pseudo-version of the true Faith. Ven. Fulton Sheen (who fittingly converted Bella Dodd) describes the desired result: a future "religion without the Cross, a liturgy without a world to come, a religion to destroy a religion, or a politics which is a religion — one that renders unto Caesar even the things that are God's."[964] In 1 John 2:22, the antichrist is described as "[one] who denieth the Father, and the Son." In the same spirit, Sheen writes:

> [Amid] all his seeming love for humanity and his glib talk of freedom and equality, he will have one great secret which he will tell no one: he will not believe in God. Because his religion will be brotherhood without the fatherhood of God, he will deceive even the elect. He will set up a counter-church which will be the ape of the Church because he, the Devil, is the ape of God. It will have all the notes and characteristics of the Church, but in reverse and emptied of its divine content. It will be a mystical body of the Antichrist that will in all externals resemble the mystical body of Christ. In desperate need for God, whom he nevertheless refuses to adore, modern man in his loneliness and frustration will hunger more and more for membership in a community that will give him enlargement of purpose, but at the cost of losing himself in some vague collectivity. Then will be the verified paradox — the very objections with which men in the last century rejected the Church will be the

---

[961] Paul Kengor, *The Devil and Karl Marx* (Gastonia, NC: TAN Books, 2020), 142–143.
[962] *The Memoirs of the Communist Infiltration into the Church* by Marie Carré, for example. Also, testimony of Manning Johnson, hearing before the House of Representatives, 1853: John Vennari, *The Revelations of the Holy Face of Jesus* (Constable, NY: The Fatima Center, n.d.), 41.
[963] Mary A. Nicholas and Paul Kengor, *The Devil and Bella Dodd: One Woman's Struggle against Communism and Her Redemption* (Gastonia, NC: TAN Books, 2022), 17–18.
[964] Fulton J. Sheen, *Communism and the Conscience of the West* (New Pekin, IN: Refuge of Sinners Publishing, 2022), 24.

reason why they will now accept the counter-church [i.e., its universality, intolerance (of heresy), dogmatism, hierarchy, belief in the devil (many atheists paradoxically believe in the demonic), etc.][965]

Sheen's observations are remarkably like the prophecies given in various approved Marian apparitions regarding a great tribulation within the Church.

As an example, and as discussed in the previous chapter, it was warned in the apparition of La Salette that "the Church will be in eclipse,"[966] as in a great crisis. This is reflected also in the revelations given to Sister St. Pierre: "The Church is threatened with a terrible tempest. Pray, pray!"[967] A period of trial for the Church is both an effect of blasphemies and heresies against the Church and an allowed chastisement by God for those offenses. "The Church is the Face of the Mystical Body of Christ now covered with wounds by the impious."[968] Crimes against the Church are crimes against the rights and majesty of God, those prohibited by the first three commandments, which have, according to Christ's revelation to Sister St. Pierre, "risen to the Throne of God and provoked His wrath which will soon burst forth if His justice be not appeased, [for] in no time have these crimes reached such a pitch."[969] These violations draw forth their own chastisement, for in wounding the Face of Christ, they are disfiguring the Face of His Mystical Body, the Church. It is a defacing of the Faith, the Countenance of Christ, making it unrecognizable. Man is suffering from his own transgressions, bringing about a crisis in the Church, making it but a shadow of its former self: its "eclipse."

Eloquent in warning of this eclipse in the Church, of this defacing of the Faith, Ven. Fulton Sheen (1895–1979), American Catholic bishop and renowned theologian, was also beloved for his intellectual acuity in relating (as correlated to this crisis) the evils of Communism, among other relevant topics of the day, shared with a vast following through his homilies, writings, radio and prime-time televised lectures of the mid-twentieth century. Referring to his radio presentations, *Time* magazine described him in 1946 as "golden-voiced"

---

[965] Ibid., 24–25.
[966] *Apparition of the Blessed Virgin on the Mountain of La Salette on the 19th of September 1846*, ed. Association of the Children of Our Lady of La Salette, reproduction of the original 1879 edition of Lecce (Béaupreau, 1976), 19.
[967] Sister St. Pierre, *Life of Sister St. Pierre*, 379.
[968] Ibid., 393.
[969] Ibid., 145.

and "Catholicism's famed proselytizer"; at its height, his *Life Is Worth Living* was viewed by twenty million people, making it the most widely watched television program in history; and he won two Emmys for "Most Outstanding Television Personality" in his later *The Fulton Sheen Program*. Yet his "public, repeated, and unabashed" denouncing of Communism in the early 1940s — during the height of World War II and when the United States and the Soviet Union were uneasy allies to defeat Nazi Germany — landed him on the Federal Bureau of Investigation (FBI) watch list under J. Edgar Hoover.[970] Beginning in 1943, he was under investigation for seditious propaganda for his critique of Communism, considered a possible danger to U.S. national security.[971] Yet after tracking his every move for more than a decade, the FBI in 1953 invited Sheen to speak at the graduation address for the FBI National Academy in Washington, D.C.; Hoover thanked him for one of the finest and most inspirational talks he had ever heard. Apt to a poetic justice, copies of the FBI reports on Sheen are filed at the Vatican and were used in his cause for canonization.[972]

Ven. Sheen's anti-vogue stance on Communism at the time makes even more compelling his methods of refuting Communist ideology with its own documents and writings,[973] showing it to be "the final logic of the dehumanization of man." Quoting Marx as saying, "We have already destroyed the outer priest; now we must destroy the inner priest," Sheen revealed an almost personal enmity he felt, and related, for what he referred to as the "collective atheism of communism" and the "destroyer of man's clerical, spiritual nature." Conversely, he was equally passionate in defending democracy and the principles behind it, citing the Declaration of Independence in its proclamation of inalienable rights given by the Creator.[974] Yet he impartially criticized all forms of totalitarianism, even involving the West, making a distinction between the antagonism of Communism and Christian civilization with an accord between Communism and Western civilization:

> Unquestionably [Communism] is the enemy of our Christian civilization.... Communism certainly is not [however] the enemy of our

---

[970] *Follow That Bishop* (documentary), Rome Reports, dir. Antonio Olivie, premiered Fort Worth, TX, April 2023.
[971] Ibid.
[972] Ibid.
[973] Ibid.
[974] Ibid.

Western bourgeois, capitalistic, materialistic civilization. The truth of the matter is: Communism is related to our materialistic Western civilization as putrefaction is to disease. Many of the ideas which our bourgeois civilization has sold at retail, communism sells at wholesale; what the Western world has subscribed to in isolated and uncorrelated tidbits, communism has integrated into a complete philosophy of life.... Our Western bourgeois world is un-Christian; Communism is anti-Christian.[975]

Sheen holds that the "elements of destruction" of Communism were those of capitalistic civilization, put together to become "a new kind of thing," an immensely horrifying thing when the effects are "worked out on a world-wide scale."[976]

The analogy of capitalism being putrefaction while Communism is the disease, the ills and effects becoming almost interchangeable in their assault of the body of mankind until it succumbs to evil ideology on a global scale, is apt in understanding the dangers of Communism — and capitalism, as well as man's obligation to do his part to cure the disease. And certainly, inherent in the Holy Face devotion is a call for the faithful to help renew the societal structure, using Catholic principles. *But this is not the most essential message in the revelations of Christ given to Sister St. Pierre regarding Communism.* Therein, it is Sheen's latter point and one other: Communism is the enemy of the Church and of Christ, for while other ideologies may be un-Christian or godless, Communism epitomizes anti-Christian, *anti-God* ideologies, embracing the sins most offensive to God, those forbidden by the first three commandments. And as such, there is an implicit understanding that engaging in spiritual battle with the enemy is the first and most important line of defense: all other maneuvers by man are useless without first making reparation.

---

[975] Sheen, *Communism*, 49. "The individual atheism of our bourgeois civilization became the collective atheism of communism.... Communism is potpourri, a hodgepodge of all the cheap, deistic,... atheistic, agnostic thinking of the Eighteen Century, and what Leon Daudet called the 'stupid nineteenth century.'... Karl Marx, its founder, patched the dialectics of a Hegel to the materialism of a Feuerbach, to the sociology of a Proudhon, to the economic problems born of liberalism and out of it came the philosophy we call 'the enemy' of our Western civilization. Every single idea of communism is Western Bourgeois in its origin." And, Ibid., 52.

[976] Ibid.

Indeed, reparation to the Holy Face is the *most noble and the most necessary work of our times*,"[977] for God is demanding a new effort, a new cooperation on the part of man, whose object is to repair these most loathsome crimes of modern society (as even manifesting within the Church) that He describes as "deep rooted impiety and absolute incredulity."[978] Christ deputed Sister St. Pierre:

> I have made known to you that I hold you in My Hands as an arrow. I now wish to speed that arrow against my enemies, and I give you wherewith to combat them, the weapons of My Passion — My Cross of which they are the foes, and the other instruments of My tortures. Meet them with the artlessness of a child, and the courage of a valiant soldier, and receive for this mission, the benediction of the Father, of the Son, and of the Holy Ghost.[979]

She asked the Blessed Virgin to be the depositary of these divine weapons, which had been given to her by her beloved Son. Christ said, "The weapons of my enemies scatter death, but Mine give life."

And certainly, Communism does scatter death; it has been accurately described as "the killingest idea ever."[980] No other ideology is as deadly, killing an estimated one hundred million people to date. Victims span Russia, China, Vietnam, North Korea, Cambodia, Eastern Europe, Latin America, Africa, and Afghanistan. The ideology's "accomplishments" of human annihilation outnumber those of Nazi fascism by a factor of ten. This is not to mention the "wretched poverty, rank repression, and sheer violence" of Communism.[981] The facts portray a regime that epitomizes death and devastation. For even more than its socioeconomic-political dangers, it is, as Fulton Sheen states, a philosophy of "life": an anti-God ideology designed to infiltrate every fiber of man's existence.

Its ideals have not only infiltrated all aspects of humanity in explicitly designated Communist states but have been largely embraced throughout the world. The reign of a "secular" state, whether socialist or capitalist, has integrated even into Western civilization. Communism is an error that "spreads," as

---

[977] Sister Mary St. Peter, *Life of Sister Mary St. Peter*, ed. Rev. P. Janvier (France, 1884), 312.
[978] Ibid., 311–312.
[979] Ibid., 294–295.
[980] Paul Kengor, *The Politically Incorrect Guide to Communism: The Killingest Idea Ever* (Washington, D.C.: Regnery, 2017), 9–13.
[981] Ibid.

Our Lady of Fatima warned. This is evidenced in an onslaught of social and cultural evils that are contrary to the last seven commandments, which pertain to the rights of one's neighbor. But they stem from what is worse: evils that are contrary to the rights of God, effectively declaring with Friedrich Nietzsche, "God is dead."[982] The violation of the first three commandments is endemic, even when not overtly presented as such.

Thus, Communism does not just kill people or make their lives miserable. Its ideology is anti-human, anti-family, and anti-God. It strikes at the very image of God in man, corroding human dignity by destroying freedom and individual rights, undermining the nuclear family, and stamping out religion — most expressly, Catholicism. In fact, there were twice as many martyrs in the twentieth century as there were in the previous nineteen centuries of Christian history combined, the great majority of these having given their lives for Christ at the hands of Communist regimes.[983] Karl Marx held that "Communism begins from the outset with atheism."[984] And Vladimir Lenin stated, "Communism abolishes eternal truths, it abolishes all religion, and all morality."[985] Indeed, Communism is the enemy of humanity — and Christianity: God's antagonist.

One could even argue that the Church is to Christ as Communism is to the antichrist. Indeed, Ven. Fulton Sheen stated in the 1940s, "The conflict of the future is between an absolute who is the God-Man and an absolute which is man-god; between the God who became Man and the man who makes himself god; between brothers in Christ and comrades in the anti-Christ."[986] Communism, as premier anti-God-Man-and-pro-man-god "dogma," is the ultimate nemesis of the Holy Face of Christ, which is the emblem of both the God-Man (Christ) and the Godhead itself.[987] As such, Communism is the logical face of the antichrist. In the Holy Face devotion, God requests that the "brothers of Christ" participate in an explicit, modern means to counter the death and dark

---

[982] An expression coined by this German philosopher to indicate his belief that the Enlightenment had essentially eliminated the possibility for the existence of God.

[983] George Weigel, *The Fragility of Order: Catholic Reflections on Turbulent Times* (San Francisco: Ignatius Press, 2018), 47.

[984] Karl Marx, *Economic & Philosophic Manuscripts of 1844* (Moscow: Progress Publishers, 1959), accessed November 7, 2023, https://www.marxists.org/archive/marx/works/download/pdf/Economic-Philosophic-Manuscripts-1844.pdf, 44.

[985] Vladimir Lenin, *Collected Works*, vol. 25, *The State and Revolution* (1918), accessed November 7, 2023, https://www.marxists.org/ebooks/lenin/state-and-revolution.pdf.

[986] Sheen, *Communism*, 22.

[987] Sister Mary St. Peter, *Life of Sister Mary St. Peter*, 243.

of the "comrades in the anti-Christ," restoring life and light to the masses,[988] reviving the Face of Christ in man. God chooses that modern man play a role in the Holy Face "face-off" with Communism, engaging him in the spiritual warfare of the age.

Sister St. Pierre "entered upon the arena" of celestial combat by opposing the fury of the enemies of God with the Cross and the instruments of the Passion.[989]

> To animate His servant in this mystical combat, the Savior reveal[ed] to her the designs of these secret societies, and their anti-Christian principles.... He said to her: "The soldier, who knowing the origin of the war in which he is enlisted to be the injury offered his King, burns with indignation to avenge it, and intrepidly arms himself for the fray. Think, now, my daughter, of the outrages inflicted on Me by this society of Communists; it is they who have dragged Me from My Tabernacles, profaned My Sanctuaries, and laid hands upon the anointed of the Lord; but their machinations are in vain, their designs shall be foiled! Have they not committed the crime of Judas? They have sold Me for money! Let not this knowledge be sterile in you, for I acquaint you with it to animate you to the combat. Act in a spirit of simplicity, for if you reason too much, you thereby fail to be a proper instrument in My hands. Think more of the glory that will be rendered Me by the Celestial Court, for having combated such enemies with so puny an instrument!"[990]

Christ encouraged Sister St. Pierre, promising her (and all who undertake this combat) a "Cross of Honor," which would "open Heaven to her," were she but faithful.

As the editors of Sister St. Pierre's autobiography alluded, anti-God ideology is not exclusive to Communism. "Vladimir Lenin, the godfather of Bolshevism, considered himself a democratic socialist before he called himself a communist."[991] In fact, Lenin and Marx use socialism and Communism synonymously, as steps in a progression.[992] Socialism follows where Communism leads. At best, even moderate socialism is the proverbial camel's nose in the tent, where the body of Communism follows close behind. Popes have

---

[988] Ibid., 320, 324.
[989] Ibid., 295.
[990] Ibid., 296.
[991] Kengor, *Guide to Communism*, 167–168.
[992] Lenin, *State and Revolution*, 68.

consistently warned Catholics about the specific dangers and errors of socialism. They pointed to a variety of irreconcilable offenses to Catholic doctrine — concerning in large part its denial of the dignity of the human person and his fundamental rights.

Pope Leo XIII in 1878 first warned of socialism's threat to man, marriage, the family, and the fabric of social life.[993] In 1907, Pius X warned of the heresy of modernism, which is intrinsic to Communism and socialism, wherein the Church is made subject to the State.[994] Benedict XV in 1914 reminded the faithful take note of socialism's many errors.[995] Pope Pius XI in 1931, seeing the inherent misalignment, forbade Catholics to be members of even the more moderate forms of socialism:

> Whether Socialism be considered as a doctrine, or as a historical fact, or as a movement, if it really remains Socialism, it cannot be brought into harmony with the dogmas of the Catholic Church.... The reason being that it conceives human society in a way utterly alien to Christian truth. Christianity always upholds the basic dignity of human personality and its fundamental rights. Material goods, necessary as they are, are not an end in themselves, but a means to that higher end of man, the super-natural union of man with God here and hereafter. A system that ... subordinates the individual to the State cannot have the support of the Church.[996]

Pope St. John XXIII in 1961 held that no Catholic could subscribe even to moderate socialism,[997] and Pope St. John Paul II affirmed Pope Leo XIII, among other

---

[993] Pope Leo XIII, encyclical letter *Quod Apostolici Muneris* (December 28, 1878), accessed November 5, 2023, https://www.vatican.va/content/leo-xiii/en/encyclicals/documents/hf_l-xiii_enc_28121878_quod-apostolici-muneris.html, no. 8.

[994] Pope Pius X, encyclical letter *Pascendi Dominici Gregis* (September 8, 1907), accessed November 6, 2023, https://www.vatican.va/content/pius-x/en/encyclicals/documents/hf_p-x_enc_19070908_pascendi-dominici-gregis.html, nos. 24–25.

[995] Pope Benedict XV, encyclical letter *Ad Beatissimi Apostolorum* (November 1, 1914), accessed November 5, 2023, https://www.vatican.va/content/benedict-xv/en/encyclicals/documents/hf_ben-xv_enc_01111914_ad-beatissimi-apostolorum.html, no. 13.

[996] Pope Pius XI, encyclical letter *Quadragesimo Anno* (May 15, 1931), accessed October 12, 2023, https://www.vatican.va/content/pius-xi/en/encyclicals/documents/hf_p-xi_enc_19310515_quadragesimo-anno.html, no. 79.

[997] Pope John XXIII, encyclical letter *Mater et Magistra* (May 15, 1961), https://www.vatican.va/content/john-xxiii/en/encyclicals/documents/hf_j-xxiii_enc_15051961_mater.html, no. 34. Pope Pius XI further emphasized the fundamental opposition between

ways, by emphasizing the good of private property as necessary in protecting foremost the working man.[998] Pope St. John Paul II and Benedict XVI are known to have each suffered under socialist oppression via Communist and Nazi regimes in their respective Poland and Germany. Indeed:

> Communism deprives individuals of their inalienable rights. It is a totalitarian, atheistic ideology pursued for the stated purpose of ushering in a classless utopia — a better, even perfect, world.... [Yet in the case of] Stalin's Russia to Pol Pot's Cambodia to Hugo Chavez's Venezuela, communism has ushered in not the promised workers' paradise but the closest thing the world has known to hell on earth.[999]

Besides being ungodly, socialist Communism has largely — if not absolutely[1000] — achieved the very inverse of its stated goal: for an ideology that believes that the ends justify the means, the Marxists' "means" appear as the dismal "end" for the masses victimized by the regime — a hellish far cry from utopia.

Advocating for social "equality," yet achieving the very inverse of its stated goal, was initially the case with the French Revolution, "which showed for the first time that a [modern] powerful state could be used as a tremendous anti-Christianity

---

Communism and Christianity and made it clear that no Catholic could subscribe even to moderate socialism. The reason is that socialism is founded on a doctrine of human society that is bounded by time and takes no account of any objective other than that of material well-being. Since, therefore, it proposes a form of social organization that aims solely at production, it places too severe a restraint on human liberty, at the same time flouting the true notion of social authority.

[998] Pope John Paul II, encyclical letter *Centesimus Annus* (May 1, 1991), citing Pope Leo XII, encyclical letter *Rerum Novarum*, no. 99, accessed November 5, 2023, https://www.vatican.va/content/john-paul-ii/en/encyclicals/documents/hf_jp-ii_enc_01051991_centesimus-annus.html, no. 12. "His words [Leo XIII's] deserve to be re-read attentively: 'To remedy these wrongs (the unjust distribution of wealth and the poverty of the workers), the Socialists encourage the poor man's envy of the rich and strive to do away with private property, contending that individual possessions should become the common property of all ...; but their contentions are so clearly powerless to end the controversy that, were they carried into effect, the working man himself would be among the first to suffer. They are moreover emphatically unjust, for they would rob the lawful possessor, distort the functions of the State, and create utter confusion in the community.' The evils caused by the setting up of this type of socialism as a State system — what would later be called 'Real Socialism' — could not be better expressed."

[999] Kengor, *Guide to Communism*, 10.

[1000] A full discussion of "socialism" experimentation in other States, which do, however, have great economic — and sometimes religious — freedom, is beyond the scope of this text.

machine."[1001] Like all forms of modernist-nihilist-rationalist thought, the Communist ideology had its roots in the Enlightenment.[1002] Its big debut, however, dates to the first totalitarians of the Jacobins who used the French Revolution as a jumping point to initiate the Reign of Terror. This 1790s "reign" used the infamous guillotine to decapitate thousands of dissidents of the "democratic" revolution, including hundreds of Catholic priests and nuns, an intensification of the persecution of the Catholic Church by the then-new French government. Robespierre, the brain behind the tactics of terror for the good of the "republic of virtue," was in the end himself put to the guillotine when "members of the assembly turned against their master, out of fear of being next on his list."[1003] Despite Robespierre's own methods turning on himself (a phenomenon not uncommon in the realm of thought wherein "truth" and "morals" are believed to be arbitrated by man), the Jacobins were admired by Lenin.

An apostatized Christian, Lenin, as the leader of the Bolsheviks, overthrew the Russian Republic in 1917 — just twenty-five days after the Miracle of the Sun in Fatima. He founded the Soviet Union and instituted his own Red Terror during the 1918 Russian Civil War. Lenin in turn was admired by Trotsky, his minister of foreign affairs. Both desired to turn Russia into a terror-like, repressive, and murderous machine for the machinations of their cause. Marx, already an unabashed author of demonic prose and poetry,[1004] was there with the perfect "how-to" guide. *The Communist Manifesto*, written by Marx and Engels in 1848, served as a blueprint for Marxism-Leninism in Russia, Maoism in China, and twenty-first-century socialism in Chavez's Venezuela.[1005]

It was also in the year 1848 that Sister St. Pierre died. Though the Russian Revolution had not taken place and the *Manifesto* had not yet been written when she received the revelations pertaining to Communism, the term *Communism*, as noted previously, was already used in the early 1840s to denote any of a variety of socialists, liberals, or nihilists, "assuming different names at different

---

[1001] David Carlin, "Since the Reformation," The Catholic Thing, August 7, 2020.
[1002] Diane Moczar, *The Church under Attack: Five Hundred Years That Split the Church and Scattered the Flock* (Manchester, NH: Sophia Institute Press, 2013), 92.
[1003] Ibid., 96.
[1004] Anne Hendershott, "A Disturbing Guide to the Devilish Karl Marx," *The Catholic World Report*, August 17, 2020, https://www.catholicworldreport.com/2020/08/17/a-disturbing-guide-to-the-devilish-karl-marx.
[1005] Kengor, *Guide to Communism*, 23.

epochs to suit the caprice of the moment."[1006] Pope Leo XIII in his encyclical on socialism, *Quod Apostolici Muneris*, likewise spoke of

> that sect of men who, under various and almost barbarous names, are called socialists, communists, or nihilists, and who, spread over all the world, and bound together by the closest ties in a wicked confederacy, no longer seek the shelter of secret meetings, but, openly and boldly marching forth in the light of day, strive to bring to a head what they have long been planning — the overthrow of all civil society whatsoever.

Like Satan, Marxism rebels against God "by destroying the world as it exists [to create] a new world in which God is destroyed and man is elevated."[1007] Likewise "creating a new world" — even if it be make-believe — and suiting the caprice of the twenty-first-century "moment," adherents of moral relativism, spawning from modernism, in which each man decides for himself "his" own truth and morality, are proverbial frogs in a pot of slow-boiling Marxist ideology, protagonists of the man-god, antagonists of the God-Man. While the revelations given to Sister St. Pierre could not have *in her understanding* referred to then-future Communist regimes of Russia and China, for example — since the revelations were given to her some seventy years before the Communist Revolution in Russia — the seeds of those revolutions were already in place, going back at least to the Jacobins and their Reign of Terror and pertaining to the thought that fueled the reign, to the earlier period of "Enlightenment."

The theology of the Reformation led to the philosophical thought of the Enlightenment, wherein reason was considered the primary source of knowledge. The Reformation had substituted "faith alone" and the "Bible alone" for the authority of the Church and her tradition. Yet the freethinking ideology concurrent with the French Revolution took anti-Church concepts a step further, substituting, in effect, a new faith, the "autonomy" of reason for the authority of Church dogma and Christian society. Having separated morals from faith, the "autonomy of reason" led to a steady decline in morality and a contempt for the authority of the Church.

The Holy Face devotion was revealed to Sister St. Pierre by Our Lord in response to the "enlightened," freethinking notions concurrent with the French

---

[1006] Ibid., 318.
[1007] Hendershott, "Disturbing Guide."

Revolution, which left an aftermath of atheistic and blasphemous ideology, now the norm. Many like Voltaire were both Freemasons and freethinkers,[1008] and the slogan of the French Revolution, "Liberty, Equality, Fraternity," was originally Masonic.[1009] Warned against in the apparitions of Our Lady of Good Success, Freemasonry is a secret society that bears a special hatred for the Catholic Church; its avowal to destroy the Church is well established, even manifest in its mantra to "overcome Throne and Altar" — that is, monarchies and Catholicism.[1010] As early as Pope Clement XII and as recently as Pope Benedict XVI, popes have condemned Freemasonry and issued the penalty of excommunication for those Catholics who become members.[1011] And while the French lodges of Freemasonry were doubtless more extreme than some, its constitution remains anti-Church and anti-papacy, as were the freethinkers.

Leo XIII succinctly summarizes the history of rationalism (which may be seen as a summation of the ills and effects of the Reformation, the Enlightenment, Freemasons, freethinkers, and socialists) in *Quod Apostolici Muneris*:

> That most deadly war which from the sixteenth century down has been waged by innovators against the Catholic Faith, and which has grown in intensity up to today, had for its object to subvert all revelation, and overthrow the supernatural order, that thus the way might be opened for the discoveries, or that the hallucinations, of reason alone.... Hence, by a new species of impiety, unheard of even among the heathen nations, states have been constituted without any count at all of God or of the order established by Him; it has been given out that public authority neither derives its principles, nor its majesty, nor its power of governing from God, but rather from the multitude, which, thinking itself absolved from all divine sanction, bows only to such laws as it shall have made at its own will.

[1008] *The Catholic Encyclopedia* (New York: McGraw-Hill, 1965), s.v. "Freethinkers." Voltaire was enrolled in the Lodge of Nine Sisters in Paris in 1778.

[1009] Alex Davidson, "The Masonic Concept of Liberty: Freemasonry and the Enlightenment," Pietre-Stones Review of Freemasonry, accessed January 17, 2019, http://www.freemasons-freemasonry.com/Davidson.html.

[1010] Marianna Bartold, *Fatima: The Signs and Secrets* (Lapeer, MI: KIC, 2014), 77. Taken from John Vennari, *The Permanent Instruction of the Alta Vendita* (Rockford, IL: TAN Books, 1999), 14.

[1011] Joseph Ratzinger, Congregation for the Doctrine of the Faith, "Declaration on Masonic Associations," November 26, 1983, http://www.vatican.va/roman_curia/congragations/cfaith/documents/rc_con_cfaith_doc 19831126 declaraion-masonic_en.html.

Rationalism in which "truth" is understood through argumentation paved the way for modernism in which "truth" is understood as dynamic and even as perceived by personal feeling, which has further devolved into today's moral relativism and wokeism in which there is no objective truth at all — only individual "truth," "morality," and even "reality"!

Relativism and other postmodernisms share with socialism, Communism, atheism, and satanism the denial of the absolute truth of God, manifested in natural law, which allows for the deduction of the universal, God-given values and rights of men. They have other noteworthy common denominators: Lenin, Marx, Engels, and Trotsky, for example, were all Freemasons.[1012] Communism shares tactics of infiltration with Freemasonry, modernism and the various postmodernisms, and, as mentioned, its anti-God, anti-family, and anti-man system has in fact become the deadliest in the history of man.[1013] These systems of thought are grave offenses to the Triune Divinity and have the *explicit purpose* of the de-spiritualization of Christian civilization. They are warned about in Isaiah 5:20: "Woe to you that call evil good, and good evil."

Communism is an unprecedented affront to the majesty of God in its *overtly* atheistic and blasphemous foundation. Mankind is to "repair" its (and all) offenses against the Almighty in reparation to the Godhead, defeating via spiritual, not material, combat — resulting in the conversion, not death, of the enemy. Christ instructed Sister St. Pierre to combat Communists (and all "by any other name" would-be Marxists). She would begin by placing her soul in Our Lord's hands, then pray: "Eternal Father, I offer Thee the Cross of Our Lord Jesus Christ, and all the instruments of His Holy Passion,[1014] that Thou mayest put division in the camp of Thy enemies, for as Thy Beloved Son hath said, '*a kingdom divided against itself shall fall.*'"[1015] She also utilized the virtues of the holy name of God as an offering for their conversion. And she additionally made the invocations: "Let God arise and His enemies be dispersed, and all that hate Him fly from before His Face. Let the thrice Holy Name of God overthrow their

---

[1012] Jüri Lina, *Under the Sign of the Scorpion: The Rise and Fall of the Soviet Empire* (2002), 72, 98, 136. Stockholm: Referent Publishing.

[1013] Kengor, *Guide to Communism*, 9–13.

[1014] Our Lady appeared at La Salette, wearing a crucifix upon her heart, surrounded by the sharp instruments of the Passion, the hammer and sharp pincers. This was surely a symbolic cojoining of the messages of La Salette with the revelations given to Sister St. Pierre.

[1015] Sister St. Pierre, *Life of Sister St. Pierre*, 295.

designs. Let the Sacred Name of the Living God sow dissension among them. Let the terrible Name of the God of Eternity annihilate all their impiety."[1016] Continuing this shower of "spiritual missiles," she adds, "I wish not the death of the sinner, but that he be converted and live. Father, pardon them, for they know not what they do."[1017]

Inspired by her revelations, Sister St. Pierre also composed the Chaplet of the Holy Face, which is recommended in the *Manual of the Archconfraternity of the Holy Face*. The most often repeated verse in the chaplet, said thirty-three times, as reparative homage for all the suffering which Our Lord (has)[1018] endured especially in His Face through each of His five senses, is "Arise, O Lord, and let Thy enemies be scattered, and let those who hate Thee flee from before Thy face!" St. Athanasius relates that the devils, upon being asked what verse in the Scriptures they feared the most, replied the aforementioned (Psalm 67:2) and that it always compelled them to take flight. The chaplet ends with the invocation, "O God, our Protector, look on us, and cast Thy eyes upon the Face of Thy Christ."[1019] It is considered a minor exorcism to be used in the defeat of Communism.[1020]

Our Lord forewarned Sister St. Pierre that "Satan would do everything in his power to stamp out the devotion."[1021] He also related:

> Lucifer willingly abandoned to his subordinates the charge of the other troops of sinners, as for instance, the lewd, the intemperate, the avaricious, but the blasphemers, he kept as his favorite flock.... Saint Michael and the holy angels will protect you; with My cross which I give you for your shepherd's crook, you will become a terror to Hell.[1022]

Undeniably, *all* are called to become "terrors to Hell" by means of this great work of reparation, for God has commanded the faithful to take part in this celestial combat and has thus armed them with His singular weaponry. They share in the

---

[1016] Ibid., 297–298.
[1017] Ibid., 298.
[1018] Ongoing, renewed suffering of Christ's Face due to blasphemy (per the revelations to Sister St. Pierre) is possible as He is head of the Mystical Body of Christ.
[1019] *Manual of the Archconfraternity of the Holy Face* (Tours: Oratory of the Holy Face, 1887), 232–235.
[1020] See the appendix for full instructions.
[1021] Sister St. Pierre, *Life of Sister St. Pierre*, 140.
[1022] Ibid., 257.

work of St. Michael and his warrior angels — and will likewise in their victory.[1023] For according to Christ, the "machinations [of the Communists] are in vain; their designs shall be foiled."[1024]

Ven. Sheen writes:

> Never before in history has there been such a strong argument for the need of Christianity, for men are now discovering that their misery and their woes, their wars and their revolutions increase in direct ratio and proportion to the neglect of Christianity. Christians realize that a moment of crisis is not a time of despair, but of opportunity. The more we can anticipate the doom, the more we can avoid it. Once we recognize we are under Divine Wrath, we become eligible for Divine Mercy.... The thief on the right came to God by a crucifixion. The Christian finds a basis for optimism in the most thoroughgoing pessimism, for his Easter is within three days of Good Friday.[1025]

God is pleading with man, warning him, demanding of him, to engage in the spiritual significance of the times: to "face-off" with Communism in all its manifestations. Given the unparalleled iniquity of the era,[1026] God implores modern man to do his part toward the salvation of the masses, the restoration of peace to the nations, and the renewal of orthodoxy to the Faith in satisfying justice to draw mercy. Man's is a cosmic battle in which all must choose sides, for God gives the sobering admonition, "Woe to those [cities that] do not make reparation!"[1027] Yet the warning also gives hope, for the inverse is true: protection for those cities and people that do make reparation. The devotion is still largely unknown in these times. A devotee may be the only — or one of a few — in his city or region making reparation. When Christ revealed to Sister St. Pierre the graces flowing from the Golden Arrow prayer (and which may be obtained especially in offering the wounded Countenance of Christ to the Father in reparation), He cautioned: "Be careful how you appreciate [this] favor, for you will be held accountable." To those who have been given knowledge of these celestial armaments and aids to mercy for the masses, there is a real responsibility as members of Christ's Mystical

---

[1023] Ibid., 141.
[1024] Ibid., 295.
[1025] Sheen, *Communism*, 44–45.
[1026] *Life of Sister Mary St. Peter*, 159.
[1027] Ibid., 147.

Body and the communion of the saints to use them. Yet there is a worthy reward even in the present, for Our Lady makes the promise, "In proportion as God's army, the Defenders of His Name, increase in number, so would that of Satan, the enemies of the Church and State, decrease."[1028]

Sister St. Pierre writes:

> In God's own appointed time all will yield to the sway of His sovereign power. Oh! how excellent this Work! And how sublime! What benefits inestimable are reserved for the defenders of the Holy Name of God!... In our sacred militia, the Cross of Jesus Christ is the sole weapon with which we combat the enemies of His Name, and this Sacred Name Itself, full of virtue and strength, our Divine rampart.... Let us address ourselves with a boundless confidence to the glorious Virgin Mary, supplicating her, the Queen of the armies of God, and more terrible to the demons than an army in battle array, to place herself at our head.[1029]

Our Lady of the Holy Name of God, lead us in the spiritual combat to defeat Satan! *Sit nomen Domini benedictum!*

> *May God arise and let His enemies be scattered*
> *and let all those who hate Him flee before His Face!*
> *May the thrice Holy Name of God overthrow all their plans!*
> *May the Holy Name of the Living God split them up by disagreements!*
> *May the terrible Name of the God of Eternity*
> *stamp out all their godlessness!*
> *Lord, I do not desire the death of the sinner,*
> *but that he be converted and live.*
> *Father, forgive them for they know not what they do.*
>
> — Prayers of Sister St. Pierre to defeat Communism

[1028] Sister St. Pierre, *Life of Sister St. Pierre*, 397.
[1029] Ibid., 304–305.

Chapter 9

The Death and Legacy of Sister St. Pierre

*The Lord taketh pleasure in them that fear him:
and in them that hope in his mercy.*

—Psalm 146:11

*To entreat Yahweh to calm His wrath, Moses conducts himself
before the Lord "as a friend before his friend." This will be one
of the two great tasks of every prophet of the Holy God: to
unveil His Face to men hurrying to be converted to idols, to
appease the Face of that God, of whose Love men make for.*

— Louis Van den Bossche, secretary of state of Pius XII

THE FIVE-MONTH PERIOD IN which Sister St. Pierre enjoyed mystical contemplations of Mary as Mother of God, Mother of Man, and Mother of Mercy were but a respite in her life of spiritual burdens, a preparation for her last trials. She suffered alone as the depositor of God's messages concerning reparation to the Holy Face, for at Carmel, only the mother prioress and her secretary (who would eventually succeed Mother Mary of the Incarnation as prioress) knew of the weighty, heavenly communications given to Sister St. Pierre. All other sisters were ignorant of "the mission with which she was charged and the interior pains which she hid under a smile and an amiable word."[1030] For the usual way in which Our Lord led her was by continual mortifications, such that she rarely received spiritual consolations, and the revelations given to her by Our Lord caused her to suffer greatly in that they often made known to her the justice of the wrath of God.[1031]

Yet she did have the memory of the enormous consolation of her spiritual experiences concerning the mysteries of the divine maternity, and toward the end of her life, she received two more, specifically concerning her beloved Carmel. St. Teresa of Avila, great reformer of the Carmelite Order, appeared to her and related that she had been deputed by God to combat the enemies of the work of reparation and revealed to Sister St. Pierre that the work would be the "honor of Carmel." She affirmed that the work was very much in accord with the spirit of the Carmelite vocation: for the glory of God and the needs of the Church.[1032] She asked Sister St. Pierre to continue in her obedience toward her superiors and disclosed that she herself would be a most powerful protectress of the work. The Virgin Mary also appeared to Sister St. Pierre as the Queen of Carmel, promising to protect her "houses" (Carmelite convents) in the days of calamity.[1033] The Virgin requested her to recite the hymn "O gloriosa Virginum" as many times as there were Carmelite convents in France, in honor of her divine maternity. Our Lady told her that she would "water the flowers of Carmel in pouring down upon them the celestial dew of mercy" and that "the more God's army grows in number, the more Satan's army will be enfeebled."[1034]

Warned by Christ about a year prior to her death that the end of her life was near, Sister St. Pierre felt on Good Friday of 1848 the weight of divine justice pressing down upon men.[1035]

> Recent events in France excited anew her fervor and zeal. Beholding the advent of the calamities she had announced [the French Revolution of February of the same year], she felt prompted to an act of truly heroic charity and devotion. At three o'clock, Good Friday, when prostrate on

---

[1030] Louis Van den Bossche, *The Message of Sister Mary of St. Peter*, trans. Mary G. Durham (Tours: Carmel of Tours, 1953), 167.
[1031] Ibid., 168.
[1032] Ibid., 169.
[1033] Ibid., 172.
[1034] Ibid., 172.
[1035] Ibid., 174.

the ground to adore Jesus Christ dying on the Cross, it was revealed to her that the Divine wrath was about to descend upon men. Immediately, renewing her act of perfect abandonment, she offered herself to God as a victim to appease His irritated Justice. It really seemed as if the Lord had been awaiting only this last and generous offering, ere immolating His courageous victim, for immediately, was developed that long and painful ailment which caused her final dissolution.[1036]

She at once contracted pulmonary consumption (tuberculosis), additionally suffering an ulcerated throat, devouring fevers, and the inability to take nourishment during the last two and a half months of her life. Her inability to change position caused bedsores, and the toll of her ailments caused her body to become skeletal, with only her face remaining fresh and rosy. She was described by her doctor as "reduced to a state of complete nullity, ... but the face [was] of an entirely heavenly beauty.... The disease ... only embellished the features of Our Lord's happy privileged one, features hitherto not remarkable."[1037]

As Sister St. Pierre approached nearer to death, she spoke to her mother prioress:

> My Mother, I shall remain upon earth a little longer, because my soul is not sufficiently purified; but during this time, I am going to suffer cruelly, because Our Lord has fastened me to the cross, and I shall stay here till my last sigh. Do not give me any more care or comfort; I must occupy myself only with suffering and I only wish to think of my eternity. I desire to remain alone with my God, because I can hardly speak any more; people think that I sleep, but no, I am solely occupied with Him. Soon I shall see His adorable Face, soon I shall sing His praises for all eternity. Oh, how I shall pray then for the Church, for France, for the Community, and for the Work of Reparation. My career is finished, as God has made me understand, because the Work of Reparation is created, and it is only on that account that He put me into the world. Now, I have nothing more to do, only to suffer; one must enter into God's designs.[1038]

[1036] Sister St. Pierre, *Life of Sister St. Pierre*, ed. Rev. P. Janvier (Baltimore: John Murphy, 1884), 422.
[1037] Van den Bossche, *Message*, 174.
[1038] Ibid., 176.

She died as she lived, a true victim for Christ, totally immolated for the work for which He had deputed her. Conscious to the end, her last words were, "Jesus, Mary, Joseph! Come, Lord Jesus. *Sit nomen Domini benedictum.*" It was Saturday, July 8, 1848, but a few short months after she initially contracted the disease. She was thirty-one years and nine months old and had spent eight years and eight months in the Carmel of Tours.

Though routinely strict and severe to Sister St. Pierre exteriorly, the prioress had long since interiorly held her in the highest regards. She wrote a year and a half before her death:

> This child in her candor, is really a masterpiece of grace, which is her unique incentive. She has a right judgment, a solid spirit naturally tending to good, an imagination easy to dominate, a character sweet, docile, and gay, a germ of virtue already very developed, an already eminent degree of perfection, acquired by an absolute fidelity. We admired her regular conduct, which made her a model of exactitude, her spirit of simplicity, uprightness, and obedience, her sustained practice of charity. Add to these qualities her deference toward her sisters, her mortification of the spirit and the senses. In a word, to distinguish all the religious virtues in her, we can assert that she did not commit any fault so to say, or even voluntary infidelity and how, despite the most severe and minute examen, I believe it would be almost impossible to have a well-founded reproach to make against her.[1039]

Added to this account is the fact that while her sisters in Carmel were ignorant of the extraordinary graces with which Sister St. Pierre was favored, they already considered her a saint.[1040]

When Sister St. Pierre was asked by the prioress whether she had had any fears concerning the work of reparation — as to whether she had been mistaken or followed her own ideas, rather than the inspirations of God, she replied:

> No ... that I may have been mistaken, I have always allowed; but I can positively declare, now, when on the point of appearing before the Lord, that I have never acted herein by my own spirit; it cost me very much indeed; but I did nothing except by the Will of God and to accomplish His designs. All that I wrote by order of our Superiors, was in the

---

[1039] Ibid., 181.
[1040] Sister St. Pierre, *Life of Sister St. Pierre*, 439.

sincerity of my soul, and I would be willing to attest it with my blood. By the grace of God, having nothing with which to reproach myself herein, I am perfectly tranquil.[1041]

Louis Van den Bossche, secretary of state for Pope Pius XII, wrote:

> In the last analysis, it is the life and the person of Mary of Saint Peter herself which forms the best guarantee of the supernatural authenticity of these communications. Her heroic obedience, her faultless humility, her uprightness, and her natural simplicity, as well as the habitual profundity of her interior life, confirm her testimony.[1042]

The circular (lengthy obituary) relating her life, death, and virtues expounds at length on the beauty of her soul, attested to by her mother prioress, Sister Mary of the Incarnation. (The full circular as given to my great-great-grandfather has been translated from the original French copy as an appendix to this book.)

As is illustrated so beautifully in the circular, Sister St. Pierre's final trials took her to the depths of her personal reparation for the salvation of others — and herself: "Effectively, this interesting victim began a new mission of suffering, the level of hardship of which one can only in vain begin to characterize."[1043] She understood that God was purifying her entirely in this world "so as to give her immediate entrance into Heaven." She writes:

> Such is God's sanctity, that I had supposed myself destined to remain in Purgatory until the end of the world; but no, I have only to suffer a little longer here. Let us enter into the designs of God. Oh! how true it is, that He has means of satisfying His Justice unknown to man![1044]

She did suffer severely, however, and was even subject to renewed attacks by Satan. One demon, she believed, was ever tempting her to impatience and rebellion to God's will, "whispering in her ear insults and blasphemies, and even thoughts of despair."[1045] At last, she was relieved of her torments by putting on a

---

[1041] Ibid., 431.
[1042] Van den Bossche, *Message*, 73.
[1043] Circular of Sister Marie de St. Pierre by Mother Mary of the Incarnation, 1948. See appendix.
[1044] Sister St. Pierre, *Life of Sister St. Pierre*, 432.
[1045] Ibid., 435.

little Gospel of the Circumcision (a secondary devotion that had been revealed to her concerning the power in the holy name of Jesus — as distinguished from the name of God the Father, which is the primary focus in the Holy Face devotion). The virtue of the holy name of Jesus dispelled the demon, and all temptation vanished in an instant.

As stated, all Sister St. Pierre's convent sisters held her as an object of general veneration, beholding her as a saint, though they were ignorant of her rare supernatural gifts and heavenly communications: all, except one. Though this sister could find no fault in Sister St. Pierre, she felt that a life so simple and ordinary should not merit such praise. A month prior to the death of Sister St. Pierre, this nun had prayed that if she be as holy as she is reputed, "make it known to me by affording me such relief [this nun being very ill at the time], that I may follow the regular observances of the Community."[1046] Though her prayer was immediately answered, granted so uniformly that to the surprise of all, she could, from that moment, take part in the exercises of the choir, the nun remained unconvinced. It was only after the death of Sister St. Pierre that her opinion changed, brought about by a dream that greatly disturbed her:

> It seemed to her that she and all her companions were assembled around the bed of the dying Sister, who, expiring before her eyes, was suddenly resuscitated under the form of a little child, the most beautiful she had ever seen. Stepping down from the bed, it kissed each sister present except herself, then disappeared forever.[1047]

The next day at Holy Communion, the sister's opinion was fully changed. "The life of her holy companion recurred to her mind with such evidence of sanctity as she had seemed to have utterly overlooked, and she regretted not having appreciated so inestimable a treasure until it was removed from their midst."[1048] This was not the only apparently miraculous occurrence surrounding the death of Sister St. Pierre.

It was noticed during the entire visitation of Sister St. Pierre's body in the choir of the convent that the four large candles, each fixed near a corner of her coffin, did not wane in substance, despite continually burning in a strong draft,

---

[1046] Ibid., 440.
[1047] Ibid., 441.
[1048] Ibid.

such that other candles held by the sisters "flickered and wasted very much indeed."[1049] Several persons also noticed that the pieces of Sister St. Pierre's personal articles of clothing, which were saved as mementos, "exhaled a very defined balsamic odor, not, however, resembling any known perfume, but an indescribably celestial balm as it were, which, penetrating the soul, incited it to love of God and virtue."[1050] Additionally, a woman was healed of a fatal crisis when a piece of Sister St. Pierre's veil was placed upon her.[1051]

Archbishop Morlot, who had blessed Sister St. Pierre during her final days, gave the following testimony:

> I hear with the liveliest emotion of sorrow of this good Sister's death; but she is to be congratulated and not pitied. Let us cherish the hope that she will continue in heaven, where her influence will be far more powerful and efficacious than when in the flesh, that which she began, and for which she labored so earnestly on earth. She will protect your beloved House, the diocese and France!... I entertain the sweet confidence that she will.[1052]

Upon reading the circular relative to Sister St. Pierre, the archbishop added:

> I have read with great interest the notice you sent me. I doubt not of the salutary impression its perusal will produce in all the Convents of your Order, and with you, I cherish the unshaken confidence, that this chosen soul having led a life of faith and prayer on earth, and practiced those beautiful virtues which distinguish the true Spouse of Jesus Christ, will now, in the possession of glory and happiness, efficaciously plead our cause with the Lord.[1053]

These were the sentiments shared by all and especially by Ven. Dupont. He, too, read the circular of Sister St. Pierre's death and was overcome with joy. He believed it would make a great impression upon the Christian world, "and excite it to implore pardon and mercy."[1054] He referred to addressing his petitions to God

---

[1049] Ibid.
[1050] Ibid., 442.
[1051] Ibid., 443.
[1052] Ibid., 443.
[1053] Ibid., 443–444.
[1054] Ibid., 445.

through Sister St. Pierre to be "one of his secrets for obtaining graces."[1055] The epitaph of her tomb in the monastery (now relocated to the Oratory of the Holy Face, located next to the tomb of Dupont) read, "Lord, Thou wilt conceal her in the secret of Thy Face."

The "secrets" of the Holy Face were indeed lived and shared by Sister St. Pierre as well as by her successor, St. Thérèse of Lisieux. The Carmelites had in common "the same overmastering desire that the treasures of grace hidden in the Sacred Image of the wounded Face of Our Lord should be revealed to the world.... [And] the seal of the Church's approval has been placed upon their efforts, for Archconfraternities have been blessed and approved by the Sovereign Pontiffs Pius IX, Leo XIII, and Pius X."[1056] Pope St. John Paul II alluded to dedication of the third millennium to the Holy Face, and he declared St. Thérèse a Doctor of the Church in 1997. Though elements of St. Thérèse's great spiritual contributions can be traced to the revelations received by Sister St. Pierre (as discussed previously at length and which could only add to their richness of heavenly insight), knowledge of Sister St. Pierre has seemingly decreased in proportion to St. Thérèse's increase, such that today the Little Flower is arguably the most popular intercessory saint after Mary and St. Joseph, while by comparison, almost no one would recognize the name of Sister St. Pierre. Still, they remain especially and forever connected in the spiritual unfolding of things by their extraordinary love for, and recourse to, the wounded Face of Christ.

It is perhaps fitting that the foremost proponent of reparation to the holy name and Face of God should herself remain — at least for a time — in obscurity, "nameless" and "faceless," and this was her express desire while living. But let us hope that that time has expired, for it is perhaps only in this era, from a hindsight perspective, and with the benefit of successive saints and devotions to Christ and Mary, each augmenting and complementing the pinnacle Holy Face revelations, that the full treasury of this reparation to the Godhead may now be appreciated. It is only now, on the cusp of the newest "worst of times" — the "malice of men in open rebellion against itself" in full spiral, some 150 years after Christ first warned of the consequences if men did not

---

[1055] Ibid.

[1056] Sister Mary Emmanuel, *Life of Sister Marie de St. Pierre of the Holy Family, Carmelite of Tours, 1816–1848: A Forerunner of St. Thérèse of Lisieux* (London: Burns, Oates & Washbourne, 1938), 13.

heed His request[1057] — that the effects of neglecting the devotion are being realized, as well as the ever-increasing necessity of it as remedy.

The depth and breadth of Sister St. Pierre's spiritual influence upon Christ's Mystical Body (via the revelations and mystical experiences given to her by Christ) is perhaps only now more fully appreciated by the fruit of her spiritual insights. Her most important contribution was the insistence of offering the suffering Face of Christ to the Father on behalf of sinners to draw down mercy for them "as an essential, organized element of Christian Life."[1058] The suffering Holy Face as the sensible sign of reparation, most efficaciously combining the power of God with the cooperation of man, was *revealed by Christ for the first time in the Holy Face revelations.*[1059] Reparation of the head for the members[1060] also reflects the mysterious solidarity of the members in the unity of Christ's Mystical Body,[1061] each being called to fulfill his duty in the universal obligation of co-redemption within the context of the communion of saints. This understanding is foundational to the requests of other devotions to Christ and Mary. Indeed, the efficacy of reparation to the Godhead for the most radical, blasphemous offenses of the time complements the devotions to Christ's sacred humanity as well as the Marian apparitions — all while being foundational to them.

The aforementioned influence that the life, revelations, and spiritual experiences of Sister St. Pierre had upon St. Thérèse has helped to form perhaps one of the most universally appreciated and adopted forms of piety in our era.[1062] This is even more true of total consecration to Mary, as promoted foremost in modern times by St. Louis de Montfort, yet "confirmed" by Sister St. Pierre's same understanding, concurrently revealed most decidedly in the revelations and mystical experiences bestowed upon her: mysteries

---

[1057] Though the initial threat to France was thwarted by men heeding the call to make reparation for offenses against the first three commandments, it is clear in the revelations that the work of reparation was to be ongoing and for the whole world.

[1058] Sister Mary Emmanuel, *Life of Sister Marie*, 1.

[1059] Ibid., 6.

[1060] Our Lord to Sister St. Pierre: "I have taken upon my head the sins of mankind, that my members might be spared." Ibid., 290.

[1061] Ibid., vii.

[1062] St. Thérèse's autobiography, *Story of a Soul*, has sold millions of copies in many languages the world over. "This phenomenon is an extraordinary event in the field of publishing as well as in the life of the Church." Dorothy Scallan, *The Whole World Will Love Me: The Life of St. Thérèse of the Child Jesus and of the Holy Face (1873–1897)*, ed. Emeric B. Scallan, S.T.B. (Rockford, IL: TAN Books, 2005), ix.

surrounding Mary's divine maternity included that Mary is *the* most efficacious way to Jesus and "legatee of the immense riches [Christ] has acquired for [man] ... the admirable channel through which all His infinite merits would flow to the Holy Church, His spouse."[1063] Man is to employ Mary as Co-Redemptrix, Mediatrix, and Mother of Man to aid in the Virgin's defeat of Satan by one's total recourse to her. He is to exchange his merits with hers, utilizing her as the "mediator to the Mediator of Christ" before God in making offerings of reparation to draw mercy for sinners, toward the conversion of the whole of humanity. Finally, the "treasures" of the Holy Face cap insights of the great Carmelite mystics, becoming the very "honor of Carmel," as prophesized by St. Teresa herself, aiding all who would apply these treasures to themselves, in taking on the very likeness of God.

The work, recalling "the eternal presence of Christ's Face and the necessity of Veronica's gesture,"[1064] is a sister devotion to Fatima in its universal call for reparation to bring about the defeat of Communism and reverse the effects of the "errors of Russia." Sister St. Pierre's mother prioress writes,

> The Work revealed to the admirable virgin whose history we have just related, is, at the same time, as she herself says, "a necessity of justice and a warrant of mercy." Let our efforts be in common; let us unite ourselves in striving fervently to appease the Divine Justice; then indeed will it be our consolation to experience only the effects of Mercy, even more abundant and fruitful, in proportion as the Reparation has been prompt and fervent.[1065]

[1063] Sister Mary St. Peter, *Life of Sister Mary St. Peter*, ed. Rev. P. Janvier (France, 1884), 374–377. There is indication that Sister St. Pierre did not have access to the writings of St. Louis de Montfort, which had been mysteriously hidden for approximately one hundred years prior to her time in Carmel and published only in 1843 — though not receiving ecclesiastical approval until later. (The first pope to endorse Montfort's writings was Pius IX (1846–1878). Regardless, she espouses the same understanding, only uniquely referring to Mary as the Divine Mother "legatee" of "[Christ's] immense riches [which] He has acquired for us during His laborious life, and His dolorous Passion, that she might become the admirable channel [versus "mediatrix"] through which all His infinite merits would flow to the Holy Church, His spouse." And, Ibid., 374. "Jesus belongs to Mary together with all His treasures of grace, and Mary belongs to mankind, with all her tenderness ... that she may lavish on us the most heavenly favors." And, Ibid., 375.

[1064] Van den Bossche, *Message*, 208.

[1065] Sister St. Pierre, *Life of Sister St. Pierre*, 456.

The synthesis of the gifts of the devotion comprise some of the most crucial elements of Catholic spirituality that have been introduced in the modern era.[1066] Indeed, the revelations and mystical experiences given to Sister St. Pierre have resulted in an unknown soul — a hidden face — affecting the entire body of the Church and having the whole world as its beneficiary, for as Pope Bl. Pius IX proclaimed, "Reparation to the Holy Face of Jesus is a divine work, destined to save modern society."[1067]

> *The weapons of our warfare are not carnal, but mighty to God unto the pulling down of fortifications, destroying counsels.*
>
> — 2 Corinthians 10:4

> *May [Sister St. Pierre's] example cause God not to veil His Face and that we may never merit the terrible warning of the prophets: "One day they will invoke the Lord, but He will not answer them, and on that day He will hide His Face from them because of the evil of their conduct" (Micah 3:4), but may we be able, with the saints, to behold "The open face, to reflect as in a mirror the splendor of the Lord and to see ourselves transformed into this same image, ever more and more radiant, through the action of the Spirit of the Lord" (2 Corinthians 3:18).*
>
> — Father Bernard, B.R.O., O.P., preface of *The Message* by Louis Van den Bossche

> *Is not the Veil of Veronica before all, the picture of a soul drawn toward the Sorrowful Face of Christ and sufficiently purified so that He may be able to impress His Divine resemblance upon it?*
>
> — Louis Van den Bossche

[1066] Michael Gaitley, M.I.C., *33 Days to Merciful Love: A Do-It-Yourself Retreat in Preparation for Consecration to Divine Mercy* (Stockbridge, MA: Marian Press, 2016), 28. As discussed in chapters 4 and 5, there is, for example, the affirmation of St. Louis de Montfort's "true devotion to Mary," as well as reparatory offerings complementary to the "Offering to Merciful Love [as] one of the best kept secrets of the Catholic Church..., the culmination of the central teaching of the greatest and most popular saint of modern times — a Doctor of the Church."

[1067] Sister Mary Emmanuel, *Life of Sister Marie*, 144. Also, Sister Mary St. Peter, *Life of Sister Mary St. Peter*, 338.

Memento [not yet considered a relic since she is not canonized] of Sister St. Pierre made from her hair and clothing and sent from the Carmelite monastery to her (only) surviving sibling, my great-great grandfather

Appendix I

The Cross of Lorraine

The Cross of Lorraine, a double cross-pieced cross, a variant of the Christian cross and first attributed to Justinian II, has become associated with St. Joan of Arc and is symbolic of freedom and patriotism in France (perhaps especially following World War II). It has also become a symbol of resistance against heresies and moral corruption within the Church, all making it a very fitting choice of the Cross of the Archconfraternity of the Holy Face, established in 1885.

The Archconfraternity, having its center in the archiepiscopal city of Tours where it had its origin, adopts as a principal sign of decoration for its members a cross with two arms arranged in the manner shown in the engraving below. On the center of one of its sides is inscribed the monogram of Christ surrounded with the words: *Pius IX*, 1876 [the date of approval of the earliest version of the

The Cross of the Archconfraternity of the Holy Face
(Taken from the Manual of the Archconfraternity of the Holy Face)

work of reparation, though not as comprehensive as the archconfraternity established in 1885 by Pope Leo XIII], and upon the arms of the cross: *Sit nomen Domini benedictum.* On the obverse is seen engraved, on the center, the Holy Face, above which is the inscription of the Cross: *INRI*, and beneath: *Vade retro, Satana.* The associates are advised habitually to wear this cross as a safeguard; during pilgrimages and at public ceremonies, it is well to have it placed where it can be seen on the breast. The Archconfraternity is an army; the cross, such as has been described, is its standard. It is to be worn with confidence; it will help to conquer enemies and to repair losses. But it is not absolutely necessary that the cross should be worn; according to the rule, it may be replaced by a medal or a scapular of the Holy Face.

Appendix II

Circular of Sister Marie de St. Pierre

In gratitude for the generosity of Christian Colby-Kelly, Ph.D., a resident of Canada, for translating this document. The original was in French, buried in old letters and documents saved by Sister St. Pierre's brother, Prosper Eluere, and passed down through the generations. Evidently sent to Prosper by the Carmelites, this is likely the first printing of the Circular of Sister Marie de St. Pierre since its original distribution after her death.

J. M. J.

MY VERY REVEREND AND MOST HONORED MOTHER,

A very humble and respectful salutation in Our Lord, who has just given us a share in the bitterness of His Chalice, plunging us into the deepest grief in taking from us our most dear and well-loved Sister Marie de St. Pierre of the Holy Family, professed from our house, and aged thirty-one years, nine months, and four days, and having been received into the religious life eight years and just under eight months ago.

My Reverend Mother, the loss of our dear sister is a most sorrowful sacrifice for us, and in this circumstance our submission to divine will is total consolation for us. Yet to comprehend the depth of our sorrow it is necessary to understand, as well as we do, the one for whom our tears originate. We have no doubt of your sympathy to our grief, since we have already traced, albeit weakly, a sketch of this excellent model of all virtue. It is to our dear sister that we can apply this word of Scripture: *In a Short Time She Crafted a Long Career*.[1068] For while her life was so short in years, there was enough in it to fill a book. Since I am limited at this time to writing a short description, I will focus here on her main qualities.

Our dear Sister Marie de St. Pierre was born in Rennes on October 4, the same day as the death of our Mother St. Teresa, into a devout and respectable family whose piety was exemplary. Even as a child she was already privileged by God, and received *blessings of His sweetness*. When she was as young as six years old, she was already actively combating her faults. She loved seclusion, contemplation, and prayer, so much so that her virtuous parents ensured from an early age that she was trained in the Christian virtues. One could say that in her interior life the Holy Spirit was her greatest teacher. From that time on she had the utmost horror of the slightest faults, as she bitterly chastised herself for the least childhood shortcomings. For her older sister often found her in tears, and when she asked her the reason for them, she naïvely responded, *I'm crying about my sins*. She dreaded so much even the appearance of evil, that at the age of eight years, she was so worried about the contents of a history book that had been loaned to her, that before opening the book she took it to her parish priest to ask his advice. Upon learning from him that the book wasn't bad but that it was frivolous, she immediately returned it; she had not even read the first page. Wise beyond her years, it can be said that she matured more in relation to God than in relation to man. In this way, she unknowingly prepared herself for the plan God had for her. In reading of Our Lord's sufferings, her heart was deeply touched. She frequently walked the Way of the Cross with much piety, yet her great attraction was for prayer. Despite not knowing any methods of prayer, she attentively recited silent prayers, expecting to learn those saintly exercises. God gave her that opportunity; she was only ten when she received solid instruction on this subject. The Word of God was for her profound, and it opened her spirit and heart to the divine light, quickly rendering her competent in the science of saints.

[1068] "Being perfected in a short time, he fulfilled long years" (Wisd. 4:13, RSVCE).

For a long time, in pious action, she aspired with zeal to see the favor of that day of her First Communion, and that happy day occurred when she was ten and a half years old. Her feelings on that occasion were qualifiedly different from those seen ordinarily in children of her age. Already grace had entered her heart in secret prayer, according her the knowledge of *the sweetness of the Lord*. At that time, she also received bountiful heavenly gifts, and it is difficult to describe the fervor of that young, burning heart, united with and forever of God. That is how this dear child began to infiltrate the secrets of divine love and how her soul, filled with inexpressible consolations, came to understand that she should belong, without reserve, to Him who had so generously given Himself to her. Faithful to the celestial call, she then courageously entered the path planned for her and endeavored, as she herself has said, to serve the Lord *in spirit and in truth*. At twelve years of age she lost her mother, and like our Mother St. Teresa, she ran right away and threw herself at the feet of the Blessed Virgin Mary, praying that Mary take hold of her in the place of the mother God had taken. Mary indeed adopted that innocent soul, and also gave her appreciable proofs of it through the course of her life. The virtuous father of our dear sister, charged with a large family, confided this child to the care of two of his aunts, maiden aunts of great piety who managed a youth home. In their pious household, she progressed in virtue, becoming a model of virtue to her companions, even serving as mistress of the interior path, tasked with teaching them to love the practice of prayer in union with God. Our dear sister was not limited to the souls that surrounded her there. She sought every opportunity to practice works of mercy, given her means — assisting the poor, visiting the sick, and attending to the dying, these were her favorite occupations as long as they didn't hinder the duties of her vocation.

A life so perfect, nevertheless, would not suffice to satisfy the appeal of such an elite soul. Early on she had understood *the secret of the Kingdom of Heaven* and from the bottom of her heart she heard the oracle of her Divine Teacher, *he who will not renounce everything will not be my disciple*.[1069] Not long after her First Communion, the desire for the religious life grew so much in her heart that it became the sole object of her thoughts and wishes. In order to reach that end, she fasted and made short pilgrimages in honor of the Virgin Mary and St. Joseph. She also

---

[1069] "So therefore, whoever of you does not renounce all that he has cannot be my disciple" (Luke 14:33, RSVCE).

called on St. Martin, bishop of Tours, to whom she had a great devotion, and visited a chapel dedicated to him. There, in the presence of the relics of such a great saint, she prayed the most fervent of prayers, imploring him to receive her in his diocese as a religious, without even knowing if there were Carmelites there. She was continuously perplexed, however, by unceasing oppositional obstacles to her vocation. Inspiration came to her to make a pilgrimage to a famous chapel to the Holy Virgin near Rennes (Notre Dame de la Peinière). There, more than ever, she felt her Divine Mother's very special aid, and by the graces she received there, she knew without a doubt that God had called her to serve Him by the practice of evangelical counsels.

All of her wishes centered on Carmel. And imagine, the very week after that pilgrimage, her confessor, doubtless to test her, decided to enter her into another religious order. But Our Lord, always full of mercy and goodness, eased her worry, as on the ninth day after her return from her pilgrimage and after receiving Holy Communion, she repeatedly heard these words, *You will be a Carmelite,* and she believed that Our Lord added, *Carmelite at Tours.* She related this to her director immediately, who recommended her to us, unbeknownst to her. How great was her surprise on hearing him say, *My daughter, you have been accepted among the Carmelites of Tours,* when she had been up until then still ignorant that there were Carmelites in Tours.

It was true, for by a quite remarkable coincidence, that worthy member of the clergy had just received a letter from us informing him that we would accord this dear child an entry into our house. That day was for her one of the most beautiful of her life, but it would cause her sorrowful sacrifices: to leave her cherished family, in which she was clearly abundantly loved, especially to leave her father who had a great claim on her affections; this was a dreadful blow to her heart. Nonetheless, with no lack of courage she forged on, and as a good Christian father, her good father consented to his daughter's vocation and brought her immediately to us.

She left for Rennes on the day of the feast of St. Martin, whom she regarded as her deliverer, and at the age of twenty-three entered our order on the eve of the day of the feast of the saints.[1070] She often had recourse to ask their intercession, placing herself under their protection anew, and she straightaway and generously embraced all of the practices of religious life with fervor. Notice, my

---

[1070] Nov. 13, the vigil of the great feast of All Carmelite Saints, Nov. 14.

Reverend Mother, that from that first day until the day of her death, she didn't yield for a minute; we never perceived in her behavior any cooling, any other way, and not one single day went by without her rapidly advancing toward the summit of the Holy Mountain.

It didn't take us long to appreciate the candidate that Providence had entrusted to our care, and indeed, her loveable simplicity soon led us to know her intimately. From that time on, the dear child confidently deposited her soul into our hands, abandoning all of herself in blind obedience. Also, we had in her more of a perfect religious to guide than a postulant to train. Not long after her entry with us, she received a very particular grace with great effect to her soul. That inner illumination gave her such a high sense of our holy vocation that anything she had heard before fell to nought in comparison, and she so perfectly comprehended the spirit of the duties of the vocation that she quivered incessantly for fear of failing at the least of her duties. She abandoned herself completely to Our Lord to achieve His designs, and she endeavored to act with as much courage as loyalty.

That is how our dear postulant prepared to be garbed in the holy habit, which she received with an inexpressible happiness and appreciation. In return for this grace for which she felt herself unworthy, she gave new flourish to her fervor, and during her novitiate, she was so exacting, so humble, so mortified, that we could not look without admiration, or surprise even, upon the strides she made in virtue. Throughout that time, she consecrated herself in a particular manner to the holy childhood of Our Lord, who had always been the object of her partiality. Thus, knowledge of the manger became the sole occupation of her spirit. The Child Jesus, her ideal, rendered her astute to honor Him and to imitate Him faithfully. Finally, the day arrived that she had so desired, that of her profession. We can but imperfectly describe the inclination she brought to that holy act. But to give you an idea of it, my Reverend Mother, suffice it to say that she avowed that during the whole retreat preceding the moment of her sacrifice, she had only at most twice lifted her eyes. Unified by the indissoluble links of the Divine Spouse with her soul, our dear Sister Marie de St. Pierre put all of her resources into seeking to please Him, and to fulfill the duties of her dear vocation with all possible perfection. It is hard for us to point to which virtue this dear sister excelled at most. Tracking them all down is a task that is beyond my capacities. I would then prefer to consign myself to those that principally constitute the spirit of our holy state.

Our beloved Sister Marie de St. Pierre exuded charity to an eminent degree. Her tender, steadfast piety inspired her to a real and ardent love of God. The glory of God and the saving of souls were the grand motivation for her actions, and the sole objective of her prayers. One can say that this zeal moved her all of her life, but that it really began to consume her from the moment in 1843 when, surrounded by a supernatural[1071] light, she came to know that God's anger would strike mankind due to man's numerous crimes against His divine majesty. Strongly compelled by grace, she offered herself to God to mollify His judgment and deter His wrath. The loss of souls affected her so very much that sometimes she could not contain herself, and she would break down in sobs.

Nonetheless, her heart swelled in Our Lord's love, honoring His sainted humanity in all its mysteries, while that of His birth and inner life held for her incomprehensible charm. In the same way, she directed all her affections toward the Blessed Sacrament. A hundred times a day, and possibly more, she honored Him in her thoughts, having composed a spiritual exercise that she frequently recited, in adoration of the Blessed Sacrament as well as for Holy Communion. She attended the Holy Sacrifice of the Mass with apt attention, appearing completely absorbed in God; during Holy Oblation we often saw her cry a flood of tears. It was especially at Holy Communion that her devotion to the Eucharist took, if I may say, a marvelous ascension. She prepared for receiving the Eucharist with extraordinary care in pious practices the day and even the night before, in adoration with fervent ejaculatory prayers toward the Host to be received, and calling upon the Blessed Virgin Mary and all the angels and saints to make ready the abode of the anticipated heavenly Host. But when she received the Eucharist! Oh! Lost in the abyss of Him, she forgot everything in the joy of intimate communion with Him, and it sometimes seemed to her that she no longer resided on earth; her normal home was in the Sacred Heart of Jesus. It was in that ardent furnace that she mined many illuminations and favors for herself and for others. It was there that she discovered a treasury of graces and mercy, and it was there also that she sought refuge from her sorrows, running to Him for all of her needs.

We spoke of her devotion to the Blessed Virgin Mary at the time she began her religious life. Her love for the Divine Mother grew markedly once she had

---

[1071] On the subject here discussed, as we have said here or will say later, we declare the inspirations, graces, and events that we report herein have no other authority than our purely human thoughts, as we wish to conform ourselves to the ordinary rules of the Church in this regard.

consecrated her life forever to the Blessed Virgin Mary in her Carmelite Order. Her fervor brought her to honor pious industry, and she often talked of spreading the Faith in all hearts. By the intercession of the Blessed Virgin, she received in turn innumerable favors and illuminations on the prerogatives of the Blessed Mother of God. Also the object of her tender affection and devotion were St. Joseph, whom she called her good father, and our Mother St. Teresa.

I have spoken of her other virtues. Our dear sister was graced with a rare degree of humility. In the world, she had occasion to exercise this mother of virtues, and her soul, nourished as it were, on the bread of humility, found more nourishment there than most people who praise each other in the most flattering ways. It was easy to see the truth of this since she was quick to thank us for humiliating her, doing so with a profusion of heartfelt warmth and recognition of her feelings, that infused us with edification. In addition, my Reverend Mother, we lavished upon her this food of which she was blessedly hungry. We did this both to support and to ensure God's plan for her, and as to protect the precious gifts of which her soul was enriched. With help from this grace, she was able to become entirely devoid of pride, and her inner searches in accordance with our work were the object of the cruel battle for souls seeking to practice humility. As for our dear sister, she sincerely believed herself the last, the most imperfect, the least capable of all, and even if she did receive praise, never did her heart lift as a result.

What can I say about her obedience? That she was whole and perfect, unhesitating, and unquestioning; she submitted with childlike simplicity to all that was asked of her. Her thoughts, her will, the inner illuminations she received, all were discarded once she had the least knowledge of her superiors' intentions. She acted toward them with such great faith that she spoke of them as if to God Himself, and in fact received orders and advice from them as if from God. To the deep respect she had toward her superiors was added limitless confidence in them, a tender love, true gratitude, and blind submission. This obedience was so constant in her that our dear sister was able to witness in her last illness, *My consolation in dying is to have always obeyed.*

Her reverence was such that those who looked at her were penetrated by it; it only sufficed to see her to feel elevated to God, for she appeared to be foreign to all her surroundings. This is so true, because even after her profession, she didn't know which positions the others occupied in the choir stalls and at the refectory table, and she appeared to be surprised at things happening right under her nose. From that came her intimate and constant union with God, who was never out of her sights. To use her expression, her soul was tightly united with Our Lord, being happily close at His feet. But this Heaven-filled life was not exempt from trials and tribulations, and we even believe that, in God's plan, those she rigorously and interiorly endured contributed to shortening her life.

Sister Marie de St. Pierre practiced mortification perfectly and extensively. They consisted mainly of the elimination of any unnecessary satisfactions, as well as by seeking deprivations that she could commonly impose on herself. And so she unceasingly sought out opportunities for sacrifice, being adept at finding them and even quicker to use them to totally immolate herself and so arrive at the inner death that was her principal characteristic. Her discipline in this regard was admirable. Faithful to the smallest detail of this grace, it could be said that she was a slave to this virtue, but she knew from experience that therein lay the secret to happiness in a religious soul. Also, what of her love of silence and for consistency? It was almost impossible to find fault with her on that basis, so exacting was she that one could almost see her as a living measurement ruler. One had only to follow her attentively to come to know and love her works. And as she eminently possessed the kind of thinking of Our Blessed Lady, and the saintly free thinking of a true Carmelite, she knew perfectly how to ally charity and the joyfulness of interior virtue. At recreation times, she was sweet and kindly, and her companions were glad to be in her company because they always benefited from it. She also knew how to shy away from individuals, or to exchange with them, depending on the circumstances, though she often suffered extremely violent feelings at the interruption of her interior occupation with God. She was predominantly drawn to the hidden life with her simple demeanor, so little affected, so against distinctiveness even for good, that it appeared to everybody that these virtues came easily to her. My Reverend Mother, I will conclude this portrait with one last trait. We think, with good reason, that this soul has preserved the purity of her innocence since she lived in the world as if she was not of it. From the time of her entry into our house, we have never seen her sin voluntarily, as attested to by all in our community. Our reflection on this does detriment to this simple account of the truth, so I would hasten to shorten it.

Our dear Sister Marie de St. Pierre filled the posts of second and first porter, even doing both alone for some time, to everyone's satisfaction. Thus, through her dedication, she was very serviceable to us, and she earned the esteem and affection of all those with whom she had frequent connections in those posts. She will be sorely missed there. Those duties went completely against her natural inclination, and she exercised them with great aversion. But she didn't remonstrate, either with her frequent recruitment, nor due to the disruption of the calm of her soul, as a result of her soul's purity. It was even when the heaviest of her occupations overwhelmed her that she experienced the greatest graces from Our Lord. Our dear sister could have continued to serve the Faith, for she had the gift of excellent judgment, much tact and perfect discretion, a cheerful and very fair character, essentially the precious qualities that made her a natural in the Carmelite life, as requested by Our Blessed Mother.

In 1843, as we have said, God favored our dear sister with intimate communications on the subject of France. He conveyed to her the knowledge that due to the sins of man, His anger had been inflamed, and that He would catch men out with much more rigor than ever before. At the same time, He inspired her to see a great way of disarming His wrath by the institution of work of reparation. As well, she saw in the Sacred Heart of Jesus the longing, even the need, to offer mercy, on condition of the reparation of outrageous sins against His Divine Father. She received vivid illuminations of the sweet Face of Our Lord, as an object sensitive to the reparation, just as the Sacred Heart of Jesus is the sensitive sign of His love for us. Moreover, in one of His communications with her, Our Lord gave her this consoling promise: *Because you have honored My Face, covered with wounds by sinners, I will renew in you at the hour of your death the image of God, and all on earth who contemplate the wounds of My Face will see it one day in Heaven radiant with glory.*

What prayers, what tears, what sufferings there have been for our dear sister as a result of her inspirations! Although it cost her extremely, she confessed everything to her superiors with the greatest naïvety, and we cannot say enough about the deference and docility with which she listened to their opinions and observations, and she submitted to their decisions. For quite a long time we didn't give credence to what she was saying, fearing illusions on her part in so delicate a matter, and to examine with greater certainty the path of God in her. So we asked her informally, without seeming to attach much importance to it, to write it all down. My Reverend Mother, we regret not being able to cite some passages of interest that she wrote, as we have already here passed the limitations of a pamphlet. Although blessed with singular graces, our dear sister labored to keep her writings hidden so that nothing external could be added to them. In addition, in her lifetime the community was always ignorant of the wonderful gifts with which the Lord honored His spouse, the grace she had requested of God.

In the first years of her religious life, our dear Sister Marie de St. Pierre fulfilled all holy observances without detriment to her health. She even seemed quite strong, and we were hopeful of having her for a long time. But as soon as she offered herself up to Our Lord, she weakened and often suffered ill health. There was apparently nothing specifically amiss — at least her last malady did not appear then. This year she observed Lent until Holy Week. But at the time of the Church's remembrance of the Passion of Our Lord on Passion Sunday, she began to experience the anguish of the sickness that would take her from our affections.

Our dear sister always thought that her mission on earth would not be long, but for about two years she had clearly known from Our Lord, as He told her, *As soon as the work is established, I will not leave you on the earth for long.* She received knowledge of this again and again on different occasions. On March 30 of this year, Our Lord told her again, *Your pilgrimage will soon be at hand! The terms of the battle approach, and you will soon see My Face in Heaven! I will purify you to make you worthy.* On hearing these words, she prostrated herself, saying, *Lord, I only deserve Hell.* What is more, on Good Friday at three o'clock, as our dear sister was in adoration of the dying Jesus Christ, she felt the heavy weight of divine justice dwelling on mankind, then she renewed her devotion to sacrifice herself for Him. Her offering was promptly received. She was immediately struck with a serious and cruel sickness that would soon bring her to the cusp of death. Her chest was the most stricken, yet there were other discomforts added to that. Her throat was ulcerated so she could only take liquids in small amounts, and a continuous and raging fever engulfed her, as the nights rolled on when she was deprived of any rest. Whatever position she lay in her bed proved another torture, so that she had to stay in one place for long periods of time, causing bedsores to accompany all of her other sufferings. Those sores healed somewhat after a time, but there was no relief as her body took on a skeletal aspect, her skin tight on her bones, which were as dry as though they had been through a blaze. Her face alone remained fresh and rosy.

An affront to nature and against all expectations, this state was prolonged, yet it had no ill effect on our dear sister's temperament. In equal measure she was accepting and patient, her union with God constant; she was generous and her spirit of sacrifice was unchanged. From the beginning of her illness we told her, *Pray then, that Our Lord will ease you a bit, if He doesn't want to heal you.* No, she replied, *in terms of suffering and sacrifice, I have never asked anything in particular of God, but also I have never refused Him anything.*

By the time she entered the infirmary, her mind was all occupied with thoughts of God's judgment, and she viewed herself as weighed down in the scales of justice. Seeing only her faults for which to seek pardon from God, one could say she was forgetting the favors she had been graced with. From such a pure soul such a sentiment of humility can be easily understood considering the intense light of God's holiness that filled her, and her own sense of her lowliness. Indeed, the greatest of saints have been tested with the same apprehensions. This notion was so keen to our dear sister that her frame bore its imprint. She seemed completely absorbed by these thoughts and on several occasions we saw her shedding tears, and we asked her the cause. *My Mother,* she said to me, *I ponder God's judgment and I cry for my sins.* She walked thus with her Divine Teacher entering the Garden of Olives, and following Him all the way to Calvary. This outlook stayed with her, but in no way kept her from feeling the tenderest confidence, and a desire for Heaven. Her forthcoming death caused her to tremble with joy. *My hour has come,* she said. *Soon all my bonds will be broken. When will I be contemplated, O heavenly sojourn? When, O my God, will I see You face to face unveiled?* If we spoke to her about Heaven, her face became enlivened. *That's what I aspire to,* she said, transported. And she added the most beautiful words she remembered from the Canticles on the subject. To look at her, it seemed as though a beam of beatification had already penetrated her soul. Throughout her illness, she had been like a child in our hands and in those of the charitable nurses who attended her. She was simple, docile, and innocent. Also, when we asked her if something caused her pain or discomfort, she said, *No, my Mother, by the grace of God, for I suffer all that He wants and I do all that He wants.* In discussing these sentiments, we remembered the Child Jesus and the graces she had received by this mystery, and she responded, *The Divine Teacher has already taught me the science of the nativity, and now the science of the cross.* Alas! She had done as much as to dampen her lips on the bitter chalice from which she must drink to the dregs.

In the first days of June, our dear sister became so ill that she herself asked for the last rites. The doctor had said from the start of her sickness that she was in imminent danger of death, so we had hastened to satisfy her requests. Thus, she received Holy Viaticum and Extreme Unction with the greatest sentiments of piety, and she asked the forgiveness of the community in the most touching manner. She received Holy Viaticum as often as her health and our rules permitted, after which she sighed happily, having found therein all strength and all consolation.

Friday, June 16, our dear sister suffered an attack so acute that we thought it would be her last, and we began praying for the recommendation of her soul. But while reciting, we saw something supernatural happen to her, the effects of which were noticeable. First, she joined only in our prayers of fervent elevations, weakened as it were, by her sufferings. But in her words, *Maria, mater gratiae, mater misericordiae,* she suddenly stretched out her arms toward Heaven as a child throws up his arms to his mother as soon as he sees her. She stayed in that position a long time, yet a few minutes earlier her arm was so weak and stiff that she couldn't make the Sign of the Cross. After that, in two different instances she crossed her arms, to die as a victim, and when we tried to dissuade her, she said, *Leave me as I am. It is a duty for me.*

She took a crucifix as well as a small illustration of the Infant Jesus (that never left her side) in her hands and then kissed each, one by one. She then held them tightly over her heart, then holding the Infant Jesus as high as she possibly could, she pronounced in a solemn and low voice, *Eternal Father, I offer You once again this adorable child, Your Divine Son, in atonement for my sins and for those of all mankind, for the needs of the Holy Church, for France, for the Reparation!* (In this, she spoke of the work in reparation for blasphemy and for the profanation of Sundays.) *Holy Jesus, I add, I leave this work in Your hands; it is for this I have lived, and for this that I die!* She asked God for forgiveness for her faults. Then, while crying bitter tears, she thanked the community for the care we dispensed, adding, *Oh, my sisters, how happy it is to die a Carmelite!* She asked for our blessing, testified to her gratitude for the care given to her soul, and then said, *The hour has come. O Jesus, come.* After she added to that somewhat, crossing her arms across her breast: *My Father, I give up my soul into Your hands.* For several minutes she remained in contemplation, then returned to her normal state. This moving scene, of which I have but touched the surface, lasted more than an hour, and having witnessed this wonder, the community was only able to voice its admiration in tears shed.

The next Sunday, on the feast of the Holy Trinity, our dear patient had the pleasure of receiving Holy Viaticum. In that Communion, Our Lord spoke again to her soul. When I went to see her a few minutes later, she said, *My Mother, I will stay a little while longer on the earth, because my soul is not yet purified enough, but in that time I will suffer cruelly, for the Lord has attached me to the cross. I will stay there till my last breath. Don't give me any more care, any relief. I must occupy myself only with suffering, and I want now to only think of my eternity. I desire to stay alone with my God, for I am almost unable to speak. One may think that I am sleeping, but no, I am exclusively occupied with Him. Soon I will contemplate His adorable Face, soon I will sing His praises for all eternity. Oh! How I will pray then for the Church, for France, for the community, and for reparation!* I then asked her some questions that she answered solemnly and with precision. Then she added, *My mission is finished, as God has made me know, for the work of reparation is done, and it is only for that work that He has brought me into the world. Now all I have left is to suffer, to fulfill God's plan. Oh, how very true it is that His justice has means unknown to man to be satisfied!*

Effectively, this interesting victim began a new mission of suffering, the hardship of which one can only in vain begin to characterize. And still, this generous and faithful soul did not want any more care. *No,* she said, *let God act.* Nonetheless, she bowed to obedience rather than to the needs of nature, and she entered into a more ordinary life, taking and asking for what she needed. Yet nothing could provide her with either a remedy or an easing of her sickness. On the contrary, whatever we did seemed only to add new distresses. Nevertheless, not one complaint issued from her mouth. At times, her pain caused her to cry out in wails of anguish that were always countered with expressions of acceptance and edifying words, such as, *My God, how I suffer, have pity on me, help me, don't abandon Your little servant; I am Your victim, You know, Lord, remember this.* Then in a voice that can't be described, she cried out above her wails, *Oh! How terrible the rigors of divine justice are! My God, how Your designs are rigorous! If one knew what one had to endure! O my Divine Spouse, how bitter You are to me, You who are so sweet!* In her moments of desolation, we reminded her that she had offered herself up to God to accomplish His designs. *Yes,* she replied, *and I don't take it back. My God, I want all that You want, as much as You want, and if need be, I consent to suffer till the end of the world.* When we asked her where she was suffering the most, *In all the parts of my body,* she said. *It is a complete martyrdom. My bed is a purgatory where I burn; a fire consumes me and every second feels like a century. I don't ask God to shorten or lessen my suffering, but when will the moment come when I will be united with Him forever? Request that I be granted patience, I beseech you. I want no more than my crucifix, my eyes are constantly fixed on Him, for He helps me in my suffering. My love has been crucified, and I am crucified with Him.*

Against expectations, the terrible agony continued on. And this, despite our dear patient's receiving the doctor's most devoted and attentive care, well worthy of our gratitude. Our beloved sister had to have received physical and spiritual powers from God nearly beyond the natural in order to endure her condition. In the midst of all of the pain, she maintained a profound peacefulness, a level and calm soul. While her face had been altered by suffering, it reflected sweet joyfulness anew, in moments of brief letup from her pain. She loved to hear talk of God, and feared losing God's presence due to the violence of her sickness, so she charged us with often offering up her suffering to Our Lord.

Our dear sister was honored with a visit from the monsignor archbishop, as that distinguished prelate who unceasingly accords us his benevolence had consented to come to give her his blessing. She received it with the greatest gratitude, her happiness was complete. Father Superior was also good enough to come several times to encourage her with his fatherly counsel. These acts were powerfully consoling and well appreciated in the grateful heart of our beloved sister.

We can't remember without tenderness all the marks of respect, of trust, of kindheartedness that our dear child filled us with, especially in her last minutes. The most touching expressions of love and gratitude flowed from her sensitive and loving heart. After her formidable battle through which we gave her succor, she repeated, *Oh! How good it is to relate all to my superiors!* Yes, my Reverend Mother, this privileged soul came up against attacks from Hell but only, I presume, as a victim. It was necessary for everything in her to partake in that holocaust. In addition, near her last days when we asked her how a victim should die, she answered, *Sacrificed.*

As the end approached, her suffering became more keenly felt. On the seventh of this month, a Friday, she was in complete agony, yet she was cognizant almost till her last breath. Our chaplain, whom our dear invalid held in great esteem and trust, came to hear her Confession and to commend her soul to Heaven because we feared she would not get through the night. That last night proved to be very grueling for our dear dying patient; she often requested holy water, and she united to God in fervent aspirations. We stayed close to her since it proved to console her, and she pleaded with us to not leave her. When morning broke, I left for a minute, and while I was gone, she expressed a wish to be repositioned. She was told that I had recommended that she not be moved, except if she suffered too much; then we would try, keeping in mind our intention. *No, then!* she said. *Obedience!* To any of the things that we suggested to her, she responded smiling and lowered her crucifix tightly over her heart, saying, *He is mine and I am His. What happiness to suffer!* She then asked us, *My mother, when?* I added, *When the Spouse comes, isn't it?* She replied with an affirmative sign, and I told her, *Soon, my child, in a few minutes.* This seemed to satisfy her as she gathered her thoughts, remembering that Our Lord had communicated a promise to her a long time ago to reestablish on her soul the image of God at the hour of her death. She wanted to renew her baptismal vows, and symbolic of the grace she desired, she requested holy water, made the Sign of the Cross on her forehead, and joining her hands, added, *I renounce Satan and his pomps and his works, and I wish to belong to Jesus Christ forever.* Just before that she had appeared to be in an arduous fight, but after that little observance, her face took on a heavenly aspect, one could say as of a child drawn out from the baptismal water, or an angel descended from Heaven only to there return. From that moment on until her last breath, she never ceased to pray; she was covered in death sweats and already icy cold, and even so, her cold and deathly pale lips repeated, *Jesus, Mary, Joseph. Come, Lord Jesus. Sit nomen Domini benedictum.*[1072] Those were the last words she spoke that we were able to understand. Her lips continued their movement, but without intelligible issue. Soon she could no longer hear us and her eyes closed, and as a last trait of resemblance to her Divine Master, she let out a cry and gently expired.

This precious death occurred on the eighth of this month around noon, with all the community and myself present. Our dear Sister Marie de St. Pierre had asked the Blessed Virgin if she would present her soul to God. She died on a Saturday. She had desired to not die in nighttime in order not to frighten all the sisters when they discovered her. That charitable desire was also fulfilled, so true it is that Our Lord, so full of goodness *fulfills the will of those He loves.*[1073]

Despite the profound sadness we were plunged into on the separation of this most cherished soul, we experienced a feeling of consolation and hope. We felt called to invoke her, rather than to pray for her. Her face exuded an appearance of peace and happiness. Her limbs that had been stiff through her sickness and by her excessive thinness became soft and supple as a baby's. It pleases us to say that even the public paid homage to her mortal remains, which many touched with their objects of piety during her exposition. Also, numerous people accompanied her to the cemetery and gave many blessings to her memory, and many tears fell. (We don't have the comfort of keeping all of our dear sisters

---

[1072] Blessed be the name of the Lord.
[1073] Psalm 145:19 (RSVCE).

among us.) From all over France we received requests for objects that she had used. *The Lord exalts and raises up the humble and the meek.*[1074]

Pray be so good, my Reverend Mother, to add to the already announced Requiem Mass of our Holy Order an invocation of the patron saints of our dearly departed, the hymn "O Gloriosa Virginum," and the verse *Sit nomen Domini benedictum*. This charitable act will produce ample rewards, I have no doubt.

Please receive, my Reverend Mother, renewed assurance of my affection and deepest respect, for which I am honored to be, in Jesus and Mary,

> My reverend and very honorable Mother,
>
> Your most humble and obedient servant,
>
> Sr. Mary of the Incarnation
>
> Carmelite Religious Ind.

From our Monastery of the Incarnation and the Holy Family of the Carmelites of Tours, July 25, 1848.

P.S. We request your prayers, my Reverend Mother, in aid of the soul of our dear sister Louise Vegnier, extern sister, deceased last July 28, only forty years old. She had served the community with great devotion for seventeen years, spreading the odor of sanctity of Our Lord Jesus Christ. Her end, like her life, was holy and edifying.

[1074] Psalm 147:6 (RSVCE).

Appendix III

How to Say the Holy Face Chaplet

The following explanation and instructions are based upon the *Manual of the Archconfraternity of the Holy Face,* compiled by Abbé Janvier and with the approbation of the archbishop of Tours, France, 1887.

The photo was taken of a Holy Face Chaplet sent from the Carmelites of New Orleans to my great-great-grandfather, Sister St. Pierre's eldest brother, in 1885, the same year the Archconfraternity of the Holy Face was approved for the world by Pope Leo XIII. The Carmelites also sent him a copy of the first biography of Sister St. Pierre, which they had translated from the French to English.

The annotated photo and instructions were graciously contributed by Jule Lane.

Original 1885 version of the Holy Face Chaplet

Holy Face Chaplet

1887 Archconfraternity Holy Face Manual

The little chaplet of the Holy Face has for its object the honoring of the five senses of our Lord Jesus Christ and of entreating God for the triumph of His Church and the downfall of Her enemies. It is well to recite it everyday. This Chaplet comes from Sister Marie de Saint Pierre, a Carmelite nun of Tours, France.

The first 30 beads recall to mind the 30 years of Christ's private life. They are divided into 5 groups of 6 beads each with the intention of honoring the 5 senses, which have their seat principally in His Holy Face, and of rendering homage to all the sufferings which our Lord endured in His Face, through each one of these senses. The set of 3 beads recall to mind the public life of our Savior and have for their object the honoring of all the wounds of His adorable Face. The Gloria is repeated 7 times in total in honor of the 7 last words of Jesus upon the Cross, and the 7 sorrows of the Immaculate Virgin.

Holy Face Chaplet Explanation

258 UNVEILING THE SIXTH STATION OF THE CROSS

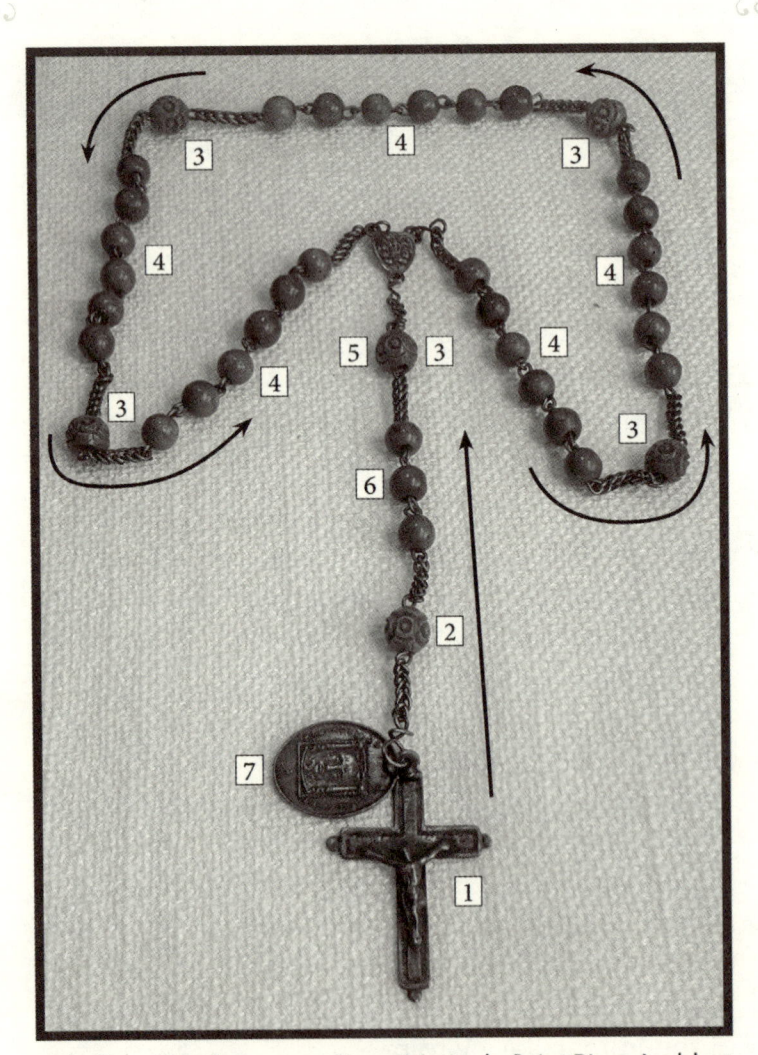

Holy Face Chaplet sent to Sister Marie de Saint Pierre's eldest brother, Prosper Eluere, in 1885 by the Discalced Carmelites of New Orleans, who were also the editors of the English version of her first biography.

Holy Face Chaplet Annotated